IMMORAL TRAFFIC

This insightful ethnography delves into the complex intersection of India's anti-prostitution law and global anti-trafficking campaigns, and how they impact sex workers in both voluntary and involuntary situations. *Immoral Traffic* examines the role of legal actors and NGOs in implementing these interventions, revealing the mix of paternalism, humanitarianism, punitive care, bureaucracy, and morality in their efforts. Through a sequence of interventions prescribed by India's anti-prostitution law, the book follows the experiences of sex workers, from rescues to courts to carceral shelters. It sheds light on the ways in which donor-driven NGOs draw upon this law to implement anti-trafficking agendas, and how these interventions are navigated by women removed from the sex trade. Detailed and eye-opening, this book is a valuable resource for scholars and students of anthropology, law and society, gender and sexuality studies, South Asian studies, global studies, and critical studies of NGOs and humanitarianism.

Vibhuti Ramachandran is an assistant professor of global and international studies at the University of California, Irvine. Her work connects the anthropology of law, NGOs, and the Indian state, and her broader interests include gender and sexuality, care and punishment, and labor and migration. The University of California's Hellman Fellowship supported the completion of this book.

CAMBRIDGE STUDIES IN LAW AND SOCIETY

Founded in 1997, Cambridge Studies in Law and Society is a hub for leading scholarship in socio-legal studies. Located at the intersection of law, the humanities, and the social sciences, it publishes empirically innovative and theoretically sophisticated work on law's manifestations in everyday life: from discourses to practices, and from institutions to cultures. The series editors have longstanding expertise in the interdisciplinary study of law, and welcome contributions that place legal phenomena in national, comparative, or international perspective. Series authors come from a range of disciplines, including anthropology, history, law, literature, political science, and sociology.

A list of books in the series can be found at the back of this book.

CAMBRIDGE
STUDIES IN
LAW AND SOCIETY

Awarded the

Joseph W. Elder Prize in the Indian Social Sciences

by the American Institute of Indian Studies and published with the Institute's generous support.

AIIS Publication Committee:

Sarah Lamb, Co-Chair
Anand A. Yang, Co-Chair
Sonal Khullar
Gabrielle Kruks-Wisner
Preeta Mani
Tulasi Srinivas

Immoral Traffic

AN ETHNOGRAPHY OF LAW, NGOs, AND THE GOVERNANCE OF PROSTITUTION IN INDIA

VIBHUTI RAMACHANDRAN
University of California, Irvine

CAMBRIDGE
UNIVERSITY PRESS

CAMBRIDGE
UNIVERSITY PRESS

Shaftesbury Road, Cambridge CB2 8EA, United Kingdom

One Liberty Plaza, 20th Floor, New York, NY 10006, USA

477 Williamstown Road, Port Melbourne, VIC 3207, Australia

314–321, 3rd Floor, Plot 3, Splendor Forum, Jasola District Centre, New Delhi – 110025, India

103 Penang Road, #05–06/07, Visioncrest Commercial, Singapore 238467

Cambridge University Press is part of Cambridge University Press & Assessment, a department of the University of Cambridge.

We share the University's mission to contribute to society through the pursuit of education, learning and research at the highest international levels of excellence.

www.cambridge.org
Information on this title: www.cambridge.org/9781009490290

DOI: 10.1017/9781009490313

When citing this work, please include a reference to the DOI 10.1017/9781009490313

First published 2025

A catalogue record for this publication is available from the British Library

Library of Congress Cataloging-in-Publication Data
NAMES: Ramachandran, Vibhuti, author.
TITLE: Immoral traffic : an ethnography of law, NGOs, and the governance of prostitution in India / Vibhuti Ramachandran.
DESCRIPTION: 1. | New York : Cambridge University Press, 2025. | Includes bibliographical references and index.
IDENTIFIERS: LCCN 2024013569 | ISBN 9781009490290 (hardback) | ISBN 9781009490313 (ebook)
SUBJECTS: LCSH: Prostitutes – Legal status, laws, etc. – India. | Prostitution – India. | Human trafficking – India.
CLASSIFICATION: LCC KNS4224 . R36 2025
LC record available at https://lccn.loc.gov/2024013569

ISBN 978-1-009-49029-0 Hardback

In loving memory of my mother, Sadhana Ramachandran (1955–2024),
who supported my research and writing every step of the way.

Contents

Figures

Tables

Preface

Students, colleagues, and friends often ask me how I came to this project. The motivations for the broader areas of study seem clear to those who know my personal and academic background. I am from India, I was trained in anthropology, with a strong focus on law and society and gender and sexuality studies, and I am now in a global studies department. But what got me interested, specifically, in nongovernmental organizations (NGOs), the Indian anti-prostitution law, and the global anti-trafficking regime whose impacts and intersections this book traces?

I came to this research as an anthropologist of law, NGOs, and the Indian state. I am not an anti-trafficking activist and have never worked for an anti-trafficking NGO, apart from the volunteer tasks I performed while doing research for this book. Nor have I been involved in sex worker rights advocacy against the harms of anti-trafficking interventions, though I have kept abreast of key developments around it in India and brought its critical perspectives to this book. The best way to introduce this book is through some significant and somewhat disjointed moments from my early years of graduate study that came together to shape my research.

In the mid-2000s, I was closely following two legal and political developments in India through media reports, legislative efforts, court cases, and public debates. In March 2005, the Indian state of Maharashtra (of which Mumbai is the capital) ordered the closure of dance bars across the state. The working-class women who worked at these bars danced to Bollywood film songs while male customers drank alcohol and showered them with cash. Many bar dancers were the sole earners for their families. Some told researchers and reporters that they did sex work too, though most said they didn't. The Maharashtra government, however, was on a moral policing mission and insisted that the dance bar economy was a front for prostitution and needed to be shut down. The ban was also reportedly prompted by police and politicians' appetites for bribes from the bar owners and their retaliation when those appetites were not satisfied. Shaped by multiple motives, the ban construed the bars (and the dancers) on the one hand as immoral and on the other as sites of sex trafficking from which women needed to be rescued.

While prominent anti-trafficking NGOs in Mumbai supported the ban, bar owners and the bar dancers' union protested it on grounds of discrimination. They argued that if the sexually charged "item numbers" in Hindi films by well-paid elite actresses were permitted in cinemas and five-star hotels, then banning the imitation of the same dances by much lower-paid working-class women in non-elite bars was discriminatory. The Bombay High Court, and later the Indian Supreme Court, ruled the ban unconstitutional on these grounds, but over 75,000 women had already lost their livelihoods.

The Mumbai dance bar ban became the focus of my master's thesis at the University of Chicago on the policing of women's sexuality in India. I examined the discriminatory moral policing of the ban, the bar dancers' resistance to it, and the court judgments, situated in the cultural politics of censorship around sexuality, morality, and class in India. In that mid-2000s moment, it was significant that both the Bombay High Court and the bar dancers' union drew an explicit distinction between working-class women making ends meet by merely dancing in bars and the immorality of sex work. Indeed, the bar dancers argued that the ban would push them into prostitution, which they construed as a far worse fate – both immoral and exploitative – than bar dancing. In the public debates around the dance bar ban, the possibility or absence of sex trafficking, the relative respectability of different forms of gendered performance and labor, and the perceived immorality of sex workers, were all points of reference. Although the doctoral research this book builds upon focused on anti-trafficking and anti-prostitution interventions, the dance bars made their way back in, as the reader will see in Chapters 5 and 6.

Around the same time as the Mumbai dance bar ban, a different legal development was unfolding in New Delhi. I followed it with great interest, given its connections to and departures from the dance bar debates. In 2006, thousands of Indian sex workers marched to Parliament to protest an amendment to the anti-prostitution law, the Immoral Traffic (Prevention) Act (ITPA) of 1956. The government proposed this amendment, which sought to criminalize the clients of sex workers, owing to lobbying by anti-trafficking NGOs. The NGOs were reportedly influenced, in turn, by two closely linked agendas that were globally pervasive in the mid-2000s. One was the Swedish or Nordic model of criminalization that considers prostitution inherently exploitative and expands criminal penalties to everyone involved in the demand for sex, including clients. The second was the US-led anti-trafficking regime; in particular, India's poor ranking by the US State Department's annual *Trafficking in Persons (TIP) Report* for not doing enough to curb sex trafficking.

Those analyzing these developments saw the proposed amendment to Indian law as a move by Indian NGOs and the government agencies they worked with to improve India's ranking on the US *TIP Report*. The Nordic and US approaches equated prostitution with sex trafficking, while India's ITPA law was more ambivalent, treating sex workers as both immoral and victimized. By amending its anti-prostitution law to include the criminalization of clients, India could show that it was enacting stricter penalties against those purchasing sex, whom the Nordic model and US anti-trafficking regime firmly place among the perpetrators of sex trafficking.

Opposing this move to amend Indian law to criminalize clients, Indian sex worker rights groups questioned why they had not been consulted on the proposed amendment. They had been organizing since the late 1990s in the context of HIV/AIDS prevention and calling for a distinction to be made between voluntary sex work and sex trafficking. Their argument against the proposed amendment was that criminalizing clients would adversely affect voluntary sex workers' livelihoods, harm HIV/AIDS prevention efforts, and push the sex trade further underground, with the result that sex workers could not seek any assistance from government agencies or NGOs. The amendment ultimately lapsed before it could be passed by the Indian Parliament.

Tracking developments around the dance bar ban and the proposed ITPA amendment introduced me to a tumult of legal developments, moral panics, and public debate around sex work, sex trafficking, and related questions in India in the mid-2000s. I learned about a contested political field to which Indian state agencies, global anti-trafficking campaigns and donor-driven Indian NGOs, sex worker rights groups, and bar dancers' unions came with vastly different perspectives. I began to comprehend both the Indian sociolegal and political contexts, and the global donor and policy regimes steering these developments. And I became attentive to how efforts against bar dancing, sex trafficking, and sex work coalesce, how NGOs play a key role in shaping them, and how law is central to the construction and resistance of these efforts.

In 2009, Sally Merry, my PhD advisor at New York University (NYU), was working on a National Science Foundation-funded project on the politics of human rights indicators – how efforts to quantify human rights performance become a form of global governance – the subject of her 2016 book *The Seductions of Quantification: Measuring Human Rights, Gender Violence, and Sex Trafficking*. Sally asked me if I would like to be her research assistant in India for this project, where I would focus on the politics of the poor ranking given to India on its anti-trafficking performance by the US State Department's *Trafficking in Persons Reports*. She was curious about India's response to this form of stick-wielding global governance being unilaterally imposed by the US. I was already aware of the US' role in funding and shaping global anti-trafficking campaigns and of the *TIP Reports*' impact on NGO efforts and law reform in India. Given the intersections with my research interests and my eagerness to learn more about Sally's work, I jumped at the opportunity and conducted research in India for her project over two summers (2009 and 2010).

Through interviews with US embassy officials, Indian government representatives, and anti-trafficking NGOs in New Delhi, I learned that the Indian government clearly resisted US interference. Though it did not officially take cognizance of the US *TIP Report*, it took issue with an external entity evaluating India's anti-trafficking performance. India's poor ranking on the *TIP Report* had caused political concern. In July 2009, an Indian legislator asked a question in Parliament about how this ranking would impact its global reputation. The Home Minister,[1] P. Chidambaram, acknowledged that sex trafficking, which he referred to as the "immoral trafficking" (per the terminology in Indian law) of women and girls into prostitution, was a major problem, but emphasized that India was fighting it "as an enlightened nation, not because somebody else points it out to us." Thus articulated, India's resistance as a postcolonial nation questioning the need for "enlightenment" by Western nations was framed by its history and politics of anticolonial nationalism. Given this resistance, the US relied heavily on Indian NGOs to provide information, carry out its anti-trafficking agenda, and work with Indian state agencies and legal actors to do so.

In summer 2010, I also connected with a US-funded anti-trafficking NGO in New Delhi. I had scheduled an interview with its founder and chief functionary for the research I was doing for Sally. The NGO had funding from the US State Department's Office to Monitor and Combat Trafficking in Persons for a project to train Indian judges on the issue of human trafficking and how Indian law could be applied in human trafficking cases. Right after the interview, I had the opportunity to observe a meeting between this NGO and a team from the US embassy in New Delhi.

During the meeting, the NGO representatives briefed the embassy officials about the progress of the US-funded project. Eventually, an embassy official broached the topic of India's poor ranking on the State Department's *TIP Report*. India had been placed on a Watch List until the Indian government demonstrated greater effort to curb human trafficking. The embassy official explained that they were meeting with the NGO that day to "help India move up" these rankings. This reminded me of the efforts led by anti-trafficking NGOs to amend the Indian ITPA law in 2006 to criminalize clients as a bid to showcase India's commitment to legislative action against human trafficking. Knowing more about the geopolitics of the US *TIP Report* helped me gain further perspective on those developments being a likely response to US pressure to "do more" against trafficking.

The US embassy team asked the NGO to give them reasons why India should *not* be on the Watch List. A legal expert from the NGO responded that the federal government in India was doing a great deal to take initiative against human trafficking. He explained that the issue was India's federal structure, where the responsibility for law enforcement lay with the multiple state (provincial) governments, which varied in their responses to trafficking and could not easily coordinate a response to interstate trafficking crimes in the country. The NGO's explanation to the embassy officials thus called for a recognition that an anti-trafficking agenda had to be implemented within the specific structure of Indian law enforcement.

[1] The Home Minister heads the federal department overseeing law and order and internal security in India. Though each state (province) in India has its own police, the Home Ministry coordinates certain aspects of nationwide policing and oversees central policing and investigation agencies.

Reflecting on the Indian Home Minister's response to the question in Parliament about the US *TIP Report* and this meeting between the NGO and US embassy officials, I began to map out the US-driven, globally pervasive anti-trafficking agenda, the Indian government's resistance to it, and NGOs' role in implementing it within the Indian legal context. The embassy–NGO exchange centered on the role of Indian NGOs as key partners of the US-led global campaign against trafficking. It showed how donor-driven NGOs were expected not only to provide updates on the progress of their projects but also to explain what steps the Indian government was taking (steps that the NGO was expected to shape and monitor) to counter human trafficking.

Building upon that summer's research, I began to formulate my own ethnographic research project around the multiple entities and agendas shaping the governance of prostitution in India – Indian law, state institutions, NGOs, and global humanitarian agendas and funding circuits. While the role of the US and its *TIP Reports* continued to be of interest and relevance, I wanted to situate the increased presence and power of US-funded anti-trafficking NGOs within a longer and broader story. My interdisciplinary academic training and the shifts I have outlined in my research trajectory led me to the conjuncture of multiple interventions governing prostitution in India. How do donor-driven, globally pervasive anti-trafficking campaigns intersect with India's long history of anti-prostitution regulation? How does anti-trafficking campaigns' eclipsing of distinctions between sex work and sex trafficking square with Indian law's ambivalence about prostitution as both immoral and exploitative? How do these conflations and ambivalences shape contested meanings around prostitution in the Indian sociolegal context, and in interactions between Indian legal actors, NGOs, and sex workers? And how do the women targeted by these intersecting interventions navigate, respond to, and resist them? These are the questions that animate this book.

The questions framing *Immoral Traffic* are therefore different from the moments I have recounted here, as are its ethnographic sites. However, those early moments have shaped the directions my research has taken, leading up to this book. They have steered me toward an exploration of how Indian anti-prostitution law, a global anti-trafficking donor and policy regime, and Indian NGOs converge to govern prostitution in India, and how the women these efforts target respond to them.

Those early moments stayed with me during the doctoral research this book draws upon. They make interesting returns and thread through this book. The ITPA, India's anti-prostitution law, which was almost amended in 2006 owing to pressure from Indian NGOs and global anti-trafficking regimes, and resisted by sex worker rights groups, is central to this book. Indeed, the book reprises this law's name in its title. *Immoral Traffic* follows the sequence of interventions from rescues to shelters that this law prescribes and NGOs help to implement. The US *TIP Reports*' impact on and incongruity with the Indian sociolegal context are palpable, especially in Chapters 3 and 4. The issue of coordination between police across states that the

NGO raised with the US embassy team emerged during my research across multiple sites – rescues, courts, and shelters. I continued to track the work of the New Delhi NGO whose meeting with embassy officials I had observed for Sally's project on human rights indicators. The same NGO led the rescues, court proceedings, and judicial training session discussed in Chapters 2 and 3 of this book. A Mumbai anti-trafficking NGO that supported the dance bar ban in 2005 also pushed for the establishment of a Special Court under the ITPA in 2008. This Court, with which I begin the book, is the focus of Chapters 4 and 5. And the Mumbai dance bars continued to be targets of both anti-trafficking intervention and moral policing, as Chapters 4 and 5 will show. These sites, entities, and developments connect the book from what led me to the project, to how it eventually developed, and to what I learned along the way.

Acknowledgments

RESEARCH ACKNOWLEDGMENTS

The ethnographic research at the core of this book would not have been possible without the NGOs, police officers, judges, prosecutors, lawyers, and state officials who generously shared their time and perspectives with me. I have chosen not to name most of them to maintain anonymity and confidentiality, but I am deeply grateful for the access and support they provided, and the interest many of them took in my research in the midst of their busy schedules. I am especially thankful to the members of the New Delhi anti-trafficking NGO who allowed me to observe their work closely, the Mumbai magistrate who graciously permitted me to observe the ITPA Special Court, her predecessor who facilitated my initial research access to the Court and to the Mumbai protective home, and the superintendent and staff at the protective home who allowed me to volunteer there at a time when the institution was under intense scrutiny.

I am much indebted to the women – survivors of trafficking, voluntary sex workers, and those who denied involvement in prostitution – I met during and after rescues, in court, and at shelters. My access to these processes meant that I was sometimes asked to "counsel" or inquire with them or keep them "productively engaged." Apart from "passing" as an NGO worker or legal actor, these forms of involvement inevitably positioned me as an authority figure, not someone rescued women could speak with freely. I remain immensely grateful to those who were willing to speak with me, and learned a great deal from the silences and refusals of those who were not.

While conducting fieldwork in India, conversations with several scholars, researchers, and activists helped me think through various aspects of this book. Oishik Sircar, Suman Saha, and Annie George provided rich insights on the tensions between sex worker rights activism and anti-trafficking interventions. Anuja Agrawal was always generous with her time and suggestions. Her work on prostitution in the Bedia community helped me develop my analysis in Chapter 2. I had the privilege of speaking with (Justice) S. Muralidhar about his early work as a human rights lawyer. His investigative report during that time on the Agra protective home, and the insights he provided during our conversation, have informed my analysis of protective custody in Chapter 6. In Mumbai, I am grateful for conversations with Manjima Bhattacharjya, Flavia Agnes and her team at Majlis, and Meena Gopal and other members of the Forum Against Oppression of Women on the politics of dance bars and forced raids.

I am truly fortunate that Saie Shetye, then an MPhil student at the Tata Institute of Social Sciences, conducted research at the Mumbai Special Court at the same time as me. We shared the joys and challenges of research at the Court, laughing, commiserating, and collaborating along the way. Saie also often translated or summarized Court proceedings in Marathi for me and has permitted me to use a table from her MPhil thesis in Chapter 4. I have learned so much from her.

I would like to acknowledge Save the Children India (STCI), a Mumbai anti-trafficking NGO, and their funders, the Kamonohashi project, for hiring me as a consultant for their study on factors impacting the prosecution of trafficking cases in Mumbai and Maharashtra. I analyzed the judgments that STCI's legal team collected and the interviews that Saie Shetye conducted for the study. This provided me access to judgments and interviews beyond my own research to analyze. I have included some of these cases in my analysis in Chapter 3.

The Wenner Gren Foundation for Anthropological Research funded my ethnographic research. NYU's MacCracken Graduate Fellowship funded the completion of my doctoral dissertation. The University of California's Society of Hellman Fellows funded the development and completion of the book manuscript. Aure Schrock from Indelible Voice provided editorial feedback and support. As I completed, revised, and updated the book manuscript, I received excellent research assistance from several students at the University of California, Irvine: Vinootna Kakarla, Danielle Tassara, Nandini Sharma, and Madeline Cole.

PUBLICATION ACKNOWLEDGMENTS

Some of the chapters in this book include material I have previously published in journal articles and public-facing essays. My contribution to a symposium on New Directions in Legal Anthropology for *Law and Social Inquiry* contains some of the arguments I have developed further in the book's Introduction and Chapter 1, and some of the ethnographic moments I have expanded upon in Chapters 2 and 3. Chapters 3 and 4 include arguments and some ethnographic material from my article in the journal *Social Sciences*. Chapter 6 is a longer version of my article in the journal *Contemporary South Asia*. Some of the ethnographic moments I expand upon in Chapters 2 and 6 find mention in two essays I wrote for *Open Democracy*.

I want to express my gratitude to Mark Massoud, Rachel Stern, and Jens Meierhenrich, the series editors of *Cambridge Studies in Law and Society*, for their interest in and support of the manuscript. Mark Massoud has been incredibly generous with his own helpful and discerning editorial suggestions. The peer reviewers' comments indicated a close and careful reading of the manuscript. I am thankful for their time and attention. I am also truly thankful to the staff at Cambridge University Press, especially Matt Gallaway and Jadyn Fauconier Herry, who have been an absolute pleasure to work with.

ACADEMIC ACKNOWLEDGMENTS

My somewhat unlikely path to academia began in college. When I was majoring in journalism at Lady Shri Ram College, Deepti Priya Mehrotra supervised my honors thesis on street theater. Her mentorship helped me discover the joys of ethnographic research, and her work deepened my interest in gender and sexuality studies. At the Delhi School of Economics, where I pursued a master's in sociology, I developed an interest in the anthropology of the state through the work of Anand Chakravarti, and in carceral studies through the work of Mahuya Bandyopadhyay. They heightened academia's appeal for me. I began to explore the policing and censorship of women's sexuality in India while pursuing an interdisciplinary social sciences master's at the University of Chicago. My interest in the Mumbai dance bar ban, and the broader questions it led me to explore, were shaped by working with William Mazzarella as my thesis supervisor. At Chicago, Rochona Majumdar also provided significant mentorship and support.

At NYU, where I earned my PhD in anthropology, I gained immensely from the mentorship of my doctoral committee. Tejaswini Ganti honed my attentiveness to films and television shows as contexts and methods for anthropological research (see Chapter 6). Rayna Rapp encouraged me to explore the breadth of the subfield of feminist anthropology, which she herself played a pivotal role in building. Teja and Rayna were both wonderfully supportive mentors as I completed my dissertation amid medical crises and caregiving responsibilities.

I owe a tremendous debt of gratitude to my PhD advisor, the late Sally Merry, whose contributions to the anthropology of law, human rights, and law and society have given me both direction and inspiration. In the three years since she passed away, I have felt her loss profoundly. She was that rare and wonderful blend of a brilliant and prolific scholar with heartfelt care and concern for her colleagues and students. Sally read everything I sent her – from an article draft to the smallest of grant applications. She always had astute and substantive feedback, often accompanied by the important and helpful, but difficult question, "but what do you *mean* by X sentence?" She was a stickler for clarity and comprehensibility in the expression of ideas, which she modeled in her own writing. I still hear Sally's voice in my head when I read over something I'm writing and find myself asking the "what do you *mean*" question.

Sally's graduate seminar on law and society gave me the tools to envision my project. She showed me and my fellow graduate students (not to mention sociolegal scholars beyond NYU) how to study the micropractices of law while also examining the transnational politics of human rights, gender justice, and global governance. While I was at NYU, Sally was developing a project on the politics of human rights indicators, which culminated in her book critiquing these "seductions of quantification" (2016). I worked with her for two summers (2009 and 2010) as a research assistant, focusing on the US State Department's *Trafficking in Persons Reports* in India. As explained in the Preface, this became the point of entry through which I formulated my own research across multiple interventions governing prostitution in India.

This book bears the imprint of Sally's mentorship both academically and personally. I wrote the doctoral dissertation that led to this book under often challenging personal circumstances. Despite her busy schedule and travel, Sally went above and beyond to provide support when I had to take time off. She cared enough to help with things as mundane and time-consuming as paperwork that I sometimes did not even have the bandwidth to think of or remember.

Beyond NYU, I have benefited from several scholars' engagement with my work. Srimati Basu and Svati Shah served as the external members of my doctoral committee. I am thankful for their time and feedback. Srimati's ethnography of family courts in Kolkata and Svati's ethnography of migration, labor, and sex work in Mumbai offered much inspiration as I formulated my project, conducted fieldwork, and developed my arguments. As a graduate student in New York City, I was fortunate to connect with Elizabeth Bernstein, whose critiques of anti-trafficking interventions and insights on abolitionist feminism, faith-based humanitarianism, and law enforcement in the US have shaped my understanding of the transnational politics of anti-trafficking.

Over the years, I have gained immeasurably from the feedback of discussants and fellow panelists at conferences where I presented early versions of each chapter. I presented a draft of what eventually became Chapter 2, on rescues, at the American Anthropological Association (AAA) Conference in San Francisco and at the Law and Social Sciences Network Conference in Sri Lanka. Radhika Coomaraswamy and Katherine Lemons served as discussants at these conferences, and I am deeply appreciative of their comments.

Pratiksha Baxi invited me to present my early findings at a conference organized by the Center for the Study of Law and Governance at New Delhi's Jawaharlal Nehru University. I am grateful for the questions posed and suggestions offered by Pratiksha herself, Roma Chatterji, who served as discussant, Upendra Baxi, and Pooja Satyogi. I presented a revised version of the paper at the AAA conference in Chicago, where Sameena Mulla was a wonderfully engaged and astute discussant. These early drafts focused on the case of Sunaina Das, which I developed into a substantial component of Chapter 3, on victim-witness testimony at a New Delhi court.

I presented an early draft of Chapter 4, on evidence and testimony at the Mumbai Special Court, at the Law and Society Association's annual conference in Washington DC, where Jack Jin Gary Lee provided excellent suggestions as discussant. Chapter

5 was developed through papers I presented at a South Asia Legal Studies Pre-Conference at the University of Wisconsin–Madison and the AAA conference in Washington DC, both in 2014. William Mazzarella served as discussant for the first and Denise Brennan for the second. The insights they brought to the paper were invaluable and have helped shape the chapter. Early versions of Chapter 6, on shelter detention, benefited from the insights of Anjali Arondekar at the South Asia by the Bay graduate student conference at the University of California, Santa Cruz, and Jennifer Musto at the American Ethnological Society Conference in Boston.

Prabha Kotiswaran's prolific body of work on sex work and law in India has shaped my understanding of the complex terrain marked by tensions between sex worker rights activism and abolitionist anti-trafficking interventions. I am grateful for the support Prabha has provided over the years. In 2014, she invited me to participate in a conference on Shaping the Definition of Trafficking in the Palermo Protocol at King's College, London, where I connected with several feminist scholars – Prabha herself, Denise Brennan, Julia O'Connell Davidson, Aziza Ahmed, and Janie Chuang, among others – whose critical work on sex work, migration, and the harms of anti-trafficking interventions has been greatly insightful and generative. Prabha also invited me to participate in a virtual workshop in 2020 on Interdisciplinary Conversations on Sex Work in India, which helped me develop my analysis (especially in Chapters 2 and 3) of how NGO intervention and police investigation come together in the practice of "counseling."

I am tremendously grateful to several brilliant and supportive peers and colleagues across the academic fields I work within and across. It has been a pleasure and privilege to collaborate with them on conferences, workshops, and publications. On the politics of sex work and sex trafficking in India, I have learned so much from Kimberly Walters, Simanti Dasgupta, Mirna Guha, and Gowri Vijayakumar. Kimberly provided excellent suggestions as I developed parts of Chapter 6 into an article for a special section of *Contemporary South Asia*. Rohit De's work on the Suppression of Immoral Traffic in Women and Girls Act (1956) has enriched my understanding of the legal history that continues to shape the present. Sahana Ghosh's work has helped me understand the politics of migration and anti-trafficking at the India–Bangladesh border, especially as the vilification of Bangladeshi immigrants has further escalated since the time I conducted my research in 2012–2013. Moyukh Chatterjee and Megha Sehdev were fellow travelers in the anthropology of law in India. Deepa Das Acevedo invited me to participate in a symposium on New Directions in Legal Anthropology, which she shepherded to publication in *Law and Social Inquiry*. My essay, which gave me the opportunity to work out some of the arguments in this book, was enriched by feedback from Deepa, Matthew Canfield, and the several wonderful legal anthropologists Deepa brought together.

My fellow graduate students in the department of anthropology at NYU provided the community that made academia less isolating. Ram Natarajan, Wenrui Chen, Sneh Patel, and Carol Wang brought meaning, support, friendship, and warmth to my time in New York City. I am also grateful to have had as part of my "village" Johanna Römer, Louis Römer, Matthew Canfield, Anna Wilking, Dwaipayan Banerjee, and Vijayanka Nair.

The University of California, Irvine, my academic home since 2018, has provided the opportunity to connect with several fellow anthropologists of law. Eve Darian-Smith and Susan Bibler Coutin have provided both mentorship and generous engagement with my work. Lee Cabatingan and Jessica Lopez-Espino have both been wonderful colleagues. I presented a draft of Chapter 3 at a workshop by the Center in Law, Society, and Culture, where Swethaa Ballakrishnen and Christopher Seeds provided helpful comments. I am grateful for Victoria Bernal's feedback as I finalized the manuscript and for her own work on gender and NGOs, which has informed this book. At the Department of Global and International Studies, I am fortunate to have Long Bui, Yousuf Al-Bulushi, Brenda Nicolas, Sarah Whitt, Mamyrah Prosper, Tiara Na'puti, and Fantasia Painter among several wonderful interdisciplinary colleagues. Brenda Nicolas and Elena Agapie have been much-needed sources of support, care, and writing accountability in an exceptionally challenging year. Our department administrators, Jessica Cañas-Castañeda and Jewel Quilaton, deserve mention for the support they provide every day.

PERSONAL ACKNOWLEDGMENTS

It would not have been possible to conduct ethnographic research without the generosity and support of my family, and friends old and new. In New Delhi, my parents, Sadhana and Raju Ramachandran, and parents-in-law, Savithri and Anil Kumar Singh, provided the comforts of home. In Mumbai, Madhavi and Ameet Hariani, Anjana Thiagarajan, and Priyanka Zutshi welcomed me to their homes while I settled into an unfamiliar city. Research can be an isolating experience, but Divya, Rajul, and Pallabi in New Delhi and Saie Shetye, Rahela Khorakiwala, Radhika Rajagopalan, and Ashwitha Jayakumar in Mumbai made it so much fun.

Those who have supported me the longest have endured the absences and preoccupations that this book's decade-long journey has imposed on them. I owe so much to them. My paternal grandparents, the late Girija and T. N. Ramachandran, helped to raise me, modeling a lifelong love for learning and reading. My maternal grandmother Kamala Rana's experiences as a social worker since India's early postcolonial years have substantially shaped my research interests. She passed away just as I was completing this book. Her formidable strength and rich stories fill my thoughts. Growing up in a household of lawyers, I was determined not to become one, yet I ironically, perhaps inevitably, developed enough of a vicarious interest in the law to study it ethnographically. My parents, Sadhana and Raju Ramachandran, have selflessly supported all my choices and endeavors. Though the courts and procedures I observed were not their domain, they were often my sounding boards for questions about Indian law. In response to my endless queries about criminal legal procedure, my brother Chaitanya handed me his law school textbooks before returning to the go-to quips and random silliness he has passed on, for better or worse, to my adorable nephews. My sister-in-law, Krishna, and her family made Mumbai feel like home.

Sameer and Aadya mean the world to me. Sameer has been my rock for more than two decades – from before I ever thought I would write a book, to its completion. He has been there for me with care, cheer, and patience for my innumerable requests for tech fixes. Indeed, beyond mere "fixes," he turned my hand-drawn sketches of the courtroom and shelter into the images in Chapters 4 and 6. We have navigated life, academia, family, and so much more together (and maybe one day I'll embrace AI). Our daughter Aadya has seen me work on this book since she was born. She now knows that every time I say I have finished it, there is probably more left to do. After all, her second grade class published their book while I was "still working" on mine.

As a feminist anthropologist, I want to end in recognition of care, all too often rendered invisible in academia. I wrote both the dissertation and the book amid crises and care – care that I provided, shared, and received. My mother battled cancer and endured the toll of its treatments, yet found the capacity to support me as I experienced a complicated pregnancy involving multiple hospitalizations. My incredibly brave daughter spent months in neonatal intensive care after her preterm birth. I am completing this book while my mother continues to valiantly battle cancer and its complications. Indeed, I wrote these acknowledgments in a hospital waiting room as she received chemotherapy. At times, this book has taken a back seat while I prioritized caring for my loved ones. At other times, I have prioritized this book and relied upon the caregiving others in my family shouldered, and the labor of care providers. I am profoundly thankful to all of them. Many of us navigate academia with multigenerational caregiving responsibilities, and are also, in turn, supported by others. My journey reflects these experiences, and my book bears their imprint.

Introduction

The ITPA Special Court is a small, unassuming space tucked away at one end of the fourth floor of the run-down Mazgaon Courts complex in southern Mumbai. A petition by a US-funded Indian anti-trafficking nongovernmental organization (NGO) helped to initiate its establishment in 2008 as the first and only court to prosecute cases under India's anti-prostitution law, the Immoral Traffic (Prevention) Act of 1956 (ITPA). Its nondescript appearance, otherwise indistinct from other courtrooms in the building, and the bureaucracy of law and piles of paperwork central to its functioning, render this court seemingly unremarkable in the Indian sociolegal context. Yet, as I found out, it is an extraordinary site where evidence and testimony are focused on proving commercial sexual transactions, procedures and judgments are shaped by moral assumptions and evaluations, and hints of global concern about sex trafficking in India pop up every once in a while via reports, brochures, and visitors.

Since it came into existence, global donor agencies and policymakers and Indian anti-trafficking NGOs have devoted considerable attention to this small Mumbai court. It finds frequent mention in the US State Department's annual *Trafficking in Persons Report* for "clearing the backlog in trafficking cases and ordering a record number of convictions against traffickers and brothel owners" (2011: 49). From time to time, as I sipped the *cutting chai* the court's magistrate generously called for in her chambers, a copy of the US *Trafficking in Persons (TIP) Report* on her table would remind me of the global interest in the court amid our conversations otherwise focused on Indian legal procedures and patterns of cases. In the months I spent observing this court, further forms of global attention occasionally emerged. Members of a Japanese aid agency funding NGOs in Mumbai showed up one day to observe the court's proceedings – struggling to figure out its layout and procedures, and missing a translator, yet curious about its possibilities. Their primary objective, which they had worked toward in Cambodia and were now pursuing in India, was to fund Indian NGOs to support sex trafficking survivors to testify against traffickers in courts like this one.

The significant global interest in this small Mumbai court is deeply connected to this type of donor support for "victim-witness testimony." To meet donor expectations, anti-trafficking NGOs encourage women they rescue from the sex trade to testify at this court against those accused of sex trafficking and other crimes under India's ITPA law. Though facilitating such testimony is a key component of NGO efforts, magistrates and prosecutors at the court lamented that "victim-witnesses" rarely testified. In eight months observing the court, I saw several other prosecution witnesses – police officers, NGO representatives, and even decoy customers – come to testify. I saw camel-colored envelopes with cash, reams of documents, and even unopened condom packets regularly produced as evidence of prostitution,[1] but rarely did "victim-witnesses" show up. This disjuncture between the patterns of evidence at the court, on the one hand, and the expectations of foreign donors and efforts of the NGOs they fund, on the other, showed me how India's anti-prostitution law and global anti-trafficking campaigns converge, yet remain incongruous in their focus and priorities.

Behind the courtroom, in the magistrate's chambers, I observed a separate procedure prescribed by India's ITPA law. Here, NGO representatives assist the magistrate in conducting inquiries with women brought in after raids and rescues. During these inquiries, the magistrate and NGO workers questioned, "counseled" and censured the women, seeking to elicit accounts of sex trafficking, while many women denied being involved in prostitution at all. In these interactions, victimhood was assumed, imposed, debated, and resisted in far more complex and ambivalent ways than the figure of the vulnerable, helpless Third World sex slave saturating global campaigns against sex trafficking. The interactions I observed combined accusations of immorality, concern at the women's exploitation, and suspicions about their identities – especially about the possibility of them being immigrants from Bangladesh who were in India without documents or with forged documents. The inquiries evinced how deeply this court's activities were rooted in the Indian sociolegal and South Asian sociopolitical contexts. Yet global interest occasionally reared its head in this aspect of the court's work as well. For instance, a Canadian filmmaker associated with one of the NGOs once showed up to seek permission to observe the inquiries, a day after landing in India. She was deeply interested in hearing the women's accounts, while also mystified by how they constructed them in response to the hierarchical dynamics of the inquiries.

These moments at the Mumbai Special Court introduced me to the complex ways in which global anti-trafficking campaigns and Indian anti-prostitution law come together, and Indian legal actors and foreign-funded NGOs work together, to govern prostitution in India. They also reflected the distinct genealogies, logics, perspectives, and roles of these interventions and entities. And they brought forth how

1 In Chapter 4, I explain how the prosecution marshals these forms of evidence toward proving transactional aspects of prostitution, rather than sex trafficking, in ways that reinforce deeply moralistic assumptions and satisfy the evidentiary requirements of Indian procedural law.

sex workers' accounts, silences, absences, and denials were central to these intersecting interventions, often resisting their premises and solutions. In my memories of fieldwork, these moments at the court jostle with the loud whir of the ceiling fan that drowned out the proceedings while providing relief from Mumbai's sweltering heat, and the sweet-bitter taste of the *cutting chai* I sipped in the magistrate's chambers.

Immoral Traffic takes its readers to the Special Court and multiple other sites in New Delhi and Mumbai where women removed from the sex trade are processed, addressed, and offered forms of assistance prescribed by Indian law and implemented by Indian legal actors and NGOs. At these sites, foreign-funded, donor-driven NGOs carry out an anti-trafficking agenda, while also performing tasks that Indian anti-prostitution law has long assigned them, in newly intensified and expansive ways. This book is an ethnography at these intersections of law, NGOs, the Indian state, and the global "anti-trafficking industrial complex."[2]

AN ETHNOGRAPHY OF INTERSECTING INTERVENTIONS

India is often the setting for images and accounts, constructed and circulating in media reports and policy and donor networks, that drive US-funded anti-trafficking interventions in the Global South. From the *New York Times*' Nicholas Kristof's reports and op-eds (2004a, 2014b, 2015) to a *National Geographic* documentary featuring US journalist Lisa Ling,[3] Indian sex workers are depicted as helpless victims forced into the sex trade, from which they must be rescued by outside intervention. Western journalists, including Kristof and Ling, often cover and even participate in anti-trafficking rescue operations in India. Pressure from a transnational anti-trafficking regime has fueled the expansion of anti-prostitution initiatives in India, from rescues to efforts to strengthen the prosecution of alleged traffickers in court, and shelter-based protection and rehabilitation programs.

Though global media and donor interest begins with and usually lingers in the drama of raids and rescues in metropolitan Indian cities, it also reaches less hypervisible sites, such as the Mumbai court I have just introduced my readers to. Other Indian institutions, such as shelters for women rescued from the sex trade, also feature in the US *TIP Reports*. These portray shelters as safe, protective, and even empowering spaces, even as they acknowledge the egregious abuses reported at these institutions.[4] These forms of interest and attention exemplify how global

2 Bernstein (2018); Hoefinger (2016); Walters (2020). Quoting sex worker activist Carol Leigh, Elena Shih explains this term as the circulation and accrual of benefits by those who are working to stop trafficking, though the benefits to trafficked people are debatable (2023: xii).

3 National Geographic (2007). *Slave Girls of India*.

4 Indian shelters for rescued sex workers are discussed in the India country narratives of the 2012 and 2019 *TIP Reports* in particular. In this book, my ethnography of one such shelter is the focus of Chapter 6.

media, policy, and activist efforts especially since the year 2000 are framing the issue of prostitution in India as sex trafficking, to be addressed through rescues, law enforcement, criminal justice interventions, and economic rehabilitation.

Funded by globally influential entities such as the US State Department, and implemented by Indian NGOs, anti-trafficking campaigns have brought foreign funding, emotive appeals, new motivations for rescues, and a new focus on law enforcement and criminal justice to an already complex history of concerns around prostitution in India and solutions devised to deal with it. Since the early 2000s, the State Department has been funding NGOs in India and other Global South countries to train legal actors to treat prostitution as sex trafficking, rescue sex workers from brothels, prosecute alleged traffickers, encourage sex workers to testify against them, and urge sex workers to pursue alternative livelihoods. These sites and processes, to which I take my readers, are not only shaped by relatively recent, transnationally funded anti-trafficking interventions, but also by long-standing Indian anti-prostitution interventions.

The title of this book, *Immoral Traffic*, reprises the name of India's anti-prostitution law – the ITPA of 1956 – that has structured the governance of prostitution since its early years as a postcolonial nation. The ITPA reflects the Indian state's deep ambivalence toward prostitution, treating it as both immoral and exploitative. It sets out an array of morally charged, elaborate procedures to "manage" prostitution. This law is implemented by the police, judiciary, state social welfare apparatus, and NGOs in India who have been removing women from the sex trade and seeking to assist, reform, and "save" them since the late colonial period. The term "immoral traffic" captures both the historical background to this law and the ways in which current anti-trafficking NGOs draw upon it to use its anti-prostitution provisions toward an anti-trafficking agenda. Central to this book are the ITPA's provisions and procedures to "manage" prostitution, and the ways in which NGOs work within and beyond the roles it prescribes, strengthen and intensify its implementation, and encourage Indian legal actors to use it in specific ways.

Immoral Traffic draws upon ethnographic research at five different sites and processes in New Delhi and Mumbai – police- and NGO-led rescue operations, an NGO-led training session for Indian judges, magistrates' courts such as the Mumbai Special Court where I observed trials under the ITPA and inquiries with rescued women, and a state-run shelter where rescued women are sent to be detained, protected, reformed, and rehabilitated. The chapters follow the sequence of interventions the ITPA prescribes and women removed from the sex trade experience, from rescues to courts to shelters. The book is situated in encounters between those implementing these interventions and those experiencing them. The former include anti-trafficking NGOs, Indian legal actors, and state agents (police, magistrates, prosecutors, and state welfare officials). The latter are the women whom those intervening seek to rescue, reform, and assist.

Immoral Traffic tracks these sites, processes, and encounters to illuminate the convergence of global sexual humanitarianism,[5] moral crusades against sex trafficking,[6] long-standing anti-prostitution interventions steeped in paternalism,[7] and newly intensified concerns around sexual violence, gender justice, and immigration in India. It demonstrates how these multiple agendas, implemented by state and non-state actors, act in tension and in collaboration upon the perceived "problem" of prostitution. And it reveals how they deploy complex meanings around prostitution, invoking both victimhood and immorality.

At the center of these converging forms of governance are the Indian and Bangladeshi women whom I refer to as "rescued women" in this book.[8] At the sites and procedures I observed, their accounts of how they entered the sex trade ranged from being trafficked (i.e. being forced, threatened, abducted, or deceived),[9] to voluntary sex work, varied combinations of choice and compulsion, and denials of being involved in the sex trade at all. I describe them as "rescued women" because they entered the ambit of the legal system and NGO intervention via raid and rescue operations. Rescue was usually the first point of intervention, followed by multiple postrescue procedures and protective custody.

The complex experiences and choices the rescued women narrated were deeply dissonant from the narrow and mutually contradictory rubrics of immorality and

5 Nicola Mai's concept of sexual humanitarianism recognizes an "interplay between protection and control" in the way anti-trafficking interventions act upon migrant sex workers, through specific narratives of identification, suffering, and abuse (2016: 2, 3). It is "the process through which groups of migrants are represented as vulnerable to trafficking in relation to their involvement in sex work and intervened upon by local, national and international institutions and NGOs" (Andrijasevic and Mai 2016: 2).

6 Ronald Weitzer describes the dramatic, unverifiable and demonstrably false claims of US-led anti-trafficking campaigns as moral crusades that inflate the scale of the problem beyond the available evidence, primarily in response to moral anxieties and ideological concerns about prostitution, and have institutionalized them in US policy (2007: 448).

7 I draw upon Michael Barnett's use of the term paternalism to describe the exercise of power and control over those deemed to be the objects of concern in a global ethics of care across human rights, humanitarianism, development, and other projects designed since the nineteenth century to improve the lives of others. Barnett uses the term to capture the mix of care and control that suffuses humanitarian governance (2016). Locating paternalism more specifically in the "anti-trafficking industrial complex" (see footnote 2), anthropologist Kimberly Walters also emphasizes the way it fuses care and punishment, and describes it as a simultaneously classist, sexist, and casteist sense of "knowing better" than women who sell sex (2020: 314).

8 I use the term "governance" drawing upon feminist legal scholars Janet Halley et al., who emphasize that all legal power does not inhere in the state. The term "suggests multiplicity, mobility, fragmentation, a regulatory or bureaucratic legal style, as well as ready facility with non-state and para-state institutional forms" (2006: 341).

9 The 2001 UN Palermo Protocol defines "trafficking in persons" as the recruitment, transportation, transfer, harboring, or receipt of persons, by means of the threat or use of force or other forms of coercion, abduction, fraud, deception, the abuse of power or of a position of vulnerability, or the giving or receiving of payments or benefits to achieve the consent of a person having control over another person, for the purpose of exploitation. "Exploitation" includes sexual exploitation, forced labor, slavery or practices similar to slavery, servitude, and the removal of organs.

victimhood through which the ITPA and those implementing it seek to assist, represent, and reform them. Yet the book will show how, regardless of whether or not they were trafficked, they were (sometimes willingly and sometimes forcibly) removed from the sex trade, encouraged to testify against alleged pimps, brothel owners, madams, and traffickers, urged to accept legally prescribed and morally charged forms of assistance, and forcibly sent to carceral shelters and livelihood training programs.

The reader will see how, in response to these forms of intervention, some women actively sought assistance to leave the sex trade, many resisted rescue and further offers of state and NGO assistance, and yet others had choices, expectations, and aspirations that existing interventions do not envisage, endorse, or support. The book foregrounds how rescued women navigate the overlapping punitive, protectionist, reformist, and humanitarian agendas of these interventions. It also brings out how the anti-immigrant "demographic anxieties" of India's current sociopolitical regime map onto these agendas and attendant interventions,[10] and shape the treatment of Bangladeshi women removed from the sex trade in India.

AIMS OF THE BOOK

Immoral Traffic is an ethnography of the governance of prostitution at sites and procedures in contemporary India where global donor-driven anti-trafficking campaigns intersect with long-standing anti-prostitution measures, and where they are together implemented by Indian legal actors and foreign-funded NGOs. It demonstrates how these sites, procedures, and entities bring together overlapping, even conflicting concerns centered on prostitution, and approaches centered on its governance. It illuminates how they are shaped by broader developments in postcolonial India – around the deployment of law enforcement and criminal justice to address sexual violence and exploitation, efforts to assist marginalized women through both state paternalism and neoliberal women's empowerment programs, and highly politicized concerns about border control in the context of immigration from Bangladesh.

The book does not merely highlight the intersection of anti-trafficking and anti-prostitution interventions, but takes them as points of entry to offer broader insights. Though the governance of prostitution, and the contested meanings around it, are the book's structuring context, *Immoral Traffic* mobilizes ethnographic insights of these interventions to make the following contributions. First, the book reveals an excess rather than lack of legality – suffused with morality, bureaucracy, and

[10] Megan Moodie discusses how the rise of Hindu nationalism in India has fueled anti-Muslim and anti-immigrant sentiments against Bangladeshi migrants in recent years, using the term "demographic anxiety" to index a xenophobic political discourse around the figure of the illegal immigrant misusing the generosity of the Indian state and threatening law and order (2010).

paternalism – that challenges the prevalent assumptions and preferred solutions of the global anti-trafficking regime. Second, it situates the governance of prostitution in India in the complex relationship between law and NGOs. Third, it centers how these intersecting interventions impact the women they target, and how women navigate them.

First, through the design and insights of the research, the book challenges widely prevalent assumptions in global anti-trafficking donor and policy regimes about Global South legal systems and sex workers. The ethnography lingers in sites and procedures steeped in the moral panics, bureaucracy, and paternalisms of the postcolonial Indian state, Indian NGOs, and global anti-trafficking campaigns. I observed an excess rather than lack of legality shaping these sites and procedures, through donor-driven policing and criminal justice solutions, as well as long-standing punitive and protectionist Indian social welfare measures. These interventions offered highly legalistic, morally charged, and deeply gendered solutions to sex workers, rather than community engaged or economically viable options. From the vantage point this research affords, the book calls into question the global anti-trafficking regime's assumptions about Global South legal systems and actors being inherently unable or unwilling to curb sex trafficking, about law enforcement and criminal justice solutions unquestionably benefiting survivors of sex trafficking, and about Global South sex workers being always already victims of sex trafficking.

Second, *Immoral Traffic* approaches the governance of prostitution in India through the mutually reliant yet ever contingent and delicate relationship between law and NGOs. At its core, the book recognizes that Indian law has *always* imagined and involved the participation of non-state actors committed to curbing prostitution, from colonial to contemporary times. With this recognition, the book brings out how contemporary NGOs' work is shaped both by their participation in the US-funded global anti-trafficking regime and by the role and legitimacy Indian law has carved out for them. It examines how Indian law already anticipates a certain type of NGO intervention committing to curbing prostitution, which it also depends upon and legitimizes. Thus, my premise is not that the complex, messy, and contested field governing prostitution in India is new, but that it is expanding and intensifying through new modalities and combinations of governance shaping relationships between the law, state agencies, and NGOs.

Immoral Traffic highlights how law remains at the center of anti-trafficking NGOs' expanding roles in India. It demonstrates how, in their efforts to deploy Indian law toward a global anti-trafficking agenda, NGOs draw upon the role Indian law has long carved out for them, and the space its moral ambivalence toward prostitution has opened up. The book reveals how NGOs work within the roles Indian law prescribes for them, but also stretch their scope and possibilities to meet donor-driven agendas. It does not argue that NGOs have replaced India's anti-prostitution legal framework with a US-funded anti-trafficking one. Instead, it shows how NGOs are positioned between and across the two frameworks, gluing them together in the governance of prostitution in India.[11]

The book reveals not just the convergence and collaborations, but also the conflicts between NGOs, state agencies, and legal entities in governing prostitution. In doing so, it builds upon, but also departs from existing feminist scholarship critiquing the global anti-trafficking regime.[12] It illuminates how NGOs bolster, rather than weaken, Indian state institutions and procedures by providing them various forms of support. At the same time, it highlights the constitutive tensions at the heart of this convergence. It shows how relationships between Indian NGOs, legal actors, and state agencies are a constantly negotiated work in progress, an ongoing project that NGOs are perpetually building, rebuilding, ironing out, and strengthening, and one that legal actors and state agencies both depend upon and resist.

Third, the book centers how women targeted by interventions against prostitution and sex trafficking in India are processed through multiple forms of governance – the political economy, bureaucracy, and carceralities of law, the combined moralities of sexual humanitarianism and state paternalism, and anti-immigrant suspicions and accusations. It explores how rescued women navigate an ambivalent framework of contested meanings around prostitution – as both exploitative and immoral – through these expanded and intensified forms of governance. And it foregrounds the myriad strategies through which rescued women respond to them – by seizing upon the opportunities they provide, resisting them, or escaping them altogether.

With these contributions, I wrote this book for interdisciplinary audiences across the fields shaping my research – anthropologists of law, and scholars of law and society, critical NGO studies, gender and sexuality studies, critical feminist work on sex work and sex trafficking, South Asian studies, and global studies. I also wrote it for those in applied fields such as human rights and international development interested in critical perspectives on a range of projects ostensibly aimed at improving the lives of marginalized populations, especially those centered around gendered victimhood. The book's insights extend beyond critiques of anti-trafficking and anti-prostitution interventions. It illuminates how vastly different projects of varied historical, geographical, and political origins come together, both contingently and deliberately, to construct and address a given problem and "manage" those deemed to be its victims, and how those targeted by these projects experience and respond to them. I hope that both academic and nonacademic

[11] Mark Schuller describes the role of NGOs in the neoliberal global aid regime using the metaphor of a glue that results in an unplanned patchwork connecting foreign donors, Global South states, and local communities (2009: 97). For further discussion on this neoliberal context and its relevance to my conceptual framework, see Chapter 1.

[12] Discussed in Chapter 1.

readers will find resonance with similar themes across a range of humanitarian and developmental interventions in the Global South, especially on questions around gender, sexuality, and morality.

METHODS, SITES, AND RESEARCH

The book is based on fourteen months of ethnographic fieldwork in New Delhi (six months in New Delhi and eight in Mumbai) from June 2012 to August 2013, and a three-month follow-up research trip in 2014. I conducted participant observation in both cities at multiple sites, including rescue operations, police stations, NGO offices, NGO-led training sessions, courts, magistrates' chambers, and shelters. I also conducted open-ended interviews, collected and analyzed case documents and court judgments, and had informal conversations with police, prosecutors, lawyers, judges, NGO representatives, foreign donors, state welfare officials, and the women who were rescued, expected to participate in legal procedures, offered assistance, and subjected to multiple interventions by legal actors and NGOs.

I offer an overview of my methods here. Given the multiple sites across which I conducted my ethnography, each chapter additionally includes discussions of the methodological choices I made and ethical challenges I faced as an anthropologist and feminist researcher at each site, while also performing a range of volunteer tasks to earn and maintain research access. In each chapter, I reflect upon how I navigated these choices and challenges. I consider these aspects of research as worthy of discussion as its findings, and encourage my readers to think with me about methods and ethics as they travel with me to my field sites through this book.

In New Delhi, my fieldwork centered on examining the role of an anti-trafficking NGO. I volunteered with this NGO and shadowed its work. In Mumbai, I situated myself in two sites: the Special Court, with which I began this Introduction, and a state-run shelter where sex workers are sent after rescues. To understand how anti-trafficking and anti-prostitution interventions converge, and to ensure that anti-trafficking NGOs were not my only interlocutors or field site, I made a deliberate decision to balance the time I spent observing NGOs, state institutions, and legal procedures during fieldwork.

Non-affiliation with an NGO sometimes limited the nature of my access to certain legal processes (see Chapter 4). However, the multisited and multiperspectival research I was able to do across both cities offered insights into the Indian sociolegal context beyond observing NGOs alone. It also helped me maintain a level of distance from the legal actors and NGO workers I observed and interviewed, as each of them knew that my research extended beyond them. During my interviews or conversations with them, they were often curious about what I was learning at other sites, which they either did not visit themselves or did not visit as frequently as I did.

I chose to conduct fieldwork in New Delhi and Mumbai because both are metropolitan Indian cities with flourishing sex trades, and therefore prime targets for anti-trafficking NGOs. Both cities also have long-standing state institutions (police, courts, and shelters) governing prostitution, framed by myriad moral concerns. For these reasons, they were also the sites for the developments I was tracking in the mid-2000s around the ITPA amendment and the Mumbai dance bar ban (see Preface).

Linguistic reasons also shaped my choice of New Delhi and Mumbai as research sites. I have native fluency in Hindi, which is spoken in both cities. In Mumbai, the official language used by the government (and widely spoken by many of its residents) is Marathi, which I do not speak. However, most of the rescued women and many of the NGO workers at the sites where I did my research were not Marathi speakers and had working knowledge of or fluency in Hindi, and most Marathi speakers I encountered during my research also spoke Hindi. Some interactions I observed, such as courtroom proceedings involving Marathi speakers at the Mumbai Special Court where audibility was already a problem (see Chapter 4), and conversations among court and shelter staff, took place in Marathi. Though my linguistic limitations did impact my understanding of these contexts and moments, I was partly able to address the language barrier through the help of a Marathi-speaking MPhil student who was also conducting research at these sites and often translated for me.

In New Delhi, my home town, I developed rapport with a US-funded anti-trafficking NGO during the research on Sally Merry's project I discussed in the Preface. I shadowed this NGO's work in a few different ways. I accompanied its teams on rescue operations with the police, where I was also expected to assist the NGO team to rescue and "counsel" sex workers (Chapter 2). I attended a court trial, where the NGO assisted the prosecution by supporting and preparing a survivor of sex trafficking to testify against an accused brothel madam, and a judicial training session, where the NGO addressed Indian judges, including the judge presiding over the trial I attended (discussed in Chapter 3). I also conducted interviews and had informal conversations with police officers, judges, prosecutors, NGO workers, rescued women, and members of a Child Welfare Committee, to develop the analysis.

Working with the NGO in New Delhi provided access to rescues, courts, and training sessions, and opportunities to meet women it had rescued. However, this access came with challenges and limitations that need to be acknowledged in research involving NGOs. As anthropologists reflecting on the subject have pointed out, NGOs are not only ripe for anthropological study themselves, but also increasingly shape fieldwork encounters and knowledge production by facilitating access to field sites and key interlocutors, leading to awkward relationships and ethical conundrums for anthropologists (Lashaw 2012; Lemons 2017). This becomes especially significant in contexts such as trafficking where it is hard for researchers to meet survivors without "gatekeepers" like NGOs who provide them assistance (Brunovskis and Surtees 2010).

Keeping in mind the possibility that assistance providers may refer researchers only to their "successful cases" (Brunovskis and Surtees 2010: 16), the research I conducted through the New Delhi NGO could have been impacted by some of this gatekeeping. I was able to address this possibility in a few ways, some of which emerged organically as I conducted research. For one, I was also able to observe cases in which rescued women resisted the NGO's intervention. In Chapter 2, for instance, I compare a rescue in which women sought assistance to leave the sex trade with another one in which they resisted rescue. Secondly, in situations where shadowing the NGO's work led me primarily to "successful" cases (such as the court case in Chapter 3), other interviews at the same sites and procedures often provided vastly different perspectives. Apart from these fortuitous opportunities, I deliberately designed my research to balance my time between observing NGOs and observing legal institutions and procedures. The state agencies and legal institutions I observed were sites of anti-prostitution intervention, while NGOs pursued an anti-trafficking agenda. This meant that there were multiple agents of gatekeeping involved. As each site involved interventions to remove women from the sex trade and offer various forms of assistance and punitive protection, there was always some "gatekeeping" involved. I was, after all, observing forms of interaction tethered to some form of intervention and assistance – as opposed to, say, trafficking survivors who were not rescued or sex workers who were not targeted.

Conducting research with NGOs presented further challenges. It was often difficult to glean information from anti-trafficking NGOs, given that these organizations "rely on their reputation and status for donor funding" and "guard their image accordingly" (Molland 2013: 314). Examples of such information I sought, but rarely received, include how NGOs received information about trafficked women in brothels, how often women they rescued testified against the accused in court, and whether their economic rehabilitation programs were successful in helping women find secure and sustainable employment after leaving the sex trade. NGOs were not easy research subjects, as I often sensed that they withheld information or presented it in ways that would not threaten their image or credibility to their donors, fearing the global circulation of information in which I, as a researcher from the US, might participate.

I carried out the next eight months of ethnographic research in Mumbai, at two sites – the ITPA Special Court, and a state-run shelter. Conducting participant observation and interviews at these sites provided the opportunity to understand how the criminal justice system, NGOs, and state welfare bureaucracy come together to process women removed from brothels, take decisions about their custody and rehabilitation, and provide and evaluate evidence of both prostitution and trafficking.

In contrast to the New Delhi court I observed (and discuss in Chapter 3), a regular criminal court also adjudicating other cases, the Special Court where I conducted research in Mumbai exclusively prosecutes cases under the ITPA statute. At the Mumbai Special Court, I observed the two different legal processes I outlined at the beginning of this Introduction – trial proceedings in the courtroom against accused madams, brothel keepers, brothel managers, pimps and traffickers (discussed in

Chapter 4), and inquiries with rescued women and their families in the judicial magistrate's chambers with the assistance of NGO workers (discussed in Chapter 5).

My ethnographic observations of the trial proceedings focused on the testimony provided by NGO representatives, police, and (minimally) by the few "victim-witnesses" I met at the Special Court. I also conducted interviews and informal conversations with the judicial magistrate, lawyers, NGO representatives, police, and other prosecution witnesses arranged by the police and NGOs in these cases. The ethnography and interviews are supplemented by my analysis of the texts of the judgments for the overall patterns of testimony, evidence, and judicial outcomes.

At this court, I also observed inquiries the magistrate and NGO representatives conducted in the magistrate's chambers with rescued women and their families to make decisions about their custody and rehabilitation, and was sometimes asked to assist with these inquiries myself. After inquiries, the magistrate and NGO representatives often debriefed through informal chats. Along with my observations of and participation in the inquiries, these debriefing conversations also inform my analysis.

My second research site in Mumbai was a state-run shelter where rescued women are sent for what the ITPA terms "protective custody." At this site, the focus of Chapter 6, women who are either willingly rescued or forcibly removed from the sex trade are detained for uncertain periods of time and expected to participate in activities including both reform-oriented performances and livelihood skills training programs. I observed interactions between the staff (state agents from the welfare bureaucracy), NGO representatives (who came to visit the women they had rescued and to provide counseling and rehabilitation programs), and the rescued women being detained there. I also conducted interviews with the staff, NGO representatives, and the detained women. As a volunteer at the shelter, I performed my assigned task of keeping the women "productively engaged" with considerable discomfort, while finding ways (such as film screenings) to build rapport with the detained women and the staff and maintain research access.

POSITIONALITY

As a volunteer across multiple field sites, research access meant that I was expected to participate in and help with rescues (Chapter 2), "counseling" (Chapters 2 and 3), inquiries (Chapter 5), and the "productive engagement" of women placed in shelter detention (Chapter 6). Observing these sites and interventions, I constantly struggled to balance the volunteer tasks I was assigned with my anthropological commitment to understanding the complexity of the situation, and my feminist discomfort with the often punitive and always moralistic paternalism through which state agencies and NGOs interacted with sex workers and survivors of sex trafficking. In each chapter, I have centered the ethical dilemmas I experienced and how I navigated them. As they shaped my research methods, access, observations, insights, and how people responded to me, they are as important to discuss as the ethnography itself.

My positionality as an upper-middle-class urban Indian woman conducting research helped me gain access to my sites and interlocutors, while also limiting the possibilities of building rapport with rescued sex workers. To explain how I was perceived by those I interacted with, the relationship between class, gender, and perceptions of respectability in the Indian context bears discussion here. Respectability, as an "amalgam of signs, economics, and practices," embodies moral authority, and is central to the development of class categorizations (Skeggs 1997: 15). The expansive category of "middle class" in the Indian context is bound up with the normative moral authority of respectability (Ganti 2012: 142). Rather than a measurable or accurate description of an income category, "middle class" signifies the acquisition of forms of capital such as education, credentials, skills, and cultural resources (Fernandes 2006), with historical roots in colonial education and employment policies. It has primarily performative and discursive dimensions, with somewhat fluid empirical boundaries (Fernandes 2006; Liechty 2002; Mazzarella 2005). Those who have accrued the forms of capital that place them in the upper tiers of this class categorization also tend to have caste privilege.[13]

My clothes, accessories, comportment, and speech inescapably indexed my positionality as an upper-middle-class, urban professional woman.[14] For instance, the magistrate presiding over the Mumbai Special Court remarked, after observing me for a few days, that many of my *kurtas* (loose-fitting Indian shirts) appeared to be from Fabindia, a retail chain popular with urban, professional women in the broader "middle class" category, especially NGO workers, academics, and activists. As it emerged in our conversations, she took an interest in my clothes (and those of NGO workers) because we could wear colors to court, while she, like all magistrates, prosecutors and lawyers, had to wear black and white clothing – the prescribed norm in Indian courts. But my clothes also indexed, for her and others in my field sites, my class location, social status, and professional category. At the Mumbai shelter, my cell phone and handbag often drew the attention of the women detained there (Chapter 6). While my laptop-carrying handbag was seen as the coveted accessory of a woman doing "respectable" work, my cell phone (an old iPhone model)

13 The access to English language education, leading to specific forms of cultural capital in the colonial era, continues to disproportionately benefit upper caste families whose members were recruited to work in the civil services and professional occupations during colonial rule. My family's background falls within this "upper" tier of the contemporary Indian middle-class, whose access to English language education and white-collar employment opportunities over three or four generations has also been shaped by privileged status in the context of caste-based inequalities.

14 Some informants might have also made silent assumptions about my being from a privileged caste background. Though I wore no markers of caste identity, it might have been discerned from my last name (which not many in my field sites knew) or assumed to align with my class background. For discussions of the overlap between caste and class, see Deshpande (ed). 2014; Jodhka 2017.

received quizzical looks and the occasional remark for not being fancy or expensive enough for someone of my perceived class status, who lived in the US, to boot.

Perceptions of respectability are always already gendered. As feminist scholar Shilpa Phadke points out, women are expected to manufacture and demonstrate both purpose (education, employment, or consumption) and respectability (defined through clothing, symbolic markers of "good womanhood," and temporality) to legitimize their presence in public space (2007). The fact that prostitution was the focus of my research usually led those I interacted with in my field sites (including legal actors, NGO workers, and sex workers) to assume that I had some connection to NGOs or social work and was somehow invested in improving the lot of "fallen" women. In Mumbai, those whom I introduced myself to as a doctoral student often assumed that I was studying social work at the prestigious Tata Institute of Social Sciences, where many NGO workers and some state welfare staff had received their training.

As I will discuss in Chapter 1 in the context of the ITPA, efforts by female social workers from privileged backgrounds to "save" and reform women in the sex trade also mark their own assertions of respectability. This gendered respectability is something that those intervening consciously cultivate and perform, rather than something that merely exists because of their social status. The NGO workers, state agents, and legal actors processing women rescued from the sex trade constantly constructed their distinction from them through the hierarchical ways in which they interacted with them. Significantly, though the police station, courts, and shelter where I did my research were not sites of prostitution themselves, those working there brought up how its stigma carried over into these spaces meant to "manage" prostitution.

My presence as a researcher, while often easily mistaken as that of an NGO representative or social work professional, gave me a legitimate reason to be in these stigmatized spaces where, apart from those tasked with processing rescued sex workers, the presence of "respectable" people (especially women) was considered incongruous. Perceived as both "respectable" (with sex workers being the putative "Others" to this presumed respectability) and always available by virtue of "hanging out" in my research sites, I was often co-opted into the roles of rescuer, counselor, volunteer, and even as a member of the inquiry committee assisting the magistrate in Mumbai. These opportunities, though often challenging to navigate for the ethical dilemmas they posed, yielded research access.

The same "respectable" positionality that facilitated research access made it challenging to build rapport with rescued women. As the "gatekeepers" through whom I met them were always NGOs, a magistrate, shelter staff, and sometimes the police or prosecutors, the women I encountered always identified me with these figures of authority. One group of women even asked me if I was the "judge's assistant" as they had seen me helping with inquiries in the magistrate's chambers. They presented their accounts to me the way they would to these authority figures, crafted in a manner knowing that they were speaking to someone who (from their perspective) might be able to make a difference to the outcomes of their cases. In each chapter, I discuss how my presence and positionality shaped my research, offering certain possibilities and foreclosing others.

ORGANIZATION OF THE BOOK

Chapter 1 provides the sociolegal context of law, NGOs, and the governance of prostitution in India, and the conceptual framework of the book. While the sociolegal context will be relevant to all readers, the conceptual framework lays out the academic conversations the book participates in, and as such, will be of greater interest to academic readers. Chapters 2–6 draw upon my multisited ethnography, following the sequence of interventions from rescues to shelters that the Indian anti-prostitution law (the ITPA) prescribes and NGOs help to implement.

Chapters 2–4 show how anti-trafficking NGOs stretch the scope and possibilities of the roles envisaged for them in Indian law toward new donor-driven agendas that emphasize rescues, a more "sensitized" policing, and prosecution as solutions to sex trafficking. Chapter 2 highlights how rescues are swift and chaotic events, fraught with confusion and uncertainty, tensions between NGOs and police, and a range of choices sex workers make, from actively pursuing their escape to resisting rescues. Comparing two different rescues, it builds upon and departs from existing feminist critiques to foreground the tensions between NGOs and police, rooted in different gendered moral frameworks, interpretations of the law, resources, and priorities of intervention. It explores how these tensions are constantly negotiated, and examines their impact on the construction, navigation, and contestation of victimhood through ethnographic observations of two very different rescues.

Chapters 3 and 4 center on court trials of those accused of sex trafficking. As I explained with my opening description of the Mumbai Special Court, training rescued sex workers to testify against the accused is crucial to anti-trafficking NGOs' efforts, and is given top priority by their US donors. However, both chapters situate NGO-led prosecution-focused interventions in the Indian criminal justice context to show how they play out in much more complex ways, driven by a much wider range of factors than US donors' anti-trafficking priorities.

Chapter 3 explores the perspectives of Indian legal actors and NGOs, the complexities and contingencies impacting "victim-witness testimony" in the Indian criminal justice system, and the challenges faced by those who do testify. It weaves together ethnographic insights about the broader pattern of rescued sex workers' resistance to testify, with an ethnographic account of an atypical case where a trafficked woman testified against an accused madam in a New Delhi court. It tracks her encounters with the legal system and the NGO support she received. It also explores how NGO-led anti-trafficking training sessions for Indian judges impacted this case.

Chapter 4 draws upon further ethnographic research and an analysis of judgments at the Mumbai Special Court, where rescued sex workers' testimony is only one (albeit significant) factor shaping the outcomes of trials against the accused. The chapter illustrates how these trials are primarily shaped by the priorities of Indian law, its interpretation by the police and prosecutors, and the possibilities that requirements for "respectable" witnesses both in the ITPA and in Indian procedural law open up for NGOs. It shows how evidence and testimony at this Special Court is presented to prove prostitution rather than sex trafficking, and how NGOs, police, and other witnesses participate in what I call the choreography of these trials.

Overall, Chapters 2–4 show how the anti-trafficking agenda of NGOs and the anti-prostitution focus of Indian law come together in distinct, even incommensurate, ways to govern prostitution. Chapters 5 and 6 shift gears to explore these conjunctures at sites and processes which, while impacted by anti-trafficking priorities, reflect Indian law's ambivalence between a will to reform and punish, and a will to protect "immoral" women. Chapter 5 focuses on judicial inquiries with women removed from the sex trade, and Chapter 6 on their shelter-based detention in what the ITPA terms "protective custody." These chapters examine how anti-trafficking NGOs support, intensify, and strengthen the Indian state's entwined and contradictory projects of punitively disciplining and paternalistically protecting rescued women.

Chapter 5 focuses on NGO-assisted judicial inquiries with rescued women and decisions about their custody and rehabilitation at the Mumbai Special Court. It demonstrates how they center on the tactics of "counseling" and censure, and on morally and politically laced evaluations of identity and kinship. This chapter takes the reader to a more intimate and interactive site (the magistrate's chambers) than the adjudication of courtroom trials. By focusing on this site and process, the chapter illuminates the roles played by female judges and NGO workers in a postcolonial legal regime combining state paternalism, moral reform, sexual humanitarianism, and immigration control. It shows how these inquiries are framed both by accusations of immorality and by concerns about victimhood, and how rescued women respond with narratives centered on poverty and kinship. It also shows how Bangladeshi women are targeted by, and navigate, a culture of suspicion and regime of documentation that brings anti-trafficking, anti-prostitution, and anti-immigration imperatives together.

Chapter 6 takes the reader to the simultaneous and contradictory projects of protection, detention, reform, and rehabilitation at a state-run shelter in Mumbai. It describes how women placed in shelter detention, mandated by India's ITPA law, experience this carceral institution through profound uncertainty about their release. It shows how the detained women's experiences are shaped by the bureaucratic procedures the law authorizes, and this institution's curtailment of their mobility, interaction with family or the outside world, and ability to earn a living. It examines how anti-trafficking NGOs shape this "protective custody" through programs providing (questionably useful and rarely sustainable or lucrative) livelihood skills training – programs that appeal to foreign donors, Indian judges, and state agents because of their neoliberal objective of facilitating women's exit from both prostitution and state custody. It also tracks the way Bangladeshi women are targeted by an immigration control agenda that joins the existing forms of governance converging on shelter detention, and the additional delays and biases through which this agenda plays out.

The chapter situates shelter detention within and beyond the Indian sociolegal context, drawing connections to global anti-trafficking and anti-immigration contexts. It also discusses the challenges of doing research and maintaining research access in a carceral institution. I explain, in particular, how I screened films as a way to provide entertainment, build rapport, and seek the perspectives of the detained women, while working within the restricted scope of interactions I was permitted and performing the volunteer tasks I was assigned.

Finally, I pair my ethnography of shelter detention in this chapter with reported accounts of twenty three women escaping from the shelter. By tracking tabloid reports of the incident and the Bombay High Court's subsequent intervention, I examine how the escapes became the focus of media scrutiny and judicial surveillance in Mumbai. Analyzing these responses, I argue that they ultimately extend and intensify, rather than question, the multiple forms of governance to which shelter detention subjects rescued and detained women.

Each chapter explores how rescued women navigate intersecting interventions that are ostensibly aimed at helping and protecting them, but are often experienced as deeply punitive and moralistic, and rarely align with the outcomes they seek. These outcomes range from seeking stable and sustainable employment (whether within or outside the sex trade), to marrying a partner of their choice (whether or not deemed appropriate by their families or rescuers), to taking care of themselves or their families in ways that make the most sense to them. The chapters highlight the multiple agentive strategies, structured by socioeconomic and familial circumstances, that rescued women adopt in response to anti-trafficking and anti-prostitution interventions. These include the ways they initiate or resist rescue and participate or refuse postrescue procedures (Chapter 2), agree or refuse to testify or turn "hostile" as prosecution witnesses (Chapters 3 and 4), selectively withdraw or reveal information, and perform and narrate their accounts and identities (Chapter 5), strategically conform to or resist reformist projects and rehabilitation programs, and escape state custody (Chapter 6).

From rescues to courts to shelters, the book follows the sequence of interventions India's ITPA law prescribes and women removed from the sex trade experience. While this law and its procedures structure the book, my aims are broader. *Immoral Traffic* explores how global anti-trafficking campaigns and India's anti-prostitution legal framework intersect, through the work of the state and non-state actors implementing them, and through the sites, institutions, procedures, and encounters set up to govern prostitution in India. It illuminates how they bring together a range of concerns and approaches centered on or adjacent to prostitution – such as transnational sexual humanitarianism, moral policing, and the paternalist approaches of the Indian state and NGOs – with broader aspects of the Indian sociolegal and sociopolitical contexts, such as law enforcement and criminal justice, neoliberal women's empowerment programs, and border control in the context of immigration from Bangladesh. The book uses these convergences and intersections as points of entry to center the ways in which rescued women navigate them, critique the prevalent assumptions and preferred solutions of the global anti-trafficking regime, and explore the complex relationship between law and NGOs in India.

1

Law, NGOs, and the Governance of Prostitution in India

CONTEXTUAL FRAMEWORK

The US-Led Anti-Trafficking Regime

Since the early 2000s, India has been a prominent focus of concerns about sex trafficking in the Global South. From the US State Department's annual *Trafficking in Persons (TIP) Reports* to a slew of well-publicized media reports and documentary films on the topic, Indian sex workers are depicted as helpless, virginal girls abducted from remote villages, and forced or duped into prostitution. Since 2002, India has ranked poorly on the State Department's *TIP Report* (an annual report mandated by US anti-trafficking law: The Victims of Trafficking and Violence Protection Act of 2000), which ranks countries based on the US' assessment of their anti-trafficking efforts, with repercussions on the flow of aid dollars.

Spearheading global concerns about sex trafficking, and using the *TIP Report* as an instrument of global governance, the US State Department has taken it upon itself to strengthen legal responses to the issue, especially in Global South countries.[1] Sociolegal scholars studying the impact of the *TIP Reports* have described them as an instance of the US playing "global sheriff" (Chuang 2005) and as a "seductive form of knowledge" that functions as an instrument of global governance (Merry 2016), in response to moral anxieties rather than factual accuracy (Weitzer 2007).[2] Current US-led concerns around sex trafficking stem from an amalgam of anxieties during the Bush administration around organized crime and immigration, conservative Christian values around sexuality, and the proximity to power of "abolitionist" feminists who see all prostitution as violence against women (Bernstein 2018).

Beyond the US wielding its geopolitical stick through the *TIP Reports*, the politics of representation through which India features in the *Reports* bear discussion.

[1] In 2004, the Bush administration gave funding priority to Brazil, Cambodia, India, Indonesia, Mexico, Moldova, Sierra Leone, and Tanzania (*TIP Report* 2005: 27).

[2] See also Blanchette et al. (2013) for a similar analysis of moral panics in Brazil.

Indian girls and women are frequently the faces and narratives of sex trafficking in the *Reports*, which recycle colonial-era assumptions, bereft of context and nuance,[3] about vulnerable, victimized Third World women.[4] The *Reports* also reprise a colonial-era legal orientalism that assumes and bemoans the inferiority, corruption, and inefficiency of non-Western legal systems.[5] They echo the assumptions about corruption and a lack of transparency and accountability that have become a morality-laden, colonially derived explanatory trope for Global South states in global development-speak (Mathur 2017: 1801).[6] The reason the *TIP Reports* provided for placing India on a Watch List in the early to mid-2000s is its status as a country that has a significant number of victims of human trafficking but has "failed to provide evidence" of increasing efforts to combat it.[7]

The problems the *TIP Reports* identify with the Indian legal system include both a lack of resources and a lack of commitment. Citing NGOs as sources, the *Reports* note that the Indian police are overburdened, underfunded, and lack necessary resources (2018: 223). Similarly, they note (again citing NGOs) that Indian judges and courts do not have the resources to "properly prosecute cases" (2016: 201). The *Reports* criticize the Indian legal system for its "overburdened" courts, "a weak understanding of the laws, and lack of commitment and awareness (of human trafficking) by some local authorities" (2011: 189). Though recent *Reports* have recognized increased efforts to combat human trafficking in India, they continue to highlight low levels of law enforcement action and a low rate of conviction of traffickers, relative to the scale of human trafficking in India (2016: 200).

In critiquing the US *TIP* discourse here, my aim is to shift attention away from India's depiction in global media and policy circles as a hotbed of trafficking where the state cannot keep up with anti-trafficking priorities set up in the Global North. The book focuses, instead, on the ways in which the Indian state, NGOs, and the anti-trafficking donor regime converge, in collaboration and in contradiction, to act upon prostitution. As I explained in the Introduction, the book challenges the prevalent assumptions and preferred solutions of the global anti-trafficking regime by revealing an *excess* rather than lack of legality in these intersecting interventions. As the book

3 As discussed by several postcolonial feminist scholars, such as Kapur 2005; Mani 1998; Mohanty 1984; Sinha 2006; and Spivak 1988.

4 For a trenchant critique of such representations in the *TIP Reports* and their reductive assumptions about the sex trade, sex workers, and "saviors," see Baker (2013).

5 For critiques of such forms of legal orientalism, see, for example, Chimni 2006; Darian-Smith 2013; Hussain 2003; Rajagopal 2008; and Ruskola 2013.

6 Nayanika Mathur discusses how an "excessive focus on corruption detracts from the core issues of how the Indian state actually functions, what it does, when, how, and why" (2017: 1801). In a similar vein, I treat such explanatory tropes as the geopolitically driven, colonially derived forms of power/knowledge that they are.

7 In 2012, the *TIP Report* moved India off the Watch List to Tier Two, on account of India having ratified the United Nations (UN) Convention against Transnational Organized Crime, and its supplementary Protocol to Prevent, Suppress and Punish Trafficking in Persons in 2011.

will show, their convergence intensifies a procedural bureaucracy across law enforcement, criminal justice, and social welfare as multiple agendas and agencies seek to rescue, protect, "counsel" and rehabilitate women, and prosecute traffickers.

Though the *TIP Reports* evaluate government efforts, they rely on NGOs for information (Merry 2016). The concerns they list indicate how heavily the US leans on NGOs as sources of information and agents of change. It is primarily through NGOs that a US-driven, globally pervasive anti-trafficking campaign seeks to shape the Indian legal system's responses to prostitution (qua sex trafficking). As I explained in the Preface, the Indian government has expressed its resistance to US interference via the *TIP Reports*. In this context, the State Department thus relies heavily on Indian NGOs to provide information, carry out its agenda, and work with Indian state agencies and legal actors to do so. Along with producing the *TIP Reports*, the US State Department funds anti-trafficking NGOs in India (and other parts of the Global South) to engage in a range of donor-driven interventions, including training Indian legal actors to treat prostitution as sex trafficking, rescuing sex workers from brothels, assisting in the prosecution of alleged traffickers in courts, encouraging sex workers to testify against alleged traffickers, and urging sex workers to take up alternative livelihoods. It is through these NGOs that the US-driven anti-trafficking industrial complex seeks to "fix" the Indian legal system, which has, in fact, long had its own anti-prostitution law through which state and nonstate actors intervene in the sex trade.

Law and Prostitution in Postcolonial India

India has had a long history of legal reform and social welfare measures devised, and attendant discourses mobilized, to deal with the "problem" of prostitution. Its postcolonial law and legal history present a complex and morally ambivalent imagination of prostitution. British feminists, Indian nationalists, and Indian women's groups opposed the colonial state's tolerance of prostitution. The late colonial period saw a shift from the segregation of brothels – tolerated to cater to the sexual needs of the British military, and regulated by colonial-era Contagious Diseases Acts – to legislation aimed at the "suppression" of prostitution. Various provincial Suppression of Immoral Traffic Acts were enacted across India during this time, influenced by a range of motivations: transnational anxieties about a sexual traffic in white women, entwined concerns about vice and venereal disease articulated by elite women's groups in India and Britain, and middle-class nationalist public opinion about "fallen" women in India.[8] This intersection of multiple concerns around prostitution is seen across global contexts.[9] Owing to an expansive colonial

[8] As discussed in detail by several historians of colonial Britain and India, including Legg 2014; Levine 2003; Tambe 2009; Walkowitz 1980; and Whitehead 1995.

[9] For example, in English Canada, where moral reform projects intended to curb sexual exploitation eventually became primarily centered on the morals of young working-class women (Valverde 2008: 168, 176).

definition of prostitution, myriad historical and sociopolitical currents have shaped the Indian legal framework on prostitution.[10] Indeed, the term "prostitute" had an excessive archival presence in colonial India, where the concept was deployed to govern, explain, and describe social life and define new modes of inquiry (Mitra 2020: 18). It was applied with definitional fluidity to a wide range of women stigmatized as sexual deviants, marked as aberrant, sexually unchaste, outside of respectable society, socially ill, criminally dangerous, or sexually unbound (6).

Beyond prostitution, India's colonial history of Western intervention to construct and save vulnerable female subjects, and its postcolonial assumption of paternalism and protectionism toward marginalized women, make it a productive site from which to explore how the global furor about sex trafficking in the past two decades maps on to historical constructions of gendered victimization. Feminist scholars have discussed the colonial zeal to "save" Indian women from what were construed as the victimizing customs of their native culture, and negotiations of these concerns by late nineteenth-century social reform efforts by both colonizers and Indian nationalists.[11] At a later historical juncture, scholars consider the Partition of the subcontinent in 1947–1948 at the time of India's independence a significant moment in the emergence of the figure of the abducted woman whose displacement and sexual violation ruptured families and kin networks and rendered her a victim in need of legal remedies and welfare from the state.[12] This complex legacy of concerns shapes the laws, institutions, and practices of the postcolonial Indian state, preceding the current wave of anti-trafficking efforts and partly incorporating them into a broader paternalism and protectionism toward marginalized women. Such paternalism remains integral to the identity of the postcolonial nation-state (Sharma 2008; Sunder Rajan 2003), now reinforced and intensified by NGO-mediated humanitarianism (Walters 2020).

The UN Convention against Trafficking in 1949 conceptualized a "traffic" in persons and the "exploitation of prostitution" as intrinsically linked.[13] Having ratified this UN Convention, India enacted the Suppression of Immoral Traffic in Women and Girls Act (SITA) in 1956 soon after its independence from Britain to demonstrate its compliance with the terms of the UN Convention.[14] The SITA's definition

[10] Indian reformers and nationalists in the late colonial and early post-colonial periods also launched moral campaigns and legislative reform that often aligned with colonial and missionary civilizing logics to oppose practices categorized as "traditional" forms of prostitution (such as *devadasi* and *tawaif* performances), targeting them as "barbaric" customs that victimized Indian women. See, for example, Arondekar 2012; Joshi 2001; Kannabiran and Kannabiran 2003; Oldenberg 1990; Soneji 2011; Srinivasan 1985.

[11] Mani 1998; Sinha 2006; Spivak 1988.

[12] Butalia 2000; Das 2007; Kapur 2010.

[13] Unlike its successor, the UN Protocol against Trafficking of 2000, which addresses the exploitative aspects of prostitution, and does not repeat the explicit condemnation of prostitution (Dottridge 2007).

[14] This acronym interestingly also spells the name of Sita, a mythical figure from the Hindu epic, the *Ramayana*, who was married to Lord Rama, abducted by the demon king Ravana, and rescued by Lord Rama and his army. In the *Ramayana*, and in the political and public discourse that often

of "prostitution" as the sexual exploitation or abuse of persons for commercial purposes echoed the 1949 UN Convention. As a legislation, it built upon late colonial anti-prostitution laws, and also served as postcolonial Indian lawmakers' response to the global anti-trafficking agenda of the time.

Legislative debates around the SITA in 1956 illuminate how sex trafficking was only one of several concerns around prostitution voiced by lawmakers in the newly independent nation. Prostitution's very existence, in allowing women to become "fallen" and "destitute," was seen to impede India's ability to establish itself as a "modern" nation (Lok Sabha Proceedings 1956: 1494–1496). In 1986, the SITA was amended and renamed the Immoral Traffic (Prevention) Act (ITPA), reprised in this book's title. It retains the SITA's moral ambivalence around prostitution, observed in the legislative debates of 1986, judicial interpretations of the law and perceptions of prostitution, and the views of the police implementing it (Solanki and Gangoli 1996).

The ITPA, as postcolonial India's federal anti-prostitution legislation, defines neither trafficking nor even "immoral traffic" (the term used in its title). It defines "prostitution" as sexual exploitation, while simultaneously recognizing concerns about the threat "prostitutes" pose to "public order, decency, and morality."[15] As it currently stands, the ITPA criminalizes those who solicit sex and those who facilitate the sale of sex, as well as those who exploit women in prostitution, thus blurring the line between victim and criminal. It treats sex workers as both criminals to be arrested and penalized for soliciting customers for sex and victims to be rescued and provided care and assistance (Walters 2020: 314). Its ultimate objective is to curb prostitution (Law Commission Report 1975: 6).[16] In equating prostitution with sexual exploitation from which women must be removed, protected, and

deploys it in everyday contexts, Sita is characterized as a virtuous, victimized, abducted woman who stands for purity and chastity and whose rescue and return to her husband and kingdom becomes the primary motivation for his war against the demon king. The legislative debates around the SITA and subsequent amendments are rife with Indian legislators recognizing this chance similarity between the acronym and the figure of Sita as emblematic of the ideal, respectable, but vulnerable Indian woman whose virtue is besmirched by abduction and must be restored by her rescue (Legg 2014; Solanki and Gangoli 1996).

15 I use the term "prostitute" to reference the term used in Indian law, not as my own preferred category to reference sex workers.

16 The Law Commission of India's 1975 Report reflects how centrally the ITPA is concerned with criminalizing solicitation and "immoral" conduct in public spaces:

> The Act, thus, stops short of banning prostitution absolutely, and deals only with certain specified and concrete forms of immoral conduct. The ultimate object is, no doubt, to check prostitution … The philosophy reflected in the Act is that the law should stop only where the vice either assumes a commercialized form, so that public policy requires its suppression, or appears in a public place, so that it constitutes a public nuisance. (1975: 6)
>
> The Act is, therefore, concerned not with prostitution itself but with the manner in which the activities of prostitutes and of those associated with them which offend against public order and decency, expose the ordinary citizen to what is offensive or injurious, or involves the exploitation of others. (Law Commission Report 1975: 7)

reformed, the ITPA neither recognizes nor denies the possibility of consensual sex work outside of the framework of "immorality." Its legal imagination of prostitution in India is as much about middle-class unease at the social malaise and public nuisance that women selling sex are seen to cause, as it is about their perceived victimhood. Drawing upon ethnography, this book will demonstrate how this moral ambivalence, echoed in the ways state agents, legal actors, and NGOs interact with sex workers, continues to shape the current Indian sociolegal context, even as it is heavily impacted by transnational anti-trafficking campaigns.

The acts the ITPA criminalizes include keeping a brothel, "living on the earnings of prostitution," "procuring, inducing or taking persons for the purpose of prostitution," detaining a person in premises where prostitution is carried on, prostitution in or near a public place, and seducing or soliciting for the purpose of prostitution. Many of these acts are potentially (but not necessarily) exploitative toward sex workers (e.g. if they were forced into prostitution, if someone is living on their earnings forcefully or with duress, and if they are detained in a brothel).[17] However, as the Law Commission of India points out, the statute is centrally concerned with "immoral" conduct in public spaces (1975: 7). It primarily deals with prostitution rather than trafficking.

The moral ambivalence toward prostitution that frames the ITPA and its implementation became especially evident in an order of the Indian Supreme Court in a public interest litigation,[18] to address the "problem of sex workers in the country."[19] Some opinions articulated by the Justices authoring the order are worth quoting, to illustrate how the morally ambiguous image of the fallen woman and the victim deserving sympathy and assistance are conjured within the Indian legal framework:

> A woman is compelled to indulge in prostitution not for pleasure but because of abject poverty. If such a woman is granted opportunity to avail some technical or vocational training, she would be able to earn her livelihood by such vocational training and skill instead of by selling her body. (pp. 2–3)

[17] Reading the ITPA along with critical commentaries on it clarifies the following points. Prostitution itself is not illegal, but several activities around it which enable the sale of sex are. Technically, an individual sex worker selling sex consensually to earn only for herself, in a private and not public place, is not criminalized. However, agents or intermediaries are still penalized for benefiting from her prostitution. The intent or mere act of sexual intercourse for commercial gain is not criminalized. However, causing someone's entry to the sex trade or detaining them in a brothel, outward manifestations of the sex trade such as "seducing or soliciting," and all commercial aspects of it, such as running a brothel – are penalized (Kotiswaran 2001; Law Commission 1975; Sarode 2008; Thorat 2002). Clauses penalizing those who "live on the earnings" of a sex worker also have a punitive effect on sex workers by punishing not only pimps, agents, intermediaries, or traffickers, but also sex workers' husbands, lovers, partners, adult children, and other kin with whom they have intimate attachments (Thorat 2002).

[18] For an explanation of public interest litigation in India, see Chapter 6.

[19] The Supreme Court of India's order in the case of *Budhadev Karmaskar vs State of West Bengal*, Criminal Appeal No. 135 of 2010, dated August 2, 2011.

> Our effort in this exercise is to educate the public and inform them that sex workers are not bad persons, but they are unfortunate girls who have been forced to go into this flesh trade due to terrible poverty. Hence society should not look down upon the sex workers but should have sympathy with them. (p. 6)

The higher judiciary in India thus articulates prostitution as a "problem" caused by "terrible poverty," to be addressed by social welfare and rehabilitation measures to help "unfortunate" women who have fallen to the extent of selling their bodies. On the other hand, anti-trafficking NGO efforts funded by the US State Department often focus on a prosecutorial approach, where the blame for trafficking is placed on the criminality of individual offenders. These represent two different frameworks to address prostitution – one focusing on the state's responsibility for social welfare (to help "unfortunate girls") and the other on the criminal justice system. Both frameworks come together in the sites and processes where this book will take its readers. The book shows how, along with their relatively recent donor-driven efforts to work with the police and prosecution (Chapters 2–4), anti-trafficking NGOs support Indian state agents and legal actors at sites and processes where the ITPA's intent to reform "immoral" women is manifested (Chapters 5 and 6).

The ITPA lays out the following procedures to both reform and assist prostitutes,[20] in which NGOs have long participated. It empowers the police to "remove" women from brothels – a provision which anti-trafficking NGOs reframe as a provision for rescue (Chapter 2). It also mandates judicial inquiries with women thus removed from brothels to evaluate their "character," "antecedents," and "genuineness," and the "suitability" of their families to take charge of them (Chapter 5). These inquiries lead to decisions about whether to send the women home to their families or remand them to state protective custody (Chapter 6).[21]

Anti-trafficking NGOs in India

India has a long history of nonstate actors and elite women's groups being heavily involved in curbing prostitution from a deeply moralistic, gendered, and paternalist social welfare perspective. From colonial to contemporary times, nonstate social workers have been an extended entity of governance whom the Indian state relies upon for assistance in curbing prostitution. The late colonial state in India actively sought the assistance of an embryonic and "ruthlessly reformative" colonial civil society (including Indian women's reform groups as well as imperialist feminists) to remove women from brothels, reform them, and manage rescue homes (Legg 2014).

These nonstate actors were also actively involved in shaping the colonial-era predecessors of the ITPA. The efforts of privileged Indian women to save and reform

[20] See footnote 15.

[21] As I elaborate in Chapter 6, the statute prescribes protective custody even in the case of rescued adult women, regardless of their consent.

women in the sex trade have long been entwined with the need to define their own respectability vis-à-vis poor unfortunate "fallen" women needing guidance toward a more dignified life (Dell 1999). In the decade after India's independence, women social workers and elite women's organizations played a key role in drafting the SITA and actively pushed for its enactment, even as sex workers challenged it for violating their fundamental right to practice any profession under the then newly enacted postcolonial Indian constitution (De 2018). Lawmakers and women's organizations alike emphasized women social workers' role in implementing the SITA through a special social welfare bureaucracy (De 2018; Lok Sabha Proceedings 1956). Contemporary Indian anti-trafficking NGOs, as Prabha Kotiswaran points out, continue to be persuaded by a combination of cultural nationalist and conservative politics and radical feminism (2018a).

India's anti-prostitution law thus carves out space for nonstate actors committed to curbing prostitution, into which contemporary anti-trafficking NGOs have smoothly stepped. The ITPA requires "respectable" members of "social welfare organizations" to assist the state in removing women from the sex trade, and in subsequent procedures to process, question, detain, protect, and reform them. In my ethnographic research, the role of anti-trafficking NGOs was shaped only in part by their participation in a globally pervasive donor-driven anti-trafficking agenda. It was shaped, equally, by the ITPA's dependence upon and legitimization of a certain kind of nonstate intervention committed to curbing prostitution within a larger, contested field of meanings and politics around prostitution that includes sex worker rights activists' efforts to oppose the law. The book will show how both state actors and anti-trafficking NGOs have found ways to draw upon the ITPA's specific provision for "respectable" and "experienced" women social workers "in the field of suppression of immoral traffic in persons,"[22] to assist state agencies in governing prostitution.

The governance of prostitution has expanded in scope from the late colonial period to the current context of neoliberal governmentality, owing to NGOs' donor funding and increased global media and policy attention on the issue in the past two decades. Across different global contexts, there has been a multiplication of governmental bodies in the fields of social welfare and development. The growth of contemporary NGOs is traced to the 1980s, when state social welfare programs were cut to meet structural adjustment goals, leading to a shift from welfarist states spearheading development to neoliberal arrangements marking "leaner" and more efficient operations (Edelman and Haugerud 2004). Since the 1980s, international development agencies such as the World Bank began to contract aid out to NGOs in Global South countries. In this climate, NGOs became central to the global "aid industry" in the fields of international development and humanitarian work (Schuller and Lewis 2017).

[22] Specified in Section 17(5) of the ITPA.

In South Asia, as in other Global South contexts, the development sector has seen an immense growth of NGOs funded by foreign governments and aid agencies. Western aid organizations prefer to work through NGOs, whom they see as more accountable, to bypass the perceived bureaucracy and corruption of state agencies (Bernal and Grewal 2014; Schuller 2007). Neoliberalism in this context has meant a greater involvement of NGOs in activities formerly carried out by state agencies.

Anti-trafficking NGOs bring a new framework of global sexual humanitarianism to existing moralistic, gendered, and paternalist social welfare perspectives and legal provisions against prostitution in India. The law and order and criminal justice focus of contemporary anti-trafficking NGOs, driven by US donor priorities, is new, as is their professionalization and capacity to attract foreign funding.

Most anti-trafficking NGOs I encountered in New Delhi and Mumbai started working on sex trafficking in the late 1990s. Their work began to expand around the year 2000 when global activism, funding, and legal instruments around sex trafficking were developed, established, and circulated. Though the G/TIP office of the US State Department was the largest current or past donor for many of these NGOs, their backgrounds, motivations, and other sources of funding were complex and diverse.[23] Though the anti-prostitution positions of most of these NGOs align with those of abolitionist or radical feminists who conflate prostitution with sex trafficking and do not support voluntary sex work, most NGOs I encountered did not refer to themselves as feminist organizations or make explicitly feminist claims. Some NGOs, including the New Delhi-based NGO whose work I discuss in Chapters 2 and 3, work not only on sex trafficking, but also on a broader set of human rights, child rights, gender violence, and gender justice issues, and a broader range of trafficking issues beyond sex trafficking to labor trafficking in other sectors, such as domestic work.

Among the large anti-trafficking NGOs I encountered in Mumbai (discussed in Chapters 4–6), two were Christian organizations, staffed by Indian Christians (who form a significant minority in Mumbai) and well funded by faith-based organizations based in the US. Though these faith-based anti-trafficking NGOs were somewhat newly established, in the early to mid-2000s, there were also two large nonfaith anti-trafficking NGOs active in Mumbai, which had received funding from the US as well as other Indian and foreign sources. Unlike the New Delhi NGO whose work I track in Chapters 2 and 3, these four anti-trafficking NGOs in Mumbai were focused exclusively on sex trafficking.

Some anti-trafficking NGOs I encountered in both cities had a combination of funding from smaller US donors, church communities, European sources, the Indian government, and the Japanese funding agency I mentioned in the Introduction, which had previously worked in Cambodia and had recently started

[23] G/TIP is the Office to Monitor and Combat Trafficking in Persons, which coordinates the US' global and domestic anti-trafficking efforts.

funding Indian NGOs. This agency was funding two of the NGOs I regularly encountered in Mumbai that worked on facilitating the prosecution of traffickers and the economic rehabilitation of rescued sex workers. It was also funding a startup enterprise providing livelihood skills training and employment to sex workers detained at the Mumbai shelter.

Law, Prostitution, and NGOs in India: A Contested and Evolving Field

To establish the contexts framing Indian anti-prostitution law, anti-trafficking interventions, and new legal developments in India, a few further points deserve mention. First, though the NGOs whose work I observed were primarily US-funded, the US is not the only voice or player in contemporary global anti-trafficking discourse and policy. There are other global influences shaping the Indian sociolegal context – connected to the US-driven anti-trafficking campaign, given the global circulation of its discourse and interventions, but also bringing their own experiences and perspectives to the anti-trafficking agenda. The small Japanese funding agency partnered with several NGOs in both Mumbai and Kolkata. They wished to replicate the anti-trafficking work they had done in Cambodia in India, by funding NGOs to support rescued women to testify. As I mentioned in the Preface, another globally powerful legal framework that has shaped Indian NGOs' law reform efforts, including an unsuccessful effort to amend the ITPA in 2006, is the Swedish model that (like the US) conflates prostitution and trafficking. Its main approach has been to criminalize clients while decriminalizing the sale of sex by sex workers.[24] This amendment was also reportedly shaped by India's poor ranking in the US *TIP Reports*, and the efforts of Indian anti-trafficking NGOs and government agencies they worked closely with to improve India's ranking on the *Reports* by showing that India was enacting stricter penalties against perpetrators of trafficking.[25]

Second, foreign-funded anti-trafficking NGOs are not the only driving force shaping the discourse around prostitution in the Indian sociolegal context. Though the ITPA authorizes only what it sees as "respectable" anti-prostitution NGO intervention, there is a larger, contested field of meanings around prostitution. Sex worker rights activists have made strong and concerted efforts in the past two decades to oppose the ITPA's criminalization of many aspects of prostitution. Though the ITPA denies them the legitimacy it provides anti-trafficking NGOs, sex worker rights groups in India have pushed for the law to be repealed and amended, alongside a larger repertoire of social movement strategies as subaltern citizens

[24] For a discussion of how the Indian sex worker rights movement played a significant role in preventing an amendment to the ITPA shaped by the Swedish or Nordic model of criminalizing clients from being passed in 2006, and the counterarguments they made about how this proposed amendment would affect their livelihoods and harm HIV/AIDS prevention efforts, see Kotiswaran (2014) and Lakkimsetti (2020).

[25] As analyzed by Kapur (2007), Kotiswaran (2011a), and Shah (2013).

(Kotiswaran 2013a). Recent ethnographic work by feminist sociologists in India has explored how sex worker groups' involvement with HIV/AIDS interventions efforts has boosted their collectivization efforts, especially since the mid-2000s, and reconfigured their relationship to the Indian state through increased political mobilization, rights claims, and advocacy for legal reform (Lakkimsetti 2020; Vijayakumar 2021). Sex worker rights groups have called for decriminalizing consensual sex work and recognizing its legitimacy, while launching their own efforts to prevent trafficking in the sex industry. They have also critiqued the often-misguided interventions of foreign-funded NGOs targeting voluntary sex workers in the name of curbing sex trafficking, through forced rescues that do not distinguish between voluntary and trafficked sex workers, adopt a carceral and paternalistic approach, and negatively impact HIV/AIDS intervention programs in India.[26]

I mention the sex worker rights groups here to indicate that beyond NGO-led interventions, there is a richly contested political field around prostitution shaping the Indian sociolegal context.[27] However, anti-trafficking NGOs have had a disproportionate influence on the law and its implementation. In the sites and procedures where I conducted my research, anti-trafficking NGOs, given their ready alignment with the law's description of "respectable social welfare organizations," occupied and mobilized a space that has not been made available to sex worker rights groups. This gendered politics of legitimacy and respectability extends beyond the Indian sociolegal context to global human rights advocacy, where groups that focus on sexual harm are more likely to be invited to inform policy than those that call for the recognition of sexual rights and agency (Miller 2004).

Third, though at the time I conducted most of my ethnographic fieldwork, Indian law did not address "trafficking in persons" explicitly, an amendment to Indian criminal law in 2013 adopted the UN Protocol's definition of trafficking and made it an offense.[28] This was not an amendment to the ITPA, but part of comprehensive law reform efforts,[29] prompted at the time by public furor over the widely reported and condemned New Delhi gang-rape and murder incident of 2012.[30] Since then, though the ITPA still stands as an anti-prostitution law at the time I write this, a series of new draft legislations have also been proposed and circulated (in 2016,

[26] See Ahmed and Seshu 2012; Dasgupta 2014, 2019; Ghosh 2008; Govindan 2013; Kapur 2007; Kotiswaran 2011a; Shah 2014; Walters 2018.

[27] A more detailed engagement with the ideological divide between anti-trafficking NGOs and sex worker rights groups – about whether prostitution is inherently exploitative or ought to be recognized as a legitimate form of work for those who do it consensually – is outside the scope of this book, though I have discussed my own position briefly here.

[28] See Introduction, footnote 9.

[29] The incident involving the gang-rape and eventual death of a young woman on a bus in New Delhi led to nationwide protests and substantial global attention to sexual violence in India, resulting in comprehensive reforms of the criminal law on violence against women.

[30] For a lucid discussion of this amendment, the adoption of the UN Protocol's definition, and the inclusions and exclusions involved, see Kotiswaran 2013b.

2018, and 2021) to address human trafficking (including several forms of non-sex sector trafficking), which is not defined or comprehensively addressed by the ITPA. NGOs, which have played such a central role in shaping and implementing the ITPA, have also significantly shaped these new bills. I mention these developments here to highlight anti-trafficking NGOs' expanding legal efforts beyond prostitution to other forms of trafficking, and will return to them in the Conclusion.

CONCEPTUAL FRAMEWORK

Immoral Traffic builds upon cross-disciplinary engagements with NGOs, law, gender, and the state in India and globally. It examines law's significance to the state's governance of sexuality – in particular, its concerns about public order, decency, and morals, and anxieties around nonnormative sexual identities and practices. The book takes as a point of entry insights from feminist historians and sociologists of India about sexuality's "constitutive effect" on the state, and about the state's "pornographic imagination" of those deemed sexually deviant as objects of surveillance.[31] Jyoti Puri argues, persuasively, that "sexuality's seeming threat to society is used to produce and affirm the role of the state" (2016: 11). Indeed, as Puri also notes, the governance of sexuality perpetuates and reanimates the role of the state despite states' retreat from some aspects of social life in neoliberal contexts (2016: 5).

This book extends the analysis of sexuality and governance beyond the state by placing postcolonial law in a broader field of neoliberal government, including state agencies and foreign-funded NGOs acting upon prostitution. It takes forward legal anthropology's long tradition of exploring the complex ways in which law is embedded in wider social processes (Starr and Goodale 2002). The NGO–law relationship I observed in India resonates with legal anthropologist Sally Falk Moore's prescient comments about law as a "semi-autonomous social field" that is "set in a larger social matrix which can, and does, affect and invade it, sometimes at the invitation of persons inside it, sometimes at its own instance" (1973: 720). *Immoral Traffic* brings out how, on the one hand, anti-trafficking NGOs work within the parameters set out by Indian law, and on the other hand, they also "invade" it (to quote Moore) and treat it as malleable in their efforts to reframe it. I show how, for anti-trafficking NGOs, the malleability of Indian anti-prostitution law lies both in the space it carves out for a certain type of nonstate actor and in its moral ambivalence toward prostitution.

New directions in legal anthropology retain the subfield's focus on local legal institutions and procedures, while expanding its scale to increasingly global sites and investigations of transnational legal processes.[32] Law and society scholars have also called for a more expansive and global perspective beyond state-centric or

[31] Hinchy 2019; Lakkimsetti 2020; Puri 2016; Tambe 2009.

[32] See, for instance, Clarke 2009; Goodale 2009; Merry 2000, 2006, 2016; Mertz and Goodale 2014; Starr and Goodale 2002; Wilson 2001.

state-framed interpretations of law (Darian-Smith 2013; Massoud 2015). *Immoral Traffic* pursues these new directions with an attentiveness to multiple scales of governance and the implementation of law by both state and nonstate actors, while remaining committed to the minutiae of legal practices and spaces. While the global anti-trafficking donor and policy regime often frames my analysis (as it does in my description of the Mumbai Court in the Introduction), I situate the governance of prostitution deeply and broadly within the Indian sociolegal context – the practices, institutions, and moral frameworks of Indian law, and the cultures, political economy, and bureaucracy of law enforcement, criminal justice, and state welfare agencies.

Law and society and critical NGO studies scholars have shown how humanitarian actors and international aid donors seek to intervene in Global South states by building up and even undermining legal institutions. Of particular note are critiques of how the "export" of law has become an integral part of humanitarian efforts in the Global South (Massoud 2014) and how donor-driven NGOs, despite good intentions, are eroding Global South states' capacities to govern (Schuller 2009). While informed by these critiques, *Immoral Traffic* is not set in a postconflict or aid-dependent state where new legal institutions are being set up, or where NGOs are operating in lieu of state intervention. It is based on ethnographic research in legal institutions in postcolonial India with complex histories, logics, processes, and politics, which both limit the possibilities of donor-driven NGO intervention and are shaped by it.

Finally, the book is in dialogue with interdisciplinary feminist scholars who have critiqued anti-trafficking campaigns and provided nuanced ethnographic insights on the complexities of sex workers' lives. Unlike these studies, however, this is not an ethnography of sex work. Nor is it an ethnography of sex trafficking, or even of anti-trafficking interventions alone. It explores the convergence, collaboration, and contentions between the agendas, projects, and agents acting upon prostitution, and the ways in which (both trafficked and voluntary) sex workers navigate and resist them.

NGOs, the Indian State, and a "Governmentalized Legal Complex"

Anthropologists leading the field of critical NGO studies have examined the central role NGOs play in neoliberal government, mediating between marginalized populations, state institutions, and transnational and multilateral agencies.[33] They connect the growth of NGOs in the Global South to the impact of globalization and neoliberalism on postcolonial states (Bernal and Grewal 2014; Schuller 2007, 2009). As they note, what makes NGOs anthropologically interesting is that they

[33] See, for example, Alvarez 1999; Bernal and Grewal 2014; Lashaw et al. 2017; Leve and Karim 2001; Fisher 1997; Gupta and Sharma 2006; Kamat 2004; Karim 2011; Mertz and Timmer 2010; Schuller 2007, 2009; Sharma 2008.

are not so much separate from or dependent on states as they are entwined with them (Bernal and Grewal 2014: 425).[34] A wealth of feminist scholarship on South Asia has critically examined NGOs focused on development, women's welfare and empowerment, and, more recently, LGBTQ+ issues and HIV/AIDS. Their work has provided important insights on the new governmentalities, claims, and gendered subjectivities emerging in the shifts NGOs have helped to bring about in marginalized women's relationship to the Indian state.[35] This book expands these contributions through a law and society lens, examining NGOs' efforts to glue (Schuller 2009) Indian anti-prostitution law and a donor-driven anti-trafficking agenda together.

In examining the role of NGOs in neoliberal India, *Immoral Traffic* also takes careful note of the work of anthropologists who have called into question generalized assumptions about the state, welfare, and neoliberalism (Gupta and Sharma 2006; Sivaramakrishnan and Gupta 2010). Especially generative here is the argument that unlike Western contexts where neoliberal policies have replaced welfare programs, both are propagated simultaneously in India (Gupta 2012), not by a shrunken state that has dismantled welfare, but by a multiplication of governmental bodies (Sharma 2008: 59). Indeed, in India, nonstate bodies "have always played an important role as partners in postcolonial governmental projects of development and humanitarian welfare" (Bornstein and Sharma 2016: 78). NGO interventions in law and policy are linked both to the growth of more recent neoliberal "good governance" and development policies, and to a longer history of legal and moral civil society activism (77). However, in a context where the protection of marginalized populations, women in particular, has been integral to the nation's postcolonial identity, the devolution of welfare responsibilities to nonstate actors may be partial at best.[36] Anthropological work across the state and NGOs in India thus emphasizes that global neoliberal trends play out differently in postcolonial contexts where electoral victories depend on states' identities as agencies of social welfare (Gupta and Sharma 2006).[37]

To analyze the dynamic, co-constitutive relationship between NGOs and the law, and their role in governing prostitution in postcolonial India, I have found the work of Foucauldian law and society scholars generative. Especially useful is their emphasis that law operates among a wider set of governmental actors and is

[34] Victoria Bernal notes, for instance, the "complex and contradictory power relations at work where it is no longer possible to draw clear boundaries separating governmental and nongovernmental, local and foreign, grassroots initiatives and international agendas" (2017: 55).

[35] See, for instance, the contributions on South Asian NGOs to Bernal and Grewal 2014 and Lashaw, Vannier, and Sampson 2017, and full-length monographs by Karim 2011, Lakkimsetti 2020, Roy 2022, and Sharma 2008, among others examining these themes.

[36] See, for example, Chatterjee 2004; Sharma 2008; Sunder Rajan 2003.

[37] Some scholars have argued that despite neoliberal adjustments, the state in India has not weakened, but the privatization of many state functions has meant that the political leadership is often able to divest itself of responsibility to impoverished citizens by invoking the role of other actors (Randeria 2003).

pervaded with forms of knowledge and expertise that are not strictly legal (Rose and Valverde 1998). For Rose and Valverde, law is therefore worth approaching from the perspective of government[38]: as a *legal complex*, an assemblage of regulatory agents, apparatuses and so on, acting upon a particular "problem" – which, in this context, is prostitution. Explaining how and why law matters in the regulation of sex work in neoliberal contexts, Jane Scoular calls for sociolegal scholars to theorize it through the lens of governmentality, that is, to examine how law is embedded in an extended group of regulatory agents that it authorizes, empowers, and acts alongside to construct spaces and subjects (2010: 38).

Connecting these multiple conceptual trajectories, *Immoral Traffic* situates the governance of prostitution within this broader "governmentalized legal complex." It illuminates a growing field of state and nonstate institutions, practices, knowledge, expertise, affect, morality, and anxieties acting upon prostitution. It is attentive to the way this field has expanded in scope from the late colonial period to the current contexts of neoliberal governmentality and sexual humanitarianism.

To explain my use of the "governmentalized legal complex" framework, three clarifications are worth making. One, I found that law, legal procedures, and legal institutions remain central to this broader field of intervention, and that the increasing involvement of NGOs has in fact served to strengthen the role of the law. Foucauldian scholars who situate law within governmentality argue that doing so does not mean "expelling" or diluting law's role (Golder and Fitzpatrick 1990). Indeed, law gains rather than loses its potency as it "increasingly operates alongside other normative ordering practices to shape subjects, identities, practices, and spaces" (Scoular 2010: 38). Bringing attention to how, for instance, NGOs are increasingly taking on tasks associated with policing, prosecution, and judicial inquiry, and training Indian legal actors to perform the tasks Indian law prescribes for them, this book demonstrates how foreign-funded NGO intervention is bolstering, rather than weakening, postcolonial law and state agencies.

Two, my claim is not that every entity and agenda constituting this governmentalized legal complex is always in agreement, converges smoothly without friction, or necessarily acts in concert with others. In the context of the colonial governance of sexuality, feminist historians make the important point that states themselves are hardly cohesive entities of governance. For instance, discussing efforts to control prostitution in late colonial Bombay, Ashwini Tambe steers clear of treating the

38 Several interdisciplinary scholars have drawn upon Michel Foucault's concept of governmentality (1991), an analytic he used to describe schemes, tactics, and apparatuses aimed to improve the condition of a given population, to examine a range of projects of "improvement" by state and nonstate actors. Foucauldian scholars have applied the concept beyond state interventions to those involving other authorities – civil society, philanthropists, social workers, experts, etc. Anthropologists have used the concept to extend critiques of the narrow lens through which developmentalist states "see" populations and problems (Scott 1998) to forms of expertise beyond the state, including NGOs – their simplistic technical assumptions, constitutive exclusions, and messy consequences (Li 2005).

colonial state as a uniform and unified entity, showing instead how the fissures in administration reveal the limits of empire (2009).[39] Studying the governance of sexuality in contemporary India, feminist sociologists have shown how tensions and disagreements between state agencies, and hybrid state/nonstate institutional spaces created to incorporate sex workers in India's HIV/AIDS response have inadvertently helped sex worker rights advocacy efforts (Lakkimsetti 2020; Vijayakumar 2021). In this book, I foreground the tensions and disjunctures (between state agencies and between Indian legal actors and NGOs) that mark the intersection of anti-trafficking and anti-prostitution interventions.

Beyond prostitution, ethnographers of the Indian state have dismantled the pervasive fiction of "the state" as monolithic, unified, and coherent. Instead, they center the instabilities, inconsistencies, fractures, and disjunctures within and across state agencies and practices, while contending that this very incoherence makes the state more powerful (Ferguson and Gupta 2002; Gupta 2012; Hansen and Stepputat 2001; Puri 2016). These frictions are seen beyond the state, across multiple forms of governance where the concurrence of multiple ideologies, techniques, and forms of power can be unstable, complex, and contradictory (Roy 2017: 886).

A third clarification about my use of the "governmentalized legal complex" framework is about whether, in situating law in a broader "legal complex," I frame my analysis as an "NGOization" of Indian law. Critical NGO studies scholars have, for instance, debated whether there is an "NGOization" of feminism and development in the Global South (Bernal and Grewal 2014). In India, as in other Global South contexts, the professional, technical/managerial approach to social issues taken by a new donor-driven NGO culture has been critiqued for depoliticizing social movements (Kamat 2003; Schuller 2009). The Indian women's movement has expressed concern at a donor-driven "NGOization" that has co-opted, transnationalized, professionalized, and therefore depoliticized many feminist and radical agendas (Roy 2015).

While I agree with these critiques and concerns, NGOization implies situations where NGOs have greater power and influence than whichever agency (usually the state) or set of actors previously occupied that realm, or where NGOs have taken the place of other civil society actors such as social movements. In the context of prostitution, anti-trafficking NGOs have certainly taken significant space away from

[39] Tambe finds, in the context of the Contagious Diseases Act enacted in 1870 to curb venereal disease in colonial Bombay, that though the law was implemented through an unprecedented degree of surveillance of sex workers, it failed because of rifts between the judiciary, police, and public health officials. This made evident a "disharmony between the different arms of the colonial state" (2009: 44). Similarly, Jessica Hinchy examines the fractures of colonial governance in the context of the criminalization of *hijras* (a third gender community) in colonial India (2019). Beyond India, feminist scholars have highlighted the inconsistencies and contradictions marking the governance of prostitution in other colonial contexts. Mariana Valverde finds in the case of moral reform in English Canada (1885–1925), for instance, that "the policing of prostitution was … caught up in a web of interests … that made it impossible for authorities to settle on any policy and be consistent in its enforcement" (2008: 176).

sex worker rights activists in their influence on the law and its implementation. As I have explained, this is rooted, for good measure, in the way postcolonial Indian law legitimizes only those it sees as "respectable social welfare" NGOs. However, anti-trafficking NGOs have not suddenly taken over the work or influence of state agencies, which have long depended on nonstate actors to curb prostitution. India's sociolegal history and my ethnographic research both demonstrate how law and NGOs together constitute a broader assemblage of entities and projects acting together (in tension and in collaboration) upon prostitution. I therefore prefer the "legal complex" framework as a conceptual apparatus that accommodates how anti-prostitution intervention in India has always already been "NGOized," and how law's reliance on and legitimation of NGOs, and NGOs' reliance on and deployment of law, have expanded and intensified through anti-trafficking campaigns.

Critical Trafficking Studies

This book builds upon insights from the interdisciplinary feminist field of "critical trafficking studies" that challenges the narrow definition, ill-conceived conceptual framing, and "ideological capture" of anti-trafficking discourses and policies (Musto 2016: 169–170).[40] This "anti-anti-trafficking" approach recognizes trafficking as a problem, but calls for a different approach, invoking concerns that anti-trafficking interventions can sometimes do more harm than good to those they aim to assist (Lindquist 2013: 321–322). Feminist scholars taking this approach have questioned: (1) the US government's conflation of sex trafficking with prostitution, (2) the global anti-trafficking discourse's portrayal of Global South sex workers as passive victims in need of rescue and protection, and (3) the US-driven anti-trafficking campaign's focus on law enforcement and criminal justice, instead of seeing sex trafficking as a structural problem rooted in poverty, gender inequality and discrimination, and migration gone wrong, or connected to other forms of labor exploitation.[41]

Feminist scholars across disciplines have traced the rise of current global anxieties around sex trafficking to an assemblage of US experts, activists, and legislators concerned about organized crime, immigration, and conservative Christian values

[40] Though she does not use the label of "critical trafficking studies," feminist sociologist Elizabeth Bernstein explains its premise succinctly by pointing out that "the framework of 'trafficking' (and its attendant notions of sexual victimization and exploitation) has been far better suited to the goals of aid organizations and governments than it has been to the needs of sex workers" (2018: 4). Bernstein further describes the remit of this growing area of interdisciplinary feminist inquiry by explaining her own landmark contribution as the "study of the growing cadre of humanitarian projects that have emerged to reclassify all or certain forms of sexual labor as 'trafficking' or 'slavery,' to press for laws that punish the individuals who are deemed responsible for this captivity, and to vigorously pursue sex workers' rescue" (2018: 8).

[41] See Agustin 2007; Bernstein 2018; Brennan 2014; Chacon 2006; Chapkis 2003; Chuang 2010; Doezema 2001; Fukushima 2019; GAATW 2007; Hua 2011; Kapur 2005; Kempadoo et al. 2012; Kotiswaran 2021; Mahdavi 2011; Musto 2016; Parreñas 2011; Weitzer 2007.

during the Bush administration, joining existing concerns about human rights and violence against women (Bernstein 2018; Hua 2011).[42] They have tracked how abolitionist feminists (who equate prostitution with violence against women) have gained a strong moral and ideological voice in the US government's conflation of trafficking with prostitution (Chuang 2010; Halley et al. 2006; Huckerby 2007). They have also explained how the agendas of abolitionist feminists and Christian faith-based organizations coalesced when both groups received generous funding under the Bush administration from 2001, and how they concurrently gravitated toward criminal justice solutions.[43] Although the US *TIP Report* emphasizes the importance of victim protection and assistance, a core concern remains the number of trafficking prosecutions and convictions and the quality and impact of law enforcement efforts (2010: 6). Feminist critiques have called into question how the US government does not address the socioeconomic causes of sex trafficking, regulate the labor conditions of sex work, or provide legal protection to migrant sex workers.[44] Providing robust critiques of the US-led "anti-trafficking industrial complex" for its heavily carceral, militarized, and securitized approach, feminist scholars have called, instead, for more nuanced, complex, and empirically informed perspectives on the global sex trade.[45]

Yet there remains a scarcity of empirical research on anti-trafficking interventions (Marcus and Snadjr 2013; Lindquist 2013). Anthropologists are uniquely positioned to fill this gap, peeling away layers of meaning and experiences to reveal the messy realities of people's lives (Montgomery 2013: 317) and challenge the dominant frameworks of the anti-trafficking narrative (313). Feminist ethnographies in different global contexts have illuminated several aspects of anti-trafficking campaigns in recent years, such as the complex interpretive frameworks of those tasked with implementing anti-trafficking law and assisting trafficked persons (Peters 2015), the concurrently punitive and protective approaches of anti-trafficking interventions (Musto 2016), the market-based humanitarianism anti-trafficking campaigns mobilize to attract Western consumers and volunteer tourists (Shih 2017), and the overlap between US-driven carceral approaches to curb trafficking and migration control (Vanderhurst 2022).

A key contribution of critical trafficking studies has been to explore and critique the unlikely alliance in the US between NGOs, abolitionist feminists, faith-based

[42] Alliances between certain feminist and faith-based groups to curb prostitution have a longer history beyond the US. In the context of the moral regulation of prostitution in English Canada (1885–1925), Mariana Valverde finds that "clergymen and nonconformist ministers, together with ardent Christian feminists such as the famed Josephine Butler, undertook evangelical missions to persuade both prostitutes and their customers to leave their lives of sin" (2011: 162).

[43] The production of the US *TIP Report* in an office headed by a former prosecutor and the international proliferation of the Swedish model of decriminalizing sex workers and criminalizing customers have also worked to shape these agendas and alliances (Bernstein 2018; Kotiswaran 2011a).

[44] Indeed, it imposes stringent conditions on providing such protections (Chapkis 2003; Huckerby 2007).

[45] See Bernstein 2010; Chacon 2006; Chapkis 2003; Chuang 2010; GAATW 2007; Kotiswaran 2021; Musto 2016.

groups, social service providers, law enforcement, and criminal justice in anti-trafficking campaigns.[46] Feminist scholars have theorized and critiqued these alliances in depth.[47] Ethnographic work in other global contexts, such as France (Ticktin 2011) and Brazil (Amar 2013), has also highlighted the unlikely pairing of policing and moral humanitarian agendas. In the Indian context, anthropologist Kimberly Walters has argued that the global panic over sex trafficking "animates a mode of global governmentality that fuses together otherwise contradictory registers of care and punishment in the disciplining of women who sell sex" (2020: 289).

This book builds upon, but also departs from, these insights and critiques, by situating anti-trafficking interventions firmly, deeply, and broadly within the Indian sociolegal context. In doing so, it tracks US-funded anti-trafficking campaigns as one among multiple forms of intervention against prostitution in India. While existing feminist research and critiques have focused on the connections, collaborations and coalitions between state agencies and NGOs in anti-trafficking campaigns, *Immoral Traffic* shows how the possibilities of alliance and cooperation among Indian NGOs, legal actors, and state agencies are contingent on several factors, and often fraught with tension and resistance. Fewer scholars have highlighted these aspects of anti-trafficking campaigns, a notable exception being Paul Amar, who emphasizes the temporary and tense alliances between a diverse set of actors involved in anti-trafficking rescue campaigns in Brazil (172–173).[48]

During my research, tensions and contradictions centered on the meanings of prostitution and victimhood played out most sharply in the encounters between

46 Bernstein 2018; Germain and Dewey 2017; Halley et al. 2006; Musto 2016.

47 Feminist legal scholars Halley et al. use the term "governance feminism" to describe the incremental installation of feminists and feminist ideas in actual legal-institutional power, where there is an emphasis on criminal law (2006: 340). They argue that abolitionist feminist involvement in the law and policy against sex trafficking reflects the ascendance of governance feminism (348). Elizabeth Bernstein also describes the gravitation of US abolitionist feminists and evangelical anti-trafficking activists toward solutions that support increased policing and prosecution, and state agendas of border control, terming these neoliberal alliances "carceral feminism" (2018). Jennifer Musto uses the term "carceral protection" to describe the blurred line between protection and punishment in the "complex interplay between state and non-state actors as they cooperate to identify and ostensibly help people in exploitative sex-trafficking situations" (2016). Musto describes these alliances as "a blending of criminal justice efforts with non-state assistance efforts that put a collaborative spin on efforts aimed at protection" (2016: 13). Also in the US, Tania St. Germain and Susan Dewey describe efforts to curtail prostitution as a "criminal justice-social services alliance, a punitive-therapeutic confederation of federal, state, and municipal law enforcement agencies and state, municipal, or independent nonprofit social services entities" (2017: 3). They use the term "the alliance" to refer to the "coalescence of punitive-therapeutic forces that work together to police or otherwise regulate street-involved women through arrest, incarceration, and court-mandated drug or other therapeutic treatment" (4).

48 Amar highlights the "mutability and contested, internally contradictory character of human-security governmentality" (2013: 177). His work shows how the different contradictory logics that came together in an anti-sex trafficking campaign in Brazil clashed profoundly, to a point where they could no longer be reconciled.

NGOs and police I discuss in Chapter 2. Other chapters reveal the myriad interdependencies, inconsistencies, and contingencies marking the encounters between NGOs and legal Indian law enforcement and criminal justice actors. Across the chapters, the book highlights how the relationships between anti-trafficking NGOs and state actors, though written into Indian law, are often fraught and constantly negotiated, rather than always already in coalition or collaboration.

Sex Work, Feminism, and Where I Stand

This book does not provide definitive answers to whether or not the women at the different sites and processes I observed were trafficked or what their identities "really" were. I explore, instead, how they presented their accounts to NGOs, state agents, and legal actors, how they were perceived, engaged, and processed, and how they navigated and resisted the ways in which they were interpellated. Via feminist criminologist Carol Smart (1989), I recognize the power of law's claim to truth, as well as how its accounts of women's experiences are partial and fragmented. However, and again with Smart, I do not seek to provide an alternate truth to resist the power of the law. Instead, I demonstrate how Indian and Bangladeshi women experience and respond to interventions aimed at rescuing, assisting, representing, and reforming them. The book highlights the myriad strategies through which women navigate both NGO-led anti-trafficking efforts and Indian law's anti-prostitution framework – by seizing upon the opportunities they provide, resisting them, or escaping them altogether. The women I met did not deploy the identities of either trafficked victim or sex worker as they strategized to navigate the interventions acting upon them: how to seek the outcomes they desired, or how to escape the interventions affecting their lives, incomes, and families.

I am often asked, in connection with my research, whether I support an abolitionist, anti-prostitution position or a non-abolitionist one that recognizes the legitimacy of sex work. To clarify, I came to this project, and wrote this book, as an anthropologist of law, the Indian state, and NGOs. I have not been involved in advocacy or activism on either side of the feminist debates on prostitution, which are polarized between radical or abolitionist feminists who consider prostitution inherently coercive and violent toward women and thus synonymous with trafficking (Barry 1979; Jeffreys 1997), and pro-sex work feminists and sex worker rights groups who consider consensual sexual labor a legitimate means to earn a living (Delacoste and Alexander (eds.) 1998; Doezema 2005; Pheterson 1989). In India, too, prostitution is located at what Shohini Ghosh terms the "faultlines" of feminism (2008).[49]

[49] Although, as Prabha Kotiswaran notes, the Indian women's movement has failed to include prostitution/sex work among its principal legal struggles. She underlines the fact that the mobilization of sex workers in India for law reform from the early 1990s was accomplished as a "spill-over effect" of HIV/AIDS prevention efforts (2011b). See also Sahni et al. (2008): 15–16.

I will briefly clarify the extent to which I have a position on these contentious debates. I recognize the possibilities of both sex trafficking and consensual sex work. I also acknowledge the distinction anthropologist Svati Shah points out between what is described in Hindi as *zabardasti* (force) and *majboori* (compulsion or constraints). Shah notes that force is not the same as the structural factors that shape constraints or compulsions leading someone to certain livelihood options (2014: 125, 199).

Of the women I encountered during my research, some said they were trafficked (brought by force or *zabardasti*), many provided accounts that included elements of *marzi* (choice), *majboori* (economic compulsion), or both, and yet others said they were not even involved in the sex trade. Some said they wanted to be rescued, while many said they were forcibly rescued against their will. My ethnographic accounts across the chapters cover this spectrum of coercion, choice, and denial in the narratives that Indian and Bangladeshi women removed from the sex trade presented to state agents, legal actors, and NGO representatives.

This book, though not an ethnography of sex work, is informed by a rich body of feminist ethnographic work on the complexities of sex workers' lives that calls into question the flawed assumptions of anti-trafficking campaigns that simplistically reduce sex workers to "trafficked victims." These scholars have shown how sex work involves diverse work conditions that public policies do not recognize (Dewey and Kelly 2011), and that sex workers make complex agentive choices to sell sex under structural constraints, from among limited employment choices, income-generating activities, and migration strategies.[50] Recent ethnographies in India have illuminated the diverse conditions and modes of organization of the sex trade (Kotiswaran 2011a), and sex work's imbrications with strategies of migrant labor (Shah 2014), caste and kinship ties (Agrawal 2008), practices of religiosity, sexuality, and matrimony (Ramberg 2014), and reproductive labor (Vijayakumar 2022). They have also explored sex workers' involvement in HIV/AIDS interventions (Lakkimsetti 2020; Vijayakumar 2021) and sex worker-led, community-based anti-trafficking interventions (Dasgupta 2014; Magar 2012).

This book, however, shifts focus from sites where sex is sold, from the lived experiences of sex workers, and from spaces and practices of sex worker activism, to encounters between sex workers and state agents, legal actors, and NGO workers at sites and processes where anti-prostitution and anti-trafficking interventions meet. My findings and conclusions here are based on what was observable at the sites and processes I studied – police stations, NGO offices, courts, and a state-run shelter. As I did not conduct ethnography in sex workers' homes, communities, places of work, or at sites and moments when they entered the sex trade, I cannot claim to know what their lives were actually like in the sex trade or the extent of choice and/or coercion they experienced.

[50] See Agustin 2007; Brennan 2005; Cheng 2010; Kempadoo 1998; Parreñas 2011; Zheng 2008.

Lastly, though the book critiques many assumptions and practices of anti-trafficking NGOs, state agents, and legal actors, my primary objective here is not an oversimplified claim that these entities "do no good" (Fisher 1997; Lashaw et al. 2017). I did observe anti-trafficking interventions help several women leave a life in the sex trade that was forced and exploitative, and I discuss those observations in this book. At the same time, I maintain a critical perspective, showing how these intersecting anti-trafficking and anti-prostitution interventions are deeply moralistic, paternalist and punitive, often imposed on those who do not seek the forms of assistance they offer, and do not always deliver outcomes that are useful or acceptable to those who seek to leave the sex trade.

2

A Tale of Two Rescues

Navigating Victimhood and the Politics of Intervention

Rescue operations are swift and chaotic events, fraught with confusion and uncertainty. Questions about who was trafficked into the sex trade, versus doing sex work voluntarily, or who wishes to leave versus stay on in the brothel, are not easily answered (nor usually asked). As I learned, rescues are also marked by tensions – between those conducting them and those being rescued, and between the various state agents (the police and Child Welfare Committee, abbreviated as CWC) and NGOs involved in rescues and postrescue procedures. During and after rescues, relationships between Indian NGOs, legal actors, and state agencies are a constantly negotiated work in progress – both collaborative and contested – as they come from different gendered moral frameworks, interpretations of the law, resources, and priorities of intervention. It was also evident that the women being rescued – which include those who entered the sex trade voluntarily, those who were trafficked, and several possibilities in between – make a range of choices, from actively pursuing their escape from brothels, to contesting and resisting rescues. My ethnographic observations of rescues brought out how they are shaped by these questions, uncertainties, tensions, and choices, rarely acknowledged in mainstream representations of rescues.[1]

I want to introduce these politics of intervention and navigations of victimhood through a few key moments shaping the two rescues this chapter focuses on and compares. The first set of excerpts is from my notes about a rescue operation conducted at GB Road, New Delhi, in October 2012. The second set is from interviews I conducted after a rescue operation in Kabadi Bazaar, Meerut, in July 2012.

[1] As Gretchen Soderlund points out, "While the stories abolitionists tell about their interventions tend to focus on the moment of the raid and the successful delivery of the rescued slaves to safe houses, events that occur in the aftermath of raids often belie the claim that all of the rescued women are sex slaves held captive and against their will in brothels" (2005: 65). And further, "Indeed, if news reports and policy documents are any indication, there appear to be few ways to talk about sex trafficking that do not include dramatic readings of the captivity narrative's well-rehearsed scripts: the prison-like brothel, the lured or deceived female victim, and her heroic rescuers" (2005: 77).

New Delhi rescues, October 2012:
"We cannot tell you how good we are feeling at leaving this place."
—Group of girls and women rescued from GB Road.

"Oh! She is a major! Will she 'give a statement' against the accused?"
—Police officer involved in New Delhi rescue.

"You! You are older. You look around eighteen. How could *you* let this happen?"
—CWC member involved in postrescue procedure.

Meerut rescues, July 2012:
"They have been tutored, tortured and threatened by the brothel managers not to tell the truth."
—NGO involved in Meerut rescue.

"Oh yes, those girls created a big commotion. They indulged in vulgar behavior, misbehaving and taking off their clothes. It took me hours to 'calm them down.'"
—Police officer involved in Meerut rescue.

"The police forcefully pulled us out of the brothel ("*kheench kheench kar nikala*"). They let the media photograph us in revealing clothes. Some of us barely had time to wrap towels around ourselves."
—Group of girls and women rescued from Meerut.

The first rescue operation was led by a New Delhi-based anti-trafficking NGO in collaboration with the New Delhi police. It was actively initiated by a woman who had been brought to GB Road (New Delhi's red-light area) against her will and forced to provide sex at a brothel there. The NGO had learned of this woman's presence at the brothel through a young man who came to her as a client and was now in a relationship with her. After the NGO, with some difficulty, managed to convince the police to conduct a raid at this brothel, six women who said they had been trafficked and wanted to leave were eventually rescued.

The second rescue operation was conducted in Kabadi Bazaar, the red-light district in Meerut (a town two hours away from New Delhi by car). It was led by the same New Delhi NGO and a national child rights agency in search of girls believed to have been trafficked there. Instead, a different group of young women was rescued, who vehemently resisted this anti-trafficking intervention. They said they had entered the sex trade out of choice, and described the rescue, rather than their entry into the sex trade, as a form of gendered violence. Varying reconstructions of this rescue operation through interviews with the police, NGO, and rescued women provide a rich contrast to the New Delhi rescues.

My interviews and ethnographic observations of interactions between rescued sex workers, police, and NGOs in these two contrasting rescue operations, brought forth two aspects of rescues. The first is the collaborative, yet contested relationship between NGOs and police and its impact on these interventions, and the second is the construction, navigation, and contestation of victimhood by state actors, NGOs, and rescued women. I also draw upon observations of postrescue procedures at the police station, Child Welfare Committees, and a magistrate's court, to show how these procedures and interactions shaped both the NGO–police relationship, and the constructions and contestations of victimhood that this relationship impacted.

The two sets of rescues provide starkly different examples of how NGOs, police, and sex workers navigate the politics of intervention and constructions of victimhood. The same NGO was involved in both cases, seeking to change the outlook of the local police toward the women being rescued, working actively with the police to enforce the law against the accused, and providing various forms of support to the police and the rescued women. Yet the role of the local police in each context, and their relationships with the NGO, varied in terms of their responses to the NGO's requests to intervene, the frameworks through which they approached prostitution, and their perceptions of the rescued women. Some of the women in the New Delhi case played a key role in initiating their rescues, while most of the women in the Meerut case did not wish to be rescued. Together, the two cases illustrate the complexities and politics of intervention and victimhood that mark encounters between police, NGOs, and rescued women.

ON THE POLITICS OF ANTI-TRAFFICKING RESCUES

Contextualizing Rescues

The Immoral Traffic (Prevention) Act (ITPA) retains the provisions of its colonial-era predecessors for the "removal" of prostitutes from brothels by the police, who must include women police officers or women social workers.[2] Social workers were rescuing women from brothels in India well before the growth of the current anti-trafficking movement, with historians documenting rescues even in the late colonial period (Dell 1999; Legg 2014). However, when contemporary NGOs raid brothels with the police, their role extends beyond rescuing those deemed to be victims, to urging the police to arrest the alleged perpetrators and urging the women to give statements against them to the police, and later, to testify against them in court. This inclusion of a law and order and criminal justice intent is a new dimension to the modality of rescue in the Indian context, introduced by donor-driven anti-trafficking NGOs.

The New Delhi-based anti-trafficking NGO leading both rescues I discuss here received funding from the US State Department to intervene in cases of sex trafficking, labor trafficking, child trafficking, and other related issues. It had been working in GB Road for over a decade and had expanded its work to other parts of New Delhi and other Indian states. Those at its helm had backgrounds in law and social work, and had developed strong working relationships with legislators, policymakers,

[2] For a clarification on the term "prostitute," see Chapter 1, footnote 15. For more on the requirement that women police or social workers be present during rescues, see footnote 21 (this Chapter).

bureaucrats, senior law enforcement officials, and the media. They were heavily involved in advising policymakers and training police, prosecutors, and judges on how to use Indian laws to respond to different aspects of human trafficking.

The NGO led and actively participated in the rescues of girls and women from the brothels in GB Road, working closely with the local police. The rescues were typically conducted by junior NGO workers, who had acquired considerable experience in just a few years and consulted the senior leadership when needed. The NGO also played a significant role in postrescue procedures under Indian law – supporting those rescued during appearances before a judicial magistrate if they were over eighteen, or before the Child Welfare Committees (CWCs) set up under India's Juvenile Justice (Care and Protection of Children) (abbreviated as JJ) Act if they were under eighteen, visiting them while placed in shelter detention and helping to coordinate their return to their families. Acting upon the priorities of the global anti-trafficking agenda, the NGO also worked to support the prosecution of those who allegedly trafficked and exploited the rescued women, and to encourage the rescued women to testify against them (see Chapter 3).

Two points of reference shaped what I knew about anti-trafficking rescues before observing them myself. The first was the way rescue narratives circulate in media and NGO domains. Predictably stereotyped and dramatized images and stories of impoverished and hapless rural Indian girls, duped and sold into sexual slavery, unable to escape without outside intervention, circulate through the US State Department's annual *Trafficking in Persons Reports* (*TIP Reports*), dramatic accounts by the *New York Times*' Nicholas Kristof, authors Kevin Bales and Siddharth Kara, CNN's Freedom Project and a myriad documentary films, and the brochures anti-trafficking NGOs in New Delhi and Mumbai handed me. This media and policy content routinely makes the claim that it is easy to identify trafficked victims in the Global South, and that rescue operations by dedicated outsiders swooping in to save apparent victims of sex trafficking solve the problem.

Preparing to observe rescues, my second point of reference was the extensive documentation of the harms of anti-sex trafficking rescues across global contexts and robust critiques of the mainstream assumptions in my first point of reference.[3] Critical trafficking studies scholars,[4] as well as sex worker rights activists,[5] have taken issue with global anti-trafficking discourse's portrayal of rescued sex workers from

3 In the US, for instance, the experiences of immigrant sex workers and trafficked persons during raids conducted by law enforcement have included the use of excessive force, harassment and abuse, interrogation without an attorney present, and detention. Those advocating for trafficked persons have called for approaches that recognize, center, and address their realities and experiences, rather than the priorities of law enforcement and criminal justice (Sex Workers Project 2009). For further critiques across global contexts see, for instance, Agustin 2007; Dasgupta 2019; GAATW 2007; Shih 2017; Soderlund 2005; Vanderhurst 2022).

4 See Chapter 1.

5 Ibid.

the Global South as passive victims and of rescuers as heroes and saviors. They have called into question accounts that recycle colonial assumptions and interventions, with little scope for nuance or complexity.[6] Indian sex worker rights groups, and feminist scholars and activists supporting them, have soundly critiqued the often misguided interventions of foreign-funded NGOs partnering with the police to target and harass voluntary sex workers in the name of curbing sex trafficking.[7] More recent ethnographic work in the context of anti-trafficking rescues in non-sex sector cases in India has expanded existing critiques of the simplistic and harmful assumptions, flawed solutions, politics, and procedural delays of rescue-based interventions.[8]

I did not directly witness forced rescues of voluntary sex workers during my ethnographic research in and around New Delhi. However, it is important to recognize how prevalent they are. A petition filed before the New Delhi High Court by fifteen adult sex workers in GB Road alleges that a police–NGO team from another state forcibly took them out of the brothel and away from their children against their will. The police sought their custody to take them back to their home state, but the sex workers went to court to exercise their choice to stay in New Delhi, where their children went to school (*Tara vs State* 2013).[9] In my research in Meerut, interviews with sex workers who reported being rescued against their will provide an indirect perspective on forced rescues.

Observing Rescues

I spent six months shadowing the work of the US-funded, New Delhi-based anti-trafficking NGO at multiple sites in and around New Delhi. This included spending time at the NGO office, looking at case files, and accompanying NGO teams on rescues (such as the New Delhi rescue in this chapter) and postrescue procedures and interactions (such as the New Delhi and Meerut cases in this chapter, and a case where the NGO encouraged a rescued woman to testify in court, see Chapter 3). I also had the opportunity to observe training sessions the NGO led for Indian judges (discussed in Chapter 3) and meetings between its senior leaders and US embassy officials about the *TIP Report*, the ITPA, the NGO's initiatives, and

6 See, for instance, Agustin (2007); Chuang (2010); Doezema (2001); Kapur (2005); Soderlund (2005).

7 See, for instance, Agnes (1996); Ahmed and Seshu (2012); Dasgupta (2014, 2019); Ghosh (2008); Govindan (2013); Kapur (2007); Kotiswaran (2011a and 2011b); Pai et al. (2018); Shah (2014); Walters (2018).

8 See, for example, Agarwal (2021); Ramachandran (2019).

9 The New Delhi High Court viewed the rescued women as victims, but ruled that they could not, as adults, be forcibly taken away if they did not wish to leave, as this violated the constitutional guarantees of the right to equality before the law and the right to a life with dignity in India. *Tara vs State of Delhi*. Criminal writ petition no. 296 of 2012. Judgment of the New Delhi High Court dated April 13, 2012.

so on (discussed in the Preface). I also observed the NGO's participation at events and discussions with the UN Office on Drugs and Crime and with Indian government agencies. Through these opportunities, I observed how this NGO worked with multiple entities – state institutions, legal actors, US and other foreign donors, and the women it rescued.

During my six months tracking its work with the police and courts in and around New Delhi, this NGO conducted two sets of rescues in GB Road,[10] and had already conducted the one in Meerut. As a volunteer, I helped meet the NGO's staffing needs across its different interventions. I therefore spent at least half my time observing anti-trafficking rescues in non-sex sector contexts, such as domestic labor, as I have discussed elsewhere (Ramachandran 2019). This provided a sense of the different dimensions of the NGO's work beyond the focus of my research. It helped me to develop a broader understanding of how donor-driven, anti-trafficking NGOs intervene in – and are resisted by – the postcolonial Indian legal system in multiple contexts possibly involving exploitative labor practices.

Across these rescues and postrescue procedures, I often wrestled to navigate my roles as an anthropologist observing them and a volunteer expected to participate in them in more direct ways than I was prepared for or comfortable with. I settled upon modified ways to do so, to maintain my research relationships and access, while being as respectful as I could to the NGO workers and police, and especially the rescued women I was expected to "talk down" to. These dilemmas, and my efforts to address them, were central to my participant observation of rescues.

A RESCUE IN NEW DELHI

Garstin Bastion Road is New Delhi's "red-light" district, named after a British officer during colonial rule. Despite being renamed after a Hindu Arya Samaj leader, Swami Shraddhanand, in 1966, New Delhi-ites still refer to it as "GB Road," with the knowing glances and hushed tones that index the mention of a place associated with sex and immorality. Historical geographer Stephen Legg has chronicled how GB Road emerged during the interwar years, at a time of transition between the colonial state's segregationist and suppressionist policies toward prostitution. Colonial authorities evicted the city's sex workers from the central bazaars, following residents' complaints about social, physical, and moral "hygiene" (2014: 1394–1395). Despite sex workers' resistance, they were banished to GB Road, where they became targets of rescue efforts by women's groups, to whom the colonial state entrusted their care (2014: 4917–4918).

10 In addition to the rescues I discuss in this chapter, I observed the rescue of another woman who had been trafficked from GB Road from West Bengal. It played out along similar lines to the rescues discussed in this chapter, demonstrating the fraught relationship between police and NGOs, and the bureaucracy of post-rescue procedures.

GB Road is located close to the New Delhi railway station, and more recently the New Delhi Metro station.[11] Today, a visitor passing through is unlikely to see any immediate signs of being in a red-light district. When I first walked over from the New Delhi Metro station with an NGO worker, I saw a busy thoroughfare with heavy traffic, and hardware and sanitary ware stores announcing their presence on the first floor. On first sight, it is still very much "a space of utter indistinction" (Legg 2014: 1175–1177). GB Road's unremarkable and dilapidated cityscape hides a brisk business taking place on the upper floors.[12] All one can see from the street is a row of balconies, where women may lounge during the day, or occasionally beckon to men passing by on the street below (Soofi 2012: 135–137). Though it is still perceived as the city's main red-light district, it has reportedly seen considerable decline in the numbers of both sex workers and clients, as the sex trade has moved to non-brothel locations.[13]

The Rescue

In late October 2012, while New Delhi was in the thick of celebrating the festivals of Dussehra, Navratri, and Durga Puja, the NGO received information about two women who had been forced into prostitution at a brothel in GB Road and who wanted to escape. The NGO had a network of informants in GB Road, about whom I never managed to learn much, as this information was fiercely guarded.[14] I did learn that some were young men who were regular clients at the brothels, and occasionally developed feelings for and relationships with the women they met there. Some of the women confided in these clients that they were forced into prostitution and wanted to escape.[15] The information in this rescue came from one such client, who was in a relationship with Bishakha, a woman who had been trafficked to GB

11 New Delhi's partly underground rapid transit system.

12 In 2004, researchers Sen and Nair, police officers who coauthored a UNIFEM-USAID-National Human Rights Commission Report on human trafficking (with a sex trafficking focus) counted ninety-three brothels on GB Road, and around twenty to twenty-five women in each, amounting to approximately 2,300. They also reported that women working in GB Road brothels were mostly from the states of Andhra Pradesh and West Bengal, with some from Nepal and Bangladesh (2004: 388). A typical brothel or *kotha* in GB Road is run by an owner, a madam, brothel managers dealing with the finances, pimps (typically men), and *didis* or *ayahs* (women who do odd jobs) (388). Clients include schoolboys and college-going men (388–389), late shift workers, rickshaw drivers, and daily-wage laborers (Soofi 2012: 50–51).

13 Increasingly, sex workers and pimps in India are soliciting clients through the use of mobile phones, the internet, and social media. The sex industry has also expanded to physical spaces beyond brothels. See Sen and Nair (2004: 415) and Soofi (2012: 532–534). See also Rakshase et al. (2022).

14 I remain unsure of whether they were paid or received any other incentives from the NGO, as I was not privy to the discreet conversations about this aspect of the NGO's work.

15 In the other GB Road sex trafficking case I had the opportunity to observe (see footnote 10.), the NGO was approached by the father of a young woman who called home to say she had been taken to GB Road against her will and had been forced into prostitution there.

Road and asked him to help her escape. Not only did Bishakha want to take the client's help to leave the brothel, but she even sent with him a photograph of another, much younger, girl who was in the brothel with her, whose escape she also wanted to facilitate.

Neha,[16] an energetic and determined young NGO worker in her early twenties, took charge of the case. She was just out of social work school and had been working with the NGO for over a year, first as an intern and then as an employee. Her colleagues described her as *dabangg* (fearless),[17] determined, and highly experienced with conducting GB Road rescues, despite her young age. She had met with the informer/client to verify and develop the information, and showed me the photographs of the women we would be looking for. Bishakha looked to be in her early twenties. The friend Bishakha wanted to help looked younger, possibly a minor.

Neha contacted the police only after she had all the information she needed. The NGO staff preferred not to approach the police with information about rescues ahead of time. They explained that some police personnel allegedly tipped off the brothel madams and pimps about impending rescues in exchange for bribes.

The inspector in charge of the police station, a gray-haired man in his fifties, at first expressed reluctance to conduct the rescue for logistical reasons. It was a busy time owing to the festivities going on in the city, with Ramlila Maidan, the large public grounds under this police station's jurisdiction, being the venue for the city's largest Ramlila performance.[18] The inspector said the police station was short-staffed, with most personnel on duty at Ramlila Maidan, and all vehicles already in use. Several important political figures were to come for the Ramlila performance that day, which meant extra security arrangements. However, the inspector was from the same North Indian state as Neha, so she hoped to draw upon their common cultural and linguistic background to strengthen the prospects of collaboration. Ultimately, she was able to convince him that this would be a "good case," because she had strong information that indicated the women wanted to leave the brothel.

Despite the close working relationship the NGO had developed over time with this police station, rescues often entailed having to convince the police to conduct them. I had observed this while shadowing the NGO during a previous rescue operation in GB Road. That rescue, too, took place during a busy time for police deployment in the city, and ended up being delayed by two or three days. The police had been deployed to a large political agitation led by yoga and Ayurveda

16 All names have been changed to protect the anonymity and confidentiality of my interlocutors.

17 Also the name of a (then) recent blockbuster Hindi film starring the popular "action" muscleman actor Salman Khan as a police officer.

18 A folk dance-drama reenacting stories from the Hindu epic, the Ramayana, based on the life of the mythological deity Rama, whose victory over the demon king Ravana is celebrated during the Dussehra festival. See also Chapter 1, footnote 14.

guru and self-styled anti-graft campaigner Baba Ramdev at Ramlila Maidan.[19] Then came August 15, India's Independence Day, a national holiday. The NGO was getting increasingly concerned about the plight of the trafficked woman in that case, whose stay in GB Road was being prolonged as the police were unavailable.[20] When the NGO attempted to meet the same police inspector and request his assistance for that rescue, he first informed them that he was in court, and then that he was running a fever and would be staying home. Anxious to conduct the rescue without further delay, Biren, a hard-working NGO worker and Neha's immediate supervisor, contacted a senior police officer for assistance. An hour later, the police inspector arrived, still reluctant to conduct the rescue and livid at Biren and the NGO for contacting the senior officer, who had insisted that he cooperate. After the raid, one of Biren's bosses came to the police station and managed to placate the inspector, emphasizing the value of the police–NGO partnership and how it would benefit society. Biren, too, worked hard to mend bridges with the inspector, praising him repeatedly for his role in finding the trafficked woman in that case.

This time, Neha had found her own strategies to navigate this fraught relationship, leveraging personal connections and the potential strength of the case. A small police team was assembled for the rescue. We piled into a jeep with them and headed to GB Road. No woman constable was available to join. Neha and I, being women, were considered adequate to meet the legal requirements of women being present during the rescue and postrescue procedures.[21] After parking the jeep, we walked past the ubiquitous hardware stores lining GB Road, up a dimly lit stairwell, using the light from our cellphones to improve visibility, to a crowded second-floor brothel. Neha knew the exact cubicle in which to find Bishakha and the other girl Bishakha had told the informer about, on a makeshift mezzanine level accessed through a rickety ladder off the front room. Neha immediately began searching for them and emerged within minutes, with Bishakha and her younger friend (Noopur) in tow, clad in salwar-kameezes and wearing a mix of fear and relief on their faces. Both were immediately willing to leave the brothel and said they did not want to do this *kaam* (work).

19 Ramdev is also a self-appointed conservative Hindu voice against homosexuality, having filed a petition in the New Delhi High Court (and later approached the Supreme Court) to oppose the decriminalization of homosexuality in India.

20 Even though this police station was designated as an Anti-Human Trafficking Unit by the Ministry of Home Affairs, it did not have dedicated staff with no other responsibilities, nor enough vehicles to conduct a large rescue. For more on this previous rescue, see footnotes 10 and 15.

21 Section 15 of the ITPA details procedures to "remove" women from brothels. It gives police the power to search premises without warrant, and specifies that such a search must include at least two women police officers. It further specifies that the interrogation (an interesting choice of word, implying an association with criminality) of a woman or girl removed from a brothel be conducted by a woman police officer. If no woman police officer is available, the presence of a "lady member of a recognized welfare institution or organization" is required.

After asking whether they knew others who might also want to leave, Neha began looking for Rozy, a friend they were concerned about. Having been involved in rescues at GB Road for more than a year, Neha knew the nooks and crannies of each brothel like the back of her hand. She headed off again, accompanied by one of the policemen. Following Neha's instructions, I remained in the brothel's front room with Bishakha, Noopur, and another policeman, to ask the several women of varying ages gathering around us if any of them would also like to leave.

The policeman stood near the doorway, not interacting with anyone. I had learned that male police wanted to avoid confrontation with the brothel madams, due to harassment allegations during previous rescues. Bishakha and Noopur stood near me, darting nervous glances at two older women whom the police and Neha referred to as *nayikas* or brothel managers. These two women had initially stood in front of the girls and women gathering around us, blocking our view of them. When Neha had asked the two *nayikas*, firmly but politely, to let us talk to the girls and women, they had moved away, but their presence and occasional glares clearly intimidated some of those gathered there.

Struggling to balance my role as an anthropologist and NGO volunteer, I kept a low profile and followed Neha while she conducted the rescue. This was only my second visit to GB Road. I had neither expertise in conducting rescues, nor the ethical inclination to participate to this extent without knowing more. However, I wasn't in a position to jeopardize the access the NGO had granted me, nor to deny the work expected of me. So I stepped, reluctantly, into the role of rescuer. I decided to merely ask the women gathering around me if they wanted to leave, and to leave the rest to Neha when she returned from her search for Rozy. I addressed the women closest to me and those peering at me from further away, in Hindi, asking if anyone would like to leave. Two young girls, Ayesha and Mamta, stepped up immediately, saying that they had been brought to the brothel forcibly (*zabardasti se*), and asking to leave with us.

Following Neha's example, I asked whether they knew of anyone else who might wish to leave. Ayesha and Mamta indicated that in the group sitting on a bench nearby there were two young women (also Bengali, like themselves) who had also been forced into prostitution – Asha (in a white and blue kurta and jeans) and Beauty (in jeans, a blue tank top, and heavy make-up). I approached Asha and Beauty and asked if they wanted to leave. Asha was hesitant, saying she wanted to stay. Beauty shook her head. I decided not to press them further and waited for Neha, who soon emerged with Rozy, the girl she had been searching for.

Neha sat down with Asha and Beauty, adopting the tone of a friend offering counsel, albeit a persuasive and persistent one with authority. She told them that no one would force them to leave if they did not want to, but that this was their opportunity to escape, so they should not waste it. Asha changed her mind after some hesitation. First, she asked where we would take her. Neha assured her she would be taken back to her parents. She asked Asha again whether she was brought to GB Road against her will, to which she nodded "yes." After some further hesitation, Asha straightened up, looked at us, and said, "*main bhi aapke saath aaoongi*" ("I will come with you, too"). Beauty, however, did not want to leave. Neha again asked her whether she was there by choice or by force. Instead of answering that question, Beauty replied, in Hindi, "*main yaheen theek hoon*" ("This is where I am alright"). The word *yaheen* combines *yahaan* (here) with *hee* (only). Beauty's words implied a comparative framework – that she was better off here than elsewhere. The police were in a rush to return to the police station and began hurrying us up. The reasons for their haste included their desire to avoid confrontation with the brothel managers and madams, their fear that the rescued women might change their minds if they stayed in the brothel any longer, and their eagerness to showcase the successful rescue in the media. Given the limited time we had and Beauty's reluctance to leave, Neha decided not to press her any further. We left without her.

Beauty's friends Ayesha and Mamta, upset that she did not want to leave, insisted that she, like them, had been forcibly brought to GB Road. Though relieved that Beauty was not forcibly rescued, I wondered whether her refusal to explain how she got there was the result of pressure from those running the brothel (the explanation the NGO workers gave me), or her own decision, or stemmed from other reasons. In the short duration of the rescue, there was no way to know why Beauty did not want to leave the brothel. Pondering her decision, I was reminded of anthropologist Denise Brennan's observation that "ultimately, every individual evaluates exploitation – what can be endured and what goes too far – by different criteria" (2014: 1739). Brennan's discussion of a "subjectivity of coercion" helps to explain the choices that both voluntary migrant workers and trafficked persons may make not to leave exploitative situations, or to wait them out.[22]

This set of rescues illuminates the complexity of choices that women in the sex trade made at the time of rescue. Bishakha actively pursued her escape with the help of her client, Ayesha and Mamta quickly chose rescue as the best option for them, Asha took her time to weigh her options carefully, and Beauty refused rescue and opted to stay on.[23] In the short span of time (an hour at most) in which the rescues were conducted, it was challenging to ascertain who was a trafficked person and who was willing to be rescued.

22 Brennan's careful analysis helps to understand the choices that some who work in abusive and exploitative conditions make not to leave those conditions, "in terms of tactics and strategy, not consent or resignation." It is not about lacking consciousness of subordinate treatment, or accepting it, but more a matter of "the timing of when or how to challenge it," keeping in mind that different individuals may have "vastly different capacities for waiting out abuse." Brennan points out that the accounts of trafficked persons that may seem to reflect passivity can be better understood as "stories of rational calculation," including stalling (2014: 1642–1643, 1727–1731).

23 My findings resonate here with those of Pankhuri Agarwal, who studies rescues in the contexts of both bonded labor and sex trafficking. Agarwal also notes the complex choices those being rescued make about whether, when, and why they should or should not leave exploitative work conditions (2021).

Neha was sensitive to these questions owing to a combination of her personal rescuing "style" and the NGO's pragmatism. Preparing rescued women to testify against the brothel madams, pimps, and so on was a key strategy that the NGO adopted, in line with the prosecutorial focus of US-funded anti-trafficking efforts.[24] NGO staff told me they knew that women who resisted rescue did not later testify against those running the brothel. The NGO did not, therefore, consider it worth forcibly rescuing them.

As we descended the dimly lit stairwell, this time with the rescued girls and women, and crammed ourselves into the police jeep, they began to express relief. As soon as we started driving away, they started smiling and chatting. Two of them waved their hands at the busy street in a "goodbye" gesture. Ayesha, the most talkative in the group, clapped her hands in joy and exclaimed, "Bye-bye, GB Road!" She pressed my arm and said, "*Didi, hum bata nahin sakte kitna achcha lag raha hai yeh jagah chhod kar*" ("Didi,[25] we cannot tell you how good we are feeling at leaving this place").

Politics of Intervention

When we returned to the police station, Neha and I were given access to the interrogation room to speak with the girls and women. This was labeled as a "counseling" session, intended to produce a "counseling report," which, as it turned out, entailed ascertaining facts about the women's identities and families, and finding out about how they were trafficked. All six of them turned out to be from different districts in the state of West Bengal – five from South 24 Parganas district and one from Howrah. Three of them had been lured to New Delhi on the pretext of being recruited to jobs, one was drugged by some newfound friends, and two were brought to New Delhi by men whose names they remembered as Raju and Rahul,[26] who had promised to marry them.

The rescued women told us the names of the brothel owner and managers (*nayikas*) who forced them into prostitution. Some said they had been beaten and threatened by them. Each reported being forcibly confined to the brothel, not being allowed to go out, and not receiving any money, which was all kept by the brothel madams. They did not even know how much they were owed. None were in touch with their families in their villages, as the brothel managers had confiscated their mobile phones, and most of them had lost their families' contact numbers. At this point after the rescue, each of them said they wanted to return home to their families in West Bengal.

[24] See Chapter 3.

[25] Kinship term for older sister, also used to indicate respect toward a women perceived to be of higher socio-economic status or with more cultural capital.

[26] These are common Indian male names that NGOs and police said traffickers and recruiters tend to assume, in order to conceal their true names and identities and evade arrest and prosecution. I discuss this tactic again in Chapter 3.

Neha began to guess the rescued women's ages based on their appearance. I learned from speaking with police and NGO staff that women who came to GB Road were often from impoverished villages with low birth registration rates. In many cases, they therefore did not have any documentary proof of age. I was also told that recruiters and traffickers furnished fake certificates of age to show that the women were older than they seemed. Though government-issued documents are accepted forms of age proof in legal institutions,[27] officials evaluating them often expressed doubts about their reliability. In cases where no documentary proof of age is available, the legal procedure to determine age entails a bone ossification test at a government hospital, per established medical jurisprudence in India (Modi 2013: 247–248). This test indicates age within a two-year margin rather than an exact estimation. Given the manipulability of age documents and the inexactitude of the ossification test, neither is considered entirely reliable, but both are accepted as legally valid. Before the bone-age test could be arranged in cases lacking other documentation of age, I observed the police and NGOs use visual perceptions to ascertain whether those they had rescued would be taken to a judicial magistrate (for adults) or a CWC (for those below eighteen).

To Neha, three of the rescued women (Noopur, Rozy, and Asha) appeared to be minors. Each said they were seventeen years old, though Neha thought two of them looked younger. Bishakha (who had initiated the rescue with the help of her client) and Ayesha looked older. Neha was sure that they were "majors," and that the sixth young woman, Mamta, looked to be of "borderline age" – either a major or a minor. Mamta told Neha that she was twenty, but when Neha had asked whether she had proof of age, she said her age was recorded in a church register in her village as seventeen. She did not know the reason for this discrepancy between her age by her own account and her age on paper, but had a vague recollection that it might have had to do with her school admission. Neha decided to treat Mamta as a minor for the time being, for multiple reasons – the possibly locatable documentary proof of Mamta being seventeen,[28] cases involving minors leading to a greater quantum of punishment to those convicted, a perception that minors were more reliable prosecution witnesses, and a precedent set by the Indian Supreme Court to consider the lower age in the age bracket (e.g. seventeen, if the age bracket determined by the ossification test is seventeen to nineteen) (Modi 2013: 247–248; Sen and Nair 2004: 260–261).

While we were taking down these details, the police inspector came in to speak to the rescued women. He could not hold back his surprise at seeing Ayesha, the first woman he saw as he entered the room. "*Arrey*, *yeh to* major *hai*!" ("Oh, she is a major!") he exclaimed. He seemed to have a hard time believing that Ayesha wanted

[27] See also my discussion of the regime of suspicion around identity documents and the politics of citizenship in Chapter 5.

[28] Ibid.

to leave the brothel, asking Neha if Ayesha was likely to "give a statement" against the accused. He said that in his experience, "majors" did not want to be rescued, and did not support the prosecution case against the accused later.[29] Across the rescues I observed, the police tended to view younger-looking women as victims of trafficking (and were thus more inclined to rescue them), and also as more reliable prosecution witnesses. Citing their experience conducting rescues, the police were of the view that older women were likely to say that they had entered the sex trade willingly and return to it after rescue. In the context of sexual assault adjudication in Milwaukee, feminist ethnographers Hlavka and Mulla have observed how adult women were "consistently cast as noncredible (witnesses) if they did not visibly demonstrate profound and spectacular trauma" (2021: 83).[30] A similar bias marked the way the police treated rescued women from GB Road who visually appeared to be adults. It was evident in the policeman's remark about Ayesha being a "major," his related assumption that she was unlikely to be a reliable prosecution witness, and his resultant hesitation to use her statement to build the case.

The police were also keen to take a minor's statement because they said it would strengthen the case and attract greater punishment under the ITPA as well as relevant sections of the Indian Penal Code.[31] With four of the rescued women being perceived as minors, the police also applied (on the NGO's suggestion) relevant provisions of the Juvenile Justice (JJ) Act.[32]

Of the minor girls in this rescue, Mamta and Asha were fluent in Hindi, while the others were more comfortable in their native Bengali. Mamta was the bolder of the two and seemed keen to bring the perpetrators to book. So the police prepared the First Information Report (FIR) based on Mamta's statement,[33] which they took down with Neha's help.[34] Mamta agreed to accompany the police to the brothel after the rescue to identify the *nayikas* whom she had named in her statement.

[29] See further discussion in Chapter 3.

[30] For the authors, this is just one of the multiple ways in which the bodies, demeanor, clothing, and activities of Black women are racialized and sexualized in US courts.

[31] NGOs and police often mentioned that the provisions and quantum of punishment under the IPC and JJ Act were stronger than the ITPA in cases involving minors. The ITPA also prescribes enhanced punishment under certain sections if the victims are minors. Police and NGOs also found the ITPA useful as it had more provisions than the other two laws to punish those connected with running a brothel (who were easier for the police to arrest than accused traffickers who were often from other states).

[32] The relevant provisions of this statute, which applies to victims eighteen years old or below, include cruelty to a juvenile or child and exploitation of a child employee.

[33] The FIR is a written complaint about the commission of a crime, the first step in the initiation of criminal proceedings in India.

[34] In the FIR against the accused brothel owner and *nayika*, the police included provisions of the IPC criminalizing the procuration of minor girls, selling minors for the purpose of prostitution, buying minors for the purpose of prostitution, and wrongful confinement for more than ten days. The FIR also included several provisions of the ITPA – keeping a brothel, living on the earnings of prostitution, procuring or inducing someone for prostitution, detaining a person in a brothel, and Section 7 (1), which criminalizes prostitution within the vicinity of a public place.

She later told us she was afraid to do this, but was determined that those who had exploited them be punished.

After briefly going over the details about their age and trafficking situation with each of the six rescued women, the police subinspector in charge of preparing the FIR indicated his delight at the NGO "counseling report" Neha and I had prepared. The report, based on our conversations with the women, already contained these details. "Oh good," he said, "I can use this. It's not like they will say anything new." By preparing the report, the NGO had thus helped to reduce the time and effort the police would have to devote to speaking to the rescued girls and women in detail.

In addition to the "counseling" report, the NGO also offered the police, the CWC, and judicial magistrates assistance in coordinating with the police in the women's home states to help locate their families. The procedure under the ITPA requires both minors and adults removed from brothels to be detained in state protective custody until they can be returned to the custody of "suitable guardians."[35] However, each Indian state (province) has its own police force,[36] leading to challenges of coordination when women moved across states. The New Delhi NGO had built strong connections with the police and NGOs in other states, especially West Bengal, where most of the women they rescued from GB Road were from. While meeting with CWC members and judicial magistrates, the NGO always expressed a willingness to assist in the "home verification" process that the police were otherwise expected to perform.[37] Indeed, after this set of rescues, the CWC directed the NGO to assist with the home verification of the rescued girls. Bishakha was deemed an adult and not a minor, and therefore taken to a judicial magistrate, not a CWC. In her case too, the NGO was informally helping the police find her family in West Bengal by tapping into its contacts there.

Overall, this form of assistance with home verification demonstrated the NGO's pursuit of the donor-driven goals of strengthening law enforcement and criminal justice responses to sex trafficking, as well as the expansion of its work into tasks that fell in those domains. Though it was eventually the New Delhi police who (on the magistrate's orders) successfully coordinated with the West Bengal police to locate Bishakha's family, the NGO took considerable initiative in this home verification process. Neha from the NGO surmised that the police had made a greater effort than usual because of the perceived likelihood of this case resulting in convictions, as the rescued women had provided statements against the accused.

Echoing the friction prior to conducting the rescues, the aftermath of the rescues also saw such moments of collaboration matched by moments of tension and efforts to smooth them over. After we had spoken with the rescued women and dinner had been arranged for everyone, it was almost 10 p.m. A woman constable was going to take the women for a mandatory medical examination, and asked us to leave,

35 This aspect of the ITPA is discussed in detail in Chapters 5 and 6.

36 For a detailed explanation, see Sengupta (2010: 720–722).

37 This process and the role NGOs are playing in it is further discussed in Chapters 5 and 6.

saying that the police would take care of things. Neha's bosses at the NGO decided that it was best to comply, to maintain a good relationship with the police. The next day, we learned that the medical examination at a government hospital took all night. Early in the morning, the rescued women were back at the police station, tired after a sleepless night. They told us they were not provided breakfast, yet were expected to speak with the senior police officials who had showed up to meet them, and the media who had been invited to be briefed about the successful rescue.

Neha and her bosses at the NGO were upset about this. She asked the police to provide the women a meal, waited till it had been arranged, and left it at that, despite seething with rage. She knew that if she made this a bigger issue, the police would retort that the NGO could have taken care of the women's meals and stayed, knowing fully well that the NGO was dependent on the police and a government-run shelter to provide these postrescue facilities. After their initial reluctance to conduct the rescue for the logistical reasons they had cited – the busy festival season, scarce resources, and limited personnel – the police were now keen to showcase the rescue operation as their own, though much of the groundwork had been done by the NGO. The NGO stepped back to let the police bask in the glory of the rescues. Neha explained that this was important to maintain a good working relationship with the police. Letting the cops revel in good publicity, and picking battles with them carefully, helped to cement that relationship.

Another tense encounter took place around the transportation of the rescued women to a government-run shelter. The police had decided (given the shortage of vehicles) that the accused *nayika* who had been arrested would travel in the same vehicle as the rescued women, as the jail and the shelter were located in the same Tihar complex in west New Delhi. The presence of the *nayika* created fear and discomfort among the rescued women, who had already started hearing from the police that they would end up spending a long time at the shelter. Their suspicions that they were being taken to "jail" were compounded by the fact that the *nayika* was traveling with them. When Neha protested at this way of doing things, the subinspector in charge replied sarcastically that the NGO should provide the police a vehicle if they were so concerned. The NGO had indeed provided vehicles for many of the rescues it was involved in, but did not have one available at that time. Seeing only one woman constable accompanying the *nayika* and the rescued women, Neha was concerned that the *nayika* would try to threaten them not to say anything against her at the CWC and magistrate's court later. Though it was a tight squeeze in the police car, Neha decided to ride along with them to make sure this did not happen.

Navigating Victimhood

The morning after the rescues, Neha and I reached a CWC in east New Delhi, where rescued minors from GB Road were taken, per procedure, before being sent to the government-run shelter. The CWC is a judicial body mandated by the Juvenile

Justice (JJ) Act to make decisions about the custody, well-being and rehabilitation of "children in need of care and protection."[38] In contrast, those deemed eighteen or above are produced before a magistrate's court.[39] The CWC (per the JJ Act) or judicial magistrate (per the ITPA) determine whether and when rescued girls and women will be sent back to their families or to a shelter after rescues.[40] The criminal case against the accused is conducted in a trial court in a separate process, before which victims' statements are also recorded by a magistrate per India's Criminal Procedure Code.

After the four minor girls arrived with the police team, the all-women group of CWC members welcomed them into a large office room harshly lit by white tube lights. They began consulting the NGO's "counseling report" while asking the girls about what had happened to them. They tried to set the girls at ease by addressing them in a manner meant for children much younger than seventeen. The CWC members' use of incongruous, diminutive terms of endearment such as *gudiya* ("doll") and *bachche* ("child") caused the girls to chuckle.

The CWC members drew a clear connection between victimhood and innocence–rendered most evident in Mamta's case, where they had trouble making that connection. The courageous Mamta, who had returned to the brothel with the police to identify the accused, and who had told us she was twenty as far as she knew but seventeen according to her church certificate, did not appear childlike. She had a broader build than the other girls, looked physically stronger, and exuded more confidence.

When the CWC chairperson caught sight of Mamta giggling aloud at something Neha had said, she started scolding Mamta loudly. "You! You are older. You look around eighteen. How could *you* let this happen?"[41] The chairperson beckoned the confused Mamta to her and asked her how she came to GB Road. She clicked her tongue and chided Mamta for not knowing better than to go away from her village with some boy.

If a woman rescued from GB Road did not look like a child, the perception of innocence inextricably linked to victimhood was thus diluted. She became,

38 Each CWC consists of a chairperson and four other members, of whom one is to be a woman. The members are selected based on qualifications including postgraduate degrees in social work, psychology, child development, education, sociology, law, criminology, and, "where such a person is not available, a person with at least a graduate degree in any of the social science disciplines" (JJ Act, 2000, Section 22 (i)). Other qualifications include a teacher, doctor or a social worker "who has been involved in work concerning children" (JJ Act, 2000, Section 22 (ii)). The members of the CWC are expected to have a minimum of seven years of experience in their fields. The CWCs are set up to conduct inquiries to ensure the necessary care and protection of a "child," defined as someone who has "not completed their eighteenth year of age" (JJ Act, 2000, Section 2 (k)). The committees are meant to provide a "child-friendly" space which does not look like a court room; for example, the committee members do not sit on a raised platform and there are no witness boxes (JJ Act, 2000, Section 24 (3)).

39 NGOs and police described the act of bringing rescued girls and women before a magistrate or the CWC, in Indian English legalese, as "producing" them before these judicial bodies. This usage reprises the language used in the relevant statutes such as the ITPA and the JJ Act.

40 As I demonstrate in Chapters 5 and 6, rescued women are not given a choice in the matter.

41 In Hindi, "*Arrey! Tum to badi umar ki ho, attharah ki lagti ho, tumne yeh kaise hone diya?*"

instead, the target of suspicion and censure.[42] Mamta was blamed for committing "mistakes" in her choices to migrate and pursue a romantic relationship, which led to her being trafficked to GB Road. Instead of being offered the same compassion demonstrated toward the younger-looking girls, she was seen as being too bold, too cheerful, and too "mature" to fit the "innocent victim" paradigm. It was evident that the CWC's perception of victimhood entailed seeming not only childlike and innocent, but also passive, withdrawn, and reticent. In contrast, Mamta, owing to her appearance and demeanor, was perceived to have the capacity to have "known better," an agency she was chided for not exercising to prevent being trafficked.[43] The CWC's perceptions of Mamta echoed the misgivings the police inspector expressed at the police station about Ayesha being an adult and therefore, less likely to be a victim. Ultimately, despite these misgivings, the CWC decided to treat Mamta as a minor pending her furnishing the church document establishing her age as seventeen.[44] The CWC directed the NGO, which had offered to assist with the home verification, to start the process for Mamta to be sent back to her family in West Bengal.

This CWC had ordered, per established procedure, that the minor girls stay at the state-run shelter at the Tihar complex until they could be sent home to their families in West Bengal. I attended a second CWC session at the shelter, with Nidhi, a different NGO worker, while Neha was occupied elsewhere. The CWC members spoke with the girls before beginning the long bureaucratic process of sending them back home. Knowing that even a short stay at a government-run shelter demoralized rescued girls and women,[45] the NGO wanted to be there to support them. This entailed urging the girls to tell the second CWC all the relevant details again, and not to change their statements despite possible intimidation by the accused *nayika* or frustrations caused by their stay at the shelter.

[42] These responses to Mamta resonate with insights from those who have critically analyzed constructions of victimhood in the anti-trafficking context. Critiquing the Victims of Trafficking and Violence Protection Act (2000) in the US, Wendy Chapkis takes issue with its heavy reliance on "narratives of female powerlessness and childlike sexual vulnerability" (2005: 63). Radhika Coomaraswamy, former UN Special Rapporteur on Violence against Women, notes and critiques the power of such stereotypes:

> Overwhelmingly, the law continues to be fueled by moral considerations. As such, it may be that the only trafficked women who will be provided protection are those who fit into the stereotype of the young virgin "who was snatched off the streets by unscrupulous criminals, drugged, taken across an international border, raped and then chained to a bed or at least severely beaten to engage in sex for money, paid to her captors." Both local and international media tend to feed into this portrayal of the appropriate trafficking victim as a young, virginal girl subjected to extreme violence and cruelty. (2000: 28)

[43] Observing interactions between victims of trafficking and those tasked with assisting them, researchers Brunovskis and Surtees highlight the role of clothes, behavior, and demeanor in perceptions of who should be entitled to sympathy and assistance (2008: 59).

[44] In the cases of the other three girls who were visually perceived as minors, the CWC ordered that the bone ossification tests be conducted for confirmation.

[45] Discussed in detail in Chapter 6.

The second CWC proceedings made it further evident that twinned assumptions about innocence and passivity were the prevalent frame through which victimhood was perceived. Here, the chairperson looked at Noopur and Rozy and commented about how young they looked. While talking to Rozy, she asked whether condoms were provided for her in the brothel. The girls confirmed that condoms were not used. Shaking her head and adopting a tone of concern, the chairperson asked Rozy how many customers came to her during her time in GB Road. The answer was twenty, in just a few days. The chairperson clicked her tongue and made no effort to hide her shock.

On the other hand, though supported by the NGO, Mamta continued to face unsympathetic and inconsiderate treatment from the second CWC and staff from the government-run shelter. She was once again treated differently for her relatively mature appearance and demeanor. When the chairperson called her to be interviewed, she smiled shyly. The chairperson's attitude was starkly different from her behavior with Rozy and Noopur. "*Arrey, jab mardon se nahin sharmaati ho, toh humse kya sharmaana*!" ("Oh come on, when you don't shy away from men, why act shy with us?") She read Mamta's smiles to index an association with both sexual agency and willful immorality. Her line of questioning was so accusatory that Mamta immediately grew subdued, except to reply quietly that she had been drugged at the time.

Echoing the previous CWC's questions about why she "didn't know better," the chairperson then asked Mamta why she did not raise a fuss on the train while being taken away from her village. This questioning tactic reminded me of the "hue and cry" doctrine that defense lawyers in sexual assault trials use to cast doubt on a survivor's testimony and make the case that an allegedly forced sexual encounter was actually consensual.[46] Mamta's treatment at the CWC felt more like a cross-examination by a defense lawyer for the accused trying to raise suspicion about her character than a procedure intended to make decisions about her "care and protection."

Mamta's age became an issue of contention between the NGO and state agencies. While the chairperson was talking to Mamta, staff from the shelter, nursing anger at a complaint the NGO had made about them not providing basic toiletries to the girls, remarked that Mamta was actually twenty, but "had been tutored" by the NGO to say that she was younger. Nidhi, the NGO staff member who had come to this hearing, was otherwise a quiet and even-tempered young woman. She nearly lost her temper at these allegations, replying that the NGO was doing its job truthfully and the government ought to do its part.

The CWC eventually set the same procedures in motion for Mamta to be sent home to West Bengal as those for the other girls, because she was legally considered a minor. However, while the NGO treated her as a victim, the treatment she received from state agencies was in the register of suspicion and accusation rather

[46] Indian anthropologist Pratiksha Baxi has examined this defense strategy extensively in her ethnography of rape trials in India (2014). I discuss this further in Chapter 3.

than empathy. And though the NGO, police, and CWC worked together after the rescues, their collaborations were mired in these conflicting approaches, centered on divergent constructions of age, victimhood, and prostitution.

Bishakha and Ayesha, being treated as adults, were taken to a judicial magistrate for their statements to be recorded. Just over a week after the rescues, I joined Neha at the labyrinthine Tis Hazari District Courts complex in New Delhi to meet them. The NGO, again, wanted to encourage the women to give the magistrate all the details they had given the police. If they changed their statement compared with what they had told the police, it would not bode well for the prosecution in the future, an aspect of anti-trafficking intervention in which the NGO was deeply invested.

When they arrived at the court from the shelter, Bishakha looked pale, withdrawn, and worn out – very different from her relieved expression on the day of the rescue. At that time, she had seemed happy at leaving the brothel, though reluctant to talk about her family in West Bengal. She eventually mentioned that she was married and had a child back in the village, but hesitated to provide information that would help to locate her family. That day at the Tis Hazari court, her mind seemed far away, and she began to cry. As we sat there outside the magistrate's chambers, she began to ask Neha about the client who had helped her to escape the brothel. She had feelings for him and longed to meet him before returning to West Bengal. She begged Neha to give her his number. Sensing that she would be judged harshly for making the choice not to go home, she reassured us that she would go home, but wanted to see her client/partner just once. She sobbed that he had done so much for her, she just wanted to say goodbye. Neha told her she could not help with this while Bishakha was in state custody. She stalled by saying that once the home verification was done, things would get sorted out. The client also made several efforts to meet Bishakha, calling Neha repeatedly to find out her whereabouts.

Later, I asked Neha what she made of the situation between Bishakha and the client, and what she thought the outcome would be – whether Bishakha would go home or get together with him. Neha, a much younger woman than Bishakha, shook her head and said that Bishakha was "too emotionally involved," and was making a big mistake by "thinking only in the short term" and placing all her trust in a man she had met in GB Road. "Anyway, it's better we don't get involved in all this," she told me in English. "They don't know what is best for them. I need to keep counseling her." She did not think this relationship was in Bishakha's best interest.

As it turned out, Bishakha chose to be with her client/partner rather than return to her family in West Bengal. Six months later, after moving to Mumbai for the next leg of my fieldwork, I was in New Delhi for a personal visit. I caught up with Neha over lunch for an update. All the rescued girls and women had gone home. The NGO had helped to trace and verify many of their families. Bishakha's family had come to New Delhi to claim her custody, which the court granted them, but she did not want to go back with them and stayed on in New Delhi with the client.

One day, Bishakha and the client had shown up at the NGO office. He had told the NGO staff that he intended to marry her. "Major *hai kya karein, sabki apni apni* choice *hoti hai*" ("She is a major, what to do? Everyone has their own choices"), Neha said with resignation and more than a hint of disappointment. Following her own advice, she did not get further involved. As an adult, Bishakha's choices were seen as less malleable than a child's, and the possibility of marriage seemed to lend some respectability to what was seen as a morally inappropriate relationship.

Bishakha's story made it clear that after being trafficked, she had met a man she wanted to be with, and wanted to leave the brothel to build a new life with this man, away from GB Road and away from "home." She sought a different outcome from the rescue – one that she had herself initiated – than returning to her home and family, as prescribed by the law and implemented by state agencies. By helping with home verifications, the NGO was also deeply invested in the latter outcome. However, the choices Bishakha made after rescue did not fit the neat, paternalistic outcomes that the law and those implementing it envisaged for women who left the sex trade.

"Home" was not an easy outcome to navigate even for those who sought such a return. The other woman deemed to be a major, Ayesha, was also concerned about going home, but for a different reason. Unlike Bishakha, she wanted to go back home, but she felt a great deal of shame and trepidation about what to tell her family – in particular, her teenage son – about where she had been. What would he think when he found out about her? She talked at length about how she had been trafficked to GB Road and had tried to run away from the brothel many times, but was stopped by the brothel managers on every occasion. A couple of months after the rescues, a policeman from her district in West Bengal had visited the shelter to take another woman back home. This serendipitous meeting hastened Ayesha's home verification and eventual return home.

The GB Road rescues were not the romanticized tales about heroic saviors and hapless victims that circulate in anti-trafficking discourse. Though these were indeed cases of trafficking, they demonstrated contrasting perceptions of victimhood by NGOs and state agencies. Mamta, though supported by the NGO, was not perceived by state agencies as a true victim. The GB Road rescues also demonstrated how women like Bishakha sought outcomes that diverged from the solutions offered to them. After initiating her escape from the brothel, she pursued a relationship of her choice, rather than the protection of the state, NGO, or her family.

A RESCUE IN MEERUT

In July 2012, a massive rescue operation was conducted in Kabadi Bazaar, the red-light district in Meerut, a town two hours away from New Delhi by car. It was led by the New Delhi NGO whose work I was tracking and a national child rights agency, in search of girls believed to have been trafficked there from the states of Assam and West Bengal. Instead of the trafficked girls the rescue teams were looking for, a different group of young women was rescued, and a case made out against the alleged traffickers. This group of women vehemently resisted rescue, saying they had entered the sex trade out of choice. For them, it was not their entry into the sex trade but the act of rescue that was a form of gendered violence. Varying reconstructions of this rescue operation by the police, NGO, and rescued women brought to light how the politics of intervention and navigations of victimhood played out very differently from the New Delhi rescues.

Politics of Intervention

Meerut is a small town where the anti-trafficking police unit, recently set up through the federal government, was described to me by police and NGO representatives alike as rather skeletal. Unlike New Delhi, the local police did not have experience dealing with sex trafficking cases,[47] and were, by their own admission, not well versed in the provisions of the ITPA. Yet Meerut's proximity to the capital meant that the local police faced pressure from the federal government to demonstrate that the newly set up anti-trafficking unit was doing its job. It also meant that the New Delhi-based NGO and child rights agency wielded considerable influence in the rescue operation and postrescue procedures. The police depended heavily on their guidance about how to proceed. Anthropologist Beatrice Jauregui points out that the police in India have "provisional authority" in a shifting field of resource exchanges and subjectivizing forces (2016). In the context of anti-trafficking interventions, I found that the police leveraged connections with the NGO and child rights agency to save face and evade censure from the federal government.

I learned just how closely the New Delhi-based NGO had worked with the Meerut police when I asked about the specifics of the FIR.[48] Among other punitive clauses, it made out a case of solicitation against the brothel managers.[49] This piqued my curiosity, knowing that Indian police had been roundly criticized by anti-trafficking NGOs, human rights reports, the US State Department's *TIP Reports*,[50] as well as sex worker rights groups for applying this section of the ITPA to criminalize sex workers (HRW 1995; Sen and Nair 2004; *TIP Report* 2009: 156). Wondering about how and why the Meerut police had applied this solicitation clause against brothel managers instead, I scheduled an interview with the local police chief in Meerut. A sincere, overworked official in a town with a high crime rate, he admitted he hadn't had the

47 Unlike GB Road in New Delhi, where many rescue operations had been conducted, especially since 2000–2001, when anti-trafficking NGOs first became active in the city.

48 See footnote 33.

49 Section 8 of the ITPA criminalizes "seducing or soliciting for purposes of prostitution" in and around a public place.

50 See Introduction and Chapter 1.

time to study the ITPA law in detail. "Madam, why don't you ask the NGO people about this? They gave us a format on how to frame this FIR, and we copied it."

He connected me with the police officer investigating the case, who obligingly looked through my copy of the ITPA with me. Pondering for a minute, she said the NGO representatives had explained to her that the solicitation clause was a "revictimization of victims." To prevent what they termed a misuse of this clause, the NGO representatives had told her that it should be used against the brothel managers and not the victims. I knew from observing training sessions led by the NGO that it encouraged the application of the ITPA as an anti-trafficking (rather than just an anti-prostitution) legal instrument. I had observed NGO workers urge the police not to use the ITPA's solicitation clause against sex workers, and encourage the police to view them as victims of sex trafficking. NGOs described the very application of the solicitation clause as a misuse of the law.[51] The Meerut police officer echoed this phrasing while explaining how the NGO had trained her in the application of the ITPA and the framing of the FIR. The NGO had thus literally explained to the police how to document the case and how to reinterpret India's anti-prostitution law toward an anti-trafficking agenda.

However, the police's recollections of the rescue also illuminated tensions between the police and NGOs in constructing victimhood. The police chief explained his initial reluctance to conduct the rescue, as the sex workers had resisted being rescued. He described what he termed the "harassment" caused to male officers like himself by the rescued women. Shaking his head, he said (in English), "After the rescue, the girls started engaging in 'nefarious activity.'" When I asked him to elaborate, the embarrassed official reluctantly added, "Madam, what can I say. They started tearing off their blouses." According to him, the women had planned this action to incriminate the police before the media and any future judicial inquiry.

The investigating officer tasked with managing the reluctant victims (who had explained the "NGO version" of the ITPA to me) voiced a perspective closer to the concerns about immorality in the ITPA than a complete endorsement of NGO efforts to construct them as victims of trafficking. "Oh yes, those girls created a big commotion," she told me. "They indulged in vulgar behavior, misbehaving and taking off their clothes. It took me hours to 'calm them down.'" Thus, while she followed the NGO's lead on how to apply the law to investigate and document the case, she had not shifted her moralistic assumptions about women in the sex trade – assumptions that are also embedded in the Indian anti-prostitution law – to align with an anti-trafficking agenda. Embedded in the police's allegations

[51] Though both anti-trafficking NGOs and sex worker rights groups have long called for amendments to the ITPA to remove this clause (including the proposed 2006 amendment I discussed in the Preface and Chapter 1), at the time of my research it remained part of the law. However, in response to the widespread criticism of this clause being used to criminalize sex workers, the Indian government, prompted by NGOs, proposed a major policy shift in law enforcement emphasizing the need to treat women found in brothels as victims of sex trafficking, and to differentiate them clearly from criminals such as pimps and brothel managers who traffic them and must be arrested and prosecuted (MHA 2009; UNODC–Govt. of India 2007).

of "harassment" and "vulgarity" are specters of both immorality and criminality attributed to sex workers. The police saw them as threatening and unmanageable gendered subjects – women they were tasked with rescuing, but simultaneously feared and disdained.

The police's response demonstrates how the reframing of the law is never quite complete, enmeshed in a complex dynamic between NGOs and legal actors, marked by both tension and collaboration. The law's moral ambivalence toward prostitution, and legal actors' pathologization of sex workers,[52] render NGO efforts to reframe Indian anti-prostitution law to fit a US anti-trafficking agenda fraught and incomplete. Following the NGO's lead for pragmatic reasons, given its connections to government officials in New Delhi, the police enforced the law as an anti-trafficking instrument, by using the solicitation clause against the brothel managers and not the rescued women, but did not shift their moral stance on prostitution as part of this intervention.

The police also emphasized their limitations in solving the "problem" of prostitution. The police chief emphasized, during our interview, that law enforcement, with limited time and manpower, had to focus on *crime*. These "women children issues" (in his words) were more of a "social service."[53] Indeed, he concurred in part with the sex workers' description of rescue itself as a form of victimization. From his perspective, rescues could only be part of the response. The rest was the work of NGOs and other state agencies. Though he perceived sex workers in the derogatory manner described earlier rather than in support of the legitimacy of sex work, the police chief also recognized that rescues were harmful rather than helpful to these women, who should have been left alone.[54]

52 My reference here is to feminist critical security studies scholar Claudia Aradau's observations about the "schizophrenic identifications" of trafficked women (2004: 251). Aradau analyzes how those who manage trafficked women approach them simultaneously as "suffering beings worthy of pity" and "risky beings who are to be contained and disciplined" (255). She observes that "when agency exists even as a potentiality, they become risky beings" (276), going on to note that this agency is pathologized. Aradau's analysis resonates with the way the police in Meerut perceived the women they rescued. It also resonates with the way the CWCs in the New Delhi rescue perceived Mamta as too agentive to be a victim of sex trafficking.

53 Social scientists have noted that the police in India tend to treat cases involving gender violence as a low priority (Jauregui 2016: 83–84; Sengupta 2010). Jauregui points out that "police often claim – and my observations confirm – that they are too under-resourced, mistrusted, or pressurized to do everything that the law and their various constituents demand" (2016: 81–82). In total, 80 percent of police officers interviewed in Sen and Nair's 2004 study (see footnote 12) admitted that these issues received no priority or low priority. The reasons they provided for not prioritizing trafficking cases included being busy with other activities, not perceiving trafficking as serious "unlike other grave crimes," shortage of staff, especially women police (who constitute less than 2 percent of the police force in India), and lack of resources (2004: 265).

54 Elsewhere, I have noted similar concerns voiced by the New Delhi police in the context of working with the same anti-trafficking NGO to rescue young girls from domestic work (Ramachandran 2019: 346, 349).

> I will tell you, madam. Those girls were adamant that we should have let them be, let them live. They said, "*Aag mein daal diya*" ("you have put us in the fire"). I could not disagree. I can't say we are giving them a good life.

He added that rescuing women from the sex trade was pointless without "proper counseling and rehabilitation." The police chief thus placed the management of prostitution largely within the domain of NGO intervention, beyond the possibilities of law enforcement. He implied that the task called for a social and moral responsibility (through efforts such as "counseling" and rehabilitation) beyond the mandate or capacity of the police. Undeniably, this perspective stems partly from a lack of time, resources, and interest in "women children issues." But it also challenges the partnerships anti-trafficking NGOs seek to cultivate with the local police. NGOs seek to train the police as "partners" to act against sex trafficking. The police, while dependent on NGO intervention to save face during this particular rescue, pointed out that the postrescue management of victims exceeds the possibilities of their intervention. The police's refusal to take further responsibility gestures back to the postcolonial law's heavy dependence on NGOs to deal with the prostitution "problem."[55] It echoes the way lawmakers and women's organizations had imagined the law being implemented in 1956: through active and engaged non-state actors, rather than law enforcement alone (De 2018; Lok Sabha Proceedings 1956).

Contesting Victimhood

I went to Meerut with a team from the NGO to interact with the twenty-five young women who had been placed in a government-run shelter after the rescue. The shelter staff had set us up with tables and chairs at the front porch of a colonial-era building. The age determination process had not yet been completed. Visually, most of the rescued women looked to be in an age range that the NGO and police called "borderline." The police and shelter staff warned that our "counseling session," as they termed it, would be difficult. Biren, the senior NGO worker who had participated in the raid, also warned our team that the young women would act "aggressive" and insist that they were not trafficked, but entered the sex trade on their own. We were instructed not to take their statements at face value, and told that they were likely to be untrue. The NGO's perspective was that the rescued women's assertions of voluntary sex work and resistance to rescue were "lies" told owing to the trauma of victimhood. "They have been tutored, tortured, and threatened by the brothel managers," Biren briefed the team.

Thus, despite the NGO's deep investment in treating rescued women as victims of sex trafficking and in training legal actors to do the same, it also pathologized the women as lying and aggressive subjects who needed to be assisted, but also disciplined and governed. Biren explained to the NGO team that our job was to elicit the

[55] See Introduction and Chapter 1.

truth about their victimhood, and ultimately, to "convince" them to participate in rehabilitation, a term used for the livelihood training programs offered to encourage them to take up a different line of work and stay away from the sex trade.[56]

Expected to participate in this "counseling" session, I again faced ethical concerns similar to those I navigated during the New Delhi rescues. But as it turned out, the young women we interviewed had no desire to be "counseled" or convinced. In a marked contrast to the GB Road rescues, where the rescued women had described being trafficked and were eager to leave the brothel, the women detained at the Meerut shelter were seething with rage. "You people keep coming and asking us all these questions. When will you set us free?" was the first thing each of them said. They firmly asserted that they had entered what they referred to as a *khandaani pesha* (family occupation) of their own will ("*apni marzi se aaye hain*"), knowing what it entailed. No one brought them to Kabadi Bazaar forcibly, they faced no difficulties working in brothels, and they enjoyed their freedom there. While the police sought to shift the responsibility for the unwilling victims back to the "social service" realm of the NGO, the rescued women challenged the label of victimhood applied to them by the act of rescue.

Many of the women said they belonged to certain communities (from the states of Rajasthan and Uttar Pradesh) which "traditionally" practice prostitution.[57] "*Yeh hamaara rivaaj hai*" ("This is our custom"), some said resolutely. Despite intensive fieldwork with Bedias, one such community, Indian anthropologist Anuja Agrawal does not consider the question of whether the women's entry into prostitution is consensual or coerced easily answered.[58] Agrawal's work suggests that neither the assumption of victimhood that anti-trafficking campaigns operate with, nor the rationale of choice within restricted options that a sex worker rights position asserts can explain the community sanction and caste regulation of Bedia women in prostitution (2008).[59]

Three of the women in the group of twenty-five were from West Bengal, and not from one of the communities mentioned above. One of them told an NGO worker that she had indeed been exploited in the brothel, but had been warned not to say so. The other two had been reported "missing" by their families in their villages, but they

56 I discuss these programs in Chapter 6.

57 Anthropologist Anuja Agrawal, who conducted research with a Bedia community in Madhya Pradesh, cautions against treating the practice of prostitution among the Bedias as "traditional," even though it may be part of their self-representation. In her research, she found it difficult to determine exactly when and why Bedia women began to engage in prostitution as a source of income, but suggests that it was most likely a strategy the community used to build ties with local elites from whom they sought protection against the colonial state (2008).

58 Interview with Anuja Agrawal, June 2009.

59 Per Agrawal's account, the Bedia context complicates the idea of choice, as the entry of Bedia women into prostitution is not only sanctioned, but also strictly policed by the caste *panchayat*. Agrawal explains how, in this community, the source of income for the family is the sex work of unmarried daughters. She observes that women engaged in prostitution in this context are wary of implicating their families in any form of criminal investigation.

did not say they were brought to Meerut by force. Whether they had indeed been "tutored and threatened," or had made the choice to migrate and enter the sex trade, or whether their trajectories perhaps included elements of both trafficking and volition, I do not know. Like Beauty in New Delhi's GB Road, these questions remained unanswered, but in Meerut, the women said they were rescued against their will.

Most of the rescued women in Meerut not only rejected the category of victimhood, but also leveled allegations of ill-treatment at the police and NGO workers, accusing those who had rescued them of criminalizing and incarcerating them. "Why has the police 'caught' us? (*kyon pakda*)" they asked. "Why have you kept us here?" gesturing to the forbidding-looking gates of the government shelter where they had spent a month. "The police forcefully pulled us out of the brothel ("*kheench kheench kar nikala*"). They let the media photograph us in revealing clothes. Some of us barely had time to wrap towels around ourselves," they told us angrily. They described the rescue as hypocritical, alleging that some local policemen and news reporters were actually their clients. "In the brothel, they treated us like *biwis* (wives). Now they want to make us *behens* (sisters) whom they have to save." They highlighted the police's abusiveness as well as its hypocritical morality as both clients and would-be saviors.

In their narratives, the women shifted the mantle of criminality from those running the sex trade in Kabadi Bazaar, to the police and media. Reiterating that their entry into prostitution was not forced, they recast their victimhood in terms of abuse and harassment at the hands of those purportedly acting to "save" them. They described the act of rescue as tantamount to arrest. The carceral environment of the shelter,[60] and the long wait for the state to figure out their age, reinforced their perception of a simultaneous victimization and criminalization by the state apparatus and NGOs.

The interviews around the Meerut case left many questions unanswered. At what point were the women undressed, and why? The women said the police abused them by rescuing them in a state of undress. The police said the women harassed them by starting to undress themselves after the rescue. What transpired lies somewhere within, or perhaps beyond, these competing allegations. The construction and contestation of trafficked victimhood and the vexed politics of intervention played out across conflicting perspectives: the NGO's assumptions about "traumatized" yet "aggressive" victims, the women's accounts of voluntary sex work and forced rescue, and the police's reluctant intervention to rescue "nefarious" and "vulgar" women.

CONCLUSION

The politics of intervention and navigations of victimhood played out differently in the New Delhi and Meerut rescues. In both cases, the NGO worked actively with the police to enforce the law, and provided various forms of support to the police

[60] Discussed in Chapter 6.

and the rescued women. The police, for their part, demonstrated varying degrees and forms of reluctance to conduct rescues. Their reluctance stemmed from a range of factors – police infrastructure and police culture (a lack of resources, time, and staff, and a disinclination to view crimes related to gender and sexuality as high-priority matters), assumptions around age, prostitution, victimhood, and the profiles of "reliable" or "unreliable" witnesses, concerns about prosecutorial outcomes, and a recognition of the harms and futility of rescues and shelter detention.

The NGO played a pivotal part in both rescues. Its role extended across investigative, police-like work (e.g. developing a circle of client-informers in the red-light area, conducting home verifications in the rescued women's villages, mediating between the police of different states) and work considered to be very much the domain of NGOs – "counseling" and supporting rescued women. Significantly, these efforts extended to evincing trafficking narratives or convincing women to agree to certain outcomes. In the New Delhi rescues, the NGO supported rescued women in multiple ways: at the police station, CWC, and courts, advocating on their behalf when they needed food or essential items or faced intimidation, and providing a sense of continuity across rescue and postrescue procedures. Part of this support was structured around encouraging rescued women to provide consistent and reliable evidence against the accused, in pursuit of NGOs' donor-driven anti-trafficking agenda focused on arrests and prosecution. In Meerut, on the other hand, the rescued women considered the NGO a significant part of the forced rescue that victimized rather than assisted them. Observing rescues and their aftermath led me to recognize NGOs' capacity to "do good" (Fisher 1997; Lashaw et al. 2017), but also to critique the reductive and moralistic assumptions with which police–NGO teams approach rescues, and their impact on those they are meant to assist.

While actively initiating both rescues and closely monitoring and shaping postrescue procedures, the NGO was deeply dependent on the police, shelter, and judicial agencies to carry out several aspects of these interventions. It collaborated closely with the police to implement India's anti-prostitution law and other relevant statutes as anti-trafficking instruments. It depended on the police to set the law in motion to conduct rescues and initiate criminal action against the accused, but in both cases gave specific input on which legal provisions to apply against the accused. The police, for their part, depended on NGOs in a variety of ways; for example, the presence of women NGO workers during rescues helping to overcome the shortage of women police constables, and their counseling reports and home investigations helping to speed up, assist, and reduce police work.

Differences in the nature of the police–NGO relationship in the two cases shaped the politics of intervention and the constructions and contestations of victimhood I observed. In New Delhi, this was a constantly negotiated relationship, built through personal ties, a strategic use of praise and publicity, and picking battles carefully. In Meerut, the New Delhi-based NGO was a more powerful entity, given its close relationship with the federal government, and thus wielded more influence over the police in implementing the law in specific ways.

Despite these multiple forms of collaboration, the police–NGO relationship was marked by frequent moments of tension – around the priorities, resources, and purpose of intervention, and around divergent approaches to age, victimhood, and prostitution. Rescues and postrescue procedures demonstrate how the relationships between NGOs and state actors are a constantly negotiated work in progress. Both rescues depended heavily on the relationships the NGO had developed with senior police officers, who directed the police on the ground to assist the NGO. On the ground, however, it was a relationship that the NGO, in particular, was constantly rebuilding, strengthening, and smoothing over; sometimes jeopardizing, at other times placating.

At the center of rescue operations were the women the NGO saw primarily as victims, albeit often reluctant victims assumed to lie owing to trauma, or "short-sighted" victims who may pursue different outcomes than those prescribed by the law. Though the NGO's lens of victimhood was also not devoid of moralistic assumptions, the CWC and police viewed the rescued women through a more complicated lens, wherein the figure of the trafficked victim jostled against the figure of the immoral woman. When Mamta did not produce the expected account or appearance of a victim of trafficking or the women in Meerut resisted a forced rescue, they were pathologized as disruptive, over-agentive, and unreliable subjects. For their part, some rescued women, such as Bishakha in GB Road, actively sought assistance to leave the sex trade, while others, such as the group from Meerut, resisted rescue. Comparing the two rescues brings forth how rescued women's entry into the sex trade and the outcomes they sought varied greatly. They navigated in very different ways the NGO's, police's, and CWC's conflicting agendas and competing moral frameworks and assumptions around age, prostitution, and victimhood.

3

"These Girls Never Give Statements"

Victim-Witness Testimony in a New Delhi Court

VICTIM-WITNESS TESTIMONY AS AN ANTI-TRAFFICKING INTERVENTION

Since the early 2000s, spearheading concerns about sex trafficking, the US State Department, US faith-based organizations, and several global aid agencies have spent millions of dollars to fund NGOs in the Global South to carry out anti-trafficking interventions. Beyond the raid-and-rescue operations discussed in Chapter 2, these interventions include facilitating anti-trafficking prosecutions (the focus of this chapter and Chapter 4). As explained in Chapter 1, US State Department has pushed Global South countries, in particular, to strengthen legal responses to sex trafficking by framing it as primarily a law enforcement and criminal justice issue. Taking this position, the State Department perceives and laments inefficiency and a lack of "modernity," commitment, and awareness as the reasons why India has been unable to make what the US sees as sufficient efforts to combat sex trafficking through prosecution. This is instantiated by the following quote from the 2011 *Trafficking in Persons* (*TIP*) *Report*:

> Obtaining convictions in many parts of India was difficult due to many causes, including overburdened courts, the lack of modern docket systems, a weak understanding of the laws, and lack of commitment and awareness by some local authorities. (*TIP Report* 2011: 189)

As explained in Chapter 1, the State Department uses the *TIP Report*, on which India is ranked poorly, as an instrument of global governance. The *Reports* have criticized, among other issues, India's lack of efforts to prosecute traffickers. They express concern at a low rate of conviction of traffickers, relative to the scale of human trafficking in India (2012: 185; 2016: 200). Citing NGOs as sources, they note that the Indian police are corrupt, protect traffickers, and are overburdened, underfunded, and lack necessary resources (2016: 199; 2018: 223), and that courts do not have the resources to "properly prosecute cases" (2016: 201).

With these justifications, the State Department funds NGOs and pressures the Indian government to adopt a prosecutorial approach that prioritizes efforts to convict the accused.[1] To bolster what the State Department perceives as India's weak response to sex trafficking, a key remit of US-funded anti-trafficking NGOs is to work with women they rescue and with Indian police, prosecutors, and judges to increase the rate at which traffickers are convicted. Though some anti-trafficking NGOs focused more on providing services such as counseling and livelihood training after rescue, two of the largest foreign-funded NGOs in New Delhi and three in Mumbai actively worked in trial courts to support the prosecution of alleged traffickers.[2] In their advocacy material and interviews with me, they foregrounded the support they provide to rescued women to facilitate and strengthen their testimony against the accused. This US-driven and NGO-mediated prosecutorial approach foregrounds what is termed as "victim-witness" testimony as the central piece of evidence to improve the rate at which traffickers are convicted (*TIP Report* 2014: 16; UNODC 2017: 11). It is rooted in the following assumption:

> If offered access to justice, shelter, medical care, legal aid, psycho-social counseling, and other forms of assistance, "many victims step forward voluntarily and without pressure to become powerful and confident witnesses, telling their stories in court and achieving justice not only for the state … but on a personal level as well." (*TIP Report* 2007: 37)

However, contrary to this assumption, prosecutors in New Delhi and Mumbai estimated that even with NGOs' efforts to keep in touch with rescued women, to encourage them to testify, and to facilitate their travel to court, "victim-witnesses" testified in support of the prosecution in only 10–15 percent of these cases. Thus, though encouraging and training rescued women to testify against alleged traffickers is a key component of NGO-led anti-trafficking efforts, and though rescued women do sometimes testify in support of the prosecution, my interviews with legal actors in New Delhi and Mumbai revealed that this is a rare occurrence. This resonates with the findings of studies of sex trafficking cases in the US, which have also shown that those categorized as victims of trafficking rarely want to testify against the accused.[3]

1 While victim protection and assistance are also included, those studying the State Department's anti-trafficking efforts have noted that twice as much funding has been granted to organizations with a law enforcement or criminal justice focus as those protecting rights (Huckerby 2007: 236). Across global anti-trafficking efforts, prosecution has remained a key focus, with only broad and vague guidance on victim protection (Goodey 2004; Haynes 2004).

2 These NGOs also provided a range of victim support services, training sessions for Indian police, prosecutors, and judges, and programming aimed to prevent trafficking.

3 In the US, despite federal and state laws that criminalize human trafficking and support the prosecution of perpetrators, only a small number of human trafficking cases are prosecuted, and suspects are rarely convicted of trafficking offenses (Farrell et al. 2016). Farrell et al. found that with physical or corroborating evidence being hard to come by in these cases, the cases rested on the believability of the victim and their willingness to cooperate with the prosecution. However, most prosecutors and police cited an inability to locate victims, and victims' refusal to cooperate with law enforcement and/or prosecution, as major barriers to successful prosecution. The study also found that in the absence of safe and secure spaces to house victims, the police resorted to punitive practices such as arresting

Drawing upon interviews and participant observation, primarily in New Delhi, this chapter explores the multiple and complex reasons why most rescued women don't testify against the accused in the Indian sociolegal context. It situates this reported pattern within broader concerns about the "hostility" of prosecution witnesses in the Indian criminal justice system. It analyzes this broader context while simultaneously focusing on the case of a trafficked woman, Sunaina Das,[4] who did testify for the prosecution in a New Delhi trial court. By doing so, it also explores the constellation of factors that lead a small proportion of women to testify, and the challenges – socioeconomic, legal, and personal – they face. It tracks Sunaina's encounters with the legal system and the support she received from NGOs as well as Indian legal actors. Beyond her testimony, it explores how an NGO-led anti-trafficking training session for Indian judges impacted her case.

The US-funded NGO in New Delhi involved in Sunaina's case was the same NGO that conducted the rescues discussed in Chapter 2. It worked closely with the police on rescues and with prosecutors in trial courts, and also provided anti-trafficking programming for judicial officers adjudicating the trials against accused traffickers, madams, and brothel managers. Observing these aspects of the NGO's work, I learned that it used two key strategies to work with Indian legal actors to strengthen their responses to sex trafficking. The first was to provide various forms of support to encourage rescued sex workers to testify effectively for the prosecution. The second was to "train" criminal justice actors (police, prosecutors, judges) to implement India's anti-prostitution law as an anti-trafficking instrument, treat all women in the sex trade as victims of trafficking, and take punitive action against traffickers. While my discussion of the Meerut case in Chapter 2 included insights on this NGO's efforts to train the police, here I examine its efforts to train judicial officers.

This chapter critically examines anti-trafficking interventions focused on prosecuting those accused of sex trafficking, and enjoining "victim-witnesses" to testify against them. The broader pattern of rescued women's absences, refusals to testify, or turning "hostile" instead of supporting the prosecution case challenge prevalent assumptions in global anti-trafficking campaigns about Global South sex workers as victims seeking criminal justice. Sunaina Das' case challenges assumptions about criminal justice incontrovertibly benefiting trafficked sex workers.

victims of sex trafficking for prostitution to secure their cooperation to testify. Studies across academic disciplines of sex trafficking trials in the US have found that those categorized as victims of trafficking rarely want to testify against the accused. Many trafficked individuals who need assistance do not testify owing to fear of retaliatory action from the trafficker and/or a lack of trust in law enforcement (Srikantiah 2007: 201). Or someone categorized as a victim may in fact identify as a voluntary sex worker, deny the narrative of victimization imposed upon her by the police and prosecution, and refuse to testify against the alleged trafficker (Hua 2011). These critiques in the US context call into question whether efforts that primarily emphasize the arrest and prosecution of traffickers can secure rights for victims of trafficking (Fukushima 2019: 116).

4 See Chapter 2, footnote 16.

And together, the broader pattern and Sunaina Das' exceptional case challenge assumptions about the Indian police and courts necessarily lacking the resources and commitment to combat sex trafficking. They demonstrate how, in contrast to the blanket assumptions of the US-led anti-trafficking regime, the roles, motivations, and efforts of Indian legal actors and their interactions with NGOs and sex workers are complex and unpredictable.

The chapter shows how these efforts to prosecute accused traffickers and encourage rescued women to testify against them are shaped not only by donor-driven NGOs, but also by a range of factors, circumstances, and contingencies involving the Indian legal system, individual legal actors' motivations, and rescued women's complex experiences, choices, and perceptions of justice. Building upon Chapter 2, it further demonstrates how the possibilities of successful collaboration among NGOs, legal actors, and sex workers are unusual rather than typical, contingent upon several factors, and often fraught with tension and resistance.

Sunaina Das' Case as an Exception

I have structured this chapter around an ethnographic account of the case of a trafficked woman, Sunaina Das,[5] who testified for the prosecution in a New Delhi court, the efforts of the NGO and Indian legal actors who supported her, and the possibilities and limitations of these efforts. I observed this case at a trial court in New Delhi, conducted interviews with those involved in it, and observed an NGO-led training session for judicial officers that helped to shape its outcome. Tracking this case revealed the specific constellation of factors that made it exceptional, while also bringing to light the more typical pattern of rescued women's resistance to testify and the range of factors shaping their decisions.

My decision to place Sunaina Das' case at the center of this chapter and its significance for my analysis bears some further discussion. The case study method is based on close empirical observation of a single subject over time, usually in reference to a wider field of cases (Darian-Smith and McCarty 2017). Conducting research on anti-trafficking interventions, Ahmed and Seshu (2012), for instance, use a single case study to illuminate a range of harmful impacts of anti-trafficking efforts on a sex worker community in Sangli, Maharashtra (2012: 158).[6]

5 Ibid.

6 The authors explore in detail the experience of one sex worker being prosecuted, and another forcibly rescued (in the same case) to demonstrate the harmful impacts of anti-trafficking interventions on a sex worker community. They explain that this case typifies the detrimental effects of raids and rescue operations on HIV programs and services and sex worker rights (Ahmed and Seshu 2012: 158).

However, a detailed case study can illustrate not just the typical, but also the exceptional.[7] Sunaina Das' case brought forth what is key, typical, and exceptional in anti-trafficking prosecutions. My interviews revealed the constellation of factors that made it exceptional, while also bringing to light the more typical pattern of sex workers' resistance to testify and the range of factors shaping their decisions. Sunaina's case also demonstrates the challenges faced by those who *do* testify, and provides insights into the impact of such participation on their lives.

My discussion of the reported pattern of sex workers not supporting the prosecution also draws upon interviews with other women I met at the New Delhi court while observing Sunaina Das' case, and research at other field sites discussed in Chapters 2 and 4–6. I draw, in particular, upon participant observation and interviews at the Mumbai Special Court with which I began this book. There, I interviewed judges, prosecutors, law enforcement officers, and NGO representatives about whether rescued women usually testified in these cases, and what their reasons for testifying, not showing up in court, or not supporting the prosecution case might be. I bring some of my findings to this chapter, but discuss them in detail along with further aspects of evidence and testimony in Immoral Traffic (Prevention) Act (ITPA) cases at this court in Chapter 4.

Some methodological challenges while conducting interviews with anti-trafficking NGOs are worth noting here. Sometimes, NGOs just didn't have the information that I sought on how often women they had rescued testified against the accused in court. The turnaround of NGO staff (often young college graduates who moved on to newer employment or educational opportunities) tended to be faster than the turnaround of cases, which sometimes made it challenging for NGOs to track the progress of cases. Though some NGOs were more forthcoming than others, it was nonetheless difficult to glean information from organizations that guard their image due to their reliance on donor funding (Molland 2013: 314). I often sensed that NGOs withheld information or presented it in ways that would not potentially threaten their reputation or credibility.

Even those funding anti-trafficking NGOs seemed to find it challenging to get this information. For instance, the Japanese funding agency I frequently encountered in Mumbai was concerned about the lack of data on how often victims of sex trafficking testified in support of the prosecution,[8] and on what factors influenced the prosecution of trafficking crimes. Eventually, they partnered with a Mumbai anti-trafficking NGO, Save the Children India (STCI), to conduct interviews to understand the "legal and social factors influencing the success or failure of prosecution of trafficking crimes" in Mumbai, and in the state of Maharashtra

7 Darian-Smith and McCarty note that case studies can be selected according to their being typical (of characteristics common to several cases), key (featuring a specific aspect or characteristic for the analysis), or exceptional (illustrating the extremes of variation in a field of cases) (2017).

8 The Japanese agency is discussed in the Introduction and Chapter 4.

(of which Mumbai is the capital) (Save the Children India 2014). STCI arranged interview access to women participating in postrescue programs through different NGOs in Maharashtra, to police and prosecutors working on their cases, to the judges adjudicating them, and to judgments in a few disposed cases. Another independent researcher, Saie Shetye, conducted the interviews, and I was hired as a consultant to analyze the judgments and interviews that were collected. Though I mainly draw upon my own ethnographic research in New Delhi in this chapter, I include some findings from this STCI study that contrast with Sunaina Das' case. Through them, I illustrate the broader set of possibilities in the Indian sociolegal context within which Sunaina's case fits, what makes Sunaina's case exceptional, and how, even with sustained NGO involvement, the constellation of factors shaping these cases can lead to a range of decisions and outcomes.

"THESE GIRLS NEVER GIVE STATEMENTS"

At the back of a small courtroom at New Delhi's Tis Hazari courts complex, a tall, broad-built, middle-aged police officer consulted a voluminous file folder on her lap as she rapidly posed questions to the petite young woman next to her. The young woman mostly gazed at the floor and nodded, occasionally looking up to provide short, tentative answers. Two years earlier, Police Inspector Ahuja had helped Sunaina Das escape from a brothel in New Delhi's GB Road.[9]

By all available accounts (from the police, the NGO who helped with the rescue and whose work I was following, and Sunaina herself), Sunaina had been trafficked to GB Road from an impoverished district in West Bengal in July 2010 and was forced into prostitution by the accused brothel madam who was now facing trial two years later. After a month of being forced to have sex with multiple clients for no pay, Sunaina (then sixteen years old) managed to persuade a client to facilitate her escape from the brothel. Thus, like Bishakha in Chapter 2, Sunaina had initiated her own eventual rescue. She gave her family's phone number to this client and asked him to let them know she needed help. Upon his doing so, her mother and uncle rushed to New Delhi from West Bengal, looking for her. The client had also informed the police of the situation, and Inspector Ahuja called the NGO to assist in the rescue (per the established protocol in these cases). The police–NGO team raided the brothel and rescued Sunaina. She later helped the police identify the accused madam, who was subsequently arrested. Sunaina was reunited with her family and returned with them to West Bengal.

On this warm September day, Inspector Ahuja was in court to refresh Sunaina's memory about the facts of the case, so that her answers during the forthcoming cross examination would not contradict statements she gave the police and magistrate after her rescue. The day before I met Sunaina and Inspector Ahuja in court, a *pairvi*

9 See Chapter 2.

officer,[10] from the police station, had come to court for the same purpose – to refresh Sunaina's memory of the details of the case. "*Dates yaad rakhna*" ("Remember the dates"), he said, wagging his forefinger at her for emphasis. I caught up with him as he left the courtroom, explaining that I was conducting research on these trials. "Ah, then you must know that in these GB Road cases, there are hardly any convictions?" Nodding, I asked him to explain why. He gave me the following perspective on cases against brothel madams accused of sex trafficking.

> See, these brothel madams are very powerful. Money is not a problem for them. They get bail very easily. Here's how it is. Basically, these girls are poor and the madams take advantage of their poverty. The defense counsel also know the "weak points" of the girls. They know how to break them. This girl's cross-examination is tomorrow (pointing at Sunaina), right? You will see, she won't say anything, she won't be able to. These girls never give statements, that's why there are no convictions.

By "not giving statements," the *pairvi* officer meant that during court trials, women rescued by police–NGO teams refuse to say they were forced into prostitution and don't name the accused. Most police officers I interviewed similarly lamented rescued women's absences, silences, reluctance to testify, or testimony that did not support the police case. "Will this girl give a statement?" was a question the police asked after every rescue I observed. This was also the context for the police inspector's concerns in Chapter 2 about Ayesha, who "looked like a major," not supporting the police case.

The male police inspector who had overseen the GB Road cases I discussed in Chapter 2 expressed his frustration about rescues not leading to convictions.

> To tell you the truth, these rescues are a thankless job … These girls never say anything against the accused. Initially they are sometimes willing to give us statements, which they later contradict by saying, "we came on our own, we want to go back to the brothel."

He explained that those who initially said they were trafficked later changed their narrative to one of consensual sex work. He went on to say that after returning to their villages, rescued sex workers were usually "not traceable," because the brothel keepers, madams, and pimps from GB Road used threats or other forms of pressure to ensure that they didn't show up in court.

Inspector Ahuja (the police officer who had rescued Sunaina from GB Road and was preparing her for the cross-examination) also described the tremendous challenges involved in locating rescued women once they returned to their villages, and in bringing them to New Delhi to testify. When I asked her why they were so unlikely to testify in support of the police case, she echoed her colleagues' views: "*Bik jaati hain. Gareeb hain.*" ("They are bought over [by the accused]. After all,

[10] Police officer who assists the Investigating Officer in ensuring the production of witnesses in court.

they are poor"). Ahuja went on to describe an instance where a rescued woman had initially "given a good statement" to the police, but later refused to recognize the brothel owner in court. In another case she described, the rescued woman had even refused to recognize her (Ahuja) in court. Ahuja recounted the case as follows:

> At the police station she had said, "I will ensure the accused is hanged to death!" Then her attitude changed so much, she turned completely hostile.[11]

Frustrations about rescued sex workers either being "untraceable" or "turning hostile" also plagued those adjudicating these cases. When I interviewed the magistrate presiding over Sunaina's madam's trial in New Delhi, protocol demanded that we not discuss this specific case. My questions to her were framed around the role of "victim-witness" testimony in GB Road cases more generally. The main problem she highlighted was that the rescued women were from villages in distant provinces. Once they returned there, they usually couldn't be traced. If they could, they rarely came to court to testify. Like the police, the magistrate also gleaned that the women were made to disappear by the friends or kin of the accused.

After some hesitation, she went on to provide her own perspective (in English) on how those who did testify became hostile witnesses for the prosecution:

> In these cases I have noticed victims *lie* also. Sometimes I can tell they are lying. These girls are scared and poor. Just recently one girl had come. Clearly she has been paid off. She just stood here, folded her hands and said to me, "Madam, I am very poor." That said it all to me. We can tell them, "say the truth," but what after that? They get a better offer from the accused. The main thing is, someone needs to *counsel* them.

The magistrate's faith in the power of "counseling" resonated with what police and NGO workers believed was the way to prevent victim-witnesses turning hostile and ensure their support of the prosecution case. In Chapter 2, I discussed in the context of the Meerut case how the practice of "counseling" from the perspective of anti-trafficking NGOs and the police seeks to extract information and attempts to persuade and convince rescued women to admit to being trafficked even when they insisted they were not. However, as evident from Chapter 2, and as I will show further, this faith in "counseling" is based on presumptions that do not acknowledge the range of reasons why rescued sex workers make hostile prosecution witnesses.

Why "These Girls Never Give Statements"

From observing rescues and trials, and interviews with NGO workers, legal actors, and rescued sex workers in New Delhi and Mumbai across my field sites, I

[11] The moralizing tone and content of the police inspector's description here is hard to translate from the original Hindi: "*Uske tevar aise badle, woh is tarah mukar gayee. Jab* police station *mein thi, tab boli thi 'main us mujrim ko phaansi chadvaoongi.'*"

discerned several possible reasons why many deemed as "victim-witnesses" do not support the prosecution case against alleged traffickers. The first possibility is that they entered sex work voluntarily, and therefore did not want to be rescued. As discussed in Chapter 2, I did not directly observe forced and indiscriminate raid-and-rescue operations where NGOs and police teams removed voluntary sex workers, there are credible reports of such situations in GB Road, and the women I met in Meerut after their rescues provided such accounts. This possibility also emerged in my conversations with other rescued women I met at the New Delhi court and with sex workers at a Mumbai shelter (Chapter 6). The police I interviewed at the Mumbai Special Court (Chapter 4) also expressed the view that the adult women they rescued were unwilling to testify as they had not wanted to leave the sex trade in the first place, and wished to return to it.

A second possibility is that they did not enter sex work voluntarily, but eventually came to terms with it and/or were earning a sustainable livelihood from it. Simanti Dasgupta provides a rich description and analysis of this possibility, drawing upon her fieldwork in Kolkata's Sonagachi red-light district (2019: 137–138). Some of the detained sex workers I met at the Mumbai shelter (Chapter 6) pointed out that even though they were forced or deceived into the sex trade, they did not want to be rescued and wished to move on with their lives rather than assist in the prosecution of the accused.

A third set of possibilities centers on the women indeed being trafficked, but either not wishing to testify or not being able to do so, for a range of reasons. Many simply did not have the information needed to strengthen the prosecution case. I learned from NGO workers that several women they rescued from GB Road reported being drugged along the way, hampering their ability to remember details. Mamta, in Chapter 2, had also mentioned this to the Child Welfare Committee. The women did not remember the names of the perpetrators, locations, timelines, and so on. The perpetrators were also skilled at never revealing their real names. Women trafficked from the eastern state of West Bengal to New Delhi often named a ubiquitous "Raju" or "Rahul" (common male names) who brought them from their villages to the city. Those from the southern states of Andhra Pradesh and Karnataka similarly named "Laxmi" (a common female name).[12]

The explanation Indian legal actors gave me most frequently was that trafficked women were threatened or "bought over" by the accused to say nothing, to lie, or to refrain from taking names. In some of these instances, the women were related or closely connected to the accused. Police in Mumbai mentioned several examples where the trafficker was a neighbor, relative, friend, boyfriend, or spouse, against whom rescued women were unwilling to testify. The STCI study included a case from Mumbai where an NGO had rescued a girl who was trafficked by her own parents. In her interview for the study, the NGO worker involved in the rescue reported

[12] See Chapter 5.

that the girl was reluctant to reveal their involvement and refused to testify against them. Another example comes from a judgment of the Mumbai Special Court, in which a woman from West Bengal had been trafficked to Kamathipura, a red-light area in central Mumbai, by a friend of her husband's, with the collusion of her husband. They had deceived her into thinking that she would be employed in domestic work. Though she had named both the accused in her statement to the police at the time she was rescued, she did not come to testify against them in court. The prosecution case could not be proved without her testimony.[13]

The police and NGOs acknowledged that whether or not explicitly threatened, several trafficked women wanted to move on with their lives, rather than participate in the criminal justice system. They told me that many survivors consider the costs of testifying greater than the gains, and are not convinced that testifying against the accused, given the associated risks and threats, would be helpful to them. These concerns, and insufficient protection measures for "victim-witnesses," have been noted in studies of trafficking cases across global contexts.[14] Beyond sex trafficking, feminist legal ethnographers find that many of those who experience sexual violence "want very little to do with law enforcement, the legal system, or penal institutions" and "eschew the solutions offered by the courts" (Hlavka and Mulla 2021: 260). In the Indian sociolegal context, the reader will see how Sunaina Das' case exemplifies the considerable risks and challenges and prolonged proceedings that those who do testify navigate and endure. Finally, rescued Bangladeshi women (some who had migrated voluntarily and others who were trafficked) often wanted to stay on in India, as Chapters 5 and 6 will demonstrate. They preferred not to participate in the trials to avoid being sent back to Bangladesh.[15]

Hostile Witnesses, Compromise, and Counseling in the Indian Sociolegal Context

Though the pattern of those categorized as "victim-witnesses" not testifying in support of prosecution is not specific to India, it is shaped in multiple ways by the Indian sociolegal context. In India, the "hostility" of "victim-witnesses" of violent crimes, usually members of marginalized socioeconomic groups, is a widespread occurrence

[13] *The State (D.B. Marg Police Station, Mumbai) vs. Subhash Birju Yadav & Ors.* Case no. 604/PW/2010, Judgment of the Metropolitan Magistrate, Special Court for ITPA, 54th Court, Mazgaon, Mumbai dated August 1, 2013.

[14] Studies from Europe question the adequacy of protections for trafficked persons expected to testify. Given the low conviction rate in trafficking cases, they argue that those who testify are unnecessarily placed at risk of being intimidated, threatened, and attacked by their traffickers (Goodey 2004). Those researching prosecution as an anti-trafficking intervention in Europe call for the extension of victim-witness protection beyond the trial, and beyond the victim to kin or acquaintances who might also be in danger (Pearson 2002).

[15] For insights on the situations of Bangladeshi women in the Indian sex trade, especially how they are "repatriated" to Bangladesh against their will, see Bose (2018), Ganguly (2016), and Ghosh (2015).

beyond sex trafficking. It is frequently reported in trials for sexual assault, murder, caste-based atrocities, and sectarian crimes (Roy 2013).

Indian legal scholar Mrinal Satish explains the procedural background as follows. Per the Indian Criminal Procedure Code (1973), the statement that a person acquainted with the facts and circumstances of a case under investigation gives the police is not admissible in court. The rationale is that the police can coerce witnesses into providing statements.[16] Witnesses are therefore required to restate what they had said to the police during investigation before the court during the trial. At this juncture, some witnesses change their statement or deny having made the statement to the police in the first place. The main reason is a fear of retaliation by the accused in the absence of witness protection. In most such instances, the prosecution is then unable to prove its case as the benefit of the inconsistencies goes to the accused (Satish 2003).

Though the Law Commission of India has acknowledged the problem and recommended measures for witness protection inside and outside courtrooms, such programs are not yet in place (Kashyap 2013). The socioeconomic situations of marginalized groups can make offers of payment from the accused attractive, and fears of retaliation by the accused well-founded. Those working with victim-witnesses in rape cases in India have pointed out that without constant and adequate support from police, judges, and NGOs, survivors from impoverished socioeconomic backgrounds turn hostile, whereas those who have the support are far more likely to support the prosecution case (Agnes, D'Mello, and Sidhva 2014).

Several ethnographers have explained the gender politics and kin and community attachments and obligations that cause sexual assault victims to become hostile witnesses in India (Baxi 2014; Berti 2011; Roychowdhury 2019). In rape trials, Baxi describes informal settlements between the accused and the victim outside the court in which the victim agrees not to testify against the accused. While illegal, these "compromises" are common, shaped by factors such as the lack of witness protection, procedural delays, and the gendered social stigma a rape complainant faces. "Compromise" may help to ensure safety, preserve social ties, and mitigate economic precarity (2014: xlii). Ethnographic research thus shows how the Indian sociolegal context – shaped by kin and community pressures and by the accused "paying off," threatening, and intimidating witnesses – often steers witnesses toward such arrangements and solutions. In my interviews, Inspector Ahuja's analysis of "victim-witnesses" being paid for their absence or silence, and the magistrate's description of poverty as the explanation for it, referenced this "culture of compromise."

As deployed in anti-trafficking interventions, and as the reader has already encountered in the context of rescues in Chapter 2, "counseling" aims not only

16 This has a likely genealogy in the colonial mistrust of the native police (as discussed by Kolsky 2005; Lal 1999; Samaddar 2008; Singha 1993).

to support rescued women, but also to get them to admit that they were trafficked (even when they denied it), name those who allegedly exploited them, and maintain consistency across their statements and testimony. After rescues, I observed the police urge NGO representatives to "counsel" rescued women to "give statements."

Aimed at eliciting, shaping, and producing testimony against the accused, "counseling" was central to the anti-trafficking NGO's work in the criminal justice system. It was seen as an art of persuasion at which female NGO workers, female police officers such as Ahuja, and female prosecutors and judges,[17] were deemed especially adept. "Counseling" came up frequently in my conversations with police, NGOs and prosecutors, who explained that rescued women would never reveal "the truth" (presumed to be that they were trafficked) at first, and would "gradually open up only with counseling." It was presumed that women who said they did sex work willingly were lying, owing to pressure from the accused and mistrust of the police and legal system. "Counseling" was deployed to produce a shift from an initial account that might deny trafficking to one that admitted it – in other words, to produce the possibility of sex trafficking from its denial. However, "counseling" did not always produce this result, given the multiple reasons why sex workers either choose to, or are pressured to, become hostile witnesses.

The assumptions behind "counseling" and what it was intended to accomplish became clearer to me through the requests repeatedly made of me to "counsel" rescued women. Though I introduced myself to the police as a researcher, they assumed I was a member of the NGO, as I usually accompanied the NGO team. With the label of "respectable" woman ascribed to me,[18] I, too, was seen as a potential counselor. Once, when I came to the magistrate's court at Tis Hazari with Neha to meet Bishakha and Ayesha (from Chapter 2) before their statements were recorded, the police officer who came with them urged me to "please counsel them too," gesturing toward three other women the police had brought to the court that day. "Please convince them to give statements." He asked me to urge them to take the names of the accused in their statements to the magistrate, to strengthen the case.

To oblige the police and satisfy my own curiosity, I spoke (without presumption or intention to convince) to the three women (one Nepali and two Indian) seated dejectedly on a bench as they waited for a magistrate to summon them for their statements. They had all been rescued by a different anti-trafficking NGO, but the same police station. The two Indian women said they had entered the sex trade voluntarily (in Hindi, "*Hum apni marze se is line mein aaye*") and wanted to be left alone. Like the sex workers in Meerut (Chapter 2), they angrily asserted that

[17] Otherwise far outnumbered by men in the Indian legal system, but frequently assigned to these cases.

[18] An identity that the police read from my clothes, speech, etc. to assume an "educated" class location. See my discussion on positionality in the Introduction.

they had been rescued forcibly, and did not want to name the accused. The third woman, who was Nepali, did not say whether she was trafficked or entered the sex trade voluntarily, merely that she wanted to return to Nepal. She, too, did not want to name anyone in GB Road. This fleeting interaction in court did not afford the time to build rapport with these women to develop deeper insights into their situations, but it did serve to instantiate how not all women rescued from GB Road wanted to be rescued, or to participate in the arrest or prosecution of the accused.[19]

SUNAINA DAS' STORY

Sunaina Das in Court

As Police Inspector Ahuja, the NGO, and the prosecutor priming Sunaina Das for the task had hoped, and as an exception to the typical pattern of cases, Sunaina testified in full support of the prosecution case against the madam. Contrary to the *pairvi* officer's pessimistic prediction, she did not turn hostile. During the examination-in-chief, conducted prior to my fieldwork, she answered the prosecutor's questions with clarity and detail, narrating how two young men had lured her from her village in West Bengal, drugged her, pulled her on to a train to New Delhi, and sold her to the accused madam at GB Road, who forced her into prostitution. She provided details of how she was trafficked, sexually and financially exploited, and beaten. She even named and identified the accused madam. Here is a short excerpt from her testimony.[20]

SD: In the evening, that lady took me to a *kotha* (brothel) and handed me over to the accused present today in court (correctly identified). I was kept in the *kotha* run by the accused. There were several other girls also. I was forced into prostitution by the accused. She made me do *ganda kaam* (dirty work) with different persons.

COURT QUESTION: What do you mean by *Ganda Kaam*?

SD: Accused used to force me to have sexual intercourse with different persons. Whenever I used to refuse, accused used to beat and abuse me. She also used to keep all the money earned by me.

Sunaina's cross examination was held in camera. The NGO had arranged a lawyer to assist the prosecutor, who remained in the courtroom with Sunaina during the proceedings, while I stepped out with her family and the NGO workers.[21] When the lawyer and Sunaina emerged an hour and a half later, they told us the defense

[19] See also my discussion of *Tara vs. State of Delhi* in Chapter 2.

[20] Excerpted from the court record of Sunaina's testimony.

[21] A 2008 amendment to the Criminal Procedure Code (CrPC) allows for victims of any crime to engage their own lawyers to support and help the prosecution. I observed NGOs drawing upon this amendment, as well as the ITPA's dependence on "social welfare organizations," to authorize their assistance in sex trafficking cases and expand their work into law enforcement and criminal justice; areas in which NGOs and their donors consider local legal actors to be deficient.

lawyer had asked Sunaina why she had agreed to "roam around" with the two men who brought her to New Delhi, and why she had not protested when they took her away. The "roaming around" accusation is a common strategy for defense lawyers in rape trials in India. They characterize a woman's "roaming around" with the accused without raising a "hue and cry" as her failure to immediately report the rape. They then use this argument to imply that she consented to sex (Baxi 2014: 227–228).

The prosecutor had anticipated this line of questioning while preparing Sunaina for her testimony. In response to the defense's questions about "roaming around" without raising a "hue and cry," Sunaina explained that she *had* protested, but no passer-by could hear her. In this way, she drew effectively upon the training she had received from the NGO and prosecutor to establish herself as an "ideal victim," who was credible both because she had been under the total control of traffickers and because she had actively resisted it. My point here is not to say that this was a made-up story. Sunaina was indeed trafficked, and beyond raising a "hue and cry," had actively initiated her own rescue from the brothel. What her response to the "hue and cry" question reveals is that she knew how to provide an account that was legitimate, credible, and established her as an ideal victim with just enough agency to show that she tried to resist, rather than a more complex account that might suggest consent to the situation the prosecution was presenting as a trafficking case (Srikantiah 2007).

During the cross-examination, Sunaina also navigated tremendous anxiety. The cross-examination was done in Hindi, which was not her native language. The court had not arranged for a translator because Sunaina had been able to provide statements to the police and court in Hindi previously (with assistance from the NGO). These aspects of the cross-examination, and the difficulties she and her family faced in having to make repeated trips to New Delhi, could well have turned Sunaina hostile. Instead, a constellation of factors – partly arbitrary and serendipitous, and partly intentional – facilitated her coming to court and testifying for the prosecution against all odds.

Factors Shaping Sunaina Das' Case

In Sunaina's case, Police Inspector Ahuja was a major source of support. The police officer described her work in deeply affective terms. She told me that the first time she went to GB Road, she was repulsed by the foul smell and cramped cubicles, but also felt a deep sense of pity. She described how she started going to the brothels regularly to "counsel" the women there and assure them of her support. Not every police officer could, or would, provide this level of affective engagement. Most male police officers instead depended heavily on NGO workers for "counseling". Ahuja elaborated:

> I thought, I should take this work positively and do something good for the girls. I realized that they were not willing to be rescued because they are taught to fear the police. They are threatened [by the pimps and madams] that if you tell them [the

> police] you did not come by choice, they will put you in jail, beat you, make a case against you. See, madam, males cannot deal with these girls like I can, they cannot do the kind of inquiry I can. The way the girls can tell me things openly, they cannot tell a man. After rescues, for half an hour they just cry at my bosom.

While Ahuja was invested in increasing the conviction rate, others at the same police station had ties with those running the sex trade in GB Road. For instance, Bishakha and Ayesha, whose rescues I had accompanied the NGO team on (Chapter 2), told me that one of the police constables who brought them to court for their statements had arranged a meeting on the way with pimps from the brothel, who threatened and pressured them not to take any names in court. I do not mean to suggest that higher-ranked police always strengthened cases and lower-ranked police always undermined them, but NGOs were frequently concerned about police constables alerting brothel managers about rescues.

Ethnographic research on the police in India shows that their "social lives, practices, and narratives … are configured by the complex sociocultural, political, and legal bureaucratic worlds with which they are deeply entangled" (Jauregui 2016: 31). The *TIP Reports*' critiques of the Indian police do not situate it in this complexity. In my research beyond the context of sex trafficking, lower-ranking police officers cited long work hours and inadequate pay as reasons to not intervene in cases involving the labor exploitation of underage domestic workers in India, pointing out that these conditions structured their own work experience (Ramachandran 2019). However, motivated police officers do innovate and improvise to help those seeking redress, as seen in the context of domestic violence cases (Satyogi 2019). The role of the police in anti-trafficking interventions thus needs to be understood in the broader context of the political economy, labor conditions, and institutional culture of police work in India.[22]

Ahuja's being a woman and an especially committed and competent police officer was no guarantee that every trafficked woman she rescued would testify. Ahuja herself cited several instances when they did not. Sunaina's own strength and motivation were clearly the most significant factors shaping her support of the case against the madam. Her initiative began with her escape from the brothel and continued thereafter. Had she, like Bishakha (Chapter 2), not sought her client's help, the police and NGO would not have been able to help her. During the trial, she came to court against tremendous odds. The day of the cross-examination was the third time she and her family had to come to New Delhi from West Bengal as witnesses in the trial. The NGO and the prosecutor found it rare for a survivor and her family to be this "co-operative." The magistrate admonished the accused madam and defense lawyer for their delaying tactics, such as asking for more time and making excuses not to show up. Owing to these delays, Sunaina's mother and

[22] For further context on the New Delhi police, in particular on how colonial legacies have shaped the institution and its role, and how the police's views on sexuality are shaped by religious and racialized prejudices, see Puri (2016), especially chapter 4.

uncle had to shut down the small food stall they ran in their village – their main source of income – for multiple days each time they came to New Delhi. Indeed, their situation resonates with the immense costs that participating in the routine operations of a trial imposes on communities already grappling with precarity. Scholars working in contexts outside India have also drawn attention to these hidden costs of coming to court. In the context of sexual assault adjudication in the US, Hlavka and Mulla point out that the court recognizes certain forms of harm as legible, while not accounting for the "harms it visits upon participants and their families during the process of adjudication" (2021: 39–40).

For Sunaina's family, the most daunting part of coming to testify was the constant threats they received from the accused, both in West Bengal and on the train back from New Delhi, on the phone and face to face. Her family – her mother in particular – played a key role in ensuring that Sunaina testified. Undaunted by the repeated threats from the accused, the determined Shanti often reiterated her desire to fight for her daughter, however long it took. With translation assistance from an NGO worker, Shanti told me how she and her older daughter had both faced domestic violence. She wanted justice for both her daughters, so they wouldn't face the same fate she did. The family sat together and watched *India Fights Back* for motivation, a TV show based on real-life instances of victims getting justice with the help of police and NGOs.[23]

Finally, the NGO's intervention was crucial to the progress of Sunaina's case and to her presence and testimony. It offered several forms of support to boost her confidence. Before and during the trial, NGO staff helped Inspector Ahuja familiarize Sunaina with court procedures and jog her memory about the details she would be asked to testify about: the sequence of events, names, and so on. After rescues, the NGO workers often accompanied rescued sex workers back to their villages, kept in touch with them, and encouraged them to testify. They monitored cases from rescue to trial, keeping in touch with the police and prosecution on their progress. During the trial, they provided the material and logistical support for Sunaina and her family to come to court – paying for their train tickets, picking them up from the train station, arranging accommodation, and so on. In the absence of witness protection from the legal system, NGO workers accompanied them to court to alleviate their fears of the accused.

ANTI-TRAFFICKING NGOS AND JUDICIAL TRAINING

Beyond supporting Sunaina, the NGO significantly impacted the outcome of the case through a training session for judicial officers it organized in partnership with government agencies in New Delhi. At this session, NGOs and legal experts explained the

[23] The popular show covers not only sex trafficking cases, but also several crimes against women. In Chapter 6, I describe how I used it and other media content to conduct research at the Mumbai shelter.

issue of sex trafficking to an audience of judicial officers in New Delhi adjudicating cases against accused traffickers, brothel madams, managers, and pimps under the ITPA and Indian criminal law. A representative from the NGO was one of the key speakers at the event. Significantly, the judicial magistrate presiding over the case in which Sunaina testified for the prosecution (whose perspective on hostile witnesses I discussed earlier in this chapter) was among the attendees. I interviewed her about a week after the judicial training session took place. Observing the training session provided key insights into the NGO's impact on the magistrate's approach toward these cases, and on Sunaina's case in particular.

At the training session, representatives from anti-trafficking NGOs conflated prostitution with sex trafficking, encouraging the attending judicial officers to perceive women in the sex trade as victims and not criminals. Ms. Kumar, a lawyer representing another prominent anti-trafficking NGO, framed prostitution as always exploitative and sex workers as victims, regardless of their claims of consent. This echoed the way the New Delhi NGO had trained the Meerut police in the drafting of the First Information Report (FIR) (Chapter 2).

In his presentation at the training session, Mr. Rai from the NGO in Sunaina's case (and the rescues in Chapter 2) provided both legal expertise (educating the judicial officers about new developments in Indian law) and human rights advocacy (providing them what he presented as the victims' perspective). He devoted much of his presentation to a (then) recent amendment to the Indian Criminal Procedure Code (CrPC), which gave courts the power to order monetary compensation for victims, emphasizing that this was the most appealing incentive for victims to come and testify. "If judges order this, it will strengthen the victim, it will be *her* fight." While addressing the judges, Mr. Rai, Ms. Kumar, and other NGO representatives also provided details of provisions and precedents in Indian law that could be used to prosecute traffickers.

Urging the judicial officers to bring justice to the victims, NGOs balanced this legal expertise with emotional appeals through survivor accounts, documentary films, and news clips about sex trafficking cases. This approach in judicial training sessions resonates more broadly with the way Indian NGOs interweave technical proceduralism with moral concerns and idioms, taking "technomoral" forms in their encounters with the state (Bornstein and Sharma 2016). Mr. Rai's presentation, focused on legal provisions and procedures, was followed by a guest speaker, through whom the NGO brought a more affective frame of victimhood to the audience. Kiran was a survivor of trafficking whom the NGO had rescued from a GB Road brothel. She now worked with the NGO to rescue and "counsel" other survivors. Mr. Rai explained with pride how Kiran had identified her own trafficker while participating in another rescue. He told the judicial officers that the NGO had rescued Kiran's children from the custody of the trafficker and assisted in the prosecution of the accused, resulting in a conviction.

Kiran narrated a powerful account of how she was trafficked to a New Delhi brothel and managed to escape, highlighting the plight of others like her being forced into the sex trade by traffickers taking advantage of their poverty and promising them money, jobs, and marriage. She explained how difficult it was for trafficked women to escape, and how they faced threats and violence from brothel madams who forced them into prostitution and threatened to harm their children. Kiran urged the participating judges to pay heed to these stories and help victims. She ended with a deeply emotional appeal.

> There is not just one Kiran there. There are many girls being kept there against their will. Many girls want to get out of there. But who will listen to us? But who will listen to us?

Kiran's account had a profound impact on the judges. A Delhi High Court judge (ranking higher than the participating judges) overseeing the training session, spoke right after Kiran. Shaking his head as he stood up, he nodded at the many aghast faces and clicking tongues around him, "I don't know what to say after this. I think her wake-up call has shaken all of us." Many of the participating judges seemed visibly and audibly shocked, engaging in hushed conversations about their visceral reactions to Kiran's account and appeals.

However, it was also evident that judicial officers did not see all sex workers as victims, especially in cases where the women were earning well. During an interactive session after the training, there was a heated discussion on the question of "call girl" or escort services operating out of farmhouses in southwestern New Delhi. Some judicial officers pointed out that many of these call girls were "foreigners" (often women from former Soviet countries) who had been arrested by the police under the ITPA's solicitation clause. In response, Ms. Kumar and a Delhi High Court judge (who had worked closely with NGOs in her previous role as counsel for the Delhi government) urged the attending judges to change their mindset and treat "call girls" as victims.

"But some of these so-called victims are earning in lakhs!" commented one male judicial officer.[24] "She can still be a victim," was the response. "But what if she is a high-profile call girl and makes a statement [about being complicit in the racket]? Shouldn't we prosecute her?" he persisted, supported by a couple of his colleagues. "You should not be prosecuting her at all! Treat her like a victim!" admonished the High Court judge. The "call girls" discussion illustrates how NGOs and legal experts associated with them pushed against judicial interpretations of the ITPA that reflect its moral ambivalence toward women in the sex trade.

Also in response, Ms. Kumar urged the judges to "look beneath the surface." Drawing from her experience working with trafficked women, she said they had become so accustomed to deception by others that they might deceive the court by saying they had chosen sex work. In making this claim, she not only discounted alternative possibilities to the anti-trafficking narrative, but also framed NGOs as experts with the knowledge and experience to seek out an underlying victimhood that many sex workers might deny. Ultimately, echoing the assumptions discussed

[24] One lakh Indian rupees are roughly equivalent to $1,195.

earlier in this chapter, she emphasized that "counseling" was needed to bring out the *real* truth (of trafficking) that victims were presumed to be hiding.

Overall, the presentations at the judicial training session highlighted not just the plight of rescued women, but also, very pointedly, the role and legitimacy of NGOs. Mr. Rai framed Kiran's narrative by emphasizing the role of the NGO in facilitating rescues and convictions. He mentioned a 2008 amendment to the CrPC, that allows for victims of any crime to engage their own lawyers to support and help the prosecution. Drawing upon this amendment, as well as the space carved out in the ITPA law for support from "social welfare organizations," he used different provisions of Indian law to underline the legitimacy of the NGO's assistance in sex trafficking cases.

At the training session, anti-trafficking NGOs offered various forms of assistance to the judges, explaining, in particular, their ability to "trace" rescued women. As explained in Chapter 2 in the context of rescues, the NGO helped the police to trace or locate rescued women and their families through its contacts in states such as West Bengal, where the past two decades have seen an increase in trafficking from certain impoverished districts. It emerged through my interviews that this was a task at which both the NGO and judges deemed the police's efforts inadequate. As discussed in the Preface and Chapter 2, the police's lack of success in tracing rescued women who had returned to their home states was compounded by the fact that each state in India has its own police force. Coordination between them was mired in bureaucratic delays and linguistic differences. Beyond offering support to trafficked sex workers, it was by taking on these aspects of police work that the NGO worked to strengthen the prosecution case against accused traffickers.[25]

In his presentation, Mr. Rai had explained how the NGO was working to facilitate "victim-witness" testimony in sex trafficking trials, and asked the judges to understand the difficulties victims faced, such as having to travel from their home villages multiple times to testify and dealing with threats from the accused. During a break in the training session after Mr. Rai's presentation, the magistrate presiding over Sunaina's madam's trial came up to him to ask for more details about how his NGO was assisting "victim-witnesses." Mr. Rai told me later that the magistrate had seemed surprised to learn that the women had to make multiple trips to testify; it was not something she had given thought to earlier.

During the training session, magistrates dealing with ITPA cases were asked to discuss problems they were facing in these cases, so that they could receive input from the High Court judge supervising the session. The magistrate in Sunaina's case had four such cases before her. She brought up the issue of victims not being traceable, even after she directed the police to locate them. In response, the High Court judge (who, as I mentioned, had previously worked closely with NGOs as a counsel for the Delhi government) suggested that the magistrate ask an NGO for assistance.

[25] NGOs taking on more aspects of police work appears to be an emerging pattern in neoliberal India more generally. In domestic violence cases, for instance, the police expect victims to "drive their cases forward" with their own resources, including NGO assistance (Roychowdhury 2015).

The Outcome in Sunaina Das' Case

Though I cannot infer what the outcome would have been had the magistrate not attended the NGO-led training session, the following developments indicate that the training session had an impact on the outcome of the case. The magistrate wrapped up Sunaina's madam's case just weeks after the training session, though the case had dragged on for two years before that. Her admonition to the madam for her delaying tactics (which adversely affected Sunaina and her family), was also after the training session.

When I interviewed the magistrate (also after the training session), she had clearly begun to consider leaning on NGOs more. Though I had explained that I was not an NGO representative, she associated me with the NGO as she had seen me accompany its staff to court. The first thing she asked me, with reference to Sunaina's safety, was whether "the girl" (Sunaina) was with us (the NGO). She also asked if the NGO could help trace women in other pending cases and help the court find translators for the witnesses (including "victim-witnesses") in those cases. Having seen the NGO accompany "victim-witnesses" in multiple cases and having attended the training session, the magistrate was beginning to respond and seek the NGO's assistance. She shared the NGO's frustration at the police's inability to trace the rescued women, and expressed a willingness to have NGOs perform this investigative role instead. I conveyed her message to the NGO's senior leadership. They were excited about these prospects and said they would set up a meeting with the magistrate the next time they came to court.

A year after Sunaina's cross-examination, and three years after she was trafficked, the magistrate convicted the madam under provisions of the ITPA that penalize procuring and detaining a person for prostitution and confining an abducted person. The speedy disposal of the case (in comparison to the slower movement of cases in the Indian legal system more generally) was due to the fact that this was a fast-track court. The magistrate noted that Sunaina's testimony "inspired confidence," a "truthful disclosure of facts by a victim of human trafficking which she narrated before the court upon an opportunity given to her to state so." The magistrate not only convicted the accused madam, but also ordered that she pay a fine to Sunaina as victim compensation. Following the criminal law amendment about monetary compensation that Mr. Rai had emphasized in his presentation at the judicial training session, the Delhi government had also devised a new victim compensation scheme. The magistrate ordered the local Legal Services Authority to award Sunaina further compensation under this scheme.[26]

The magistrate's approach and decision, shaped by the NGO-led training session and her exposure to the NGO's work, was somewhat exceptional. A comparative case from Osmanabad, Maharashtra, in the STCI study, reiterates the significance

[26] *State vs. Padma*. Case no. 16 of 2012. Judgment of the Additional Sessions Judge, Special FTC-2 (Central), Tis Hazari Courts, New Delhi, dated September 25, 2013.

of the role of the magistrate and the NGO-led training session in Sunaina's case.[27] In the Osmanabad case, a magistrate disregarded the testimony of the "victim-witnesses," who had been supported by an NGO and had provided strong testimony against the accused. That magistrate had not participated in anti-trafficking training, and the case resulted in an acquittal despite strong "victim-witness" testimony.

Although, like Sunaina's case, the Osmanabad case had been an exceptional example of both "victim-witness" testimony and family support, it resulted in an acquittal owing to the magistrate's presumptions and prejudices. That judgment showed that the magistrate had been convinced by the defense's arguments about the woman's character that used the "roaming around" accusation. An interview with the trafficked woman's mother in the STCI study brought forth the family's sense of the system failing them, despite their valiant efforts to resist the pressure to "compromise."

> I feel that everyone involved in the case may have been bribed. I feel this way as even I was offered a bribe. Sometimes I wish that I should have taken the money and withdrawn the case. Here we lost the case as well as made enemies.

The Osmanabad case demonstrates how "victim-witness" testimony is only one ingredient of an anti-trafficking conviction. The STCI study included three cases of trafficked women giving detailed accounts of their exploitation, but the system failing them – in one case owing to a lack of support from the police, and in two cases (including the Osmanabad case) owing to judicial prejudices around prostitution. What Sunaina's case demonstrates, in contrast, is a delicate and contingent coalescence of multiple factors – not just the NGO's efforts, but Sunaina's own motivation, and the cooperation of the Indian legal actors involved.

Sunaina's case also brings up the significant question of whether convictions truly deliver justice. The judgment was a complete contrast to the Osmanabad case in terms of judicial recognition of trafficking versus judicial decisions based on moralistic assumptions about prostitution. However, the conviction did not significantly change Sunaina's life. The victim compensation remained mired in bureaucratic delays. Sunaina and her family had to travel to New Delhi yet again to claim the money from the court, which did not give it to her pending paperwork that Police Inspector Ahuja needed to submit, but was delayed owing to her transfer to a different police station. It is worth noting here that the delay was because of a change in the police officer's responsibilities, not the incompetence or disinterest frequently mentioned in the US *TIP Report*. Finally, Sunaina received Rupees 50,000 (about $600) about two years after the madam's conviction.

This outcome was ecstatically received by the NGO representatives who gave me the news. Sunaina, however, had disappeared. During the trial, she had returned to school back home in West Bengal, but then stopped going because rumors had

[27] *State of Maharashtra vs. Anjali Shahaji Sul and others*. Case no. 123 of 2010. Judgment of the Adhoc Additional Sessions Judge-1, Osmanabad District dated October 8, 2012.

spread in her community about her being a "bad girl." She had escaped GB Road, but not the stigma around prostitution. Returning home, a postrescue solution that the law prescribes and that she herself had wanted did not, therefore, put an end to the challenges she faced. The NGO was trying to help her find a job, but because of her limited education and remote location this was proving difficult. Sunaina wanted to study – she mentioned wanting to become a lawyer after her experience of the trial – and to earn an income, but the moral judgments of her community, and her continued lack of access to education and employment, prevented her from building the life she wanted. Then, she apparently left home to marry a neighbor her family did not approve of. Later, her mother came around to the marriage and was scrambling, with meager means and heavy debt, to arrange the money to organize a grand wedding.

CONCLUSION

The ethnographic accounts of NGOs, courts, and "victim-witness" testimony in this chapter challenge prevalent assumptions about the victimhood of all sex workers, about Global South legal systems necessarily lacking resources and commitment, and about anti-trafficking solutions rooted in criminal justice incontrovertibly benefiting trafficked women. Instead, I have examined criminal justice-based anti-trafficking interventions from the perspectives of those implementing and experiencing them. Their perspectives have brought to light the multiple factors, complexities, and contingencies shaping these interventions in the Indian sociolegal context that US policy formulations and donor priorities do not recognize when emphasizing a prosecutorial approach.

Multiple actors, institutions, and procedures structure the possibilities and limitations of anti-trafficking interventions. The pattern of most rescued women turning hostile indicates that it is rare for NGOs' and Indian legal actors' efforts and rescued sex workers' choices to support these efforts, to coalesce. There is no magic formula, but a range of situations and motivations, both intentional and serendipitous, that occasionally, as in Sunaina's case, bring these factors together "just right." Sunaina's case illustrates the constellation of factors – partly constructed through NGO efforts and partly based on individual motivations or resources – through which some rescued women who were trafficked testify in support of the prosecution.

Anti-trafficking policy formulations and donor priorities emphasize a prosecutorial approach with little recognition or discussion of these factors, complexities, and contingencies shaping criminal justice. They do not acknowledge the limited possibilities of criminal justice in helping those who were trafficked to rebuild their lives, or sex workers' decisions about whether or not to participate. Interestingly, the 2019 *TIP Report* acknowledges that victims of trafficking are "often reluctant to testify against traffickers due to inadequate witness protection and the lengthy judicial process" and "face systemic barriers in pursuing justice, including victim blaming by law enforcement, challenges to successfully filing FIRs, and poor access to services" (238). This acknowledgment does not, however, reflect any recognition of the complexities of sex work, or a sufficiently thorough understanding of the Indian legal system, or consideration of the possibility that those who were indeed trafficked might seek different outcomes.

In India, the prevalence of "victim-witnesses" turning hostile is shaped by the exigencies of the sociolegal context. However, the claims of incompetence, lack of commitment, or lack of resources made in the *TIP Reports* and in donor, policy, and NGO circles, while substantiated in some instances, are a reductive and overgeneralized analysis of this context. Sunaina's case highlights an exceptional situation in which a trafficked woman received support from not just an NGO, but also from the police, prosecutor, and judicial officer, who shaped the outcome of the case in significant ways. Though my interviews indicated instances of lack of support from Indian legal actors in other cases, the systemic issues that emerged are not merely a matter of motivation, competence, or even resources. Though the Indian criminal justice system is indeed plagued by the absence of adequate witness protection and an often lengthy judicial process, the procedural issues shaping it are much more complex. They include, as I have shown, the multiagency coordination required (between police across states, in granting monetary compensation, transfers of police and prosecutors, etc.), the political economy of testifying (the sheer cost of traveling to court and the financial situations that make "hush money" from the accused an attractive proposition), and the "culture of compromise" shaping marginalized groups' engagements with the criminal justice system.

Apart from these aspects of the sociolegal context, sex workers' subjectivities, choices, and perceptions of justice vary. This chapter has brought together insights from Sunaina Das' exceptional case of "victim-witness" testimony and the broader pattern of rescued women refusing to testify against the accused. This comparative approach has shown how the individual situations, experiences, and motivations of sex workers, their families, and Indian legal actors shape decisions about testifying. Some, such as Sunaina, narrate trafficking and choose to testify despite the pressure from the accused, procedural and personal challenges. Others become untraceable, refuse to testify, or turn hostile, navigating these pressures and challenges differently to protect themselves and their families. They reject criminal justice as an anti-trafficking solution, due to varied combinations of choice and coercion.

Sunaina's case counters the assumptions in the US *TIP Reports* and framing US-led anti-trafficking campaigns about passive, infantilized Third World sex workers as victims (Kapur 2005) and about an indifferent or incompetent Global South legal system. Instead, it illustrates the limitations of a prosecutorial response to sex trafficking that prioritizes "victim-witness" testimony and the conviction of traffickers. Buoyed by the support of the NGO, police, and prosecutor, and the strength of her own motivation, Sunaina's testimony helped the prosecution secure a conviction. However, Sunaina's case also demonstrates how the convictions and financial compensation that criminal justice can deliver do little to improve the lives of trafficked women. Though it reflected the NGO's success at both "victim-witness" support and judicial training, the madam's conviction and the financial compensation did not significantly improve Sunaina's socioeconomic status or rid her of the social stigma she continued to face. From the perspective of the US-driven, NGO-mediated, and criminal justice-focused anti-trafficking campaign, Sunaina's was a "success story." However, this perspective takes the conviction of the accused, the supportive roles played by the NGO and legal actors, and Sunaina's decision to testify as the only parameters for success. While these efforts are certainly commendable, the fact that testifying in court could not significantly alter Sunaina's situation deserves scrutiny. These on-the-ground realities need to be recognized and carefully examined to evaluate whether and to what extent prosecution as an anti-trafficking strategy is helpful to those who seek to rebuild their lives after being trafficked.

Finally, focusing only on the factors that set Sunaina's case apart from those who do not testify provides an incomplete picture. The similar circumstances that *all* trafficked women face at the prospect of testifying need to be acknowledged. Among those who were indeed trafficked (i.e. not voluntary sex workers), the cooperative "victim-witness," the hostile witness, and the untraceable non-witness all face similar challenges posed by the criminal justice system, the accused, and their own circumstances. These challenges remain unaddressed in anti-trafficking strategies focused on prosecution. While NGOs do offer other forms of support, the prosecutorial focus of anti-trafficking interventions takes funding, efforts, and priorities away from more substantial forms of educational, employment, and socioeconomic assistance which could help survivors of trafficking build more secure futures.[28]

[28] This resonates with insights from other global contexts. Critiques of anti-trafficking interventions in the European context, for instance, have called for survivors of trafficking to be served not merely through criminal justice, but also through social assistance and employment opportunities (Berman 2010). Researchers examining the US and European situation have questioned the practice of temporary visas, social services, health benefits, or employment options being conditional on a trafficked person's willingness to be a prosecution witness (Haynes 2004; Pearson 2002; Sadruddin et al. 2005). Overall, these studies critique how victim assistance is tied to cooperation in the case against traffickers, and raise the question of whether anti-trafficking efforts centered on prosecuting traffickers benefit or harm trafficked victims. Beyond the trafficking context, Hlavka and Mulla draw upon their ethnography of sexual assault adjudication in Milwaukee to argue against the assumption that the justice delivered by courts provides accountability, helps with processing trauma, or facilitates ways to heal (2021: 260). Instead, they support noncarceral forms of accountability that center healing, repair, community, and transformative justice (261–263).

4

Proving Prostitution

Evidence and Respectability in a Mumbai Court

Chapters 2 and 3 explored two aspects of the prosecutorial focus of NGO-led anti-trafficking interventions: encouraging rescued women to testify against the accused, and training police and judges to treat all prostitution as sex trafficking. Situated in the ITPA Special Court in Mumbai with which I opened this book, this chapter examines different aspects of prosecution-focused interventions in Indian courts. While the New Delhi court where I observed Sunaina's case also adjudicated several other types of cases, the Mumbai court is the only Special Court in India that exclusively prosecutes cases under the Immoral Traffic (Prevention) Act (ITPA). This chapter explores the complex interplay of NGOs, police, evidence, and testimony at this Special Court, driven by factors and influences including and beyond US anti-trafficking priorities.

On the one hand, what I learned at the Mumbai Special Court resonated closely with what I learned at the New Delhi court in Chapter 3. Here, too, NGOs foregrounded the role of "victim-witness" testimony and highlighted the support they provided to rescued women to ensure and strengthen their testimony against the accused. And here, too, prosecutors and magistrates voiced concerns about the absence, silence, and "hostility" of rescued women as "victim-witnesses," in contrast to the NGO narrative.

On the other hand, I also found that NGOs' participation at the Special Court was neither entirely dependent on "victim-witness" testimony, nor solely on proving sex trafficking as prioritized by foreign donors. This chapter demonstrates, instead, how NGO participation is shaped by Indian law's assumptions about prostitution and gendered respectability, Indian legal procedures around evidence and testimony, and the Mumbai police's strategic application of these assumptions and procedures. It shows how NGOs, in turn, shape and reinforce these assumptions, procedures, and strategies – by serving as prosecution witnesses themselves.

Before I began my research at the Mumbai Special Court, my expectations of what I might find were shaped by its frequent mentions in the US *Trafficking in Persons* (*TIP*) *Reports* and the role of anti-trafficking NGOs in the court's inception and daily proceedings. Descriptions of the Special Court by NGOs I met during preliminary research had given me the following three impressions: that the court primarily handled sex trafficking prosecutions, that several victims of sex trafficking deposed in these cases after being "counseled" by NGOs, and that this "victim-witness" testimony led to the convictions of traffickers. While I did not assume that my research would confirm this neat picture, I did expect that it would primarily center on the politics of anti-trafficking interventions, and was surprised when this was not the case. The insights I gleaned from observing the Special Court and analyzing its judgments over eight months were quite far removed from the first two impressions outlined here. The third impression – on the relationship between convictions and NGO-facilitated "victim-witness" testimony – turned out to reflect, at best, only one aspect of how trials play out at the Special Court.

This chapter explores the following puzzle. The US *TIP Reports* cite the Mumbai Special Court for its high conviction rate. Yet, my interviews, observations, and analysis of judgments at the Mumbai Special Court revealed a similar pattern to New Delhi–rescued women rarely testified against the accused. If rescued women are not testifying, how are these cases resulting in convictions? This chapter examines how not just "victim-witness" testimony, but also the testimony of other prosecution witnesses (police officers, NGO workers, and decoy customers), material evidence (cash, packets of condoms and tissues), and medical reports shape ITPA cases and their outcomes at the Mumbai Special Court.

The chapter reveals how, in the absence of, or sometimes in addition to, the testimony of "victim-witnesses," NGOs work to strengthen the prosecution case against alleged traffickers through a much less publicized strategy: NGO staff themselves serving as prosecution witnesses. It explores the requirement of respectability, especially that of non-state witnesses, built into the letter and procedure of postcolonial Indian law, how it facilitates NGO interventions, and how its implementation is, in turn, shaped by NGOs. While NGO intervention at the Special Court is greatly driven by US anti-trafficking priorities, the chapter shows how it proceeds primarily through forms of evidence and testimony thus structured by Indian law.

Studying the Special Court brought forth how the ITPA is primarily an anti-*prostitution* legislation, with elements of trafficking (such as luring or detaining someone in prostitution) joining several other provisions which have more to do with curbing prostitution than sex trafficking. In Mumbai, the police are heavily involved in implementing these anti-prostitution provisions of the ITPA, for reasons I will discuss. The chapter demonstrates how this anti-prostitution focus of the ITPA law, paired with the requirements of India's procedural law, connects raids and rescues to trials, and shapes what I call the choreography of trials at the Special Court.

THE SPECIAL COURT

The ITPA Special Court is a small courtroom at one end of the fourth floor of the run-down Mazgaon Courts complex in southern Mumbai.[1] The corridor outside the courtroom is usually abuzz with conversations between those accused in these cases (usually pimps, madams, brothel keepers) and relatives, friends or acquaintances accompanying them, their lawyers, or the court staff. Police personnel often walk or wait in the corridors, arriving to serve as prosecution witnesses, accompanying the accused from jail, or (less often) accompanying rescued women to testify in the trials or to the magistrate's chambers for inquiries (see Chapter 5). NGO-appointed lawyers attend the Special Court nearly every day. They assist the prosecution by accompanying rescued women and preparing them to testify on the few occasions when the women came to the court. More frequently, they make written applications on the women's behalf and provide extensive citations of precedents for the prosecutor to use in his arguments.

The courtroom has two entrances (see Figure 4.1), one in the back, where there are benches for the accused to sit, behind a wooden railing, and one at the front, from which anyone entering is expected to bow in obeisance to the magistrate who sits at the dais. To the magistrate's right sits a court staff member who announces the cases by number as they come up for hearing, and the names of the accused, seated at the back of the courtroom. To the magistrate's left sits the court stenographer, or sometimes the court clerk, to whom the magistrate dictates the court proceedings in English after translating from the Marathi or Hindi used by lawyers and witnesses. To the stenographer's left is the witness box. Opposite the dais is the lawyers' table, where the prosecutor, NGO lawyers, defense lawyers, and their interns and juniors sit. At the lawyers' table is the cause list (a list of cases to be heard that day), a copy of which is also posted outside the courtroom. Behind the lawyers' table, in the middle of the courtroom, are two small rows of plastic chairs, where the witnesses who come to testify sit, and where I sat. The witnesses for the prosecution are usually the police and NGO representatives involved in the raids, decoy or bogus customers

[1] The Mazgaon courts complex is a fairly new building (built in the late 1990s). It had to be evacuated in July 2013 (toward the end of my fieldwork) and its courts (with their staff, offices, and records) and lawyers transferred to the Sessions Court building at Sewri in central Mumbai. Lawyers and the court's magistrate had often told me that the building was in danger of caving in at any time, with multiple incidents of slabs collapsing on other floors. Requests from the courts' lawyers to the Bombay High Court calling for a structural evaluation of the building finally led to the evacuation and subsequent transfer of the courts. There was a gap of a few weeks during the move to the new building when no proceedings were conducted. After the court moved to Sewri, I subsequently observed its proceedings at the new location for about a month from July to August 2014 before the end of my fieldwork. This situation demonstrated how infrastructure issues, government decisions, and challenges to the daily existence of a court – not the intrinsic inefficiency of the Indian legal system that the US *TIP* Report frequently assumes–slowed the progress of cases.

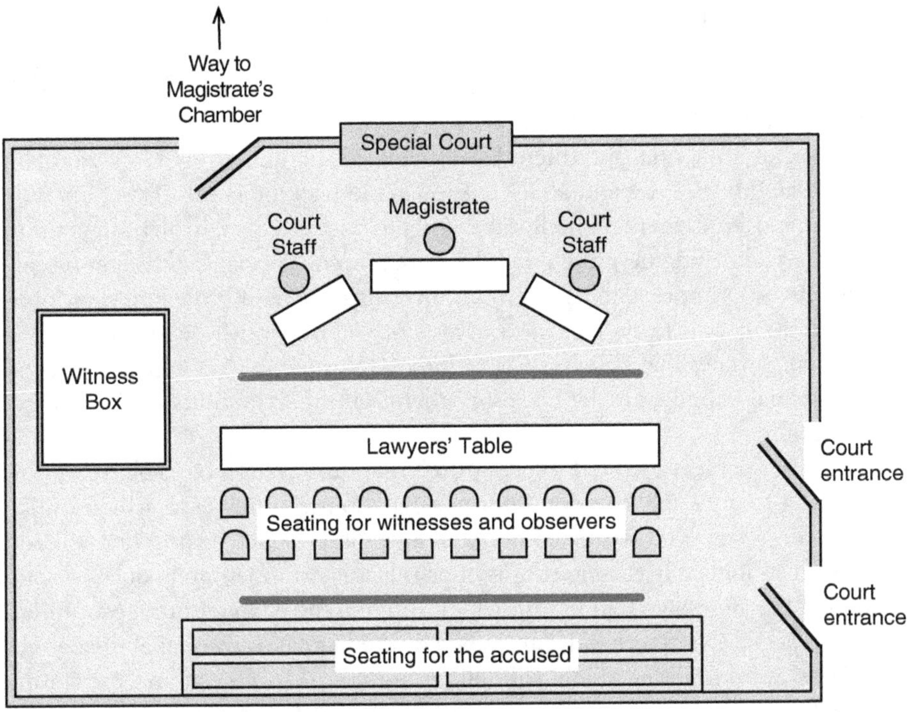

FIGURE 4.1 Layout of the Mumbai Special Court (author's illustration).

who help the police conduct the raids, and occasionally others, such as government doctors who conducted medical examinations of the rescued women. A ceiling fan, much needed in Mumbai's humid weather, whirs above, often drowning out the court proceedings with its loud noise. The walls are bare, except for a calendar, a photograph of Gandhi, and a sign in Marathi asking all present to keep their cell phones switched off.

Due to its frequent mention and recognition in the US *TIP Report*, this small local court has attracted considerable global interest among anti-trafficking experts, activists, and policymakers. Before the Special Court was established, the 2005 *TIP Report* expressed concern that the "level of prosecution remains inadequate relative to Mumbai's role as the largest center for sex trafficking in India." It blamed the slow progress of sex trafficking prosecutions on Mumbai's lack of special "fast-track" courts for these crimes, and frequent acquittals on lost evidence and unavailable witnesses (p. 124). Legal experts in India have also called for fast-track courts as much-needed solutions to speed up the progress of cases. The premise is that if a court is dedicated to a specific type of case (here, the ITPA), the backlog will be cleared faster. The Mumbai Special Court was set up partly for this reason. Its presiding magistrate explained that the court effectively functioned as a fast-track court, as she tried to complete trials within six or seven months of the filing of the charge-sheet.[2]

The Special Court was set up in 2008 as the first and only court in India adjudicating cases under the ITPA alone. Its existence was shaped to a significant extent by Prerana, an influential and (then) US-funded anti-trafficking NGO in Mumbai. When I asked magistrates and NGO lawyers about why the court was set up, they referred me to a judgment of the Bombay High Court in a case involving a petition by Prerana.[3] This judgment included the setting up of Special Courts among several directives to improve the prevention, investigation, and prosecution of inter-state trafficking, and to protect the interests of victims from rescues to trials.[4] It instructs magistrates and Sessions Court judges to expedite trials in cases of commercial sexual exploitation by disposing them within six months of the charge-sheet being filed.[5]

Some interlocutors credited a second judgment of the Bombay High Court as also leading to the establishment of the Special Court. In that case, which unlike the first was not an NGO-initiated petition, a woman rescued against her will and detained in a shelter had escaped after her release was indefinitely delayed. She petitioned the Bombay High Court, which ordered the Maharashtra government to set up Special Courts (already prescribed by the ITPA) to ensure that the correct procedures were followed, such as holding inquiries (Chapter 5) and preventing inordinate delays in protective custody (Chapter 6). This case brings out the organic connection between courts and shelters under the ITPA, and between the long-standing occurrence of women escaping protective homes and the bureaucratic aspects of law driving their escape.[6]

2 The police document of accusation that initiates trial proceedings in India.

3 The city named Bombay in the colonial era was renamed Mumbai in 1995 by the Shiv Sena, a regional political party based on Hindu nationalism and local Maharashtrian nativism and Maratha caste identity, which wanted the city to reflect these sociopolitical identities rather than the legacy of Portuguese and British colonialism. However, the High Court still retains the name "Bombay."

4 *Prerana vs. State of Maharashtra*, Criminal Writ Petition No. 1694 of 2003. Judgment of the Bombay High Court dated April 18, 2007.

5 In the Indian judicial hierarchy, magistrates preside over trial courts. The Sessions Courts are the courts to which appeals against trial court judgments can be brought.

6 *Ms. Khushi Harkishan Malhotra vs. State of Maharashtra*. Criminal Writ Petition No. 2037 of 2004. Judgment of the Bombay High Court dated September 8, 2005. The relevant details of this case are as follows. In October 2004, a woman was sent into shelter detention after the police forcibly rescued her from a hotel room on the grounds that she was involved in prostitution. Prior to her escape from the shelter, she had appealed to the Sessions Court against being placed there for more than twenty-one days (beyond the time specified by the ITPA). After her appeal was rejected, she appealed to the Bombay High Court, which found that the magistrate had not followed the proper procedure under the ITPA. The woman had been sent to protective custody without an inquiry being conducted. The High Court directed the Maharashtra government to expeditiously set up Special Courts, to ensure that the correct procedures were followed.

In 2010, two years after the Special Court was set up, the US *TIP Reports* began referring to it as an "anti-trafficking court."[7] The *Reports* appreciated this court's role in clearing the backlog in trafficking cases, and ordering a record number of convictions against traffickers and brothel owners (2011: 49). In 2011, the US State Department selected this court's magistrate among its *Trafficking In Persons* "Heroes." Though the Special Court prosecutes cases under the ITPA, India's anti-prostitution law, the *TIP Reports* describe it as an anti-trafficking court, reflecting the US State Department's agenda.

At the Special Court, the accused facing trial are typically madams, brothel keepers, managers, and pimps, rather than those trafficking women from other states or countries. They are charged under the following ITPA provisions: Section 3 (keeping a brothel or allowing premises to be used as a brothel), 4 (living on the earnings of prostitution), 5 (procuring, inducing, or taking a person for the sake of prostitution), 6 (detaining a person in premises where prostitution is carried on) and 7 (running premises for prostitution within 200 meters of a public place). These sections primarily criminalize the facilitation of prostitution. In certain situations, offenses under these sections can amount to sex trafficking – for example, if rescued women were forced into prostitution, if the accused were living on their earnings under duress, or if they were being detained. However, for the accused to be convicted for most of these crimes (except Section 6), it was not essential under the ITPA to prove the exploitative aspects of prostitution.

Observing the Court

Though the Special Court is a public place and anyone may sit there, I took prior permission from the presiding magistrate to observe cases. Due to my overall appearance and demeanor of someone studying or doing research (notebook and pen, paying keen attention to the proceedings, reading judgments during breaks in the proceedings, etc.), NGO lawyers and police officers who were in court to testify for the prosecution would often strike up a conversation with me. I was able to build a rapport with them, as well as with the magistrate and prosecutors owing to the assumptions of "respectability" around my presence. The defense lawyers and their juniors and interns, on the other hand, were always rather suspicious of me. They initially asked if I was a journalist. Then, seeing me come to the court almost every day over several months, most assumed I had some connection to NGOs, frequently

7 The 2010 *TIP Report* further notes that the Mumbai Special Court recorded convictions in at least eighty-one cases, and was "remarkable in eliminating the backlog of old cases" (p. 173). The 2011 *TIP Report* cites a higher number of convictions, 164, a majority of which are described as being for sex trafficking (p. 189). The 2012 *TIP Report* cites 242 prosecutions and 125 convictions, again describing them as "sex trafficking" cases (p. 185).

asking me which NGO I was from. I was careful to keep my interactions with them to a minimum, as I was concerned that the NGO lawyers, prosecutors, and magistrate might start to mistrust me if they saw me hobnobbing with the defense lawyers. They tended to view the defense lawyers in poor light because of their delaying tactics and the alleged and unethical practice of preparing some rescued women to navigate the inquiry process (Chapter 5) while also representing the accused brothel or bar owners in the same case in court.

I situated myself in the courtroom and observed the proceedings, rather than following cases through an anti-trafficking NGO. This was a deliberately different strategy from my approach to the New Delhi fieldwork Chapter 3 was based on, in order to achieve a balance in my research between NGO interventions and Indian legal institutions and processes. Thus, though affiliation with an NGO might have increased my chances to observe in-camera proceedings at this court as (explained later), I chose not to do so, and focused on observing the court proceedings. This methodological decision meant that I could not observe the rare instances of "victim-witnesses" testifying at the Special Court, but it gave me the opportunity to observe patterns of evidence and testimony beyond what I might have learned from observing NGOs alone.

I did not interact with rescued women much during the trial proceedings, for two reasons. One, as mentioned in the Introduction, I rarely saw rescued women come to testify in the eight months I observed the Special Court, for reasons discussed in Chapter 3 and further examined here. Two, due to my non-affiliation with any of the NGOs involved, I did not have permission from the magistrate to observe in-camera proceedings in the rare cases where rescued women testified. The way I usually came to know that a rescued woman was about to testify in camera was when I saw her arrive, accompanied by an NGO representative and/or police officer, and the court staff had the courtroom emptied and closed its doors until the testimony was over. I was usually able to find out from the NGO lawyers or prosecutor afterwards whether the rescued woman had supported the prosecution case.

Audibility (or rather the lack thereof) was a significant challenge. The acoustics of the court were such that sitting in the row of seats behind the lawyers' table, I could hear only some of what the witnesses were saying. The whir of the ceiling fan was often louder than the court proceedings. The magistrate's dictation to the stenographer (in English) was somewhat easier to hear, but not entirely audible. These problems with audibility resonate with the experiences of other anthropologists studying Indian courts (Baxi 2014: xxxii).

I also faced some linguistic limitations. In Mumbai, the official language used by the government (and widely spoken by many of its residents) is Marathi, a language I do not speak. Most of the rescued women and many of the NGO representatives were not Marathi speakers, and most Marathi speakers I encountered during my research also spoke Hindi. Hindi and English were the primary languages used in my interviews. However, with the court proceedings largely conducted in Marathi, in a space where audibility was already a problem, my linguistic limitations compounded the difficulty of understanding what was being said. I was able to address this partly through the help of Saie Shetye, an MPhil researcher from Mumbai's Tata Institute of Social Sciences, who was also conducting research on ITPA cases at the court and often translated for me.

The difficulty of following cases from start to finish was another major challenge. The duration of trials at the court, though faster than many trial courts in India owing to its Special Court status, was too long to be able to observe cases from start to finish. The timeline from the filing of the FIR to its disposal by judgment ranged between ten months and thirteen years, with most cases taking between two and four years for the judgment to be delivered. For this reason, to discuss trial patterns, I supplement my ethnographic observations and interviews with an analysis of judgments of disposed cases.

The judgments were not easy to procure. The process involved writing an application to the court office separately for each judgment, standing in long lines to buy stamps to attach to each application, and then paying for the photocopies, for which one had to earn the good favor of the overworked and often reluctant court staff. Frustrated by this process, Saie – my fellow researcher – and I divided up the cases among ourselves and shared the task of applying for them. Even so, the process of collecting the judgments, which could only be done during the hours the court was open, took time away from observing the court. Occasionally, we were able to get copies of judgments of cases from the NGO lawyers.

After going through this trouble for several months, toward the second half of my fieldwork in Mumbai, we suddenly and serendipitously got all the judgments we needed on a USB drive. The New Delhi gang-rape and murder case of December 2012 had led to calls for a nationwide evaluation of the Indian criminal justice system in cases of violence against women.[8] The Maharashtra Judicial Academy was seeking information on trial courts' conviction and acquittal patterns. It ordered all courts dealing with gender violence cases to conduct and provide a detailed analysis. The Special Court's magistrate asked us, as researchers, to help with the analysis, knowing that we needed the judgments for our research anyway, and intending to spare the already overburdened court staff this additional task.

Once in a while, hints of the significant global interest in the Special Court would show up in the form of foreign visitors, whose visits generated much curiosity at the court. Those who did not look phenotypically Indian received a lot of attention, such as members of the Japanese aid agency funding some of the NGOs active at the court or a Canadian filmmaker associated with an NGO who was conducting research for a film about violence against women. To them, in turn, the chaos of an

[8] See explanation in Chapter 1, footnote 29.

Indian court, and the sheer numbers of people milling around, were perplexing. I often found myself in the role of a cultural, linguistic, and legal translator, explaining what was going on at the court through my own initially limited experience.[9]

NGOs, POLICE, AND VICTIM-WITNESS TESTIMONY AT THE MUMBAI SPECIAL COURT

Two of the anti-trafficking NGOs most active at the Mumbai Special Court received their funding from US faith-based organizations.[10] A third NGO had funding from US and European sources, the Indian government, and the small Japanese funding agency. In my interviews with them, these NGOs tended to foreground the indispensability of "victim-witnesses" as part of the prosecutorial strategy central to their anti-trafficking efforts. NGO lawyers highlighted the support they provided to rescued women to ensure and strengthen their testimony against the accused, and emphasized the need to follow up with rescued women and keep them motivated to participate in the criminal justice system. They told me that these efforts strengthened the cases considerably.

The NGO lawyers who came regularly to the Special Court told me that they often did the bulk of the prosecutor's work in these cases. Echoing the concerns cited in the US *TIP Reports*, many described the inadequate and indifferent responses of the police, prosecutors, and state-run shelter where rescued sex workers were sent as the main reasons why they needed to intervene. One NGO lawyer said the state machinery did not want to devote time, resources, or energy toward getting rescued women to testify. Another observed that "police cannot train women to give evidence," because they did not have the motivation, skill, or time to build rapport with the women.

One NGO, funded by the Japanese donor agency, notes in its brochure that "the idea of testifying against the traffickers does not appeal to the victims."[11] To address this

[9] Members of the Japanese funding agency often asked for my input to understand these cases. They had previously worked in Cambodia, where they funded anti-trafficking NGOs to support rescued women to testify in court. They wished to pursue similar interventions in India. However, they told me the NGOs they funded could not provide data on how often victims of sex trafficking testified in support of the prosecution. As mentioned in Chapter 3, they partnered with a Mumbai anti-trafficking NGO, Save the Children India to conduct interviews to understand the "legal and social factors influencing the success or failure of prosecution of trafficking crimes" in Mumbai, and in the state of Maharashtra (Save the Children India, 2014). For the interviews, this NGO arranged access to women participating in post-rescue programs through different NGOs, to police and prosecutors assigned to their cases, to the judges adjudicating them, and to judgments in disposed cases. Saie Shetye, then an MPhil student, was hired to conduct the interviews, and I was hired as a consultant to analyze the interviews and judgments.

[10] For a critical analysis of the key role played by US-based Christian "justice"-oriented organizations in global anti-trafficking campaigns, see Bernstein (2018). For a critical analysis of one such organization in India, see Govindan (2013).

[11] This organization worked on training police, prosecutors, and judges to provide an "enabling environment" and "assistance" to victims.

challenge, it partnered with other NGOs funded by the Japanese agency to develop a project involving Dance Movement Therapy for survivors of trafficking at shelters.[12] The purpose of the project was to "provide coping mechanisms that will enable rescued survivors of trafficking to face the judicial process and minimize trauma." I received this brochure at a presentation to which the NGO invited me, its partner NGOs, the Special Court magistrate, and the NGO's Japanese funders, to explain the intended use of Dance Movement Therapy to "increase the confidence levels of the survivors."[13] This purported connection between Dance Movement Therapy and women testifying in court was not backed by research, but some NGOs and their funders found it appealing nonetheless, probably because it was a popular global trend among NGOs at the time. I was struck, however, by how dance was apparently considered appropriate as a therapeutic mechanism to get women to "open up" and develop the confidence to testify, but not as a respectable income-earning strategy (see Chapters 5 and 6).

Overall, NGOs tended to highlight positive stories about victim-witness testimony. Similar to Neha's approach to rescues (Chapter 2), several NGO representatives told me they only rescued girls and women they knew from their informants were victims of sex trafficking and would be willing to testify against the accused. A lawyer from the International Justice Mission (a large, faith-based, and US-funded NGO) whom I often met at the Special Court told me that about 60 percent of the women the NGO rescued testified as prosecution witnesses owing to its efforts.

Only one NGO lawyer at the Mumbai Special Court acknowledged the possibility that some rescued women may not have been trafficked, or that they were initially trafficked, but wished to remain in the sex trade instead of being rescued. That lawyer's more nuanced understanding of sex work and/or willingness to share it with me likely had to do with the fact that she had her own practice handling other cases and worked for the NGO only part time. She seemed more invested in strengthening the cases she was assigned than in the donor-driven aspects of anti-trafficking campaigns that conflate sex trafficking and sex work:

> To be honest, in maximum cases, they turn hostile ... Not all are victims. If they say they came into the sex trade by choice, I let them be ... I am concerned with minors, and those adults who say they were forced. I want to help them.

Though other NGO representatives and lawyers either did not share this nuanced understanding or did not feel comfortable providing it to me, they did acknowledge that some women they had rescued refused to testify as they had "moved on" in life (gone back to their homes in other states, got married, etc.) and the idea of testifying

12 Dance Movement Therapy seemed to be a popular mode of intervention among many NGOs at the time of my research. It was also being used in other contexts, for example, with domestic violence survivors.

13 The first three expected outcomes of this project included "to master courage and self-confidence to identify the traffickers," "to effectively confront the traffickers during trial in court," and "to overcome the fear of social stigma and mental set-back of being a victim of an unpleasant act that often causes the victim to either remain silent or to change her testimony in the court."

did not appeal to them. On rare occasions, rescued women deposed via video conference with the help of NGOs after returning to their home states.[14] NGO representatives also admitted that in a few cases they had "lost track" of those they rescued. Some women had returned to the sex trade after being rescued (for which NGOs used the term "retrafficked") or became "untraceable."

In contrast to NGOs' emphasis on the role of "victim-witness" testimony, my interviews with the magistrate, police, and prosecutors at the Mumbai Special Court yielded accounts of rescued women rarely testifying in support of the prosecution case. They echoed the lament I was familiar with from New Delhi – that rescued women were "hostile witnesses." In response to my question about how often rescued women testified in these cases, the magistrate at the Special Court replied "*na ke barabar*" ("virtually never"). She often pointed out to me that she had convicted the accused based on other forms of evidence and testimony in several cases. NGO lawyers also gave me examples of cases where rescues had led to convictions without the rescued women testifying. As I will show, rescued women's testimony was not essential to proving the case against the accused if other evidence was available, especially the testimony of other prosecution witnesses present at the rescue.

The Mumbai police officers I met at the Special Court voiced similar concerns and explanations about hostile witnesses to those discussed in Chapter 3. A police inspector for the Social Service (SS) Branch put it as follows[15]: "if she was willing to be rescued, then her testimony is good, not otherwise." The police expressed the view that most adult women whose rescues they were involved in were willingly involved in prostitution, as their livelihood depended on it, and were therefore "unwilling to cooperate" with the prosecution. Infusing these perceptions of the women's economic decisions with a strong dose of moralism, police officers told me many of the women they rescued were "used to easy money" and did not want to make the effort to do something else (e.g. pursue training programs for alternative forms of livelihood at the shelter after rescues).

The police pointed out that even in cases of trafficked women who were not forcibly rescued, the chances of them coming to Mumbai to testify after returning to their homes in other Indian states, or in neighboring Nepal or Bangladesh were slim. Echoing what I had heard in New Delhi, the greatest challenge the Mumbai police noted was that "victim-witnesses" could not be traced, especially when several years had passed since their rescue. In cases of trafficked women, the police often brought up how the length of time it took for cases to be completed impeded their ability to convince "victim-witnesses" to testify. They made the related point that the long duration of trials provided plenty of opportunity for the women and their families to be "bought over" by the accused.

14 I came across a total of three such cases in my analysis of judgments in Mumbai.

15 A specialized wing of the Mumbai police that conducts anti-prostitution raids, discussed further later in this section.

The police also surmised that having escaped both trafficking and the stigma of prostitution, the women feared that their names would be tarnished by coming to court and testifying against the accused. They brought up how trafficked women often wished to lead "respectable" lives as married women after rescue and saw little benefit in testifying in court about what had happened to them. Explaining this to me, one police officer asked the rhetorical question, "why would I want to disturb her married life?" The moral lens through which the police viewed these cases thus considered rescued women being "respectably" married an outcome that served the women better than coming to court to testify against the accused.

The three different prosecutors I met at the Mumbai Special Court also emphasized that rescued sex workers usually did not support the prosecution case. I spoke to a new prosecutor who assumed duty at the court in April 2013 just two weeks after he started work. He expressed surprise at what a small proportion of rescued women testified in support of the prosecution case. A few months later, with more experience handling these cases, he estimated that rescued women would show up to testify only 10–15 percent of the time, that too mostly in cases where an NGO had rescued them, stayed in regular contact with them, "counseled" them to testify, and facilitated their travel to and presence in court; a coalescence of factors similar to Sunaina's case in New Delhi.

Analyzing my interviews, I wondered how to reconcile the high percentage of "victim-witnesses" testifying, as reported by NGOs such as the International Justice Mission (IJM), with the low percentage reported by the magistrate, prosecutors, and police, and corroborated by my observations at the court. I looked for answers in the Special Court's judgments in cases completed in 2012 and 2013. This analysis yielded some answers about the relationship between NGOs, "victim-witnesses," and case outcomes. However, paired with my interviews and observations, it also revealed how cases at the Special Court were shaped by factors beyond NGO intervention and "victim-witness" testimony – the role of the Mumbai police, the anti-*prostitution* (rather than anti-trafficking) focus of the ITPA, and other forms of evidence and testimony.

Tables 4.1 and 4.2 provide an overview of the outcomes of cases at the Special Court.[16] Table 4.1 was compiled by Saie Shetye,[17] my fellow traveler in observing the court proceedings, who remained in Mumbai and observed the court longer than I did and analyzed a larger volume of cases for her MPhil. thesis. The analysis of case patterns in relation to NGOs, police, and "victim-witness" testimony at the Special Court that follows in Table 4.2 is my own.

The difference between the number of convictions in Tables 4.1 and 4.2 is that some convictions included in Table 4.1 were on charges of pimping, touting, and

[16] The difference between the "convictions" column and "number of accused convicted" and likewise between the "acquittals" column and "number of accused acquitted" is that many cases had multiple individuals among the accused.

[17] Saie Shetye (2014).

TABLE 4.1 *Overall disposal of ITPA cases by the Mumbai Special Court in 2012 and 2013.*[18]

Year	Number of cases tried	Number of cases disposed by judgment	Convictions	Acquittals	Number of accused persons convicted	Number of accused persons acquitted
2012	404	27	22	5	50	93
2013	454	51	26	25	64	56

Source: Shetye (2014).

TABLE 4.2 *Outcomes of cases involving ITPA Sections 3–7 at the Mumbai Special Court.*

Year	Number of convictions	Number of acquittals	Total cases disposed
2012	14	4	18
2013	13	20	35

soliciting, which I did not study in detail either ethnographically or via judgments. The accused in those cases mostly pleaded guilty and were set free after paying a fine. Those cases were usually handled in the afternoons and did not involve the hearing of evidence, unlike cases with charges under ITPA sections 3 (keeping a brothel or allowing premises to be used as a brothel), 4 (living on the earnings of prostitution), 5 (procuring, inducing, or taking person for prostitution), 6 (detaining a person in premises where prostitution is carried on), and 7 (running premises for prostitution within 200 meters of a public place). This latter set of cases went to trial and were the focus of my ethnographic research at the court as well my analysis of judgments.

Turning to Tables 4.3–4.8 (see next two pages), the reader might wonder what the non-NGO cases were. The judgments revealed that most cases adjudicated at the Special Court resulted from anti-prostitution raids conducted by the Mumbai police, and only a small number from rescues involving anti-trafficking NGOs. Connected to this was my discovery that the high number of convictions were for *prostitution*-related rather than sex trafficking-related charges. In cases with no NGOs involved, the police typically charged the accused with provisions of the ITPA that criminalize different aspects of running the sex trade, rather than

18 Cases disposed by judgment only include convictions and acquittals and do not include those cases that may have been compounded (combined with others) or transferred to another court.

TABLE 4.3 *Proportion of NGO involvement (in cases involving ITPA Sections 3–7) at the Mumbai Special Court.*

Year	Disposed cases in which an NGO was involved in the rescue operation	Disposed cases in which an NGO was not involved in the rescue operation
2012	6/18	12/18
2013	10/35	25/35

TABLE 4.4 *Relating NGO involvement to outcomes (in cases under ITPA Sections 3–7) at the Mumbai Special Court.*

Year	Number of convictions in cases where NGOs were involved in rescue and prosecution	Number of convictions in cases where NGOs were not involved in rescue and prosecution	Total number of convictions	Number of acquittals in cases where NGOs were involved in rescue and prosecution	Number of acquittals in cases where NGOs were not involved in rescue and prosecution	Total number of Acquittals
2012	6	8	14	0	4	4
2013	10	3	13	0	20	20

TABLE 4.5 *Patterns of victim-witness testimony (in cases under ITPA Sections 3–7) at the Mumbai Special Court.*

Year	Number of cases in which victim-witnesses did not testify	Number of cases in which victim-witnesses testified	Testified and supported prosecution case	Testified but turned hostile
2012	9/18	9/18	5/9	4/9
2013	16/35	19/35	8/19	11/19

TABLE 4.6 *Relating victim-witness testimony in support of prosecution to case outcomes (in cases under ITPA Sections 3–7) at the Mumbai Special Court.*

Year	Convictions in cases where victims testified in support of prosecution case	Acquittals in cases where victims testified in support of prosecution case
2012	5/5	0/5
2013	6/8	2/8

TABLE 4.7 *Relating victim-witness testimony in support of prosecution to NGO involvement (in cases under ITPA Sections 3–7) at the Mumbai Special Court.*

Year	NGO involved in cases in which "victim" testified and supported prosecution case	NGO not involved in cases in which "victim" testified and supported prosecution case
2012	2/5	3/5
2013	6/8	2/8

TABLE 4.8 *Relating absence or hostility of victim-witnesses to case outcomes (in cases under Sections 3–7) at the Mumbai Special Court.*

Year	Convictions in cases in which "victim" did not testify or turned hostile	Acquittals in cases in which "victim" did not testify or turned hostile
2012	7/14	4/4
2013	7/13	18/20

aspects related to sex trafficking. These findings are especially significant given the Special Court's recognition in the US *TIP Report* for its high rate of convictions in sex trafficking cases, the key role a US-funded anti-trafficking NGO played in its establishment, and the constant presence and efforts of anti-trafficking NGOs at the court.

The main reason I discerned for the large number of police-led anti-prostitution raids in Mumbai (compared to New Delhi) was that the Mumbai police had a specialized branch – the Social Service (SS) Branch, which had no equivalent in the Delhi police – dedicated to conducting raids under the ITPA and certain local laws. The SS Branch was set up in the 1970s to deal with issues including domestic violence and sexual harassment. It raids several establishments – not just brothels in red-light areas, but also bars, massage parlors, and beauty salons (see Table 4.9), which it targets on the suspicion of being dens of prostitution. The SS Branch's activities thus drive up the number of police-led anti-prostitution raids in the city.[19]

[19] See also footnote 15. The bar raid cases I analyzed through judgments and observed in court were police-led, and rarely had NGOs involved. However, some NGOs were involved in bar "rescues," especially on the outskirts of Mumbai, where they alleged that minor girls were made to have sex with customers and detained at apartments from which they were brought to the bars and taken back. Also significant in this context is the fact that anti-trafficking NGOs have, in the past, supported the Maharashtra government's ban on dance bars in 2005 (which have since resumed business), as explained in the Preface. Dance bars were establishments where women danced to Bollywood

TABLE 4.9 *Locations of raids in cases involving Sections 3–7 at the ITPA Special Court, Mumbai.*

Year	Cases involving bars, parlors, etc.	Cases involving brothels in red-light areas
2012	2 (1 parlor, 1 guest house)	16
2013	14 (3 bars, 6 parlors, 2 salons, 1 flat, 2 guest houses, 1 car)	21

The Mumbai police, especially the SS Branch, has been sharply criticized by the media and concerned citizens for indiscriminately targeting establishments such as bars, pubs, restaurants, and discotheques on mere suspicion and false allegations of prostitution. Per these critiques, these raids are thinly veiled attempts by culturally conservative and populist right-wing politicians to curb Mumbai's vibrant nightlife and party scene with nebulous allegations of immorality, and to make bars the scapegoats for crimes in the city.[20] The raids instantiate this larger context of moral policing in Mumbai that I discussed in the Preface. Chapters 5 and 6 will explore their impact on inquiries at the Special Court, and on shelter detention. Several women I met in those contexts had been "rescued" from bars, and explained that these raids mainly stemmed from a local economy of bribes (*haftas*), given the numerous licenses, permits, and regulations involved in running bars.

To explore the role of "victim-witness" testimony, I first analyzed cases in which NGOs were involved in the rescues. The Special Court's judgments showed that most such cases resulted in convictions. NGOs were mostly successful in getting rescued women to testify for the prosecution in these cases (see Tables 4.3, 4.4, and 4.7), and NGO involvement also increased the chances that rescued women's testimony would be strong enough to help secure convictions (see Tables 4.6 and 4.7). It also emerged from the analysis that police-only cases had, on balance, fewer convictions and more acquittals than NGO-involved cases, and less likelihood of "victim-witness" testifying. Nevertheless, both convictions and "victim-witness" testimony were possible in police-only cases (see Tables 4.4 and 4.7).

songs while male customers were served alcohol, which the government sought to ban on grounds of "obscenity" and "public nuisance" and of allegedly being pick-up points for prostitution (Agnes 2005; Lakkimsetti 2016). The ban on dance bars centered on the state government "imagining, invoking and attempting to impose a moralized relationship between public space and cultural value," but was also deeply connected to the "increasingly extortionate regime of bribes, licenses, and taxes that the state government and the city police force had imposed on the dance bars" (Mazzarella 2015). Prerana, an anti-trafficking NGO that supported the dance bar ban, was, pertinently, the same NGO whose petition to the Bombay High Court led to the setting up of the ITPA Special Court. Its pretext for supporting the ban was that those running dance bars exploited and trafficked minor girls, who needed to be rescued. Prerana thus mapped its anti-trafficking agenda on to a ban based on allegations of obscenity and "nuisance," and, for good measure, police and politicians' efforts to extort more money from the bar owners (Agnes 2005).

20 See, for example, Faleiro 2014; India Today 2012; Koppikar 2013; Mid Day 2012.

The relationship between NGOs, "victim-witness" testimony, and case outcomes at the Special Court needs to be situated in the context of the high proportion of cases brought to the court after police raids rather than NGO-initiated rescues. This helped me square the NGO IJM's estimate of "victim-witnesses" testifying in 60 percent of their cases with the prosecutor's estimate that "victim-witnesses" testified only 10–15 percent of the time. I read these estimates from my interviews alongside Tables 4.3, 4.4, and 4.7 generated by my analysis of judgments. Through this exercise, I gathered that since NGOs were involved in a small proportion of the overall number of cases at the Special Court, it was the relatively high percentage of NGO-supported "victim-witnesses" testifying *within this category* to which the NGO lawyer referred, and the relatively lower percentage of cases of "victim-witnesses" testifying in police-only cases to which the magistrate, prosecutor, and police referred.

Comparing the number of convictions across NGO-involved and police-only cases revealed an uneven pattern. In 2012, police-only cases resulted in a slightly higher number of convictions than NGO cases (Table 4.4). In 2013, on the other hand, NGO-involved cases resulted in far more convictions than police-only cases. Though there is an unevenness here, the acquittal patterns are also significant to the analysis. Across both years, all acquittals were in the police-only cases. Taken together, these patterns reinforce the overall trend of NGO involvement increasing the chance of convictions in these cases.

Relating supportive "victim-witness" testimony to case outcomes demonstrated that overall, across both years, cases in which "victim-witnesses" testified in support of the prosecution mostly led to convictions (see Tables 4.5 and 4.6). There was a high likelihood of acquittals in cases in which rescued women did not testify or did not support the prosecution case (see Table 4.8). However, another interesting pattern that emerged from the analysis was that around half the convictions in both years were in cases in which rescued women did not testify or did not support the prosecution case. This made it clear that while "victim-witness" testimony strengthened the likelihood of convictions, convictions were possible if other forms of evidence and testimony supported the prosecution case.

Comparing "victim-witness" testimony across NGO-involved cases and police-only cases again revealed an uneven pattern. In 2012, there was an almost equal number of police-only and NGO-involved cases in which "victim-witnesses" testified in support of the prosecution case (see Table 4.7). In 2013, however, the proportion of NGO-involved cases in which "victim-witnesses" testified was far higher than that of police-only cases. The low number of police-only cases in which rescued women testified in support of the prosecution case is especially significant given that police-only cases formed a much higher proportion of cases brought to the Special Court than NGO-involved cases (see Tables 4.3 and 4.4).

My ethnographic observations of the court corroborated what Indian legal actors had told me – that "victim-witness" testimony was, indeed, a rare occurrence. What I also learned was that this applied especially to police-only cases.

As I have mentioned, in the eight months that I observed the court, I rarely saw "victim-witnesses" come to testify in ITPA cases. I saw police officers, NGO representatives, decoy customers, and various other prosecution witnesses come to testify. I saw camel-colored envelopes with cash, unopened condom and tissue packets, cell phones, and reams of documents being produced as evidence. On one occasion, I even saw a television set being carried into court, in a case in which the prosecution argued that sexually explicit films were being shown to clients during the provision of sexual services. However, in contrast to other prosecution witnesses and other forms of evidence, rescued women came to the Special Court only six times during the time I conducted research there.

Tracking down what happened on those six occasions, I found out that NGOs worked closely with the two women who testified in support of the prosecution case. The four women who did not ultimately support the prosecution case were in police-only cases. This indicated that "victim-witnesses" supported by NGOs were more likely to testify than those without NGO support. On the four occasions rescued women came to testify in police-only cases, the prosecutor, after speaking with them, decided that they would make "hostile" witnesses and did not have them testify. They either told him that they were doing sex work voluntarily or denied that they were involved in it at all.

In one of those four cases, involving a raid on a beauty salon, the prosecutor, predicting that the women would turn hostile, caught sight of me sitting in the courtroom as usual. He asked if I could "counsel" the two women to testify against the accused for inducing them to do prostitution (ITPA Section 5), and for living on their earnings from prostitution (ITPA Section 4). Unlike the sustained interaction and training that NGOs provided to the women they rescued, the "counseling" in police-only cases tended to be done only at the court right before the case came up for hearing. The prosecutor or a woman constable from the police station involved in the raid would usually just read out the contents of the rescued woman's statement to the police after the raid and attempt to gauge if she would stick to that version. If they sensed that she was likely to turn hostile, she was dropped as a prosecution witness.

A police inspector from the SS Branch explained that if the case was strong but there was no NGO involved, his team made every effort to urge the woman to testify. But in his view this task was better performed by NGOs, as they were able to regularly stay in touch with the women and "counsel" them. This reminded me of the Meerut police's view that dealing with rescued women in ITPA cases involved forms of social service that were the domain of NGOs (Chapter 2). The Mumbai prosecutor's intention in asking me to "counsel" the women from the beauty salon seemed to be a combination of wanting to "outsource" the problem to me – read as an NGO-adjacent person, and assuming that I was, by dint of this, more likely to be successful at "counseling" than him.

I was, yet again, torn between my curiosity as a researcher, the need to build and maintain rapport with the legal actors I met frequently at the court, and the methodological and ethical choices that I was comfortable with. On the one hand, I wanted to learn more about rescued women's resistance to supporting the prosecution case. On the other hand, I did not want to be placed, once again, in a position where I was helping to "manage" women removed from the sex trade. I reminded the prosecutor that I was not an NGO representative, and that I could ask the women questions on his behalf, but did not feel comfortable asking them to say something that was not their own account. My concerns did not seem to be of much relevance to the prosecutor. He was busy with multiple cases and seemed relieved to have found someone he saw as capable of "counseling" the women. He had already discerned that the women would turn hostile, and was making what seemed like a last-ditch effort to try and save the case.

When I spoke to the two rescued women in the Mumbai prosecutor's office, both said the place where the raid was conducted was just a beauty salon, where they had been watching television at the time of the raid. They expressed shock that the police had made out a prostitution case against those running the salon. I relayed these accounts to the prosecutor, who proceeded to drop them as prosecution witnesses.

Echoing my experiences of being deemed capable of "counseling" in New Delhi and Meerut (Chapters 2 and 3), I had once again been called upon to do so. And I saw, once again, how rescued women resisted such forms of interaction aimed at persuading them to change their narrative. My interactions with the prosecutor were not as frequent or sustained as my interactions with other interlocutors at the Special Court (the NGO lawyers and the magistrate), affording little opportunity to build rapport. When asked to help, my approach to "counseling" was clearly not useful to the prosecutor, and he did not ask me to help him again.

Overall, my analysis of judgments, interviews, and ethnographic observations at the Special Court indicated the following patterns: that there was a significantly higher number of police-only rather than NGO-involved cases, that NGO involvement was more likely to lead to convictions, that "victim-witness" testimony was rare, but also likely to lead to convictions, and that NGO involvement made it more likely that "victim-witness" testimony would lead to convictions. However, cases did result in convictions without NGOs, and despite the absence or hostility of victim-witnesses, if other forms of evidence and testimony supported the prosecution case. It is to these forms of evidence and testimony that I turn next.

EVIDENCE AND TESTIMONY AT THE SPECIAL COURT

The cases brought before the Special Court were crafted around certain kinds of observable evidence and testimony required by the ITPA and Indian procedural and evidentiary law that make it both easier and more important to prove prostitution than sex trafficking. The court proceedings I observed were, more often than not, far removed from offenses around trafficking. They centered, instead, on a reenactment in court of the police raid at a site that was allegedly found (and must be proved) to be a brothel. The police case and trial proceedings centered on presenting the observable, transactional aspects of prostitution through material evidence and the testimony of those involved in the raid. As a lawyer I met at a conference on sexual violence in Mumbai, who had previously worked for a Christian anti-trafficking NGO, put it succinctly, "the ingredients of trafficking are not pursued in the investigation."

The accused facing trial at the Special Court were typically madams, brothel keepers, managers, and pimps, not those trafficking women from other states or countries. They were charged mostly under the following ITPA provisions: Sections 3 (keeping a brothel or allowing premises to be used as a brothel), 4 (living on the earnings of prostitution), 5 (procuring, inducing, or taking a person for prostitution), 6 (detaining a person in a brothel) and 7 (running premises for prostitution within 200 meters of a public place). The possibility of sex trafficking exists within some of these provisions (e.g. rescued women could have been forced into prostitution, or the accused could be living on the earnings of rescued women under duress). However, with the exception of Section 6, for the accused to be convicted for most of these crimes, it was not essential to prove the exploitative aspects of prostitution amounting to sex trafficking.

This finding – that the ITPA Special Court cases centered on proving prostitution and not sex trafficking – led me to look deeper into what "victim-witnesses" typically testified to in these cases. Since, on the whole, the issue of whether or not the rescued women were trafficked had little bearing on these cases, all they were required to say was that they was involved in prostitution, that the accused introduced them to prostitution, and/or that the accused ran the brothel, and/or lived on their earnings. This explains why both "victim-witness" testimony and convictions were possible in police-only cases (Tables 4.4 and 4.7) where the accused were typically charged under ITPA Sections 3, 4, 5 and 7 – criminalizing the facilitation of prostitution, but not forced prostitution or detention, which entail elements of sex trafficking.[21]

As my interlocutors at the court frequently mentioned, rescued women's testimony was not essential to proving many of the "ingredients" of prostitution in the case against the accused if other evidence was available, especially the testimony of other prosecution witnesses present at the rescue. Observing the court and analyzing the judgments, I learned more about these other witnesses and the roles they played in the way the prosecution case was put together. The police involved in the raid were usually always called as prosecution witnesses. Indian procedural law and the ITPA also allowed for NGO representatives to become witnesses to the police raids, and then prosecution

[21] There were only two police-initiated cases in 2012 and one in 2013 in which rescued women testified about being trafficked. These cases were crafted to foreground elements of trafficking and not just prostitution. The two 2012 cases both resulted in convictions, and the 2013 case resulted in an acquittal (because the rescued woman named two other persons in her testimony, not the accused).

witnesses verifying the details of the raids in court. NGOs were thus able to make the most of the evidentiary requirements of Indian law to strengthen the prosecution case. The testimony of NGO witnesses made "victim-witness'" testimony less indispensable to ITPA cases at the Special Court resulting in convictions, and to NGOs achieving the outcomes of a prosecution-focused anti-trafficking agenda.

Choreography of the Trials

The police case was built on a documentation of the raid that was carefully reenacted by the prosecution at the Special Court. The documentation and reenactment adhered to the Indian laws of evidence and criminal procedure[22] and the ITPA. In the way the prosecution built its case at the Special Court, its witnesses were, essentially, witnesses to the raid, not to sex trafficking, or even to prostitution.

During the trial proceedings, the prosecutor would ask prosecution witnesses to describe the circumstances leading up to the raid, provide details of the raids and the premises where they were conducted, identify the accused, and verify that the physical items of evidence (cash, packets of condoms and tissues, rental documents, etc.) being presented in court in sealed envelopes were the ones recovered during the raid. The witnesses were expected to attest to the fact that a decoy or bogus customer selected a girl or woman, paid money for her to the accused, and took her into a room, leading to an inference of prostitution rather than an actual act of sexual intercourse (whether forced or consensual being immaterial per most provisions of the ITPA). The presentation of the prosecution case in court thus centered on reenacting the transactional aspects of prostitution uncovered (and indeed catalyzed) by the raid. It also centered on describing features of the premises that associated them with a brothel through deeply moralistic presumptions (e.g. condom packets and tissue paper found together, beds, partitioned rooms).

The testimony of witnesses who supported the prosecution closely adhered to a script that connected specific steps in the recording of the raid to its reenactment in court. This script and sequencing gave the trials a carefully choreographed feel. Described in italics in the following text is a pattern I identified after observing several court proceedings, rather than an account of one case. I have retained some of the language and expressions the magistrate used as she translated witness testimony into Indian English legalese and dictated it to the court stenographer.

> *Person* X (usually either a police officer or NGO representative) *received information that prostitution business is carried on at so-and-so location. Police called person Y to act as a panch witness* (a nonpolice witness required by Indian criminal

[22] Specifically, the Code of Criminal Procedure (1973) and the Indian Evidence Act (1872).

procedure) *and person Z to act as bogus customer* (a decoy working with the Mumbai police during raids). *In the presence of the panch witness, the police gave the bogus customer currency notes, which were marked for identification, to offer as prostitution money. All these steps were recorded in the panchnama* (a document describing the raid in the presence of and signed by the panch witness). *The police formed a raid team and reached the premises after receiving a signal* (usually a phone call) *from the bogus customer. Upon arrival, the raid team first met the panch witness who accompanied the bogus customer to the premises and stayed back talking to the accused after the bogus customer engaged the girl and accompanied her to a room or cubicle. The panch witness informed the police that the accused was the person who showed the girl to the bogus customer and who accepted money for prostitution from him. The police searched the accused and recovered the money paid to him or her by the bogus customer as prostitution money, identified by the marks made on the currency notes prior to the raid. The panch witness then pointed in the direction of the room or cubicle where the bogus customer had gone with the girl. The police approached that room or cubicle and knocked on the door. The bogus customer informed them that the girl was in a half-naked condition. Then a lady police constable entered the room and asked the girl to dress properly. The bogus customer informed the police that girls were shown to him by the accused, and after he selected one the money given to him by the police was accepted by the accused for prostitution. Then the police took the girls and the accused into their custody and went to the police station…*

The cases were thus built around the raid, and centered on proving that the accused offered a woman for prostitution. The reenactment of the raid through witness testimony foregrounded the transaction between the bogus customer and the accused (brothel madam, pimp, or brothel keeper) who accepted the marked money for the prostitution of the rescued women. This transaction was presented as evidence that the accused was "living on the earnings of prostitution," criminalized under the ITPA (Section 4). When I spoke to police officers who came to the Special Court to testify, they usually highlighted this provision as the main aspect of these cases that needed to be proved to secure convictions. The marked currency notes, bogus customer, and *panch* witness whose evidence could prove this transaction were of prime importance.

Among the choreographed details about the raids presented in court, I was especially intrigued by the way women were described as being found in a "half-naked" condition at the brothel. It reminded me of Ashwini Tambe's discussion of how the police sought to prove prostitution in late colonial Bombay in the context of the Contagious Diseases Act through a level of titillating detail that Tambe aptly terms the "pornographic imagination" of colonial state actors (2009: 42). When I asked police and NGO representatives at the Special Court why it was so essential from an evidentiary standpoint for the prosecution witnesses to testify that "the girl" was in a "half-naked" condition, they explained that it showed an intention of prostitution, implied by the female body being offered for sexual services. The sexual act itself was not required to have been witnessed. Prostitution was inferred by intent.[23] This inference could be made on the basis of witnesses testifying that the bogus customer selected a woman, paid the accused for her services, and took her to a room or cubicle, where they were found together by the police, with the bogus customer reporting that the woman was in a "half-naked" condition. Testimony that a woman was "half-naked," and evidence of the exchange of the marked currency, helped the prosecution to claim that the trap case centered on her being engaged for the purpose of prostitution.

Further reasons for the need to mention "half-nakedness" emerged in my conversations with the magistrate. Responding to my perplexed query about why almost every case followed the same script of rescued women being "half" and never fully naked or in physical contact with the bogus customer, the magistrate explained that it was to avoid the allegation that the bogus customer was "exploiting" the woman. That could provide fodder for the defense to argue that the police were condoning sexual assault by the bogus customer, and potentially damage the prosecution case. By attesting to the rescued woman being "half-naked," prosecution witnesses thus helped to establish that the police case was built upon a raid correctly conducted according to the established procedure, with no actual sexual act involved.

Proving Prostitution

The evidence and testimony presented by the prosecution at the Special Court were based on what was observable at an alleged site of prostitution. In my observations of cases and analysis of judgments, I began to identify what forms of evidence and testimony were presented to prove each of the relevant sections of the ITPA. I focused, in particular, on how "victim-witness" testimony related to other forms of evidence and testimony centered on proving prostitution.

To prove charges under Section 3 (that a place was a brothel, a precursor to proving that the accused was running it), "victim-witness" testimony was not required if non-police witnesses such as *panch witnesses* and bogus customers testified in support of the prosecution. Other significant forms of evidence the court accepted for offenses under Section 3 were the medical examination reports of the rescued women and physical evidence, including condoms found at the scene and the cash transacted between the bogus customer and the accused. The doctor who conducted the medical examination had to establish the veracity of the medical reports, and the *panch* witness and/or bogus customer had to attest to the recovery of the condoms, cash, etc. from the raided premises.

[23] Analyzing the judgments and speaking with police and prosecutors at the Special Court, it became clear that it was the *intention* of prostitution that needed to be proved, rather than the actual act. The Special Court's judgments often cite a 1997 judgment of the Supreme Court of India (*Gaurav Jain vs. Union of India and Others*), which interpreted the ITPA to mean that "prostitution can be proved by the mere offer of sexual intercourse for hire," and that "sexual intercourse is not an essential ingredient."

The medical reports, based on an intrusive "two-finger test" to determine the status of rescued women's hymens,[24] declared that they were "habituated to sex," which the magistrate modified to "habituated to sexual abuse." In the absence of rescued women's testimony, and sometimes in addition to it, this medico-legal reading of their bodies made deeply moralistic, gendered, and presumptive connections between their perceived sexual histories and their involvement in prostitution. The medical reports were used to establish (often successfully) that the women found at the brothel, bar, salon, or parlor were involved in prostitution. The prosecution extrapolated from this to then argue that the site where they were found was a brothel.

To prove charges under Section 4 (living on the earnings of prostitution), the forms of evidence treated as most significant were the bogus customer's and *panch* witness' testimony and the recovered cash from the transaction between the bogus customer and the accused. The judgments also gave a lot of weight to the rescued woman's testimony specifically mentioning that a share of her income from prostitution was taken by the accused. In cases where the rescued woman did not come to testify, the court took into consideration the statement she gave the police at the time of the raid, if it mentioned the share of her income from prostitution taken by the accused. Under Indian procedural law, this statement was not an admissible piece of evidence in itself. It could only be considered if it was recorded in front of the *panch* witness, who then testified in court that they heard the rescued woman give the police this information immediately after the rescue.

To make this roundabout form of evidence admissible, the magistrate relied on the doctrine of *res gestae* that informs the Indian Evidence Act of 1872, a colonial era law that continues to be in force.[25] Derived from British law, the doctrine is an exception to the rule of hearsay evidence, which is not admissible in Indian courts. The prosecution needs to establish that what was reportedly said in a prior statement is connected to the acts constituting the offense, such that they form part of the same transaction. For Section 4 of the ITPA, the relevant part of the rescued woman's statement was that the accused took a share of her earnings from prostitution. The act constituting the offense was the accused accepting money from the bogus customer for prostitution at the time of the raid. As a legacy of India's colonial history, the *res gestae* doctrine provided the possibility for Section 4 to be proved without rescued women's testimony in court. The magistrate applied it to allow for rescued women's statements to the police at the time of the raid to be brought into evidence through the testimony of other prosecution witnesses present at the raid.

[24] A test long relied upon in rape trials in India to "discover whether the female body is 'habituated to sex.'" (Baxi 2014: 268). It is used by defense lawyers in rape trials to claim that the sex was consensual rather than coerced. See further discussion in Chapter 5.

[25] The Evidence Act and Criminal Procedure Code guide trial proceedings in India. Section 6 of the Evidence Act reads: "Relevancy of facts forming part of same transaction: Facts which, though not in issue, are so connected with a fact in issue as to form part of the same transaction, are relevant, whether they occurred at the same time and place or at different times and places." In other words, facts that can be proved to form part of the same transaction are considered relevant (Sarathi 2006: 44–45).

In contrast, "victim-witness" testimony was of paramount importance for the prosecution to prove offenses under Sections 5 ("procuring, inducing, or taking" someone for the purpose of prostitution) and 6 (detention in a brothel). Though Section 5 was difficult to prove without the rescued woman's testimony, she was not required to say that she was trafficked or coerced; merely that she was involved in prostitution and that the accused had introduced her to it. Convictions under Section 5 were thus not necessarily convictions for the offense of trafficking. It was primarily in NGO-involved cases, and only in a small subset of police cases, that elements of sex trafficking were pursued. The rest of the cases centered on prostitution *tout court*. The ITPA does not require a lack of consent to prostitution to be proved as part of the offense under Section 5. In cases resulting in convictions for charges under Section 5, the magistrate dismissed the defense lawyers' argument that the woman was selling sex consensually on the grounds that consent was irrelevant and immaterial to the crime.

In the absence of "victim-witness" testimony, many cases resulted in the acquittal of the accused under Section 5. However, "victim-witness" testimony was not absolutely indispensable. I came across cases where the rescued woman did not testify, but the bogus customer's and/or *panch* witness' testimony that the accused showed women to the bogus customer for prostitution was accepted as proof that the accused committed an offense under Section 5. Thus, it was possible, under Indian law, to prove without "victim-witness" testimony that a rescued woman was introduced to prostitution by the accused.

Section 6 of the ITPA (detaining someone in a brothel) is the only clause that penalizes exploitative aspects of prostitution. At the Special Court, there were only four convictions (out of fourteen) in 2012 and three (out of thirteen) in 2013 under this section. I discerned that the reason for the low number of convictions under this section was that proving it was completely dependent on the testimony of rescued women. In their absence, or if they "turned hostile," the court did not accept other evidence or testimony as proof of detaining someone in a brothel. In most of the convictions under Section 6, the case rested on the testimony of the "victim-witnesses," all of whom were rescued and supported by NGOs. In 2012, all four convictions under Section 6 were NGO cases. "Victim-witnesses" testified in support of the prosecution in three of them. In 2013, all three detention-related convictions were NGO cases. "Victim-witnesses" testified in support of the prosecution in all of them. Thus, in the context of Section 6 in particular, NGO involvement made it highly likely that "victim-witnesses" testimony would lead to convictions.

The Bogus Customer

Bogus or decoy customers were shadowy figures whose background was never described in the judgments, nor immediately apparent when they came to testify. Occasionally, they were NGO workers. Except for those who worked for NGOs, most appeared to be men from lower income (working class or lower middle-class) backgrounds. Unlike *panch* witnesses (see the next section), they were not required to state their occupations. I gathered from interlocutors at the court that non-NGO bogus customers were sometimes men accused in other cases and/or residents of red-light areas who needed to curry favor with the police.

The police's cultivation of bogus customers as witnesses bears similarity to other prosecution witnesses in colonial India whose testimony reflected an instrumentally constructed police-driven narrative (Amin 1987: 173, 178). Historian Shahid Amin has shown how the testimony of such prosecution witnesses was shaped to narrate all the "micro-sequences" and episodes that the prosecution sought to establish as punishable acts, identify the accused at each step of the crime, etc. (1987: 179). Though such prosecution witnesses are not formally included in procedural law, colonial case records reveal their existence, the police's shaping of their testimony, and the prosecution's dependence on them (186).[26]

The police officers I interviewed at the Mumbai Special Court, referring to ITPA cases as "punter" (decoy) cases, described the bogus customer's evidence as the most important. In their experience, prostitution, as knowable through transactions witnessed at the time of the raid, could not be proved without the bogus customer participating in the raid and testifying in court. His testimony about selecting and engaging a woman for prostitution prior to the raid, paying the trap money with identification marks to the accused, and going with the woman into a room was used to prove that a place was a brothel, and that the accused were living on the earnings of the rescued woman's prostitution.

As I discovered, however, bogus customers, like rescued women, did not always show up to testify. If they did, they sometimes turned hostile, contradicting the police version by saying they did not engage a woman for prostitution or had not yet paid the trap money when the raid was conducted, or by not identifying the accused in the case correctly. The non-co-operation of bogus customers was a frequent lament of the prosecutor and the police constable of the Mumbai police's SS Branch who brought evidence and witnesses to the court. Cases often resulted in acquittals if the bogus customer did not show up or turned "hostile" when he did testify. However, sometimes cases did result in the accused being convicted for "living on the earnings of prostitution" even without the bogus customer's testimony, if other prosecution witnesses testified about the role the bogus customer played in the raid to establish that the transaction took place. These other witnesses included the police involved in the raid, the complainant (usually either a police officer or NGO representative), the "victim-witness," and/or the *panch* witness.

In NGO rescue cases, NGO workers (usually men from the NGO's lower-level staff) or others known to the NGO sometimes acted as bogus customers for the raids, and came to testify for the prosecution. I first realized this when I noticed bogus

26 In the context of Indian peasants accused of attacking a police station as part of an uprising against the colonial government, Amin shows how those initially accused turned "approvers" for the prosecution.

customers with the same names appearing in different judgments. Observing the court, I had also noticed two or three of them come to testify quite regularly. I also discovered that some of them had worked for more than one NGO over time.

I introduced myself to one of these NGO bogus customers who often came to the court to testify. We set up an interview at the office of the NGO he worked for. He told me that his work as a decoy was not limited to participating in the raid. He also "counseled" and "mentally prepared" the woman described as being found "half-naked" with him for the rescue that was about to happen. This involved explaining the police procedures and urging her to "tell the truth" with details about what had happened to her. The bogus customer explained that the women whose rescues he had been involved in were all trafficked, and that (like the GB Road cases in Chapter 2) the NGO initiated the rescues based on specific information about them wanting to escape.

NGOs were not forthcoming about their staff being bogus customers, as they did not want to publicize this fact. They seemed wary of this aspect of their work becoming known and potentially harming the cases they were involved in. The lawyer who previously worked for a Christian anti-trafficking NGO in Mumbai and had described how the "ingredients of trafficking" were not investigated in these cases told me that NGOs tried to get witnesses who they knew would keep their word and testify. These included their own workers, people they knew from church, students they wanted to recruit to their organizations, etc. However, she cautioned me that NGOs were very guarded about this aspect of their work.

I asked a senior police officer whether he thought the fact that some bogus customers were NGO workers made a difference to the outcomes of ITPA cases. He replied with a firm "yes," explaining that the NGO decoy's "hands are clean," and therefore, has greater credibility, compared to the bogus customers the police arranged who did not have "clean pasts," and often had criminal records. The NGO decoys whose testimony I observed in court certainly had the practiced and experienced air of those who knew exactly how to explain their role in the raid in the appropriate legalese. This was not usually the case with non-NGO decoys, many of whom either turned hostile or could not reproduce the relevant details according to script. The police officer's articulation of the respectability of NGO witnesses, as against the non-NGO decoy, a slippery figure marked by suspicions of unreliability and criminality, segues into the importance of the *panch* witness in Indian procedural law.

The Panch *Witness*

The *panch* witness is a figure in Indian criminal procedure who witnesses police action during a search or raid, signs a document called the *panchnama* – a record of what the witness saw during the search or raid – and testifies to this document's veracity in court. The *panchnama* and the *panch* witness are important forms of corroborative evidence. The *panch* witness' role is to convince the court that the police had not made up a false case or planted the items seized from the raided premises, and to testify to the veracity of the incriminating evidence the police claimed to have found at the time and location of the raid.

While granting an acquittal in 2013, the Special Court's magistrate listed which witnesses could testify to a place being a brothel. Citing their absence as the reason for the accused being acquitted, she wrote:

> The witnesses who can establish the fact that indeed the premises where raid was effected was brothel and that accused were getting done prostitution from the ladies at that place are, victims, bogus customer and/or panch who accompanied the bogus customer at the relevant time.[27]

In the Indian criminal justice system, the police case is required to be corroborated by "respectable" and "independent" nonpolice witnesses. All but one of the cases I analyzed that resulted in convictions had at least one prosecution witness who was not from the police (a *panch* witness, bogus customer, or "victim-witness"), and many had more than one such prosecution witness. In short, it was rare for a case to result in a conviction solely on the basis of police testimony.

The need for nonpolice witnesses to corroborate the police version of the case has a likely genealogy in the colonial mistrust of the native police,[28] and colonial lawmakers' and administrators' preference for other seemingly objective forms of evidence (Kumar 2022).[29] Like the police's cultivation of bogus customers as prosecution witnesses and the use of the doctrine of *res gestae* to circumvent the need for "victim-witness" testimony, the requirement of nonpolice witnesses bears traces of India's colonial legal history. It presents an interesting contrast to sexual assault trials in the US, where feminist legal ethnographers have found that police testimony is a fundamental form of corroborative evidence (Hlavka and Mulla 2021: 110), and that the police are viewed as inherently reliable and believable witnesses (111) in the "hierarchy of credibility" through which different prosecution witnesses are perceived (122).

In Indian law, both the Criminal Procedure Code and the ITPA require the presence of "respectable" witnesses from the locality during a raid, without defining what "respectable" means.[30] The term *panchnama* literally translates into "the written

[27] *The State (V.P. Road Police Station, Mumbai) vs. Laxmi Nivrutti Patole and Baby Vakil Ahmed Khan*, Case no. 781/PW/2011. Judgment of the Metropolitan Magistrate, Special Court for ITPA, 54th Court, Mazgaon, Mumbai dated April 5, 2013, p. 7.

[28] See, for example, Kolsky (2005); Lal (1999); Samaddar (2008); Singha (1993).

[29] Radha Kumar discusses how the evidentiary norms framing investigations into police torture in colonial India, outlined in the Code of Criminal Procedure (1898), privileged three "objective" forms of evidence – the testimony of "impartial" and "respectable" witnesses, the police's written records, and medical reports (2022). Kumar argues that, despite being purportedly "objective," these forms of evidence served to reinforce police power and preserve existing social hierarchies and attendant notions of legitimacy and authority.

[30] Section 100 (4) of the Criminal Procedure Code requires the police conducting a search to call upon "two or more independent and respectable inhabitants of the locality in which the place to be

document of a respectable person." In practice, the "respectability" required of the *panch* presented a challenge. In one of our many conversations about issues that came up with regard to evidence in ITPA cases, the magistrate explained the problem of finding "respectable" witnesses to serve as *panch* witnesses in Hindi, as follows:

> *Jo* witness *miltey hain, woh* labor, *chhote* business *wale hotey hain. Unki* limited understanding *hoti hai. Aap samajh sakti hain, woh apni* logic *se bolenge.* [The witnesses they [the police] find, they are laborers and small business owners. They have a limited understanding. You can understand, they will speak based on their logic.]

She added, in English, "No middle-class person would want to get involved in these cases." This explanation presumed a connection between the socioeconomic status and occupation of the usual *panch* witnesses the police arranged, and a "limited understanding" and "logic" that reduced the credibility of their testimony. The implication was that by virtue of their class and occupational backgrounds, *panch* witnesses arranged by the police were unreliable and ineffective witnesses.

This view resonates with the connections historians of colonial India have identified in judicial perception between the social status of subaltern witnesses and a lack of respectability and reliability. Historian Radha Kumar examines how the perceived social status of nonstate prosecution witnesses shaped the judicial legibility of witness testimony in police torture cases in colonial and early postcolonial Madras (2022). She observes that respectability, framed along the axes of race, caste, class, and gender, was associated with socially privileged nonstate witnesses. As Kumar puts it, "The words of those with social power have more judicial legibility than those without" (2022: 966).[31]

In the context of the ITPA Special Court in postcolonial India, NGO representatives were especially valuable as *panch* witnesses because of the "respectability" that they, as middle-class professionals working in the field of social service, were perceived to have in ample measure, compared with non-NGO *panch* witnesses. The requirement of "respectability" under Indian procedural law paves the way for NGOs to inhabit the role of the *panch* witness. It provides a different way for NGOs to combine the technical proceduralism of law (here, through their prosecution-focused efforts) and the enactment of virtuosity (Bornstein and Sharma 2016) along with the strategies discussed in Chapter 3. Rescuing women from sites that those implementing the ITPA manifestly recognize as *not* respectable (i.e. where no "middle class person would want to go"), NGO workers fit

searched is situated or of any other locality if no such inhabitant of the said locality is available or is willing to be a witness to the search, to attend and witness the search." Section 15 of the ITPA requires that the police search of a place believed to be a brothel be attended and witnessed by "respectable" individuals, at least one of whom should be a woman.

[31] Kumar points out, further, that the very act of participating in proceedings involving state authority reinforced the perceived respectability, impartiality, knowledgeability, and literacy of socially privileged nonstate witnesses.

the bill of "respectable" witnesses per the moralistic and classist assumptions of Indian legal procedure, in contrast to "laborers and small business owners."

That this perceived "respectability" of NGO *panch* witnesses was predicated on class privilege and education became clear from the NGO witnesses' use of English, the practiced and polished nature of their testimony, and the judicial response to them. As (mostly) English speakers and educated professionals, trained by their NGO's lawyers in the art of testimony, NGO *panch* witnesses became "experts" at testifying. Most of the time, the prosecutor barely needed to ask them any questions. They would launch into the required components of testimony on their own, going into all the required details about the raid, its timing, and its location with minimal prompting. In cases where non-NGO witnesses were Hindi or Marathi speakers, the magistrate usually translated the answers they gave to the prosecutor during the examination-in-chief and to the defense lawyers during the cross examination into Indian English legalese for the stenographer to type up. When NGO witnesses testified, the magistrate usually decided that she did not need to provide these translations, and would ask the stenographer to take down their testimony verbatim. Observing how the magistrate and prosecutor interacted with NGO witnesses in court made it clear that this "respectability" was not only ascribed to NGO representatives by virtue of the work they did, but also developed through their frequent presence in court, and their cultivation of trust and familiarity with the prosecutor and magistrate through these interactions.

I asked one NGO representative who often served as a *panch* witness and testified in court about how she managed to remember all the details from multiple raids that were usually conducted at least a couple of years before the trial began. She told me she wrote everything down after the raid because she knew she would be required to remember and reproduce the relevant details at the trial. Inhabiting the role of prosecution witness thus required additional labor and skills from NGO workers: preserving their memory of the raid, and reproducing the right details in the right format and language in court. Their ability to do so clearly enhanced their respectability and credibility as witnesses.

Along with "respectability," a credible *panch* witness is required to have "independence." This, too, often posed a challenge in ITPA cases at the Special Court. The defense lawyers questioned the "independence" of NGO *panch* witnesses on the basis that they were receiving foreign funds to conduct rescues. They also suggested that NGOs were "habitual" witnesses; that is, the same NGO representatives testified in many cases. It was evident from the judgments I analyzed, and from my observations of the court, that many *panch* witnesses (sometimes police arranged and sometimes NGO workers) were in fact regular witnesses. When accused of being "habitual" *panch* witnesses, non-NGO *panch* witnesses would deny that this was the case, even though it was well known in the court that they had testified in many cases.

As the magistrate explained, no one who was seen to meet the criteria of "respectability" in the eyes of the court was likely to want to testify in ITPA cases, unless they worked for an NGO. The *panch* witnesses the police managed to get were thus, like the decoy customers, those who seemed to have an ulterior motive to help the police. As I learned from talking to NGOs and legal actors at the court, non-NGO *panch witnesses* were rank-and-file members of local political parties, local tea stall owners and other vendors or shopkeepers with small businesses, usually in or near a red-light area.

One woman, who said she ran a tea stall and who reportedly had connections with a local political party, frequently testified in SS Branch cases as a *panch* witness. A police constable told me that she was very "helpful," as she repeated everything that the police asked her to say in court. She was thus perceived as a reliable witness for the prosecution, which was precisely what made the defense lawyers question her independence. This particular witness, a well-dressed Maharashtrian woman with an air of nonchalance, seemed unnerved by the allegations. Once, after being accused of being a "habitual" *panch* by the defense, she declared that this was the last case in which she was testifying at the Special Court. Then she promptly showed up to testify in another case a few days later. The magistrate looked over at the prosecutor and me (the only "audience" in the room), and we exchanged knowing smiles.

Unlike other *panch* witnesses, the defense lawyers' allegation of being "habitual" witnesses did not usually work against NGO workers, given the acknowledged difficulty of finding respectable and independent witnesses in ITPA cases. In a judgment convicting a brothel madam from Kamathipura (Mumbai's red-light area), the magistrate responded to an objection made by the defense that independent witnesses from the locality were not called per the required procedure.

> Defense has taken objection that independent witnesses from locality not called. While evaluating the evidence, the problem of investigating machinery in finding a witness who would act as *panch* witness, more particularly a lady *panch* witness for visiting the brothel also has to be considered. All these practical hurdles should be born in mind, while appreciating the evidence, especially when dealing with the cases involving the raids at brothel.[32]

In judgments where she convicted the accused on the basis of the strong testimony of NGO representatives as prosecution witnesses, the magistrate upheld the credibility of NGO witnesses with the following statement:

> If the NGOs are doing the work against antisocial activities and assisting the police, they cannot be treated either as habitual witness or interested witness. Their evidence cannot be doubted just because they are associated with anti-prostitution campaign.[33]

[32] *The State (Nagpada Police Station, Mumbai) vs. Prabha Shiva Gauda and Jamuna Keshar Gop*, Case no. 136/PW/2008. Judgment of the Metropolitan Magistrate, Special Court for ITPA, 54th Court, Mazgaon, Mumbai dated October 5, 2012, p. 6.

[33] Note the magistrate's use of "antisocial" and "anti-prostitution" here to describe the NGOs' work, instead of anti-trafficking, illustrating my point about the focus of these ITPA cases being prostitution as an immoral activity that poses a threat to the public.

Mumbai has a significant presence of Christian anti-trafficking NGOs (which receive funding from faith-based organizations headquartered in the US), owing to the city's large Indian Christian population.[34] The defense lawyers often used these NGOs' religious background to question whether they were "independent" and therefore credible witnesses for the prosecution.[35] To dismiss these arguments, the magistrate frequently quoted the following observations from a judgment of the Bombay High Court cited by the prosecutor:

> The learned Counsel for the appellants contended that S. works for International Justice Mission which is a Catholic NGO getting funds from US and he has to show some work to get funds.[36] I am not impressed with this contention. Whether he works for a Catholic NGO or for any other NGO is not material. The religion or denomination of the NGO is not material. What is material is the nature of work being done by the NGO … Even though there used to be a police van parked just near Shantabai Chawl,[37] the prostitution was going on and the brothel was being run without any obstruction which indicated that the police were not taking necessary action against such illicit profession.[38] If some NGO takes interest in rescue of the women involved in such profession, there is no reason to doubt the intention of the same.[39]

Significantly, this Bombay High Court judgment was provided to the prosecutor by lawyers from anti-trafficking NGOs. The case it decided centered on a rescue conducted by the International Justice Mission, a US-funded, faith-based NGO. The accused in that case had approached the High Court to appeal against her conviction. The High Court judgment and its use at the Mumbai Special Court demonstrated that a rescue by an anti-trafficking NGO helped to establish the precedent by which the testimony of NGOs was rendered credible. NGOs thus supported the prosecution case at the Special Court not just through witness testimony, but also in this citational manner. An IJM lawyer explained to me that anti-trafficking rescues were a relatively new occurrence in India at the time, so the case law they generated was being built alongside. I learned, therefore, that NGOs were not only providing citations from these precedents to the prosecutor, but also actively creating these precedents through their interventions in the Indian legal system.

34 See footnote 10.

35 Sometimes the defense questioned the independence of non-Christian NGOs as well, on the premise that they received funds for rescuing women.

36 The IJM is a Christian organization, but not Catholic. It was sometimes referred to incorrectly as Catholic by the defense counsel, perhaps with reference to a longer history of missionary activity in Bombay – which was also not exclusively Catholic, but included a range of Christian denominations.

37 Chawls are multistoried, tenement-style, low-income housing buildings in Mumbai.

38 Note the use of "such illicit profession" rather than "trafficking." See also footnote 33.

39 *Narmada Govind Kamble vs. State of Maharashtra*. Criminal Appeal No. 1055 of 2004. Judgment of the Bombay High Court dated December 3, 2009, pp. 17–18.

CONCLUSION

The high conviction rate in ITPA cases at the Special Court has generated considerable global interest in this court as an anti-trafficking success story. As I discovered, however, cases at this court centered on proving the observable transactional aspects of prostitution. Though the court is celebrated in the US-produced and globally circulated *TIP Report* for its "anti-trafficking convictions," the convictions are most often for ITPA offenses around facilitating prostitution.

Drawing upon interviews, ethnographic observations, and an analysis of judgments at the ITPA Special Court, this chapter has shown how the cases tried and adjudicated at this court are always already about prostitution, rather than sex trafficking. Most cases resulted from the Mumbai police's anti-prostitution raids, with rescues involving anti-trafficking NGOs forming a much smaller subset. The high number of convictions were for prostitution-related rather than sex trafficking-related charges. For this reason, while both convictions and "victim-witness" testimony were more likely in cases where NGOs were involved, they were nonetheless possible in police-only cases. A combination of the ITPA's anti-prostitution provisions, and the Mumbai police's strategic adherence to Indian procedural and evidentiary law, meant that elements of sex trafficking were minimally relevant to the investigation and prosecution of these cases. To prove offenses under the ITPA and adhere to Indian procedural laws, the cases brought to the Special Court centered on the observable, transactional aspects of prostitution. They involved a carefully choreographed recording of the raid and its subsequent reenactment in court.

Exploring NGOs' participation in trials at the Special Court, the chapter has shown how NGOs' strategies are driven by their foreign donors' anti-trafficking priorities, but, equally, structured and facilitated by the possibilities and procedures of Indian law. While NGOs have been able to marshal the ITPA toward an anti-trafficking agenda, their participation in the raids and trials rest upon the ITPA's anti-prostitution provisions.

The chapter has also shown how NGOs' participation in ITPA cases at the Mumbai Special Court extends beyond preparing "victim-witnesses" to testify. NGOs strengthen the likelihood of convictions in multiple ways. In a strategy kept under the radar and out of the *TIP Reports* or NGO advocacy material, NGOs draw upon Indian law's existing requirements for "respectable" witnesses and advance their anti-trafficking agenda by serving as prosecution witnesses themselves. Their interventions also contribute to an emerging body of case law legitimizing their role as prosecution witnesses.

As in New Delhi (Chapter 3), NGOs in Mumbai foregrounded the role of "victim-witness" testimony in securing convictions, while Indian legal actors reported that "victim-witnesses" rarely testified or turned hostile. Observing the Special Court and analyzing its judgments revealed very few instances of rescued women testifying in support of the prosecution. In cases involving NGOs, the number of "victim-witnesses" testifying was relatively higher and increased the likelihood of convictions. However, as the chapter has also shown, NGOs were not entirely dependent on "victim-witnesses" testimony to support the prosecution in these cases, as they also provided their own staff as *panch* witnesses and bogus customers.

My analysis also showed that cases could result in convictions despite the absence or hostility of "victim-witnesses" if other forms of evidence and testimony supported the prosecution case. With the cases being primarily about the raid conducted by the police rather than about sex trafficking, "victim-witness" testimony was not indispensable. The forms of material evidence used in these cases, such as condoms and cash, and the medical reports of the rescued women, were deployed to establish that a place was a brothel through deeply moralistic and presumptive connections between cash transactions, condom use, women's bodies, and prostitution. Testimony by other prosecution witnesses to corroborate the police's version of the raid, the recovered material evidence, and rescued women's statements was sometimes deemed sufficient to prove prostitution without "victim-witness" testimony. With origins in India's colonial legal history, the requirement in Indian law that these witnesses be "respectable" and "independent" provided the opening for anti-trafficking NGOs to inhabit this role and participate in these cases.

5

"She Is Not Revealing Anything"

Navigating Inquiries, Documents, and Kinship in a Mumbai Court

The ITPA prescribes judicial inquiries into the "age, character, and antecedents" of women rescued from prostitution and the "suitability, capacity, or genuineness" of their kin to take charge of them (even for adult women).[1] This inquiry process seeks details about the backgrounds of rescued women and how they came to be in the sex trade. Based on this information, judicial magistrates make decisions about the women's custody – either sending them back to their families or to a state-run shelter, and about their economic rehabilitation through livelihood skills training programs.[2] It is not the consent or preferences of rescued adult women, but the evaluations judicial magistrates make in these inquiries that determine where they are sent and, to some extent, for how long.[3]

At the Mumbai Special Court, the magistrate conducted these inquiries in her chambers. Per the ITPA,[4] a committee including "respectable" and "experienced" women social welfare workers in the field of suppression of immoral traffic is to assist the magistrate in this inquiry process.[5] Like rescues, inquiries are another process where the ITPA demarcates a role for nonstate actors in its implementation, into which NGOs have smoothly stepped.

During my fieldwork in Mumbai, I met with members of a progressive feminist group who wondered why only anti-trafficking NGOs and not sex worker rights

1 Section 17(2).

2 Both discussed in Chapter 6.

3 The duration of time the rescued women whose inquiries were conducted at the Mumbai Special Court eventually spent at the shelter usually had more to do with the arbitrariness and contingencies of bureaucratic procedures than with the content of the judicial orders after inquiry. But at some other courts around Mumbai, vaguely worded inquiry orders contributed to prolonging women's stay at shelters, as I discuss in Chapter 6.

4 Section 17 (5).

5 From what I observed in New Delhi and Mumbai, when rescued women were brought to regular magistrate's courts *not* set up as Special ITPA Courts for these inquiries, only the magistrate was involved, and the practice of involving "social welfare workers" was not followed. The ITPA suggests, but does not require, the involvement of nonstate social workers. The Special Court magistrate's decision to involve NGOs reflects the significant NGO presence in Mumbai and their role both in the governance of prostitution in the city and in anti-trafficking efforts.

groups or women's groups like theirs were asked to assist with inquiries. As we discovered while poring over the clauses of the ITPA together, the statute specifically indicates that the social welfare workers who may be called for assistance should have experience "in the field of suppression of immoral traffic in persons." A second reason I discerned was that the anti-trafficking NGOs were providing rehabilitation programs for rescued women (see Chapter 6) and helping to trace the women's homes and families through their networks in other states (see Chapters 2, 3, and 6). With economic rehabilitation and women's restoration to their families being prescribed by the ITPA, and anti-trafficking NGOs being the organizations providing those services, they were the ones the magistrate found useful to call upon to assist with the inquiry process.

At the Mumbai Special Court, two anti-trafficking NGOs helped the magistrate with inquiries. One was a Christian organization, receiving funds from US faith-based groups, and the other–not a faith-based organization — also received foreign funds (from smaller US donors, some European funding, and the Japanese agency mentioned in previous chapters). The magistrate explained to me that to avoid conflict of interest, these were not the same NGOs involved in the rescues that led to the cases being prosecuted in the courtroom (Chapter 4). Both the NGOs that assisted with the inquiries held in the magistrate's chambers worked primarily on postrescue "after care" interventions for rescued women. They provided counseling services at the state-run protective home and economic rehabilitation programs for livelihood skills. Nevertheless, these NGOs brought an anti-trafficking framework to the inquiry process; a process which otherwise exemplifies how the ITPA is, in both letter and implementation, primarily an anti-prostitution statute.

As for the rescued women brought in for inquiries, only some provided accounts reflecting elements of trafficking and/or forced prostitution. Resonating with narratives rescued women provided at the other sites and processes I have discussed in this book, several women said they entered the sex trade due to some combination of *marzi* (choice) and *majboori* (compulsion), often emphasizing that they did sex work to feed their families. A third set of women, who worked in bars, massage parlors, and beauty salons, maintained that they had never engaged in prostitution at all. They said the police had rounded them up on false pretexts when the managers of the establishments where they worked did not fill the police's pockets as part of regular (and illegal) *haftas* or commissions. However, the police who brought the women to the court for inquiries insisted that they had been engaged in prostitution. The magistrate and NGO workers conducting the inquiries largely presumed that the women were indeed involved in prostitution, and were being sexually and economically exploited. If the women denied either being trafficked or being involved in prostitution, the inquiry committee usually read these denials as lies, and urged the women to reveal the "truth" they were presumed to be hiding.

Inquiries are a key site and process where ambivalent constructions of victimhood are produced, negotiated, and resisted, and decisions about rescued women's custody and rehabilitation are made and contested. At the Mumbai Special Court, inquiries were carried out in the relatively intimate and interactive space of the magistrate's chambers, in contrast to the trials held in the adjoining courtroom. Though imbued with the aura and formal ritualism of judicial authority, inquiries provided insights into a realm in which NGO representatives participate as quasi-judicial actors.

Focusing on inquiries, this chapter illuminates the roles played by women judges and NGO workers in a postcolonial legal regime combining agendas of state paternalism, moral reform, sexual humanitarianism, and immigration control. In Foucauldian terms, inquiries exemplify the intersection of a disciplinary purpose, seeking to reform "fallen" women and lead them to a more "decent" life, and a governmental purpose aimed at the "care and protection" of those rescued from prostitution.[6] In implementing the ITPA, inquiries combine deeply gendered and moralistic presumptions and sociopolitical suspicions about rescued women's denials of trafficking, prostitution, and possible Bangladeshi identity.

The ITPA is framed by two inextricably entangled moral concerns – around sexual exploitation and around the seductive propensities of women soliciting sex. This chapter will show how those conducting inquiries evince this moral ambivalence toward prostitution. In their interactions with rescued women, whom they labeled as "victims," those conducting inquiries framed their concerns around both sexual and economic exploitation, and the women's perceived departures from gendered familial roles and responsibilities. Bangladeshi women were further targeted by, and navigated, a culture of suspicion and regime of documentation that maps anti-immigrant sentiments and imperatives onto anti-prostitution interventions.

The chapter examines the concerns and frameworks of those conducting inquiries, and how rescued women respond to them. It explores how members of the inquiry committee construct complicated figures of victimhood from narratives and documents fraught with uncertainties, perceived discrepancies, and suspected falsehoods. It tracks how two contrasting versions of victimhood – the "genuine" victim and the "lying" victim – are assumed and produced in response to the narratives of rescued women and their relatives, medico-legal reports, and identity documents. It illustrates how inquiries combine questioning, "counseling," advice, admonition, and evaluations of identity and kinship, and how they are framed both by accusations of immorality and by concerns about victimhood.

Multiple women with different accounts of their identities and of why (or whether) they entered the sex trade were brought to the committee for inquiries. Most often, they ended up in the same shelter for protective custody,[7] until their families or

6 In conversation with Foucauldian sociolegal scholars, I examine this imbrication of disciplinary and governmental power further in Chapter 6.

7 See Chapter 6.

guardians could come to court,[8] provide proof of their identities and relationships, and claim their custody. The chapter examines how they negotiated the inquiry process and the contested productions of victimhood through which they were perceived, addressed, and processed. It follows how they responded with narratives about poverty and illness, seeking to be absolved of what they perceived as arrest rather than rescue. Through the very framework of kinship obligations and patriarchal norms deployed to reproach them, several women framed themselves as morally responsible actors who did sex work owing to familial and financial needs.

INQUIRIES AT THE SPECIAL COURT

The Site and the Process

At the Mumbai Special Court, the inquiry process was both spatially and temporally separate from the trial process.[9] It was conducted in the judicial magistrate's chambers, adjacent to the courtroom, located off a corridor behind it. Though a more intimate, interactive space than the courtroom, the magistrate's chambers were nonetheless imbued with an aura of postcolonial legal ritualism and judicial authority. The magistrate was escorted in and out of her chambers by a member of the court staff announcing her arrival with an emphatic hush to silence anyone around. Anyone entering the magistrate's chambers, like anyone entering the courtroom, was expected to bow and request her permission to enter. The magistrate's clothes, too, signified her legal authority. She usually took off the gown she wore while on the courtroom dais once she was in her chambers, but continued to wear a black waistcoat over her white *churidar-kurta* to indicate her judicial identity and authority.[10]

The inquiry process was also shaped by the social status of the inquiry committee members. In her ethnography of domestic violence hearings in a family court in Hawai'i, Sally Merry observes that authority derives not only from the legal status, but also the social status (including features of class, gender, language, and race) of those who pronounce judgments (1994: 36). In anti-prostitution interventions in India, class intersects with caste and gender,[11] to shape what anthropologist Heather Dell terms "hierarchies of femininity" (1999). Indeed, such hierarchies exist beyond the context of prostitution to interventions in other

[8] Or could be "traced" with police and NGO assistance if they were from other states in India outside Maharashtra.

[9] The accounts provided by rescued women during inquiries do not constitute evidence against the accused in the trials. However, the fact that they were brought before the magistrate for inquiries was sometimes used by the prosecution in the trial to prove that they had been rescued. This strategy was used to counter the defense lawyers' attempts to deny that the women were rescued in the first place.

[10] The *churidar-kurta* consists of a long shirt worn with slim, gathered pants.

[11] For discussions of the overlap between caste and class, see, for example, Deshpande (2014); Jodhka (2017).

areas of women's rights and gender justice, such as domestic violence. In her ethnography with counselors working with women impacted by domestic violence in north India, Julia Kowalski describes hierarchies of class and status shaping the assumption that educated women can best address the needs of vulnerable women within institutional settings (2023: 109). In the context of prostitution, these hierarchies have long been mobilized to maintain distinctions between "respectable" and "fallen" women. Dell discusses how elite Bengali women's efforts to rescue and rehabilitate sex workers in early twentieth-century Calcutta were motivated by a need to define their own respectability vis-à-vis poor, unfortunate "fallen" women "in need of maternal intervention from above," whom they sought to introduce to a more "dignified" life (1999: 209).

At the Mumbai Special Court, "hierarchies of femininity" pervaded interactions between those conducting the inquiries and the women brought in for inquiries. The magistrate and NGO workers were from a more privileged, "respectable," middle-class social stratum than the rescued women,[12] who were (mostly) from impoverished rural backgrounds or lower middle-class and working-class urban backgrounds. The occupation, dress, comportment, and speech of the magistrate and NGO workers marked their social status as different from that of the women brought before them. The caste or religious identities of the magistrate or NGO workers involved in inquiries, or of the rescued women, were not explicitly mentioned during the inquiries.[13] However, those conducting inquiries occasionally wore accoutrements that indexed prevalent norms of gendered social respectability. The magistrate sometimes wore signs of religious and cultural identification such as a flower in her hair during Maharashtrian Hindu religious festivals. Many of the NGO workers were Christians, a significant minority population in Mumbai, but did not always display overt religious symbols. I occasionally noticed a Hindu NGO worker wearing *sindoor*, a red *bindi*, or *mangal sutra*,[14] traditional symbols worn by married Hindu women. Some Christian NGO workers wore small, often barely noticeable, crosses. Combined with their judicial (or in the case of NGO workers quasi-judicial) authority, these accoutrements contributed to their overall appearance and comportment as "respectable," educated, middle-class women.

At the Special Court, rescued women were brought in for inquiries by the police, sometimes accompanied by NGO representatives, within three weeks of their rescue as prescribed by the ITPA. Until the magistrate was available, the women waited in the corridor outside her chamber. Their arrival was not usually by appointment. Given the suddenness of rescues and the multiplicity of postrescue

12 See my discussion of "middle-classness" in the Introduction, and NGO "respectability" in Chapter 4.

13 In a few instances, the women referenced their religious identities while positioning themselves as pious and truthful (see the section on Navigating Inquiries).

14 A mark made on the forehead with red powder, a round red sticker worn on the forehead, and a specific type of necklace.

procedures, the magistrate's office was usually only informed the same day of the women's arrival for inquiries. Arriving in the late mornings, they waited till afternoon when the magistrate was available to conduct inquiries after the trial proceedings. In the meanwhile, the court clerk called the NGOs empaneled by the magistrate to send representatives to assist with the inquiries. Sometimes, if the magistrate had enough notice, the NGO representative/s would arrive in the late morning and start the inquiries while she was presiding over the court. The unpredictability around when inquiries would take place posed a logistical challenge in my research. It was next to impossible to know about them in advance and plan to attend them. Usually, the only way to find out was to hang out around the court after the trial proceedings, and check with the court clerk about whether any inquiries were likely to happen.

The court staff, magistrate, and NGO representatives referred to the rescued women as "girls," an appellation I frequently heard at other sites and processes as well. For the most part, the women brought for these inquiries at the Special Court were adults. If they did not have government-issued documents of age proof, the age verification process was sometimes done prior to the inquiry,[15] though often not completed till later.[16] Those deemed to be minors were taken instead to a Child Welfare Committee and not a magistrate's court, as explained in Chapter 2. The use of "girls" instead of "women" by those conducting inquiries did not signal their actual age, but an infantilization of what was perceived as rescued women's propensity to be led into immorality,

When the magistrate was ready to speak with them, the women were ushered into her chamber one by one and asked to sit opposite her at her large desk and answer questions. Most of the time, there was more than one woman per rescue. Depending on the number of women brought before her, the magistrate either did the inquiry herself or asked an NGO representative to speak with some while she spoke to the rest. There was a smaller room off the magistrate's chamber where the NGO representatives conducted inquiries. The magistrate usually made sure to conduct the inquiry with the woman whom the police found with the bogus customer herself.[17] She explained to me that this was the woman in each group either most likely to tell the "truth" or the most easily persuaded to admit it. She said this was because she could confront this woman with the police's claim that the accused provided her to the bogus customer for prostitution.

I observed and participated in fifteen sets of inquiries, involving approximately fifty women over five months (see Table 5.1).[18] Of these, four sets of women said they had been forced into prostitution. Three sets of women, and one woman from a

[15] Discussed in Chapter 2.

[16] However, the completion of the process in Mumbai seemed much faster than what I had observed in New Delhi (Chapter 2).

[17] Discussed in Chapter 4.

[18] As explained, most inquiries involved multiple women.

TABLE 5.1 *Groups of rescued women brought in for inquiries to the Mumbai Special Court.*

Total	Trafficked into sex work	Voluntary sex workers	Beauty salon	Massage parlor	Bar
15 groups	4 groups	3 groups	4 groups	3 groups	1 group

group which included trafficked women, articulated a version of *marzi* or choice in their narratives. They explained that they did sex work due to financial need, either because they had dependent kin such as elderly parents or children, or because they had no kin to support them. Four sets of women worked in a beauty salon. Most of them, with the exception of two or three, denied any involvement in prostitution at all. Three sets of women worked in a massage parlor, and again only two or three women acknowledged doing sex work. One set of women said they were servers at a beer bar, and again had nothing to do with prostitution.

During inquiries, the questions and assessments were based on a format designed by the magistrate (see Figure 5.1). In eliciting answers to these seemingly factual questions, the magistrate and NGO representatives placed greater reliance on their subjective assessments of appearances, character, or relationships than on the verbal answers and documents that rescued women and their relatives provided. They drew upon moral assumptions and concerns about prostitution and its impact on families and kin, paternalism toward impoverished women deemed vulnerable to immorality and sexual exploitation, and suspicion around their denials of trafficking, prostitution, and Bangladeshi identity. The inquiry committee's assessments and decisions were based on these intersecting gendered, moral, and sociopolitical frameworks.

As I found, those conducting inquiries assessed rescued women in two ways: either as "genuine" victims who readily provided accounts of being forced into prostitution or "lying" or unwilling victims who did not verbally "reveal anything" about engaging in prostitution, disputing police accounts that they were found "half-naked" with the bogus customer.[19] When women either denied being forced into prostitution or being involved in it at all, those conducting inquiries employed various tactics to elicit the "truth" that they believed the women were hiding. As I will show, the inquiry process, though explained to the women as *not* punitive (through reassuring phrases such as "you are not in trouble"), often entailed aggressive questioning tactics, and was permeated by an atmosphere of suspicion and accusation.

Beyond efforts to elicit the "truth" the women were assumed to be hiding, inquiries were always already about reform and moral correction, encouraging and convincing rescued women to leave the sex trade. Those conducting inquiries

[19] Discussed in Chapter 4.

Name :- Victim No.

Age :-

Education :-

Occup.

Previous Address:-

Present Address:

Income

Marital Status : Married /unmarried:-

Children : Son:- Daughter :

Husband :-

Family :-

Father :-

Mother :-

Sister :-

Brother:-

Other :-

Ready to work if work is provided :- Yes /No.

Want to take up Vocational Training

at Rescue Home : Yes /No

Want to go to Native :- Yes /No.

Address of Native Place Yes /No.

FIGURE 5.1 Format used by the magistrate and committee members during the inquiry process (document on file with author).

envisioned rescued women's vulnerability and immorality as twinned afflictions, to be addressed through advice and admonition. All rescued women were instructed, both verbally and in writing, to find alternative, "respectable" forms of income. The magistrate and NGO representatives often described the "vulnerability" of all women who entered the sex trade, a term by which they alluded to a combination of infantilized innocence, economic need, difficult familial circumstances, and a fall into immorality. The following quote is typical of the orders drafted after inquiries:

> No one has come to claim custody of victim … She is too vulnerable. She is in need of care and protection and training to help her lead dignified life.

Mobilizing their legal authority and social status of gendered respectability, those conducting inquiries did not merely question the women brought before them, but simultaneously "counseled" and censured them to lead a "dignified life." When asking the women if they would be willing to participate in livelihood training programs (per the format in Figure 5.1), NGO members conducting inquiries would use language such as, "*Izzat se kaam karogi?*" ("Will you do honorable work?").

Inquiries were not only intended to "counsel," censure, and assist "vulnerable" women, but also to reconstitute "normal" families or address their deviations from a normative ideal. Those conducting inquiries placed the responsibility for rescued women's (presumed) exploitation partly with their families, for not exercising the requisite care and control to prevent the moral transgressions of prostitution. They sought to extract the "truth" about prostitution from rescued women by emphasizing their identities as wives, mothers, sisters, and daughters, whose immorality had placed their family honor in peril.

Observing Inquiries

After a couple of months of observing the Special Court, I asked the magistrate if I could also observe the inquiries in her chambers. By that point, the magistrate had seen me observing the court nearly every day. She was generous with her time, answering my questions about case patterns and ITPA provisions during our conversations in her chambers. Though the caseload at the court kept her extremely busy, she took an interest in my research beyond the court. Once, when we were discussing a section of the ITPA according to which a rescued woman cannot be released to the custody of someone from a different religion,[20] I pondered aloud about whether this was shaped by concerns around abducted women during the Partition of India. I explained the overlap I had noticed between concerns around prostitution and abducted women while studying the legislative debates on the ITPA from 1956.[21] The magistrate was interested in knowing more about some of

[20] Section 17 (4)(b).

[21] I explore this point further in Chapter 6.

these insights, and even asked me to send her the debates that I had accessed from the archives. I sensed that it was now evident to her that I wanted to understand not just the court, but also the ITPA, and the Indian sociolegal context more broadly.

When I sensed that we had established a good rapport, I asked the magistrate if I could observe inquiries in her chambers. I was apprehensive that this might not work out, as I had not been able to observe in camera proceedings at the court. I was pleased and grateful that the magistrate did grant me permission to observe inquiries, her only condition being that I sit quietly at the back of the room and take notes, as I did in court. I assured her that I would make myself as unobtrusive as possible.

However, my research access across multiple field sites often came with the expectation of assistance. Inquiries were no exception. Sometimes, when the police brought rescued women for inquiries at very short notice and no NGO representative was able to come, the magistrate, seeing me sitting in court, would ask me if *I* could begin the inquiries until she became available. Just as I became a default counselor to help the NGO, police, and prosecutors (Chapters 2–4), being perceived as "respectable,"[22] and, for good measure, available, made me a fallback option to assist with inquiries when NGO members were unavailable.

During my fieldwork at the court, I was more than willing to provide assistance in exchange for research access. However, conducting inquiries myself was a far more interventionist role than I had envisaged, as my reports would be used by the magistrate to draft orders for the women's custody and rehabilitation. This presented ethical dilemmas that analyzing judgments for the court in exchange for access to them (Chapter 4) did not. I had to weigh participating in a deeply moralistic and hierarchical form of interaction against potentially jeopardizing my research at the court. Concerned that refusing to conduct inquiries, a form of assistance the magistrate sought from me, could negatively impact my access and a deeply valued research relationship, I agreed to help. Overall, I observed seven sets of inquiries (each set involving three or more rescued women) conducted by the magistrate and NGO workers, and assisted the magistrate with eight inquiries myself.

Though I could not resolve the ethical issues that conducting inquiries presented entirely, I navigated them by sticking to the provided questions (Figure 5.1) and noting down the answers as the women provided them to me, which I later compiled into a report for the magistrate. I did not approach my interactions with the women through the potent amalgam of suspicion, accusation, admonition, "counseling," and censure that suffused the inquiries I observed. However, my access to inquiries ended up being both contentious and short-lived, for reasons worth explaining before I delve into inquiries themselves.

Just as I was not the only researcher observing trials at the Special Court, I was not the only researcher observing inquiries in the magistrate's chambers. Saie

[22] See my discussion of "respectability" in the Introduction.

Shetye, an MPhil student researching the same court (Chapter 4) who also wanted to observe inquiries and also had the appurtenances of gendered respectability, was sometimes asked to conduct them as well. Saie had previously worked for an anti-trafficking NGO, was local to Mumbai, spoke both Hindi and Marathi, and spent several months observing the court, continuing her research after I had left. All of this positioned her well – indeed, better than me – to conduct inquiries. When asked to help with inquiries we took turns, and were not usually in the magistrate's chambers at the same time, unless the group of rescued women was so large that we were both needed.

One day, however, our access to inquiries as researchers/stand-in inquiry committee members was impacted by the arrival of yet another researcher. As already evident from the Japanese visitors (Chapter 4), the Special Court's frequent mention in the US *TIP Report* meant that it had generated considerable global interest. I was not surprised to see foreign visitors in the courtroom, a public place. But I was surprised one day when I went to observe inquiries in the magistrate's chambers and saw a Caucasian woman there for the same purpose.

I initially assumed that she worked for a funding agency supporting one of the NGOs at the court. However, I learned from the business card she handed me that she was a Canadian filmmaker. She told me later that she had connected with an anti-trafficking NGO in Mumbai as she was conducting research for a film about sex trafficking in India. She had accompanied the NGO's lawyer to the Special Court and asked to observe the inquiries to understand the stories of trafficked women. She didn't seem to have had any trouble gaining this access, probably due to a combination of her status as a foreign (moreover, white) visitor connected to the global anti-trafficking interest in the court and the long-standing relationship the NGO she accompanied had with the court. As a result, there were three of us in the room observing inquiries that day – myself, the Canadian filmmaker, and the NGO lawyer she came with (who usually only appeared in court and did not conduct inquiries).

It was this filmmaker's first time in India. She was in Mumbai for a short visit. Understandably, she seemed a bit bewildered and was trying to get her bearings. She did not speak Hindi (the language the inquiries were usually conducted in), so after I introduced myself, she asked if I could help translate the proceedings for her. I was willing to help, having, after all, myself benefited from my fellow researcher Saie's translation assistance from Marathi (Chapter 4). Concerned that translating during the inquiry proceedings would be disruptive, I explained that it would not be appropriate to talk during the inquiries, but offered that she could look at my notes as I wrote them down. As I scribbled fast, occasionally writing in Hindi for the sake of speed, my notes provided her a partial translation at best. During breaks between inquiries, the NGO lawyer also gave her brief summaries of what the women had said.

I do not know what (if any) conditions the magistrate or court staff had laid down for the filmmaker while granting her research access. When rescued women came in for inquiries that day, she smiled and made eye contact with them. Perhaps, with her geopolitical and racial privilege, she was not instructed to "sit quietly" as I was. Or perhaps she was, but did not realize how visibly she was responding to the interactions we were observing.

The filmmaker's overt attentiveness created a more obvious and different sort of "audience" than usual in inquiries. The group of women who came in seemed distracted by her presence as a white foreign visitor, and hyperaware that she was listening to them. Each time she smiled at them or reacted to something they said, they would glance at me and the NGO lawyer, trying to gauge our reactions.

I had not sensed this hyperawareness during the times I observed inquiries and sat in the back taking notes. Being Indian, Saie and I passed as court staff, lawyers, or NGO workers observing or conducting inquiries, not outsiders taking interest in the women's stories. But also, having cautiously navigated access to inquiries, and being mindful that this was a judicial process, we made an effort to be unobtrusive. The Canadian filmmaker, on the other hand, was not only visibly an outsider to the court, but also responded overtly to the women's stories with her eye contact and nods and smiles. I do not mean to suggest that she was deliberately disruptive, nor to argue that only Indian researchers should be allowed to access such sites, nor that all it takes to "blend in" is to be phenotypically Indian. But as a foreign visitor new to these proceedings, the filmmaker's presence had an unsettling impact on the inquiry we observed that day. I will return to that inquiry and discuss its specifics in the section on "lying" victims. For now, I draw upon it to explain how the presence of multiple observers that day, and the Canadian filmmaker in particular, ended up disrupting my future access to inquiries.

After this incident, I was only allowed to observe one more inquiry. Deepa, the court clerk, told me that the inquiry committee was concerned that the presence of too many people in the room had made the women "not open up" and "not reveal anything." She added that some NGO members of the committee had complained about this. I told Deepa that had I known there would be others, I would have skipped attending that inquiry myself to avoid crowding the room. She looked at me sympathetically and said, in English,

> See, you are different. I know you are doing your PhD. You are always sitting there like a statue, same in court also. But that day you saw no, that American lady had come ... how many people were in the room.[23]

Thereafter, the only times Saie or I were allowed access were when no NGO representative was available and the magistrate asked one of us to conduct the inquiries. As I learned through this experience, multiple researchers visiting the

[23] "American lady" refers to the Canadian filmmaker.

court, given the considerable global interest in it, could be both helpful and disruptive for inquiries. On the one hand, they could provide easily available assistance. On the other hand, they could disrupt the proceedings by crowding the room and making their presence felt. The magistrate and the court staff found a strategy to make the most of what researchers could offer and avoid the disruptions they could cause.

Saie and I continued to observe the courtroom proceedings and conduct inquiries when requested. The Canadian filmmaker did not return during the remaining six months that I observed the court. Soon after her visit to observe inquiries, the New Delhi gang-rape incident led to a national and global furor around sexual violence in India.[24] I learned later from the NGO lawyer who had accompanied her that the filmmaker then shifted her focus to that issue.

Disappointed and concerned at the loss of my carefully negotiated access to inquiries, I wanted to make sure I had not caused offense or done something wrong. I summoned the courage to ask the magistrate about this the next time she invited me to have tea in her chambers and we chatted about my research and the court. I told her I was aware that the inquiries incident had caused concerns and apologized if I had inadvertently contributed to the problem. All she said in reply, with no change in her usual demeanor, was that my presence was not a problem, because I "sat quietly," but "there shouldn't be too many people." These conversations made it clear that while my own presence that day certainly added to the crowd, the loss of access owed as much to one of the observers not "sitting quietly."

Eventually, however, my access to inquiries stopped completely. By late April 2013, when the court was shifted to another court complex (see Chapter 4), I was no longer asked to do inquiries. Though the reasons were never entirely clear, I gauged that they were more to do with me this time. Because I was interested in listening to the women's accounts beyond the purpose of the inquiry, I was not efficient at conducting inquiries, unlike the actual committee members. Deepa, the court clerk, let me know in no uncertain terms that I was taking too much time to do inquiries. "See, take it in short, no!" Deepa reprimanded me in her Bombay English. "You are taking one hour per girl. It's just too much. Wrap it up quickly, no!" The magistrate did not voice these concerns to me herself, perhaps to avoid offending me. It was certainly true that I took longer than the magistrate and NGO representatives to speak with the women, because my interest in the court was primarily ethnographic. I would ask the required questions, but didn't stop the women from telling me other things. Deepa implied that this was a waste of time for the court – a different kind of disruption than the one caused by the Canadian filmmaker not "sitting quietly," but a disruption nonetheless.

24 See explanation in Chapter 1, footnote 29.

Apart from being seen as inefficient, I was probably also seen as ineffective – not making enough of an effort to discern the "truth" that rescued women were assumed to be hiding. Though the trafficked women I spoke to shared details with me of how they had been trafficked and forced into prostitution, most women who had been "rescued" from beauty salons, massage parlors and bars denied being involved in prostitution *tout court*. I did not accuse them of lying or try to convince them to reveal an assumed "truth." I noted down what they were telling me, instead of trying to get them to reveal that they were actually trafficked and/or involved in prostitution. I did not employ the modes of accusation and admonishment that I had observed the inquiry committee use. Though no one explicitly told me this, I sensed that like my approach to "counseling" (Chapter 4), my "neutral" approach to inquiries was therefore deemed ineffective. I was not meeting the unstated purpose of inquiries – getting the women to admit that they were forced into prostitution, or at the very least that they were involved in it.

After my fieldwork, I often reflected upon my participation in inquiries, the incident involving the Canadian filmmaker, and the eventual loss of research access. I found resonance with anthropologist Miriam Ticktin's insights into her presence while observing interactions between social workers and immigrants seeking a "humanitarian exception" for illness in French immigration law (2011). Ticktin discusses how the head social worker felt that the immigrant patients who came to apply for papers perceived Ticktin, the anthropologist, as "listening" and "attentive." Despite Ticktin not asking the applicants questions, something in her body language conveyed a "different kind of listening" that encouraged them to talk more than the social worker thought was needed to get the job done (2011: 106–107). The social worker, while acknowledging that Ticktin was merely trying to observe the interactions, was concerned that the applicants talked excessively in Ticktin's presence. Like the inquiries I conducted at the Mumbai Special Court, this was disruptive to the process, as the interactions took too much time.

Ticktin's insights made me think about how the Canadian filmmaker and I both "listened differently" than the inquiry committee. In doing so, we both impacted inquiries in contrasting but also overlapping ways. She did not "sit quietly," while I did my best to be unobtrusive. Her overt attentiveness, displayed through her body language, was therefore more disruptive than my deliberately quieter presence. Yet together, she and I and the NGO lawyer crowded the room. Our presence as researchers was collectively disruptive. But we were also different in terms of what we could offer the court as researchers. She was an outsider, who could, perhaps, bring more global recognition to the court's work. I was Indian, spoke Hindi, appeared "respectable," and was constantly available. I could, therefore, be helpful to the court's daily functioning with my time and labor. When I observed inquiries conducted by others, I "listened differently" than they did, but masked it by "sitting quietly." When I conducted inquiries myself, however, the "different listening" impacted the way I asked questions, the space I provided the women to narrate their accounts, and the time these interactions took. When called upon to help, the difference between my approach and that of the inquiry committee members was probably noticeable, with mine being seen as inefficient and ineffective.

CONSTRUCTIONS OF VICTIMHOOD

"Genuine" Victims

During a preliminary visit to the Special Court to discuss my proposed research, I was sitting across from the magistrate's predecessor in the same chambers.[25] The police arrived with a girl from Karnataka (a state in southern India) who had been recently rescued, for inquiry. The magistrate asked her staff to send the girl in and to find a Kannada translator.[26] She allowed me to sit in the back and observe the inquiry.

This girl, Latha, looked young, possibly in her late teens. Dressed simply in a long blue *kurta* and *salwar*, she was quiet and looked wary. Until the translator could be arranged, the magistrate used a combination of Hindi and hand gestures to ask Latha when she came to Mumbai and who brought her there. Latha replied that a woman named "Laxmi Amma" ("Mother Laxmi") had brought her to Mumbai eight months back and sold her to the accused brothel owner. Later, with the help of the translator, Latha recalled what she could about the route through which she was brought to Mumbai, but she didn't know many details. She provided information about her home and family in Karnataka, which the magistrate noted down. The magistrate went on to ask Latha if she knew who the accused brothel owner was. Latha nodded in recognition. The magistrate had told me earlier that the accused brothel owner was a frequent offender who repeatedly managed to get out of police custody on bail. She explained, having adjudicated several cases against her, that there was usually not enough evidence against this brothel owner.

After Latha had left, the magistrate looked at me and said, pointedly, "this girl is clearly a victim, she is not into this for money … you can tell by looking at her." She added that from her experience conducting inquiries, she knew that impoverished girls from Karnataka who were rescued in Mumbai tended to be victims of trafficking and told similar stories. She also explained that "Laxmi Amma" was a common name she had seen traffickers from southern India adopt. Many women from Andhra Pradesh or Karnataka said they had been brought to Mumbai by someone

[25] As this was during an earlier visit, the magistrate presiding over the court was different from the magistrate whose work I primarily discuss in this book.

[26] The language spoken in the state of Karnataka.

named "Laxmi Amma." The magistrate said this was likely to be an adopted name, not necessarily the same person in all cases.[27]

During the magistrate's brief interaction with Latha, her concern and empathy were evident, in stark contrast to the treatment of Mamta in Chapter 2 by the Child Welfare Committee (CWC). However, I was struck by the assumptions that were made without many questions being asked. For instance, the magistrate did not explicitly ask Latha whether she was forced or deceived into selling sex. Her perceptions of Latha's simple clothing, nervous demeanor, quiet manner, linguistic and geographical background, and her knowledge about the accused brothel owner had led her to presume that Latha was a victim of trafficking. I was struck, too, by the brief amount of time and minimal amount of questioning it took for the magistrate to come to this conclusion. The questions asked had mainly been factual – about how Latha came to Mumbai and with whom, and details about her home and family. The magistrate's plan was to send Latha to a shelter for protective custody until she could be sent back to her parents in Karnataka.

The manner in which the magistrate assessed and determined Latha's victimhood and the mostly factual format of this inquiry were a marked contrast to the specters of suspicion and modes of accusation that framed inquiries with women who said they did sex work willingly or maintained that they were not even involved in prostitution. Though the same format was used (Figure 5.1), the way Latha, deemed a "genuine victim," was treated was starkly different from the tenor of interactions in those cases.

Before I discuss the latter set of inquiries, it is worth explaining that, like Latha, several women did provide accounts of trafficking during inquiries — that is, accounts of being forced, abducted, or deceptively recruited to the sex trade. Four groups of women out of the fifteen whose inquiries I observed and conducted said they had been trafficked. Among the eight inquiries I conducted myself, two sets of women gave detailed accounts of being trafficked (see Table 5.1). This indicates that a small subset of women who came for inquiries said they were trafficked. The remaining groups either indicated a complex interplay of choice, financial need, and familial obligation shaping their decisions to do sex work, or denied any involvement in prostitution whatsoever.

In one of the inquiries I conducted during my longer-term fieldwork at the Special Court, Reshma, a thirty-year-old woman from Bangalore, was a single mother who worked at a garment factory there. She told me that a smooth-talking man had befriended her at a bus stop, and brought her a cup of tea which must have been spiked, because she felt dizzy and lost consciousness soon after. When she awoke, she found herself on a bus to Mumbai, where the man handed her over to a woman. This woman took her to Bhandup,[28] and forced her into

[27] As I mentioned in Chapter 3, trafficked women from West Bengal similarly named a ubiquitous "Raju."

[28] A suburban area to the east of Mumbai.

prostitution by beating her and threatening to have her face flashed on TV as a woman of ill repute if she did not have sex with customers. Reshma was literally locked up at the brothel and not allowed to call friends and relatives. She tried to run away, but was stopped each time.

Joya, a Bengali woman in her late twenties, was also rescued by the police and a prominent Christian anti-trafficking NGO at the same time as Reshma. Also a single mother, Joya supported her child by doing domestic work. The elements of trafficking in her account, from the man at the bus stop to the woman in Mumbai, to being forcibly detained and made to have sex with customers, resonated almost entirely with Reshma's account. Joya went on to tell me how she (like the women in New Delhi discussed in Chapters 2 and 3) shared her plight with a customer, who alerted the police about her, leading to her rescue.

In yet another inquiry, I spoke with a group of three Bangladeshi girls who had been trafficked and then escaped on their own. All three seemed to be minors, so the magistrate was surprised they had not been sent to the CWC.[29] Going by their youthful appearance (they were all in pigtails), simple attire, and short stature, the magistrate immediately assessed that this was a trafficking case. She instructed me to ask them for details about the route through which they were brought, who brought them, and so on, so she could order the police to investigate accordingly.[30]

The Bangladeshi girls said they were between fifteen and seventeen years old. They had worked long hours in garment factories in Bangladesh, where they folded and packed T-shirts for multinational companies, since they were twelve or thirteen years old. The wages were very low, around 2,000 Bangladeshi Taka ($17) a month, and they needed to earn more to support themselves and their families. They said they were brought to India by agents on the pretext of employment as domestic workers, with a false promise of high salaries. The girls knew they were coming to India, but not that they would be forced into prostitution. They arrived in Mumbai after a complicated, risky, undocumented border-crossing to India from Bangladesh, and were then taken to different hotels and forced into prostitution. They managed to run away from a man who was taking them to a different location within Mumbai. At the train station, they asked him to get them something to drink. When he turned his back, they climbed onto an arriving train and sought help from a girl already on it. This girl advised them to contact the railway police, who eventually came to their assistance.

[29] The inspector said he had been directed to bring the girls to the court to be instructed about further action to be taken. The magistrate went on to write an order directing the police to take the girls to the CWC.

[30] Though the information provided in inquiries could not be used in the trial of the accused, the magistrate occasionally used it to order the police to arrest the persons named by trafficked women and investigate their role in "procuring" or "inducing" the women into prostitution, per Section 5 of the ITPA.

In each of these cases, I noted down the information the women provided, filled it out in the provided format (Figure 5.1), and sent it to the magistrate. Afterwards, the magistrate usually spoke with some of the women on her own. When we debriefed later, she described them as "genuine" cases. In each of these cases, the perceived authenticity of the women's accounts seemed to lie in their appearance and demeanor, the details they provided of their trafficking experience, the manner in which they narrated these details (often bursting into tears), and their explanations of how they were forced into prostitution, rather than denying it. Their accounts squared easily with what those conducting inquiries saw as victimhood. The considerable efforts they made on their own to leave the sex trade, like the New Delhi cases in Chapters 2 and 3, are worth noting, but they were labeled as "victim girls" nonetheless. For all these reasons, they were not treated with doubt or suspicion. Unlike the families of women suspected of lying, who were either local or had not traveled from quite as far as the trafficked women, the families of these trafficked women were not called for inquiries. It was understood that they lived too far away (in the case of Bangladeshi women, across national borders) and their means were too meager for them to travel all the way to the Mumbai Special Court.

"Lying" Victims

In the smaller room within the magistrate's chambers, twenty-two-year-old Rehana Bano was answering an NGO worker's questions about her work and family. Sonia, the NGO worker, and I knew each other from previous inquiries I had observed. She was from a Christian anti-trafficking NGO. This inquiry had a crowd of observers – the Canadian filmmaker, the lawyer from the NGO she was accompanying, and myself.

Rehana said she worked at a beauty salon in Mumbai to pay for medical treatment for her mother, who needed medicines and injections. The social worker asked what was wrong with her mother. After a long, considered pause, Rehana replied, "She has many diseases, including TB…" and began describing the cost of her mother's medicines.

Sonia shook her head, "No, you are lying. I will tell the judge you are not telling the truth." Ignoring Rehana's protests that she *was* telling the truth and was not involved in prostitution, Sonia adopted a more accusatory tone. "Then why did the police 'catch' you?[31] Why did they raid the beauty parlor?" In response, Rehana replied fervently, "The police said 'inappropriate work' ('*galat kaam*') used to happen there, but I swear, *I* never did it." After Rehana left the room, Sonia turned to me in despair. "She is not revealing anything. I don't know what to do with these girls."

Next, Sonia spoke with Rehana's sister and brother-in-law, who confirmed that her mother was ill and undergoing treatment in Mumbai. But they said they lived in a village near Bhopal (in central India), whereas Rehana had said she lived with

[31] In Hindi, "*To phir* police *ne tum ko kyon pakda*?"

them in Mumbai and helped take care of their children. Rehana had not been able to provide the documents the court asked for to prove that she lived in Mumbai. "You don't even know where your younger sister has been living?" Sonia reprimanded Rehana's sister for failing to perform what Sonia framed as her familial duty to keep track of Rehana's whereabouts. "Did you know what work she was doing?" she asked. "Madam, I did not know she was doing 'this kind of work.' If we knew, would we let her do it?" the sister responded hastily.

When the sister left, the NGO lawyer who had accompanied the Canadian filmmaker and was also observing the inquiry, remarked to Sonia, alluding to Rehana, "how beautifully that girl was lying!" As Sonia started to concur with the "lying" remark, the magistrate came into the room. She had with her a police report according to which Rehana had been found in a "half-naked" condition with a bogus customer during the raid on the beauty salon.[32] It was important to the magistrate that Rehana admit to being involved in prostitution, as she was the one among the women from the salon who the police said had been found with the bogus customer. As the police claimed that the accused provided a specific woman to the bogus customer for prostitution, the inquiry committee perceived this to be the woman in each group either most likely to tell the "truth" or the most easily persuaded to admit it.

Sonia told the magistrate that Rehana had "not revealed anything," adding that she was sure she was not telling the truth. The magistrate asked Sonia to talk to Rehana again. When Rehana returned to the room, Sonia's tone became even more accusatory than before. She told Rehana she had seen the report according to which Rehana was "with a male customer" when the police came. She asked again why Rehana was not telling the truth. She also asked her why her account did not match what her sister and brother-in-law had said.

Probably because she now felt trapped, Rehana added a new piece of information. "That time, my 'top clothes' were taken off,"[33] she said. Though she still did not say that she had sex with men at the salon, she now indicated that she was indeed "half-naked" (though not, as she insisted firmly, fully naked). Sonia seemed both relieved and annoyed. "Why did you not tell me this earlier?" she asked in a tone of rebuke. Rehana did not answer, bowing her head down and looking around the room.

The magistrate also had a medico-legal report according to which Rehana's hymen was "ruptured," which the magistrate and NGO worker saw as a contradiction of her "unmarried" status. As I discussed in Chapter 4, these reports were used to presumptively prove women's involvement in prostitution. In her ethnography of rape trials in India, Indian legal anthropologist Pratiksha Baxi discusses how these medical reports are based on an intrusive "two-finger test" to discover whether the female body is "habituated to sex." The tests are thus not specific to prostitution

[32] See Chapter 4 for explanation.

[33] In Hindi, "*Us* time *mere upar ke kapde utre hue the.*"

cases, but widely used in sexual violence cases in India to assess consent or coercion to sex. Baxi provides a trenchant critique of the way they are used to create doubt about rape survivors' testimony. She shows how defense lawyers use the characterization of a rape survivor being "habituated" to sex to suggest that she consented to the sexual encounter (2014: 268). Though the "two-finger test" has long been opposed by feminist activists in India, and the Indian Supreme Court declared it unconstitutional in 2013, there is a continued reliance on these tests in sexual assault trials, and also, as I found, in ITPA cases.

The magistrate called Rehana into her chamber to confront her with the medical report. Though she did not deploy the report to imply consensual sex when forced sex was claimed, she did use it to imply that the only explanation for why Rehana as an unmarried woman would be "habituated to sex" was prostitution. Inquiries deployed medical reports differently than defense counsel did in rape cases, though their extrapolations overlapped with the latter context. Pairing the medico-legal authority of the report with an invocation of gendered sexual normativity, inquiries sought explanations from "lying" victims about why they were not virgins, with the intention of getting them to admit their involvement in prostitution. The magistrate told us later that it was when confronted with the mention of the ruptured hymen in the medical report that Rehana finally revealed that she was doing sex work, for which she received only Rs. 200 (approximately $2.4) out of the Rs. 1,000 (approximately $12) that the customer paid for her services. Per the magistrate's account of this interaction, after finally "revealing" that she was indeed doing "inappropriate work," Rehana begged the magistrate not to tell her family about it.

In my first example explaining the perception of "genuine" victims, while describing Latha as a victim, the previous magistrate had differentiated her from women who were "into this for the money." This contrast would seem to suggest that the latter set of women were therefore *not* viewed as victims, as their participation in the sex trade was viewed as being in pursuit of money. However, the magistrate during my longer-term fieldwork often articulated the concern that "they are not admitting that they are victims." Women denying prostitution were addressed and perceived differently than "genuine" victims of trafficking because they "lied," as a different kind of victim who had let themselves fall into prostitution. They were seen to have a combination of excessive vulnerability and excessive ambition (to seek a better living) that was pathologized during inquiries along with their suspected "lying." This perceived combination of vulnerability and ambition, as Stacey Vanderhurst finds in her ethnography of anti-trafficking interventions in Nigeria, is treated as naive and misdirected, and in need of paternalist intervention (2022: 16, 69).

At the Mumbai Special Court, the inquiry committee typically dealt with women they believed to be "lying" by countering their accounts with forms of proof presumed to establish a different "truth." They confronted Rehana with the different accounts of residence that she and her kin provided and the absence of documentation about her residence to suggest that she was lying about where she lived.

They countered her claim that she was merely a beautician with the police report, according to which she was found "half-naked" with a decoy customer. And they challenged her denial of prostitution by referring to her medical report, to raise questions about why she was not a virgin.

The deeply hierarchical interactions structuring inquiries and the accusatory dynamic suffusing them resonate with anti-trafficking interventions in other global contexts. In reference to Nigeria, Stacey Vanderhurst describes how most migrant women deemed at risk of trafficking denied the intention to work in the sex trade abroad, while counselors refused to believe them and expected them to "confess" (2022: 14). In both the Indian and Nigerian contexts, denials of prostitution are met with accusations of "lying" and efforts to get women to "open up" and change their narrative.

In response to the accusations of lying and denial, Rehana selectively provided pieces of information, crafting each successive response based on whatever form of "proof" she was confronted with. In response to the police report about her "half-naked" condition, she admitted to being (quite literally) half-undressed. In response to the medical report, she perhaps saw no way out other than admitting her involvement in prostitution. However, she framed it through the obligations of kinship and her role as a dutiful daughter. Rehana continued to talk of her mother's illness and medical treatment as the reason for her selling sex. She beseeched the magistrate not to tell her family how she was earning the money, thus articulating the concerns of a virtuous and caring daughter, for whom bringing ill-repute to her family continued to be unthinkable.

Rehana's was not the only inquiry where I had observed accusations of "lying" and the perception that women who came in for inquiries were "not revealing anything" and "not admitting that they are victims." These concerns, expressed through a combination of suspicion, admonition and accusation, imbued several inquiries. However, in this particular inquiry, the inquiry committee felt that the "lying" was exacerbated by the presence of multiple observers.

After the magistrate alerted Sonia, the NGO worker conducting inquiries that day, to the perceived contradictions in Rehana's story, and Rehana provided new information about being without her "top clothes," Sonia politely asked if the three of us (myself, the NGO lawyer, and the Canadian filmmaker) could leave the room. Sonia and the magistrate had conferred, and agreed, that Rehana was probably "not revealing anything" because of the number of people present. Indeed, Rehana did not "reveal anything" about prostitution to Sonia even after we left the room. It was only after the magistrate called Rehana into the main chamber to inquire with her herself, and confronted her with the mention of the ruptured hymen in the medical report, that Rehana, thus cornered, admitted to being involved in prostitution.

While the magistrate spoke with Rehana, Sonia conducted inquiries with four other women who had been "rescued" from the beauty salon with her who also denied that they were doing anything other than working at the salon. The Canadian filmmaker, NGO lawyer, and I were allowed back in to observe these inquiries. During the inquiries, as mentioned earlier, the filmmaker made frequent eye contact with Rehana and the other women who came in after her, smiling at them and saying hello, showing concern through her facial expressions, and occasionally making a "tsk" sound when she read translated bits in my notes about the women's poverty or their relatives' illnesses. Some women, like Rehana, giggled at this overt attentiveness, and glanced over at me and the NGO lawyer to gauge our reactions. It is, of course, hard to say how this set of inquiries would have played out without this combination of multiple observers, and the "different listening" one of them exhibited (apropos my earlier discussion). Given that several women across other inquiries similarly denied both trafficking and prostitution, would Rehana necessarily have "opened up" in our absence? Perhaps not. But the presence of the three of us certainly crowded the room, clearly disrupted Sonia's work, and ultimately ended my access to inquiries.

Nonetheless, Sonia obligingly engaged us in conversation that day in the breaks between her inquiries with Rehana and the other women. When the inquiries concluded, Sonia, the magistrate, and the NGO lawyer talked at length about how certain they were that this group of women was lying. They considered their suspicions confirmed when Rehana, confronted with the various forms of "proof" deployed to counter her account, finally admitted to prostitution.

All this while, the Canadian filmmaker had been looking perplexed. She finally spoke up to ask, "But why do you all say these women are lying? I believed their stories. They are poor and say that they needed work. What is the reason for lying?" The NGO lawyer responded that the women were afraid of the repercussions of admitting involvement in prostitution. It would mean being sent into protective custody (see Chapter 6) with no source of income to provide for themselves and their children. The lawyer explained that the women thought they had been brought to the court for punishment rather than assistance, and therefore "denied everything" to prevent this punishment from falling upon them. As disruptive as the filmmaker's presence was otherwise, the need to answer her question brought forth an explicit explanation of why those conducting inquiries believed the women were "lying."

In her answer, the lawyer implied that the women were wrong in perceiving inquiries, which were aimed at initiating their protection and rehabilitation, as punishment. However, as Chapter 6 will show, most women, including those who had been trafficked, experienced protective custody and rehabilitation as highly punitive and deeply moralistic interventions that curtailed their mobilities and livelihoods. Furthermore, though those conducting inquiries spoke with the women they deemed "genuine" victims in a supportive and reassuring manner, they interacted with those they deemed to be "lying" in a manner implying that punishment was imminent. Though the committee members prefaced all inquiries with reassuring phrases such as "you are not in trouble," the modes of questioning remained interrogative and accusatory, and the deployment of "proof" to corner the women further reinforced the impression that the women were very much in trouble.

"Bangladesh"

Apart from suspicions of prostitution despite the women's denials, inquiry committee members also often made evident their suspicion that Bengali-speaking women might be from Bangladesh. This did not, of course, apply to cases where women said they were trafficked from Bangladesh, like the three girls who escaped from their captor at the train station. Suspicions arose in cases where women *denied* being from Bangladesh. Many women who had either been trafficked from Bangladesh or crossed the border voluntarily wanted to stay on in India and earn a living rather than go back to Bangladesh. Revealing in inquiries that they were from Bangladesh would have risked losing that opportunity and being sent back to Bangladesh. Owing to linguistic, cultural, phenotypic, and sartorial similarities between Bengali women from Bangladesh and the Indian state of West Bengal,[34] Bangladeshi women can easily pass as Indian (Sur 2021: 14). In this context, the inquiry committee often suspected the Bengali speaking women brought before them of "lying" when they said they were Indian.

The belief that any Bengali-speaking rescued women who claimed to be from West Bengal (of which Kolkata is the capital) might be lying, and that they could be migrants from Bangladesh instead, saturated different fieldwork sites and the concerns of multiple interlocutors. Jennifer, a social worker with a Christian NGO who often came to help with inquiries, summarized a concern I heard from many magistrates, NGO workers, police, and shelter staff in Mumbai,

> Even when we have a strong suspicion that they are from Bangladesh, they keep saying "Kolkata, Kolkata" … and when you ask them anything about where in Kolkata they are from, they won't be able to tell you.

This instantiates the pervasive culture of suspicion (Ghosh 2019; Sur 2021) and "demographic anxieties" (Moodie 2010) around those suspected to be Bangladeshi migrants in the Indian sociopolitical context.[35] Their claims to Indian citizenship were perceived as strategies to evade detection. The rise of Hindu nationalism has fueled anti-Muslim and anti-immigrant sentiments against those known or suspected to be from Bangladeshi in recent decades.[36] In the context of the paranoia fueled by Hindu nationalists around Bangladeshi

[34] Areas which, before the Partition of Bengal during the colonial period, were the eastern and western parts of the same province.

[35] See Introduction, footnote 10.

[36] For ethnographically informed analyses of the politically charged discourse around Bangladeshi migrants, see, for instance, Ghosh (2019); Moodie (2010); Sur (2021).

immigrants as "infiltrators," anthropologist Sahana Ghosh uses the term "detectability" to describe how the possibility of identifying illegal immigrants has been normalized as a social and political goal to an unprecedented extent (2019: 873).

The culture of suspicion around Bengali speakers being Bangladeshis masquerading as Indians extended beyond inquiries to the way rescued women were treated at protective homes (see Chapter 6). As a result, Bengali speaking women often felt the need to specify, even before being explicitly asked, that they were from India and not Bangladesh. One of the women "rescued" from the beauty salon with Rehana, who said she earned a paltry sum as an assistant there, was not only accused of denying prostitution, but also of lying about her nationality because she could not provide her address in what she had said was her native village in West Bengal. The explanation she provided was that she had spent more than twenty years in Mumbai. Attempting to dispel the doubts being expressed around her nationality during the inquiry, she described the train route to her village in lieu of the address. Sonia, the NGO worker, did not explicitly ask the woman if she was from Bangladesh, but conveyed incredulity through her body language and mode of questioning. In response, the woman smiled and insisted, "Madam, I am Indian, not from 'across the border' like those other girls at the protective home."

Though I did observe many Bangladeshi women being treated as victims during inquiries, they were also viewed as illegal immigrants. This created further ambivalence towards them as compared to Indian women. As discussed in Chapter 1, the ITPA evinces a deep ambivalence toward prostitution, treating it as both an immoral act and a form of exploitation. Its implementation, as reflected in the treatment of those perceived to be "lying" during inquiries, similarly approaches sex workers as victims of both immorality and exploitation. For Bangladeshi women, what Kimberly Walters describes as an "unwieldy amalgam" of "criminal-victim" (2020: 314) was compounded by further possibilities of criminality assumed around their border-crossing.

A different magistrate in Mumbai viewed Bangladeshi women through this lens, where the specter of potential criminality loomed over other possibilities, such as economic migration or trafficking. When I interviewed this magistrate about ITPA cases, she brought up how previously, Bangladeshi women in Mumbai's sex trade were apprehended as criminals. Indeed, this is still the case, with even trafficked Bangladeshi women being sent to prison under the charge of being "illegal immigrants" (Mehta 2016). However, as the magistrate explained, with anti-trafficking NGOs conducting more rescues, legal actors had been directed to treat them as victims of sex trafficking.[37]

While empathetic toward victims of trafficking, whether from India or Bangladesh, this magistrate was hesitant about making a complete shift away from

[37] Advisory on preventing and combating human trafficking in India dealing with foreign nationals, Office Memorandum No. 14051/14/2011F.VI, Ministry of Home Affairs (Foreigners Division), Government of India, dated May 1, 2012.

apprehending Bangladeshi women as illegal immigrants. She was suspicious that some of them crossed the border multiple times. "Such women who come *again and again* are not victims. Maybe the first time they were victims." In her view, crossing the border more than once without documents had to entail some knowledge or consent, and ought to be treated as a punishable offense. She added, "I am quite sure when she comes back next time, she brings another girl. So now this woman might be a trafficker."[38]

In explaining these concerns, she cited a judgment of the Gauhati High Court (in the northeastern Indian state of Assam, bordering Bangladesh) on illegal immigration. This judgment, as I read later, expresses explicit anxieties about the "cancerous growth of Bangladeshis crossing the border."[39] Indeed, with increased concerns around a "massive influx" of Bangladeshi immigrants in the past two decades, other judgments have also supported the need to better detect and deport "illegal migrants" in Indian states bordering Bangladesh.[40] The legal repertoire of those tasked with conducting inquiries is thus shaped by mixed sociopolitical messages framing their approach to Bangladeshi women, including concerns around both cross-border trafficking and illegal immigration.

Bars

In cases involving raids on bars,[41] the police claimed that the bars were pick-up points from where customers engaged the women, and then went with them to lodges, hotels, and so on for sexual services. The Special Court magistrate told me there was an additional dimension of economic exploitation (per the ITPA) of the bar owners and managers taking a commission from the women's alleged earnings from prostitution. However, most women rescued from bars continued to deny not just trafficking or exploitation, but also sex work *tout court*.

In these cases, though well aware of the moralistic frameworks through which the inquiry committee viewed the women who came for inquiries, I was puzzled by their willingness to accept the police case rather than the women's accounts. The suspicion and conjecture through which the women were presumed to be "lying" did not seem to extend to the police who conducted the rescues. To counter the police case, women who denied prostitution often said the police had falsely

[38] For a critique of the frequent conflation of migrant smuggling with human trafficking, leading to the criminalization of migration processes that are often the only pathway to survival, see Pattanaik and Sullivan (2018). The authors argue that anti-trafficking legislation and policies calling for harsher border regimes and criminalization of migrants are often shaped by an anti-migration agenda that undermines rather than protects human rights.

[39] Judgment of the Gauhati High Court in the case of *Mustt Sarabari Begum @ Syera vs. State of Assam & Ors* on July 25, 2008.

[40] See also the Indian Supreme Court's judgment in the case of *Sarbananda Sonowal vs. Union of India & Anr.* on July 12, 2005.

[41] See Chapter 4 for context.

implicated the owners of the bars and salons when the owners did not fill their pockets with the regularly expected *haftas* or illegal commissions. Having heard this from women in many inquiries, I decided to ask the magistrate about it. "But the women say the police do these raids when they don't get *hafta*," I said, on an occasion when the magistrate was voicing her concerns about women who didn't admit that they were victims.

"*Aap hafta kyon detey ho?*" ("Why do you give *hafta*?") was the magistrate's reply in the form of a rhetorical question. She did not call the fact that the police were given *haftas* into question, but urged me to think about why those running establishments such as bars or salons would need to bribe the police. She implied that they needed to prevent the police from raiding the premises as they were obviously hiding something, which she implicitly suggested was prostitution.[42]

Inquiries with women from bars often involved pointing out "mismatches" between their earnings and expenses. The women were confronted with these mismatches to suggest that they were hiding their "real" sources of income, presumed to be prostitution. Afterwards, inquiry committee members told me that they did not believe that tips earned as a server or singer in a bar could be enough to support the women's lifestyles, which the committee members considered extravagant. The magistrate gave me the example of a woman who said she had bought a dress for Rs. 10,000 (approximately $120) that she really wanted, but was too ashamed to admit this even to her mother. In focusing on these expenditures, those conducting inquiries echoed the concerns of counselors in Stacey Vanderhurst's ethnography of anti-trafficking interventions in Nigeria. Vanderhurst describes how counselors shamed migrant women for "pursuing too much," which included not just prostitution, but also their desires for material goods and comforts (2023: 110, 120).

The magistrate frequently pointed out that women in these cases never provided an explanation about their source of income. She said most women who said they were singers or servers would tell her they did not get a salary and that their earnings were from tips given by customers. In cases where they said they did get a salary, it was around Rs. 2,000–4,000 ($24–48). The inquiry committee would often ask the women how they managed to live in Mumbai on such low incomes. The magistrate often lamented that even after being confronted (her choice of verb) with such perceived mismatches, women "rescued" from bars did not admit that they were involved in prostitution.

42 Mulling over her response later, it struck me that there could be many reasons for bribing the police, including defaulting on rent, flouting myriad local laws, or violating the terms of various city permits and licenses, with prostitution being just one possibility. Ultimately, the possibilities these sites, especially salons, provided for intimacy, for example, cubicles where women could give massages to men or could be "half naked," seemed to be what led to the presumption of prostitution as the reason for *haftas*. For a description of the economy of *haftas* around Mumbai's dance bars (before they were banned in 2005) that aptly captures its ironies, see Agnes (2006).

My fellow researcher, Saie, and I sat with the magistrate in her chamber one day, chatting about a recent Indian Supreme Court judgment upholding the Bombay High Court's ruling against the Maharashtra government's ban on dance bars. As the judgment allowed these establishments to open again,[43] we were curious about how the magistrate thought this might impact the bar-related cases that came before her in trials and inquiries. Though the entire conversation is beyond the scope of this chapter, the magistrate's musings about the lifestyles of women who worked in bars as singers, waitresses, or dancers are worth sharing here to illustrate what she meant by "mismatch."

> Do they really earn so much in tips? These people have houses that cost lakhs of rupees.[44] Their children study in boarding schools. What must the annual fees be? The standard of living they have, is so much possible just from tips?[45]

Another strategy the inquiry committee members sometimes used to catch (their choice of verb) rescued women at "lying" was by asking them to demonstrate their skill at the jobs they claimed to be their source of income instead of prostitution. The purpose was to dismantle their claims about their identities and occupations. The magistrate recounted how she sometimes asked women who said they were singers to demonstrate their singing skills.

> The girls who say "I am a singer," many times I make them sing here … I tell them to sing. But till today, not a single girl has been able to sing … Till today, I have not heard a single girl sing.[46]

Shaking her head and smiling, the magistrate continued that the women made excuses about being too tense to sing or having sore throats. She recounted how one young woman acknowledged that they lip-synced to recorded music and did not actually sing at the bars. For the magistrate, the admission that they were lip-syncing automatically disproved their claim of being singers. She extrapolated that prostitution, not singing, was their source of income.[47]

[43] As discussed in the Preface, in 2005, the state of Maharashtra (where Mumbai is located) placed a ban on dance bars, institutions serving alcohol where women dance to Bollywood songs and are showered with cash tips by male customers. In what Jyoti Puri has described as the "confoundingly arbitrary" logics of the state agencies involved, the ban construed these spaces, and the women who dance there, on the one hand as immoral, and on the other, as sites that promoted sex trafficking from which women needed to be rescued (2016: 4).

[44] One lakh in the Indian numeric system equals the numeric value of 100,000 (in rupees).

[45] Saie and the magistrate were both Marathi speakers, but she spoke in Hindi for my benefit, "*Kya sach mein* tips *itni milti hain? In logon ke laakhon ke ghar hotey hain. Unke bachche* boarding school *mein padhtey hain. Unki* annual fees *kya hogi? Unka jo* standard of living *hai, kya yeh sirf tips se* possible *hai?*"

[46] In Hindi, "*Jo ladkiyaan bolti hain 'main* singer *hoon,' kai baar to main unhe yahaan pe gavaati hoon … gaane ko bolti hoon, lekin aaj tak ek bhi ladki gaa nahin payee … aaj tak ek bhi ladki ko maine gaate hue nahin suna.*"

[47] The possibility that they might not be *good* singers but could still earn an income from it was not considered.

"Dancer," too, was a form of identity women from bars presented that invited suspicion from the inquiry committee. The magistrate mentioned an incident involving the interception of a group of women from the airport by the police, who then brought them in for inquiries on the presumption that they were being trafficked. The women had said they were dancers in a cultural troupe and were going to perform in Gulf countries. "This girl came, said 'I am a dancer!'" the magistrate said in an imitative manner, implying that the woman was posturing. When the magistrate asked the woman what style of dance she did, the woman apparently replied that it was "picture-*wala* dance" ("Bollywood-style dance"). The magistrate continued,

> If you have gone for some program, why can't you explain what type of dance? If it is a cultural troupe, why only Bollywood-style dance? And why are there only women in it?

The magistrate's suspicions about the possibility of prostitution stemmed from the woman's mention of "Bollywood dance." This was enough of a red flag to confirm the police's allegations that those involved in taking the women to the Gulf were running a sex racket. When performed by working-class or lower middle-class women to make money abroad, rather than by established Bollywood actresses, the "picture-*wala* dance" bore the imprint of immorality, owing in large part to its association with the women dancing in Mumbai's dance bars.[48]

I asked the magistrate whether the women said they went to the Gulf willingly or whether she saw this as a trafficking case. On the one hand, the magistrate acknowledged that those she perceived as "lying" victims might have performed dance or sex work, or both, to voluntarily pursue monetary gain. She told me that the passport of the woman in the dance troupe she had described indicated that she had made multiple trips to the Gulf. "There is money in this," she continued, adding that going abroad provided anonymity, so the women's families would not find out what they did there. The main issue for the magistrate was not to determine whether these women were willingly or unwillingly involved in prostitution via the dance troupe, but whether someone else was benefiting from it. Instead of forced prostitution, the magistrate saw strong possibilities of economic exploitation and detention, both

48 In the petition the bar dancers' union brought to the Bombay High Court opposing the ban in 2005, they took issue with a hypocritical morality whereby Bollywood actresses could perform "item numbers" on movie screens, but the working class were branded with immorality for performing the same dances to the same numbers directly in front of men. The Bombay High Court judgment that ultimately found the state government's ban on dance bars unconstitutional also questioned the discriminatory manner in which the venues of the performances were morally hierarchized. Hotels labeled as "three star" and above and elite clubs were exempt from the ban, which was primarily imposed on establishments frequented by working-class and lower middle-class men, where working-class women danced. This context helps to explain that it is when Bollywood dance is associated with a certain class of gendered subjects and certain kinds of venues that it is branded as immoral (Agnes 2006; Lakkimsetti 2016; Puri 2016; Sanger 2006).

criminalized under the ITPA.[49] The women had told the magistrate their passports were taken away by those organizing their trips as soon as they arrived at the destination, and they were not allowed to go anywhere without an escort. The magistrate wondered why their passports would be taken away if they had gone there merely to perform, reiterating her strong suspicion of prostitution, with possible elements of trafficking, that the women denied.

IDENTITY AND DOCUMENTS

During inquiries with women from in or around Mumbai, the committee also questioned those who claimed to be their relatives and had come to claim custody of them. Often, these relatives could not produce the information and documentary proof required to claim their relationship to the women. In one case, a woman who said she was the rescued woman's mother was not mentioned on the family's ration card,[50] and could not provide details about the rescued woman's children. In another case, a man who said he was the rescued woman's husband produced documents in which his wife's name, photograph, address, and date of birth were different from those provided by the rescued woman. Sometimes, relatives would bring family or wedding photographs in lieu of documents. The magistrate and NGO representatives often expressed concern that these photographs appeared photoshopped to combine separate individual photographs into one. Showing me one such example, the magistrate remarked, "Who has made this?" implying that the accused and/or the lawyers arranged by them had done this photoshopping to help the women produce false identities and documents.

Identity documents have what anthropologist Veena Das terms the "signature of the state" (2004) and Nayanika Mathur describes as the Indian state's creation of a person's "documentary existence" (2012: 179). This stamp of legitimacy rendered such documents a form of identity proof that had to be accepted by the Special Court as true, even when those who scrutinized them strongly doubted their veracity. As anthropologist Matthew Hull points out in the context of Pakistan, documents in South Asia are "widely seen as manipulable, while at the same time they are an essential media of bureaucratic action" (2012: 4488–4490). Das, too, notes the simultaneous potency and manipulability of the "signature of the state."[51]

49 These acts are also criminalized as acts of trafficking under the UN Protocol, 2000, which India ratified in 2013 and whose definition of trafficking it has since adopted in its criminal law. See Chapter 1 for further context and explanation.

50 An official document issued in India for those eligible to purchase subsidized food grains, which also serves as a common form of identification.

51 As Das elaborates, "Once the state institutes forms of governance through technologies of writing, it simultaneously institutes the possibility of forgery, imitation, and the mimetic performance of its power" (2004: 227).

In the atmosphere of suspicion shrouding inquiries at the Special Court, identity documents were given prime importance, yet there was always an explicit recognition that they could be fake. "These are government-issued documents, but how much can I believe them?" the magistrate pondered frequently. Examples she cited included cases of both Indian and Bangladeshi women. A woman from Mumbai had a PAN card from Pune,[52] although she had never lived there and had no proof of residence there. In other cases, women who eventually said they were from Bangladesh had Aadhaar cards, that is, Unique Identification Cards issued by the Government of India for Indian citizens.[53]

Anti-immigrant sociopolitical anxieties created further doubts about the legitimacy of these documents, already perceived as easily forged.[54] The inquiry committee frequently wondered how it was possible for Bangladeshi women to have Aadhaar cards. New anthropological work has traced the possibility of Bangladeshi immigrants having Indian identity documents to political parties providing them in exchange for votes.[55] Ironically, as Malini Sur puts it, "Indian political parties continue to vacillate between enabling Bangladeshi immigrants to fraudulently acquire identity documents to vote in Indian elections, and demanding the speedy deportation of these 'Muslim illegal immigrants'" (2021: 147–148). During inquiries, the suspicion and accusation around possible slippages between Bangladeshi and Bengali Indian identities played out both in the way women were questioned, as described earlier, and in these concerns about identity documents.

In this overall culture of suspicion, framed by concerns about immorality, respectability, and illegality, proving marriage through documentation was often contentious. As Sameena Mulla observes, kinship is made and unmade through documentary regimes (2011: 353). During inquiries at the Special Court, men who said they were married to the women whose custody they came to claim rarely had marriage certificates to provide as proof. The magistrate's view was that women presented themselves as married in order to explain the medical reports according to which they were "habituated to sex." They countered the inquiry committee's presumption that this "habituation" was due to their involvement in prostitution by arguing that it was due to sexual relations respectably ensconced in marriage instead.

The need to prove marriage was often addressed innovatively. One couple said they had eloped and gotten married in a temple and therefore did not have documentary proof. The man expressed his eagerness to turn this into a "proper" legal

52 Document of a Permanent Account Number issued by the Income Tax Department in India, which also serves as a common form of identification.

53 For ethnographic explorations of this new form of biometric identification in India, see Nair (2018), Nair (2021), and Rao and Nair (2019).

54 As Moodie points out, "documentary evidence often does more to provoke questions about the possibility of its own veracity than to provide proof of anything" (2010: 534).

55 Ghosh (2019: 878); Moodie (2010: 542); Sur (2021: 14).

marriage by looking over at the woman right there in the magistrate's chamber and popping the question, "*Bol, shaadi karegi na*?" (a comically casual marriage proposal) for the benefit of myself and the NGO representative doing the inquiry, much to our amusement. When I met the woman he had proposed to later at the shelter, she reminded me of the proposal, wondering if the magistrate had taken note of it. In another case, a Nepali woman with no one to claim her custody exclaimed, in frustration, that she would "marry a random beggar,"[56] so that the court would release her from the shelter. Her response simultaneously illuminated and called into question how marriage was assumed to be the only acceptable and respectable alternative to sex work, and how furnishing proof of it seemed enough for the committee to set women free from protective custody.

Familial Ideology

The significance and deployment of kin relations – to establish identities, make decisions about rescued women's custody, urge them to admit to prostitution, and advise them to leave it for a "decent life" – was evident during inquiries. The purpose of speaking with the women's relatives was to verify the women's identities or "catch" them at lying, and to determine whether the families were genuine, suitable, and capable enough (as required by the ITPA) to take back their custody, temporarily taken on by the state.

Framing the inquiry committee's concerns was what feminist legal scholars Ratna Kapur and Brenda Cossman have termed the "familial ideology" of the postcolonial Indian state – a set of norms, values, and assumptions about how family life is and should be organized – that shapes the way law regulates women's roles (1996: 13).[57] To curb prostitution, inquiries sought to reconstitute "normal" families upholding traditional gender norms or, at the very least, to address their deviations from the normative ideal (Basu 2012). To illustrate the centrality of this familial ideology to inquiries, here are some excerpts from the magistrate's orders after inquiries,

> The victims have assured that hereinafter they will not work or visit any controversial place and take care of themselves and their family and children.
>
> From the inquiry with victims, it is found that they are indulged into immoral act due to poverty. Necessary advice and admonition is given to the victims, to adopt some decent mode of earning for their livelihood. Their respective relatives also advised to take proper care of victims.

In cases of rescued women whom they suspected to be lying, the inquiry committee sought to elicit the "truth" about being "indulged into" prostitution by

56 In Hindi, "*kisi bhikhaari se shaadi kar loongi.*"

57 Kapur and Cossman observe that "the familial ideology of the postcolonial state has shaped the judicial understanding of women being in need of protection" (1996: 17).

emphasizing the women's identities as wives, mothers, sisters and daughters, whose immorality indexed irresponsibility.[58] The operative logic was that women who came for inquiries might be compelled both to reveal the "truth" and to choose a more "dignified" path when confronted with what was construed as an assault on familial honor. Every woman with living relatives was asked, "does your family know you are in 'this line'?" (implying prostitution). This question was meant to stir guilt at having done something that would be unacceptable to their families and bring them dishonor.

For those conducting inquiries, the responsibility for the presumed sexual and economic exploitation and moral transgressions of the rescued women lay partly with families who had not been able to exercise the requisite "care and control" over wives, daughters, and sisters. Censure and admonition were not only directed at the rescued women. Families were also chided for not keeping tabs on their whereabouts and activities, like Rehana's sister. The questioning was often explicitly reproachful. For instance, "You never thought to check on what your young daughter (*javaan beti*) was doing in the big city?"

Sometimes, relatives also responded with disapproval, to distance themselves from the "immoral acts" of the rescued woman. One of the inquiries I observed involved a group of women who described themselves as stay-at-home mothers. They said that a woman in their neighborhood had lured them into providing sex to clients at her house to earn some extra money. One of these women said she did sex work to pay for her child's medical treatment, adding that she had not revealed the source of this money to her husband, letting him believe that the money had come from her family. When her husband was asked whether he knew why he and his wife had been called to court, he responded:

> I should never have brought her from the village. I brought her here so she could cook for me, and the child could be educated here. She is saying all this happened "by chance." *Izzat* (honor) is everything to me. If she is willing to live honorably, it would be fine, but not like this.

In cases where women maintained that they only did facials or massages, the question would be modified accordingly. "Does your family know that *men* used to come for these massages?" At this point, some women would start to cry and beg forgiveness, "*maaf kar do madam, galti ho gayee*" ("Forgive me, madam, I made a

58 I remain unsure of the specific reason for the usage of the phrase "indulged into" (in English) rather than "indulging in" in these orders. The use of "into" rather than "in" may capture the intent to convey prostitution as a habit, an immoral lifestyle, a vice. It may be a neologism that aptly captures the spirit of the ITPA's provisions that criminalize inducing or luring a woman into prostitution (i.e. that someone else has brought her into the trade). Or it may simply be the kind of Indian English usage or malapropism that feminist legal anthropologist Srimati Basu notes in her study of family courts in Kolkata, where the verb "consume" was used by judges in place of "consummation" of a marriage (2011: 361).

mistake"). They would plead with the committee not to tell their mother, husband, or whoever had come to claim their custody about why they had been "caught."[59] Often, they would still not "reveal" that they were involved in prostitution, but their sobs and apologies were enough to convince the inquiry committee that there was "something wrong" if they had not told their families what they were doing. Thus invoking kinship, the committee usually viewed such apologies as admissions of immorality, enough to signify the need for admonition during the inquiry and protective custody and rehabilitation thereafter.

NAVIGATING INQUIRIES

When women assumed to be "lying" insisted that they were not involved in prostitution, they often used the frameworks of either motherhood or religiosity, sometimes both, in their denials. They presented identities such as a single mother and/or a pious woman to indicate an association with virtuosity rather than immorality. Examples included, "I am Christian, I tell the truth," "I am Muslim, I never lie," "I believe in Sai Baba,[60] so I always tell the truth," and "I am the type of person who prays regularly."[61]

Women who did "reveal" that they did sex work articulated varied combinations of *marzi* (choice) and *majboori* (compulsion) that always stemmed from economic need. Sometimes, *marzi* and *majboori* were strung together in the same sentence, indicating an intrinsic connection between them. For example, "I had the [economic] need, so I came into this 'line' [prostitution] by choice."[62]

The inquiry committee usually responded by telling the women they should have "known better" than to allow themselves to be sexually and economically exploited. As feminist scholar and activist Laura Agustin points out, those concerned about trafficking believe that "poorer women are better off staying at home than leaving and possibly getting into trouble" (2007: 39). Exercising and voicing agency can make women look like "worrying autonomous agents" whose choices to enter prostitution are pathologized (Aradau 2004; Brunovskis and Surtees 2008: 62). Thus, a mere articulation of economic need did not help women who chose sex work frame their choice within the realm of moral responsibility and respectability.

The women who came for inquiries therefore included not only explanations of economic need, but also familial obligations in their narratives, responding to the familial ideology that pervaded inquiries. They often deployed motherhood to explain why they did sex work, stating that "Any mother would do it for her child."[63] I do not

59 As discussed earlier, though the women had technically been rescued and not arrested, the word "caught" or *pakda* implied being caught in the act of doing something wrong.

60 A saint figure.

61 In Hindi, "*Main toh pooja paath karti hoon.*"

62 In Hindi, "*Meri majboori thi to main marzi se is* line *mein aa gayee.*"

63 In Hindi, "*Koi bhi maa apne bacche ke liye karegi.*"

mean to suggest that this was merely a narrative or performative strategy. As feminist ethnographers have pointed out, several sex workers shoulder the material care work of supporting families and households, and take pride in being able to do so (Shih 2018; Vijayakumar 2022). In her ethnographic research with sex workers in Bangalore, Gowri Vijayakumar observes that they responded to a moral context in which making sacrifices for motherhood is a recognized and celebrated trope (2022: 671). But as she also notes, "sex workers' aspirations and material investments in motherhood" are "more complex than just rationalization or bids for respectability" (669).[64]

Responding to the same familial ideology that was deployed to reproach them, women who came for inquiries framed themselves as morally responsible actors whose "mistakes" (*galti*) were the result of their financial compulsions (*majboori*) on account of their kin. As they had no doubt gauged, saying that they earned for themselves would have likely met with greater censure for not thinking about the honor of their families. This resonates with Vanderhurst's research on anti-trafficking counseling in Nigeria, where migrant women who admitted to involvement in prostitution sometimes explained their choices in terms of providing selflessly for their families and others (2022: 117). During inquiries at the Mumbai Special Court, those who said they did sex work because of choice or economic compulsion (or both) justified their earnings either in terms of familial obligations or the failure of their kin to provide for them. Some women pointed out that it was the lack of familial protection in their lives (husbands abandoning them, brothers ill-treating them, etc.) that had driven them to "inappropriate" work for survival.[65]

Often, like Rehana, they would cite the need to pay for the medical treatment of close kin. Once, I was asked to conduct an inquiry with a tired-looking woman in her thirties who explained that she occasionally did sex work to pay for blood transfusions for her child, who had thalassemia. "Madam! Please write that down. Mention the thalassemia," she urged me. "It will help me get out of here sooner so I can take care of him." My intention is not to suggest that these illnesses didn't exist. I had no way to determine their veracity, nor was that my objective. I focused, instead, on observing and listening to how the ailments of kin were narrated and perceived during inquiries.

Those conducting inquiries found these narratives of family illnesses and the need to pay for medical treatment suspicious. The magistrate told me how, on her

64 Vijayakumar discusses how sex work makes it possible to meet the moral and economic demands of good motherhood amid the inequalities of contemporary Bangalore (2022: 666). Sex work provided her interlocutors the income to pay for their children's expenses and the economic standing to sustain family relationships on their own terms, and also a certain flexibility and secrecy that allowed them to maintain respectable femininity (667).

65 This resonates with sex workers' accounts in Vijayakumar's ethnography in Bangalore about families (especially husbands) who had failed to provide-through abandonment, abuse, financial problems, etc. Many explained how the failure of masculine protection had led them to sex work (2022: 674–675).

first day on the job, she felt really sad for a woman who cried that her mother had diabetes and heart disease. However, she eventually began to view these narratives as another way in which the women framed their "lies."

> All of them are saying this kind of thing. Everyone's mother is unwell and child needs treatment.[66] They all come prepared with these stories, to justify their acts.

The magistrate reminded me of an inquiry where the woman, Neeta, had said she was sending money home for her sister's treatment, but her relatives denied this, as Neeta did not get along with them. "Later, that girl revealed that she does not love her family. Then what is the truth, why did she do this work?" the magistrate asked me in her usual rhetorical style that my readers will be familiar with at this point in the book. Neeta had said that she was trafficked from West Bengal to Mumbai and forced into prostitution. At one point, she left of her own accord, and then returned to sex work. She initially gave the magistrate the explanation that she did so to provide for her sister's medical treatment. Later, when confronted with her relatives' denial of this explanation, Neeta reluctantly admitted to the magistrate that she returned to sex work to support herself. Thus, even a woman estranged from her family felt the need to provide an explanation that would speak to the court's familial ideology: that she had "fallen into" sex work only to be a dutiful sister. After admitting that she was earning for herself and not for her estranged family, Neeta begged the magistrate not to send her back to them.

Neeta's was a complicated story involving trafficking and eventually a voluntary return to sex work. Though she had indicated that she was once trafficked, Neeta was seen as a "lying" victim now, as there was a mismatch between her account of voluntary prostitution to help her family and her family's account of a troubled familial relationship. Her initial withholding of information, the varying versions of why she did sex work, and her estranged relationship with her family who had "no control over her," led to the magistrate's perceptions of an entwined immorality and vulnerability. The magistrate drafted an order sending Neeta to the protective home, in which she wrote, with both censure and sympathy,

> Whatever she stated during her inquiry found to be inconsistent with statement of her mother and brother. She had given incorrect information to the court and tried to mislead. When her lie was caught, she said she do not love her parents and will not go home. She never sent money for treatment of her sister as claimed by her. Her family appears to be having no control over her and not appears to be suitable to claim her custody. She is too vulnerable. She is in need of care, counseling, and training to help her to lead dignified life.

Inquiries sought to extract "truths" about prostitution by seeking to instill familial guilt. They also sought to reinstate women to the presumed idyll of their families, with their perceived vulnerability being in need of protection from the perennial

[66] In Hindi, *"In sabki maa beemar aur bacche ka ilaaj hota hai."*

threat of immorality. Women who came for inquiries explained the *majboori* (compulsion) that led them into the sex trade by presenting themselves as morally irreproachable through this very framework of kinship. In a sociolegal context marked by a culture of suspicion, invocations of gendered moral responsibility, and a paternalist familial ideology, inquiries treated rescued women as simultaneously vulnerable, mendacious, and immoral.

CONCLUSION

This chapter has shown how narratives and identities were constructed and challenged in interactions between the magistrate and NGO representatives and the women brought before them for inquiries. It has demonstrated how inquiries are framed by concerns around trafficking, the "immorality" of prostitution, a paternalist familial ideology deployed to emphasize the gendered norms of kinship, and sociopolitical concerns around Bangladeshi immigrants. When the law's ambivalence toward prostitution played out at the intersection of these concerns, those conducting inquiries grappled to impose certainty upon the uncertainty and complexity of the lives and identities of the women brought before them. Verbal accounts, identity documents, and medico-legal reports were often considered unreliable and assessed through conjecture and suspicion. Inquiries, conducted through deeply hierarchical interactions between the committee members and the women brought before them, often involved aggressive and interrogative questioning, accompanied by advice and admonition to lead a "dignified" life.

Given the institutional location in which I observed (and conducted) inquiries, I cannot claim to know the actual, underlying realities about these women's lives. I did not know who they "truly" were, or whether or not they were withholding the truth. I recognize women's accounts during inquiries as performances framed by strategic efforts to ensure optimal advantage, as Srimati Basu observes in her research on family courts in India (2015: 60). Also useful here are insights from anthropologists and historians of sex work and its regulation in India: that sex workers strategically deploy silence to resist state and nonstate surveillance (Dasgupta 2014: 111), and that sex workers have long denied prostitution as a strategy to evade forced registration and medical examinations (Mitra 2020; Tambe 2009) and negotiate stigma (Shah 2014). In engaging these insights, my intention is not to argue that all of the women who denied prostitution during inquiries were necessarily sex workers. Indeed, as Svati Shah finds in an ethnography of migrant women workers in Mumbai, sexual commerce is not necessarily or easily "knowable" even in the spaces where it is solicited (2009). Therefore, it is even less knowable in a judicial context where the evaluation of any information provided can shape decisions about a woman's custody and earning capacity. What I find persuasive, however, is the possibility that women navigating inquiries strategically deploy silences and denials in a context suffused with interrogation, accusation, and admonition, to avoid punitive outcomes.

The instability, elusiveness, and manipulability of "truth" production comes through, more broadly, in the work of anthropologists studying victim narratives in humanitarian contexts. Erica Caple James discusses women's performances of victimhood and truth-telling in the context of Haiti's postconflict transition (2010).[67] She observes that her research subjects "choose to emphasize certain aspects of their identities and experience in different settings over others in order to meet particular needs, and control the flows of information presented to individuals and institutions acting in humanitarian capacities" (2010: 109). She argues that ""truth" thus becomes partial, flexible, and contextual, rather than absolute," with the caution that the capacity to construct "truth" is impacted by unequal distributions of power.

Despite this overlap, inquiries are, of course, different from humanitarian contexts in significant ways. Though there is a "strategic performance of traumas" in both contexts, anti-trafficking interventions and humanitarian programs are also markedly different (Vanderhurst 2022: 72). Vanderhurst astutely observes in the context of anti-trafficking interventions in Nigeria that interactions do not center on migrants needing to convince authorities with their trauma narratives, but rather on the authorities trying to convince migrants that they are victims in need of assistance and intervention (2022: 72). Inquiries at the Mumbai Special Court – a process prescribed by India's anti-prostitution law and conducted with the support of anti-trafficking NGOs – resonate with the Nigerian context Vanderhurst describes. In cases where women provided accounts of being trafficked, inquiries were geared toward determining custody and rehabilitation. But in cases where women denied either trafficking or prostitution or both, inquiries were geared toward getting them to "admit that they are victims" and accept the same protective/punitive forms of custody and rehabilitation being offered to trafficked women. This was the structuring context in which identities, experiences, economic need, and morality were performed and perceived.

Observing inquiries made it clear that women responded to questions keeping both the expectations of the authorities and the legal repercussions of providing some facts versus others in mind. The chapter has shown how, just as those conducting inquiries make certain assumptions about the women brought before them and employ specific tactics to elicit "truths," women approach inquiries with specific strategies. They respond to the contents of the police case, medico-legal report, and the accusations of "mismatch," false identities, and fake relationships with what they think will appeal to the gendered moral frameworks of those conducting inquiries.

[67] James shows how suffering is commoditized into "trauma portfolios" governed by grant and audit cycles of humanitarian and development aid.

6

From "House of Horrors" to "Sensitive" Governance

Shelter Detention in Mumbai

The ITPA prescribes "protective custody" or shelter-based detention for women removed from the sex trade, regardless of whether they are trafficked or voluntary sex workers. After police raids or NGO-initiated rescues, courts detain women in state or NGO-run shelters called "protective homes." In October 2012, twenty-three detained women escaped one such state-run shelter in Mumbai by scaling the compound wall, leading to frenzied media interest, activist concerns, and judicial intervention. One of them, a Bangladeshi woman, gave an explosive interview to *Mumbai Mirror* (a local tabloid), alleging sexual assault, abuse, negligence, and discriminatory treatment of Bangladeshi women at the shelter. The exposé led to intense judicial scrutiny by the Bombay High Court by the time I started volunteering at the shelter six weeks later.

Neither the allegations nor the escapes were isolated incidents. Shelter detention in India began in the late colonial period. Reports abound from that time and from the early postcolonial period of women escaping shelters, alleging abuse and violence (De 2018: 213; Legg 2014: 1895). Indeed, in the early years of the postcolonial nation, even as Indian legislators debating the ITPA supported legally mandated shelter detention for sex workers, they expressed concern that the existing shelters were being mismanaged and were in need of close and constant supervision (Lok Sabha Proceedings 1956).

Beyond the shelters set up under the ITPA, abuse and exploitation have been reported in several "welfare institutions" for women and children in India. Sexual abuse, in particular, has garnered unprecedented attention since the New Delhi gangrape incident of 2012.[1] In 2018, physical, mental, and sexual abuse was documented at a shelter run by a politician's NGO in Muzaffarpur, Bihar, and widely reported in the media, leading to the investigation and conviction of those involved.[2] The Muzaffarpur case exemplified rapid responses from the state and judiciary to what was perceived as "exceptional" abuse. Discussions and actions around the state

[1] Discussed in Chapters 1, 4, and 5 and explained in Chapter 1, footnote 29.

[2] For an overview of the case, see Johari (2020); Salomi and Shukla (2018).

of shelters tend to die down, until the next exposé or scandal. While such scandals are not new, the fleeting attention they garner results in what anthropologist Kimberly Walters has termed the "awful distracting from the lawful," that is, public attention focusing on the scandals, rather than on systemic abuses (2016). Recent work by feminist scholars of South Asia focuses, instead, on the systemic problems with shelter detention as an anti-prostitution legal provision and anti-trafficking solution in India.[3]

In this chapter, I build upon these critiques to move beyond the scandals with an in-depth and wide-ranging analysis of shelter detention – its prescription in the ITPA, its implementation by state agencies and NGOs, and how it is experienced and resisted. The chapter analyzes the different forms of power and governance shelter detention brings together, and how they are implemented by state agencies and NGOs. Through ethnography, the chapter demonstrates multiple ways in which shelter detention curtails rescued women's mobilities and impedes their livelihoods. It shows how shelter detention in practice is shaped by constant uncertainties and delays around women's release from the shelter owing to the need for coordination across multiple agencies. It highlights multiple forms of resistance by detained women, who call into question not merely "exceptional" abuse, but the routine, ever-expanding forms of governance that authorize, implement, and supervise shelter detention. Finally, the chapter returns to the media exposé of "exceptional" abuse at the Mumbai shelter and the ensuing judicial inquiry. It argues that these forms of scrutiny ultimately amplify, rather than end, the problems with shelter detention as they seek to improve its functioning, rather than question its existence.

In the first section, I examine the ITPA's section prescribing shelter detention and the legislative debates leading to its enactment. I situate shelter detention within the Indian sociolegal context and beyond, drawing connections to global anti-trafficking and anti-immigration contexts. After this contextual exploration, I analyze how shelter detention instantiates the convergence of multiple forms of power and governance. For this conceptual analysis, I engage with insights from Foucauldian sociolegal scholars, feminist and South Asia scholars, and ethnographers of the Indian state.

The second section draws upon my ethnographic research with state-appointed staff, NGO representatives, and detained women at the Mumbai shelter in 2012–2013. Around six weeks after the escape incident, I started visiting the shelter twice a week over eight months. I performed volunteer tasks, interviewed shelter staff, and observed interactions between them and the detained women. Drawing upon my ethnography, this section provides insights on the carceral practices and morally charged efforts through which shelter detention is enforced, and how they are experienced. I show how the police, judges, state welfare officials, and NGOs enact the

[3] See, for example, Bose (2018); Das (2016); Ganguly (2016), Guha (2019); Walters (2016).

projects of protection, detention, reform, and rehabilitation that converge in shelter detention. For instance, I examine how anti-trafficking NGOs work with the state government's Women and Child department to manage the "protective custody" of rescued women by providing livelihood skills training at the shelter. I explain how these rehabilitation programs appeal to foreign donors, Indian judges, and state agents because of their neoliberal objective of facilitating women's exit from both prostitution and state custody, but show how they are rarely useful, sustainable, or lucrative for detained women.

My ethnography foregrounds how women placed in shelter detention experience this carceral institution through profound uncertainty about their release. I demonstrate how the institution and its practices, along with the bureaucratic procedures of the law, curtail the detained women's mobility, interaction with family or the outside world, and ability to earn a living. At the same time, I highlight how detained women experience, navigate, and resist these forms of carceral governance.

The chapter also examines how anti-immigrant sentiments pervaded shelter detention and impacted how women known or suspected to be from Bangladesh were perceived and treated at the shelter. I show how sociopolitical concerns around Bangladeshi women as "illegal immigrants" join the multiple agendas shaping shelter detention, and how Bangladeshi women experience additional delays and xenophobic discourses and practices. This builds upon my discussion in Chapter 5 about the simultaneous and discordant constructions of Bangladeshi women's victimhood and criminality, and how Bangladeshi women navigate and contest them.

Central to the ethnography in this chapter are my reflections on the methods, ethical dilemmas, and challenges of doing research and maintaining research access in a carceral institution. I explain how the detained women's politics of refusal became a point of entry for me to understand the harms of shelter detention. I discuss, in particular, how one woman's refusal to answer my questions provided insights into a regime where detained women were constantly expected to answer questions, while their own questions remained unanswered. I also discuss how I screened films and TV shows as a way to provide entertainment, build rapport, and seek the perspectives of the detained women, while working within the restricted scope of interactions I was permitted and performing the volunteer tasks I was assigned.

The last section of the chapter moves from my ethnography of the Mumbai shelter to the media reports of twenty-three women escaping from it and the ensuing judicial scrutiny of the shelter. In other words, I return to the scandal that catapulted the shelter to public attention. I discuss the *Mumbai Mirror*'s reports of the escapes and allegations of abuse at the shelter and track its aftermath, from an activist bringing it to the Bombay High Court's attention, to the court subsequently initiating an investigation into the shelter. I demonstrate how the media and higher judiciary focused on what was perceived as "exceptional" abuse and poor governance at an "errant" shelter. While efforts to address abuse and violence and improve the management of shelters are important, they focused, as

I will show, on improving conditions *within* the Mumbai shelter and making it more "efficient" and "sensitive," rather than questioning the legal mandate of shelter detention to begin with. I argue that these responses ultimately extended and intensified the surveillance to which detained women were subjected at the Mumbai shelter.

CONTEXTUALIZING SHELTER DETENTION

The Indian Sociolegal Context and Beyond

Shelter detention in India has a long history that precedes current NGO-led, US-funded anti-trafficking efforts and dates back to colonial forms of governance. The late colonial period saw a shift in the governance of prostitution from the segregation of brothels – tolerated to cater to the British military and regulated by Contagious Diseases Acts – to legislations aimed at "suppressing" prostitution (Tambe 2009). The work of historians of South Asia illuminates how these colonial-era laws aimed at controlling prostitution, and the scrutiny, surveillance, and detention they brought into being, have shaped the evolution of shelter detention in India.

Through the nineteenth-century Contagious Diseases Acts, the colonial state surveilled sex workers through compulsory registration, mandatory genital examinations, and medical detention to treat venereal disease in "lock hospitals" (Levine 2003). Multiple state agencies implemented these measures, and sex workers often successfully evaded them.[4] Then, spurred by imperial feminists, Indian nationalists, and Indian women's groups actively opposing the colonial state's tolerance of prostitution, the late colonial period saw the enactment of Suppression of Immoral Traffic legislations prescribing "rescue" from prostitution (Legg 2014; Tambe 2009). To rescue women from brothels and to manage and fund rescue homes, the late colonial state actively sought the assistance of an embryonic and "ruthlessly reformative" colonial civil society (Legg 2014: 334). Historical geographer Stephen Legg describes these rescue homes in New Delhi in the 1930s as "an amalgam of a workhouse, a lock hospital, and the reformatory Magdalene Homes of the pre-1900s" (2014: 1950).

The postcolonial ITPA, as explained in the preceding chapters, reflects postcolonial lawmakers' dual and paradoxical anxieties around sex workers as immoral, "fallen" women to be detained and reformed, and as victims to be protected. The ITPA's provision for shelter detention is framed by this broader ambivalence. It gives judicial magistrates the discretion to place women removed from the sex trade in "protective custody" or shelter-based detention until the "suitability" of their families or guardians to "take charge of them" is verified. Until this verification is

4 Levine (2003); Mitra (2020); Tambe (2009).

completed, they cannot be released or set at liberty.[5] The process, involving coordination with NGOs and police, can take up to three weeks. Thereafter, courts can either order the detained women's release to a "suitable" guardian or commit them to further detention for one to three years for "care and protection." The ITPA assumes that protective custody will, where possible, be followed by the "restoration" of the women to their families. In other words, connecting back to my discussion in Chapter 5 of the Indian state's "familial ideology" shaping inquiries, the ITPA ultimately intends for the onus of rescued women's protection to shift from the state to their families.

While the ITPA gives women removed from brothels "an opportunity to be heard," their detention is determined not by their consent, but by a judicial magistrate's evaluation of their "age, character and antecedents" and the "suitability" of their guardians. Indian sex worker rights groups have challenged the way the ITPA's prescription of protective custody invalidates adult women's consent (Sangram 2018: 3). Legal scholars have questioned its constitutionality vis-à-vis the fundamental rights of life and liberty in the Indian constitution (Baxi 1988: 65; Muralidhar 1999: 293–294).

Sex worker rights activists have also questioned and challenged the ITPA's assumptions about custody and guardianship. In reality, several "rescued" women are the heads of their households, the primary providers for their families, and/or the primary caregivers for those the law assumes to be their guardians. In these situations, women find themselves scrambling to produce a younger sibling or offspring, or even fake guardians, to meet this legal requirement under the ITPA. This resonates with my discussion of the production of kinship and documents during inquiries in Chapter 5. In other cases, families to whom sex workers are "returned" sometimes refuse to take them back owing to prostitution's stigma or difficulty supporting them (Sangram 2018).

The ITPA prescribes protective custody through the language and mechanism of detention, reflecting the law's broader ambivalence towards sex workers as both criminals and victims. Protective homes are managed by the state welfare bureaucracy (typically the Women and Child Department), or in some cases by NGOs.[6] The women's organizations and social workers who shaped the ITPA in India's early postcolonial years felt that shelter detention would keep women out of the sex trade more effectively than short-term imprisonment, after which they would likely return to it (De 2018: 178). Despite ostensibly not being part of the criminal justice system, shelters are prison-like institutions. Writing about an ITPA protective home in northern India under judicial scrutiny for human rights abuses in the

5 This provision applies both to adults and to minors, though the shelters for adults and minors are separate.

6 For example, Walters and Raghavendra discuss detention in and escapes from an NGO-run shelter in Hyderabad (2022).

1980s, Justice S. Muralidhar describes its functioning as that of a "penal custodial institution, with rules drawn up along the same lines as those governing prisons" (2004: 287).[7] Detained women are not permitted to leave except by court order, and then only if a suitable "guardian" comes to take custody of them or if a police escort is available to deliver them to such custody. To appeal against detention, detained women or their kin must approach an appellate court. Indian legal scholar Usha Ramanathan questions the ease with which women are institutionalized, compared with the insuperable legal hurdles to their release (1996: 200).[8] In the context of the Mumbai shelter where I did my research, and from which twenty-three women had previously escaped, feminist scholar and activist Sujata Gothoskar asks whether the state and "respectable" society wish to protect women from doing sex work or to shield *themselves* from sex workers' perceived immorality (2013).

Enacted through the apparatus and practices of detention, protective custody is also envisioned as a project and space of reform and rehabilitation. Debating the ITPA in 1956, several Indian legislators emphasized that protective homes should not merely house, but also morally reform the women sent there and rehabilitate them to leave the sex trade (Lok Sabha Proceedings 1956). The ITPA states that protective custody is meant for "care, treatments, maintenance, training, instruction, control and discipline." It thus prescribes a carceral, moralistic, and gendered regime of protection and care. The contemporary implementation of reform and rehabilitation at shelters takes place through NGO-led livelihood training programs to encourage women to leave the sex trade.

Beyond prostitution, the ITPA's prescription of shelter detention is shaped by broader paternalist presumptions in the Indian sociolegal context about women's vulnerability and incapacity to care for themselves and act responsibly outside the protection of their families or the state (Ramanathan 1996). Indeed, these presumptions are reflected in the "familial ideology" of the Indian state (Kapur and Cossman 1996) discussed in Chapter 5. Returning women to their families is the preferred solution, with the alternative being the state taking over as guardian. This paternalist approach was also seen in the newly independent Indian state's approach to women who endured forced displacement, sexual violence, and the loss of kin during the Partition of the Indian subcontinent in 1947–1948. After Partition, the Indian state attempted to recover and then "restore" these women to their families or keep them in "safe custody" if the families were unwilling to take them back (Das 2007; Menon

7 Muralidhar was a human rights lawyer and legal researcher who later became a High Court Chief Justice.

8 It is worth citing the entire quote. "It is when the law turns its attention to what it perceives to be transgressions by women that an additional concern steps in: that of non-criminal 'immorality' … Perceptions and presumptions about a woman's sexual vulnerability as well as her (alleged) sexual conduct are tendered as unobjectionable reasons for confining her in what is euphemistically termed 'protective custody.' The relative ease with which agencies of state may institutionalise women, even where reasons of crime or mental illness are absent, contrasts with the difficulties encountered by women who seek to be allowed to leave institutions" (Ramanathan 1996: 200).

and Bhasin 1993). Feminist historians' accounts of these efforts suggest that beyond managing prostitution, placing women deemed destitute in shelters has been central to the history of welfare bureaucracy and social work in postcolonial India more generally (De 2018; Menon and Bhasin 1993). Partition-era concerns continue to frame the postcolonial Indian state's policy toward women's migration, such that they are seen as economic dependents or potential victims of exploitation in need of state protection (Kapur 2010).[9]

These paternalist presumptions span the governance of prostitution and broader concerns about protecting marginalized girls and women, while controlling their perceived sexual deviance or excess. In late colonial Delhi, most women detained in a rescue home meant to reform prostitutes were not connected to prostitution, but deemed in need of protection for other reasons including abandonment, pregnancy, and mental illness (Legg 2023). Today, the ITPA continues to intersect with other Indian laws, such as the law on child marriage, that combine state protectionism and punitive control. Through shelter detention, the ITPA institutionalizes an imbrication of the punitive and paternalist regulation of women's and girls' sexuality pervading contexts beyond prostitution. Feminist sociologists have critiqued how the governance of "child marriage" polices adolescent girls in consensual relationships (Guha 2019; Roy 2017). Echoing Legg's findings in colonial India, current ITPA shelters also house adolescent girls labeled as victims of sexual exploitation, but sent there due to parental disapproval of their consensual relationships. Guha discusses how "child marriage victims" forced to stay at such shelters in eastern India experience them as punitive spaces that extend familial control and regulation of their sexuality and agency (2019: 128). Such patriarchal norms extend beyond shelter detention to other carceral institutions such as prisons, where women prisoners are perceived as both deviant and dishonorable (Bandyopadhyay and Mehta 2022: 2).

In contemporary times, as I have shown in previous chapters, the anti-prostitution sociolegal context in India is increasingly shaped by a US-led, NGO mediated transnational anti-trafficking campaign. Though shelter detention in the ITPA precedes contemporary anti-trafficking campaigns by decades, anti-trafficking NGOs have expanded its possibilities. As the reader has already seen, the State Department and US faith-based organizations have spent millions funding NGOs in India for anti-trafficking interventions. Pressure from this transnational anti-trafficking regime has fueled the expansion of initiatives including rescues, shelters, and rehabilitation programs (Das 2016; Walters 2016). In the policy discourses of this US-funded global anti-trafficking regime, shelter detention occupies a paradoxical place. On the one hand, the US State Department's *Trafficking in Persons Reports* have portrayed South Asian shelters as safe havens,[10] where survivors

[9] Concerns around kin, community and state protectionism come together to frame the vulnerable female migrant subject in other parts of South Asia as well (see Joshi 2001).

[10] See Chapters 1, 3, and 4.

of trafficking are protected and even empowered.[11] On the other hand, the *TIP Reports* have critiqued the abuses, lack of resources and facilities, overcrowding, and negligence reported at Indian shelters (2019: 237) and shelters' restriction on freedoms that run counter to international principles on victim protection (e.g. 2010: 16, 2012: 185, 2015: 186).

It is significant to note that shelter detention joins a broader spectrum of carceral anti-trafficking solutions that feminist scholars have critiqued in other global contexts beyond India. In the US, for instance, Jennifer Musto (2016) finds that anti-trafficking interventions combine protective and punitive measures, even when not attached to shelter detention. In a feminist analysis of gendered disciplinary regimes and carceral practices targeting immigrants across Asia, Maggy Lee (2014) draws parallels between shelter detention and immigrant detention. Later in the chapter, I will explore comparisons between shelter detention and immigrant detention around experiences of uncertainty and delay.

Shelter detention, in particular, exists in many global contexts (South Asia, Southeast Asia, the Russian Federation, Nigeria, Israel, and Central and Eastern Europe) as a problematic but largely unquestioned solution to punitively "protect" sex workers after anti-trafficking rescues (Gallagher and Pearson 2010). Both China and Thailand have used existing carceral institutions to carry out anti-trafficking work funded by US faith-based organizations in tandem with moral reform projects (Shih 2023: 5). In the Philippines, shelters subject sex workers and trafficked victims to disciplinary practices and moral regulation in the name of rehabilitation, while placing restrictions on their mobility (Parmanand 2021). Shelter detention in India and Southeast Asia are similarly implemented by state welfare agencies. Unsurprisingly, escapes are widely reported in Southeast Asia too (Gallagher and Pearson 2010; Lee 2014; Soderlund 2005). There are also significant parallels between the Indian and Nigerian contexts. Vanderhurst (2022) provides a close ethnographic account of the involuntary shelter detention and moralistic rehabilitation of migrant Nigerian sex workers. Many of Vanderhurst's findings echo what I observed in Mumbai – how shelter detention equates trafficking prevention with curbing sex workers' mobilities (4) and combines protection, detention, reform, and rehabilitation (9–10), and how detained sex workers adamantly protest their detention (3).

[11] For instance, the 2012 *Report* features an image of a young South Asian girl performing martial arts while US Secretary of State Hillary Clinton and Indian anti-trafficking activist Ruchira Gupta look on (27). Below the photograph is a caption indicating that it was taken during Clinton's visit to a shelter for trafficking survivors in Kolkata, India. The caption includes a quote from Clinton: "It was the way she stood so straight, looked me in the eye, and had a sense of pride and accomplishment about her." In another example, the 2019 *Report* features an image of a South Asian woman in a *salwar-kameez* (traditional attire) with her head covered looking out of a window (vii). It describes her as a Bangladeshi survivor of sex trafficking at a shelter, where "governments and NGOs often work together to provide specialized, trauma-informed care for trafficking victims."

Discipline and Governmentality

Shelter detention instantiates an imbrication of different modalities of power through which state and nonstate actors govern prostitution. To analyze this imbrication, I have found it useful to think with political philosopher Michel Foucault's concepts of discipline and governmentality. Though shelters are carceral institutions – where Foucault situates *disciplinary* power – they are managed by a state welfare bureaucracy (sometimes by NGOs) that also enacts what Foucault terms *governmental* power. However, working with Foucault's concepts requires both recognizing and challenging his reliance on Europe as a point of reference.[12] In this conceptual analysis of shelter detention, I therefore move beyond Foucault to engage with insights from historians, feminist scholars, and ethnographers of South Asia.

As carceral institutions, shelters are sites where Foucault locates disciplinary power. This form of power is enacted through surveillance in institutions such as prisons and asylums, with the aim of transforming deviant individuals into "docile bodies" through corrective and reformatory practices (Foucault 1975). Situating disciplinary power in the Indian historical context calls for attention to the specificity of colonial institutions and practices (Kaplan 1995). For instance, comparing rescue homes and lock hospitals in colonial India with the Magdalene Homes and workhouses aimed at reforming prostitutes in Victorian Britain, Legg points out that unlike in Britain, women in colonial India did not have the option of leaving these institutions (2014: 1960–1961).[13] This difference reflects how these colonial predecessors to shelter detention were more carceral than their European equivalents.[14] It also reflects how racialized logics shaped the colonial state's regulation of prostitution through such forms of surveillance and coercion (Levine 2003: 88; Tambe 2009).

Foucault also locates disciplinary power and its panoptic forms of surveillance in a broader range of institutions including schools, factories, and hospitals. In contemporary India, shelter detention is an extreme, carceral version of a broader spectrum of gendered disciplinary regimes and surveillance practices. On the one hand, such regimes and practices exist beyond the anti-prostitution law and shelter detention. On the other hand, shelter detention is unique in the way it is mandated and legitimized by law, and enforced by multiple entities: the judiciary, the police, the state welfare bureaucracy, and NGOs. These similarities and differences emerge in comparing shelter detention with privately run surrogacy clinics in Gujarat. In her ethnography, Amrita Pande (2014) found women working as surrogates for transnational

[12] As discussed, for example, by Brown (2014); Chatterjee (2018); Heath and Legg (2018); Legg (2014); Kaplan (1995); Tambe (2009).

[13] See also Tambe (2009): 33–34.

[14] See also Tambe (2009): xxiv.

clients being closely monitored by doctors and staff in dormitories. She notes similarities between surrogacy clinics and other gendered disciplinary regimes, for instance, the monitoring of women in factory work (2014: 81).[15] The monitoring Pande describes closely resembles the forms of surveillance I observed at the Mumbai protective home. However, unlike shelter detention in the prostitution context, contracted surrogates were not literally incarcerated by legal decree.

Along with disciplinary power, another Foucauldian concept that helps to explain the enactment of power in shelter detention is governmentality, an ensemble of schemes and practices aimed to improve the condition of a population (Foucault 1991). Several scholars applying and extending Foucault's concepts have argued that as tactics of power, discipline and governmentality are often entwined and coeval.[16] In colonial South Asia, discipline and governmentality coalesced in projects of social and moral reform. Historians have observed that colonial governmentality centered, in particular, on improving native subjects' conduct or habits.[17] Central to these "politico-ethical projects of producing subjects and governing their conduct" (Scott 1995: 214) was the colonial state's governance of sexuality. Feminist scholars have shown how colonial anxieties about public order, decency, and morals targeted figures such as sex workers whose nonnormative sexualities were deemed "ungovernable" and therefore requiring control through new forms of surveillance (Hinchy 2019; Mitra 2020; Tambe 2009). In contemporary India, shelter detention merges disciplinary and governmental power: managed by a state welfare bureaucracy and NGOs (not by the criminal justice system), and combining detention with protection, reform, and rehabilitation. The next section will demonstrate how these forms of power converged in programs and practices at the Mumbai shelter aimed at creating both the "docile bodies" of discipline and the "responsibilized" subjects of neoliberal governmentality.

The governmentality framework has also been useful to examine how "improvement" projects (Li 2005; Rose and Miller 1992) bring together heterogeneous actors and objects (Heath and Legg 2018: 26; Legg 2014). In India, as in other global contexts,[18] state and nonstate entities come together to regulate prostitution through moral campaigns. This point bears further elaboration. In contemporary India, on the one hand, the governance of sexuality perpetuates and reanimates the state's role despite the state's retreat from aspects of social life in a neoliberal context (Puri 2016: 5). On the other hand, NGOs have long been partners in "governmental projects of development and humanitarian welfare," from colonial

15 Researchers in other global contexts have also noted connections between gendered disciplinary practices in shelters and factories. In China, for instance, Elena Shih discusses how women at a mandatory anti-trafficking shelter found the rules policing their behavior akin to those in dormitory housing for low-wage jobs (2023: 90).

16 See, for example, Agustin (2007); Legg (2009); Li (2007); Merry (2001); Tadros (1998); Valverde (2010).

17 Brown (2014); Chatterjee (2018); Heath and Legg (2018).

18 See, for example, Amar 2013; Valverde 2008.

and postcolonial civil society activism to recent neoliberal projects (Bornstein and Sharma 2016: 77–78). Within this longer historical context, now also shaped by neoliberal models of women's empowerment, NGOs have played, and continued to play, significant roles in the regulation of prostitution.

THE MUMBAI PROTECTIVE HOME

In Mumbai, in the past three decades, concerns over both HIV/AIDS and sex trafficking have led to an increasing number of rescues by police and NGOs (Agnes 1996; Shah 2014). As discussed in Chapters 4 and 5, police have also accelerated efforts to cleanse the city of "immoral" activities in pubs, bars, hotels, and so on, leading to more women being removed in the name of rescue (Gothoskar 2013). Concomitantly, real estate developers are displacing brothels as part of land grab efforts, aided by police raiding these establishments and "rescuing" large groups of women working there.[19] These amorphous raid-and-rescue operations, stemming from a range of agendas and motivations including anti-trafficking, land grab, and moral policing, led to an increased number of women being sent to the Mumbai shelter during the time I conducted my research. As explained by police, magistrates, shelter staff, and NGOs, this resulted in considerable overcrowding at the shelter. At the time of the escapes, the number of women placed there far exceeded its capacity of 100 inmates – a situation that these interlocutors believed prompted the escape.

When speaking with me or with shelter staff, the women detained at the Mumbai shelter provided a range of accounts similar to those I heard during rescues, postrescue procedures, court appearances, and inquiries. Some described their entry into the sex trade in terms approximating trafficking (being forced, threatened, abducted, or deceived). Others said they did sex work owing to a combination of *marzi* (choice) and *majboori* (economic compulsion), and were forcibly rescued by police sweeps of "immoral" establishments, or by NGOs wrongly perceiving them as victims of trafficking.[20] These two groups included women from Mumbai and other parts of Maharashtra, from other Indian states such as West Bengal, Andhra Pradesh, and Karnataka, and from Bangladesh. A third set included mostly local women from in and around Mumbai who worked in beer bars, massage parlors and beauty salons, and maintained that they were not sex workers, let alone trafficked.[21]

[19] My interlocutors blamed land grabs for the mass raid of the "Simplex Building," from which 400 women were rescued from seventy-five brothels and brought to the shelter. For a detailed discussion of the Simplex Raid, see Pai et al. (2013). For an ethnographic account of real estate developers' eviction of sex workers as they redevelop Mumbai's red-light district into profitable real estate, see Shah (2014).

[20] See the critiques of forced raid-and-rescue operations referenced in Chapter 2.

[21] As discussed in Chapters 4 and 5, several raids by the Mumbai police targeted establishments merely suspected to be sites of prostitution. This closely resonates with shelter detention in Nigeria,

The woman who escaped and spoke to a Mumbai tabloid, though from Bangladesh, provided an account to the tabloid that fit this last category. As I learned, however, these differences around trafficking, voluntary sex work, or a denial of prostitution mattered very little in women's experiences of shelter detention.

Anti-trafficking NGOs shaped and expanded shelter detention by conducting rescues in and around Mumbai, helping judicial magistrates to conduct inquiries with rescued women,[22] conducting "home investigations" to verify if sex workers could be sent back to their families, and conducting livelihood training programs and counseling sessions at shelters. The NGOs regularly visiting the shelter were not limited to anti-trafficking NGOs, though anti-trafficking NGOs seemed to have the strongest presence. Of the anti-trafficking NGOs, around half had US funding, while others had varied sources of local and foreign funding. They included Christian organizations affiliated both with local churches in Mumbai and with US-based church groups that provided them funding.[23] Other NGOs that organized programming at the shelter did not focus on anti-trafficking, but had experience working in prisons, conducting livelihood training for various marginalized groups, and promoting awareness about HIV/AIDS and sexual health.[24]

When I first tried to find the Mumbai shelter amid the slums surrounding it, the local man I asked for directions described it as the "place where ladies are caught and taken,"[25] expressing its local perception as a carceral institution. It is housed in a compound with a heavily guarded iron gate (see Figure 6.1). A second set of gates must be unlocked by a guard to enter the building. Inside, a third set of metal grill doors separates the central hall and staff offices from the women's living quarters, into which they are locked from the outside. The detained women were usually grouped by these doors, asking for news of their release. "*Kab chhootengey?*" ("When will we be released?") was their constant query to me, to the staff, NGO workers, or police who visited. The shelter staff could not answer this question, either because the courts had not sent the necessary orders,[26] or because no police

which functions as a preemptive form of migration prevention. Women are rescued and detained as they are deemed at risk of imminent abuse, despite not having experienced any injury or danger (Vanderhurst 2022).

22 As discussed in Chapter 5.

23 See Chapter 4, footnotes 10 and 35.

24 However, none of these NGOs were pro-sex worker rights or feminist groups. In Chapter 5, I discussed how members of a progressive feminist group supporting sex workers' rights in Mumbai found that the criteria of experience "in the field of suppression of immoral traffic in persons" seemed to exclude them from participating in inquiries at the Special Court. The same group also wanted to work with the women detained at the shelter, but were unable to gain entry, as they were not part of the powerful and well-funded anti-trafficking NGO circuit, which provided the approved training sessions and other resources, and therefore had a strong working relationship with the shelter administration.

25 In Hindi, "*Jahaan pe* ladies *log ko pakad ke laatey hain.*"

26 This was usually more of an issue with other magistrates' courts in the areas around Mumbai such as Thane. The Mumbai Special Court, being focused on ITPA cases, provided clearer orders in a much more timely fashion.

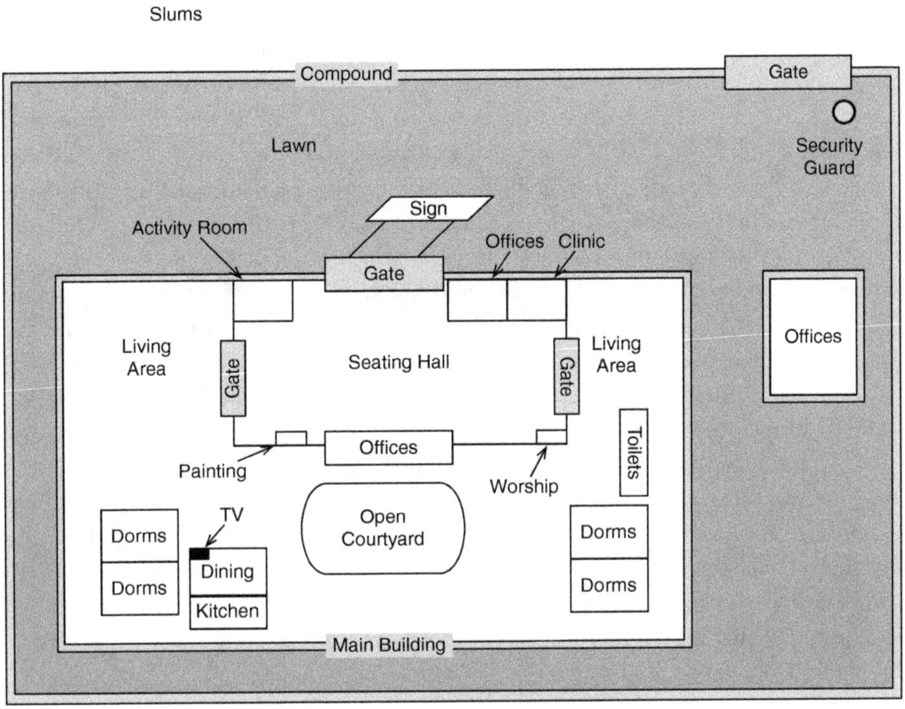

FIGURE 6.1 Layout of the Mumbai protective home (author's illustration).

escort was available to take the women back to their homes despite the court ordering their release.[27] Uncertainties and delays around court orders, police escort, and repatriation procedures led to prolonged stays at the shelter.

Day 1: Ruby's Refusal

When I first entered the protective home, the caretaker informed me that the women did not want to interact with anyone. When they saw me enter, a group of twenty to thirty women who sat watching television in the central hall started to leave the room. "Look, here they come again asking questions,"[28] they muttered to each other in Hindi. The caretaker apologetically explained that the High Court-appointed committees had been asking the women many detailed questions about the escapes and conditions at the shelter, pushing them to the limits of their patience. Making matters worse, a group of women who had been at the shelter for only a couple of weeks had been released earlier that day, while many who had been there longer still awaited their release.

[27] This police escort is a requirement in the Maharashtra State Rules implementing the ITPA.
[28] In Hindi, "*Lo phir aa gaye yeh log sawaal poochne.*"

Given this situation, I was instructed not to ask the women any questions about themselves or about the escape incident. For this first visit, I was instead asked to talk to the women about "Confidence Building" and "Correct Approach towards Life."[29] This put me in the difficult position of being introduced to the women not only from a position of authority, but also from a highly moralistic vantage point exaggerating the already inescapable hierarchies and concomitant ascriptions of respectability that framed our interactions. I prepared for the session with trepidation, racking my brains about what I could possibly say that was not entirely vacuous or pontifical, yet within the rubric of what those granting me access would find permissible. As it turned out, these ruminations came to naught. Perhaps because my visit eventually turned into a listening session the women did not object to despite the tense atmosphere at the shelter, the staff overlooked my not delivering a lecture on the "Correct Approach."

Walking toward the quickly dispersing group of women that day, I asked them to continue watching television, offering to just sit with them for a while rather than ask questions. Gradually, some returned to the television set to finish watching the film that was playing. When I kept my word about not asking questions, they began talking to me on their own about why they were upset. Some told me they had been at the protective home for three months, some for six, and some others (from Bangladesh) for more than a year.

> People keep coming and asking us questions and giving us lectures about the same things, but nobody helps us get released. That's all we're interested in. We don't want to learn anything. We just want to go home!

I recognized a young woman in a nightgown who walked past listlessly. "Aren't you Ruby?" I greeted her, reminding her that she had shown me around the shelter when I had visited months earlier to discuss research access. She had been warm and cheerful then, showing me a watercolor she had painted and offering me a cup of *chai*.[30] During that visit, Ruby had been eager to share her story with me. She crossed the border from Bangladesh with an uncle, after which another relative sent her to a brothel in Grant Road (in Mumbai's red-light area) where she did not know she would be forced into sex. Like the three Bangladeshi girls in Chapter 5, Ruby wanted to come to India to make a living through domestic work, but was trafficked into the sex trade and eventually rescued. Hers was a case of voluntary migration that turned into sex trafficking. The Special Court wanted to repatriate her to Bangladesh, but she wished to stay on in India.

In our second encounter, Ruby looked at me with faint recognition and asked when I had last visited. When I said it was six months ago, she exclaimed, "You

[29] My giving this talk is mentioned in the reports the shelter provided to the Bombay High Court as an example of the measures being taken to improve the environment in the protective home.

[30] I remain unsure whether Ruby was genuinely happy at the shelter for a short while or was presenting herself as such to remain in the shelter staff's good books.

have come again after so long and look, I am still here!" I asked if she would like to sit down and chat. "Please, spare me. I don't want to talk or listen to anyone," she scoffed, and walked away. Ruby's migration journey, prolonged detention, and refusal to speak were powerful points of entry that helped me begin to understand the harms of shelter detention.

The politics of refusal are generative and deserve ethnographic attention, as they signal an unwillingness to "play the games of the state that would signal consent" (Simpson 2017: 21; Tuck and Yang 2014). In refusing to answer "yet another set of questions," Ruby and other women at the shelter resisted a regime in which becoming objects of knowledge and being subject to power are inextricably related (Foucault 1982). They saw me, as a researcher who would ask questions, as part of this regime, which had expanded from shelter detention to the police investigation of the escapes and the judicial monitoring of the shelter. This expanded regime of governance subjected the detained women to incessant questioning, providing them nothing in return.

Through the perceptible shifts in Ruby's disposition across our two interactions, I began to comprehend the impact of shelter detention's uncertainty and delays on the women it was imposed upon. On my first visit, Ruby had been the staff's favorite, someone they relied on to be the "face" of the shelter to visitors like me, with whom she shared her story. Six months later, the staff anxiously described her as "difficult to manage" owing to her agitation at not being released. Ruby, for her part, no longer wanted to tell her story, and refused to answer questions.

Ruby was sent back to Bangladesh a few weeks later. The Bombay High Court intervention after the escapes had succeeded in fast-tracking an otherwise prolonged process. Before leaving, Ruby apparently told the magistrate who ordered her repatriation to Bangladesh that she would return to India, "if not to Mumbai, then somewhere else." Like Bishakha in Chapter 2, Ruby's desire to leave the brothel and the shelter was not to return "home." Her remarks, as reported to me by the magistrate, echo the feminist critiques I have discussed of the ITPA's assumptions around protective custody and familial guardianship infantilizing adult women. They also reflect migrant aspirations that challenge repatriation as a corollary to rescue, with shelter detention as a time and space-in-waiting.

Observing the Shelter: Navigating the "Correct Approach"

The Mumbai protective home, already a carceral space, was in an even more intense "lock-down" when I conducted my research. After the escapes, there was fastidious surveillance of who was allowed in, for how long, and what they were allowed to do. I started volunteering there around six weeks after the escapes, but owing to the ongoing police investigation and judicial monitoring, the administration was anxious to control any further "disturbance" or negative publicity. I was given strict instructions on the scope of my interaction with the women.

Anthropologists studying carceral institutions have drawn attention to the limitations of participant observation when both the researcher and the researched face constant surveillance (Bandyopadhyay 2010; Rhodes 2001). Like Mahuya Bandyopadhyay, reflecting on her fieldwork in a Kolkata prison, I was constantly aware that failure to comply with instructions and expectations would jeopardize my access to the shelter, and struggled to balance building rapport with the detained women and maintaining the expected distance from them (2010: 38–39, 50).

Before I provide further ethnographic insights on the Mumbai protective home, a discussion of my access to the institution, the ethical dilemmas I navigated, the methodological choices I made, and the possibilities and limitations I worked with is in order. I performed the role of volunteer with (varyingly successful) attempts to balance the tasks expected of me with my ethnographic objectives and feminist politics. I was allowed to visit with the understanding that I would keep the detained women "productively engaged," as the shelter superintendent put it. I was, yet again, profoundly uncomfortable to be in a position where I was essentially helping to "manage" the women, reprising the very logic of moralistic paternalism I sought to interrogate. The anthropological knowledge that emerges is a product of these struggles and dilemmas, and how the researcher navigates them (Bandyopadhyay 2010: 52).

To the shelter administration and Bombay High Court monitoring committee who gave me access to the shelter at a time when it was under tremendous scrutiny, I explained that my research was part of my study of state and NGO governance of sex trafficking and prostitution. I believe I was granted access because I clarified that I would not sensationalize the case further, but would examine protective custody from the perspectives of the detained women and the staff, and how it was shaped by the court, police, and NGOs.

While the staff knew I was a researcher, their interactions with me took place in the context of my role as a volunteer. The detained women, too, primarily got to know me in that role. The approach I settled into was to offer the women an activity they enjoyed, within the parameters of my assigned task of keeping them "productively engaged." The lack of entertainment options at the shelter exacerbated the women's mounting concerns about their continued detention. The cable connection was disconnected because the staff claimed the women fought over the remote control and the situation became "unmanageable." Over time, the television set became a primary site for my conversations with the women. On my first day, we had gathered around it instead of asking or answering questions. Later, to provide entertainment that was also acceptable to the shelter's superintendent, I brought in television shows and films to screen and discuss. I arrived at this strategy after unsuccessfully trying some "ice-breaking" games suggested by the superintendent, which the women likened to the many structured NGO-led training and rehabilitation activities at the shelter that the staff rounded them up to attend.

I knew from conversations with rescued women and their families in New Delhi and at the Special Court that many watched television shows such as *Crime Patrol* and *Savdhaan India*, dramatized reenactments of real-life instances of people getting justice against all odds with the help of good Samaritans, police, and NGOs, often focused on crimes against women.[31] I downloaded some episodes from these two shows and screened them in the shelter's dining area, initiating discussions afterwards. Often, the women would ask me to also bring *masala* (popular) Bollywood movies, which the superintendent allowed me to do as long as I screened "serious" content at other times, and as long as the women participated in discussions afterwards. Echoing middle-class perceptions about Hindi cinema,[32] the superintendent perceived *masala* films as mindless entertainment, in contrast to more thoughtful content around social justice that would provide grist for "appropriate" discussion. This perspective was also shaped by the projects of reform and rehabilitation in the ITPA's prescription of shelter detention, as discussed previously, and its implementation, as I will show.

While I endeavored to work within these parameters, the screenings and discussions often belied the *masala*/serious distinction. For one, I was able to bridge this perceived distinction in my choice of content. With their focus on gender violence and gender justice, the popular *Crime Patrol* and *Savdhaan India* provided both entertainment, which the women appreciated, and "productive engagement" with "social issues," per the shelter superintendent's instructions. But even *masala* movies, as I will demonstrate, provided opportunities for the detained women to critically reflect about the opaqueness of the legal system.

During the discussions after screening these films and shows, I tried to find indirect ways to steer the conversation toward understanding how protective custody impacted the detained women. I would typically ask them if they saw connections between scenes or themes in the content they had viewed and their own lives. In response, they spoke organically about their experiences of shelter detention, sometimes using the screened content as a frame of reference through which they articulated their sense of injustice, as the example of *Damini* will show.

The experience of collectively watching these films gradually changed the women's willingness to engage with me.[33] I was greeted with shouts of "Hi *didi*, *aaj*

31 As mentioned in the context of Sunaina Das' case in Chapter 3.

32 Bollywood film producers and actors draw similar distinctions between films for the "masses" versus "classes" Ganti (2012).

33 My use of films as the structuring context for discussion resonates with Stacey Vanderhurst's reflections on her ethnography at a Nigerian shelter, where viewing "Nollywood" films and local hip hop music videos provided fodder for her conversations with the detained women (2022: 12). There are also strong methodological parallels with anthropologist Shakthi Nataraj's research with LGBT activists in Chennai. Rather than eliciting first-person narratives – the "canned stories" that her interlocutors challenged – Nataraj used short stories and films to facilitate discussions (2022: 51, 63).

kaunsi picture laaye?" ["Which film have you brought today?"]. Before I knew it, the film would be taken from my hands, popped into the video player, and playing on the screen, while I was gently pushed into a chair so we could begin, and my cup of tea refilled more than once to thank me for the entertainment. Having mostly moved on to streaming video services for my own entertainment by then, I often struggled with the video player, much to the amusement of Preeti, an engineering student who had been forcibly rescued from a bar and detained at the shelter, who often provided me with much-needed assistance.

My growing rapport with the detained women, fueled by these sessions, did not override my participation in the expanded regime of governance or the women's politics of refusal, as previously discussed. Instead, the screenings helped me facilitate discussions without subjecting women to "yet another set of questions" from a regime where the researcher was indistinguishable from the authorities; a regime that they could not physically leave, but one that they challenged through refusal and other forms of resistance.

The detained women's gestures of affection and gratitude toward me intensified my guilt at my inability to do more than provide a temporary distraction from shelter detention's interruptions of their lives, mobilities, relationships, and livelihoods. Further, despite my efforts to develop rapport, and despite the cheer with which they eventually greeted me, I could not entirely avoid being seen as an authority figure – one of the many NGO *didi*s who visited and "lectured them." Some women also thought I was the judge's "assistant" at the Special Court whom they had seen or met while their inquiries were conducted at the magistrate's chambers,[34] and who they hoped might be able to facilitate their release. I was acutely aware of their sense that "nobody got them released," and of how, in adhering to the instructions about "productive engagement" that allowed me access to the shelter, I, too, participated in the regimes of governance perpetuating their detention.

Protection/Detention

At every visit, I was warned that the women were "upset" because their release orders, travel permits for repatriation (in the case of Bangladeshi women), or police escorts had not yet arrived. Ironically, women who had been trafficked ended up staying at the shelter the longest, because they were usually from distant Indian states or from Bangladesh.[35] They could not understand why they were being "punished" more. Though it took the longest for Bangladeshi women's paperwork to be processed from across the border, Indian women were also rarely released within the prescribed three weeks. Many ended up staying at the shelter for three to five

[34] See Chapter 5.

[35] Baitali Ganguly provides a detailed explanation of the multiple agencies involved in the repatriation of trafficked women to Bangladesh (2016: 87–88).

months. Local women from Mumbai were usually released sooner than others, as their families were able to come and apply for their custody.

Each day without news brought on crushing disappointment, destroying the women's hopes to go home in time for a specific festival, and increasing their concerns about their children's well-being and their own inability to earn while at the shelter. NGO representatives told me of several cases where trafficked women feared that if they gave evidence against the accused traffickers, they would have to stay at the shelter even longer. This is among the several significant reasons why rescued women did not support the prosecution case, as explored in Chapters 3 and 4. Sometimes, women I had previously met at the Special Court during inquiries would come running to me when I visited the shelter, crying, and asking why months had passed but they had not yet been sent home.

Detained women were allowed to phone or meet with their families once in two weeks, but the shelter staff closely policed these interactions. They checked visitors' identity documents and photographs, and spoke to callers or visitors to verify that they were "genuine" relatives and not, as Kalpana, the shelter's probation officer put it,[36] "some xyz." By "some xyz," Kalpana meant a range of male acquaintances – pimps, boyfriends, traffickers – who could be threats to the women's safety or "bad influences" on them. Every second Saturday, a long line of relatives or possible "xyz" stood outside the shelter, clutching plastic bags full of identity documents (voter ID cards, ration cards, Aadhaar cards,[37] marriage certificates) and photographs, which they showed to a guard who checked them against a list.

To interact with their visitors, the detained women also had to stand in line at the superintendent's office all day. A shortage of staff meant that not everyone was able to meet their visitors on a given day. Their mobile phones were confiscated until their release, and they were only allowed to use them when the shelter's landline was not working. The shelter superintendent explained that they discouraged the women from using the phone at all:

> Without identity proof, it is difficult to know who is on the other end of the phone conversation. It could even be the accused trying to exploit or manipulate the girls. So it is better if the girls' families come to meet them here along with the required identity proof, which we can check.

When I asked how the staff could tell who was a "genuine" visitor from who was not, Kalpana told me that apart from scrutinizing the documents they provided, she observed the "attachment" between a woman and a caller or visitor:

> If she is talking to her mother, she will cry a lot. If it is "some xyz," she will ask them about money. That's one way to tell. But it is difficult to tell when they are speaking

36 Under the ITPA, probation officers are appointed at protective homes to "inquire into the above circumstances and into the personality of the person and the prospects of his rehabilitation."

37 Explained in Chapter 5.

> on the phone in their native language. I tell them to speak in Hindi so I know what they are saying.

This type of surveillance is a prime example of how the paternalist logics of both protection and detention converge in the practices of protective custody. It also reflects how shelter staff relied not merely on the (uncertain) legality of documents but equally, on their own intuitions and moralistic perceptions to implement protective custody. This resonates with my discussion of the way those conducting inquiries assessed identity and documents in Chapter 5.

The women often questioned the logic of their enforced separation from kin and significant others, and this level of surveillance of meetings and conversations. Indeed, they described the situation as worse than prison, which would likely have allowed them more contact with kin and partners. Preeti and her friends – a group of women forcibly rescued from a bar – remarked with disgust, "Even if we had murdered somebody, we would have been better off … at least we could have gotten bail and met our families!"

Some women were the sole earners in their families and worried about their children. Others feared that their husbands or boyfriends would move on in their absence. I realized how deeply and frequently such concerns weighed on their minds when Maya, a quiet and thoughtful woman in her thirties who rarely smiled, asked to see a photograph of my husband, who I had told them was in the US. Maya had been trafficked from Bangladesh on the pretext of domestic work and wanted to go back to her husband, but was not sure if he would accept her return almost a year after she had left, against his wishes, to find work. Looking at my husband's photograph, she asked, pensively:

> *Didi*, how often do you talk to your husband? Do you see him every day on video chat? How do you know he is not with someone else? We don't have a choice, we are stuck here. But not you. Why don't you go back to him? With men, you never know…

Several women at the shelter similarly urged me to return to the US so my husband would not leave me for someone else. Meanwhile, the shelter staff (the superintendent, caretaker, probation officer, and state-appointed social workers – all women) viewed the detained women through a deeply ambiguous lens, as victims needing protection and unruly subjects needing to be managed, disciplined, and improved. They referred to the women as *ladki log* ("the girls") with a mix of infantilization and fear, reflected in their description of Ruby as "difficult to manage." On the one hand, the staff feared what they described as the women's impulsiveness and unruliness. On the other hand, they imputed a certain passivity to the women's "idle minds," "sitting around just counting the days," and so on.[38] They described their work in paternalist terms, "calming the girls down" (*shaant karna*) and "explaining things to them" (*samjhaana*). They

[38] Elena Shih's observations of moral supervision at a Chinese shelter are uncannily similar (2023: 92).

saw their role as protecting the detained women from "bad influences" while also managing their reluctance at being detained.

Despite this deeply moralistic approach toward the women, shelter staff expressed their helplessness at being unable to answer the women's questions about release. Kalpana and Sarita, two hard-working young Maharashtrian women staff, who seemed well liked among the women, explained how the uncertainties around the women's release put them in a difficult position. "The truth is, we don't know the status of their cases ourselves, so what can we tell them?" They also described the challenging task of communicating detention orders to the women, who they said became depressed and sometimes even suicidal on hearing the news.[39] Kalpana, the probation officer, explained it as follows:

> From ten to six we stay with the girls. They expect something from us. They ask us "*Didi*, what can you do for us, can you get us out of here?" We are always tense about what answer to give when they ask us these questions.

Jennifer, a young Indian woman who worked for a Christian anti-trafficking NGO and had talked about Bangladeshi women claiming to be from Kolkata in Chapter 5, echoed these concerns in describing her visits to the shelter when she came to meet women she had helped to rescue. She did not question the logic of shelter detention, but acknowledged that women experienced it as a prison, and expressed her skepticism about whether the shelter could then be effective at rehabilitation. She said to me, in English:

> It is really sad that *genuine* victims feel they are in jail. I mean yes, it's for their own safety that they are under lock and key. But it's only up to a point that you can tell them "It's for your own safety … blah blah" … but then, "Why am I under lock and key," you know, that is their question. They don't feel like victims.

"Tareeq pe Tareeq:" Inordinate Delays

The ITPA's expectation for multiple agencies – courts, police, shelter administration, and NGOs – to coordinate rescued women's return to their guardians led to inordinate delays. Such coordination involved overcoming language barriers across different states and substantial delays and lapses in the movement of paperwork. While sending women to the shelter, the Special Court often asked the staff to take NGOs' assistance for "home investigation."[40] As discussed in Chapters 2 and 3, some NGOs had a presence in other states or had developed contacts with other NGOs and police in those states in their anti-trafficking efforts. Under pressure from the Bombay High Court to reduce the time women spent in shelter detention, the

[39] There was one attempted suicide during the months I volunteered, though not while I was at the shelter, and more were reported in the media and in the High Court-directed inquiry as having taken place prior to my research.

[40] As explained in Chapter 2, this refers to locating the women's families and determining their suitability for guardianship.

shelter staff sought NGOs' assistance in this regard. However, even NGO-facilitated home investigation took several months and required substantial coordination, especially in cases involving Bangladeshi women.

Sometimes, I helped the shelter staff liaise with NGOs to visit the women's families so that the home investigation reports could be sent to the court to facilitate their release. However, these processes were often mired in communication and coordination issues between the protective home staff, NGOs in Mumbai, NGOs in the states the women came from, and the court. The shelter's official email account was often inaccessible owing to internet connectivity issues, which created further challenges. I also sought assistance from government contacts I had made in New Delhi (while conducting research there) in speeding up the repatriation of a group of Bangladeshi women. But ultimately, the law's prescription of shelter detention, and the multiplicity of agencies and procedures that its implementation requires, left little scope for the situation to improve.

My discussions with the detained women after the film screenings inevitably centered on the opaque nature and delays of the legal system as forms of injustice. One of the most revelatory moments was when I showed a *Crime Patrol* episode about a woman who was trafficked into prostitution, then rescued and returned to her family. "*Ek baat batao*, madam," ["Tell me something, madam"], said Preeti, the engineering student/bar server, when I asked her and her friends what they thought of the episode, "*Iss sab mein* court *kahaan hai?*" ("where is the court in all of this?"). She pointed out that the postrescue procedures were made to look so easy and quick on television, far from the reality of her experience with the law. The court, which she saw as the reason she was "stuck" at the shelter, was conspicuous in its absence from the television show. She recognized that this was because only a speedy depiction of justice would make for good television. The women pointed out that their long stay at the shelter was also missing from the televised depiction of postrescue procedures, which showed, instead, that "everything looks OK." On a different day, I played an episode about sexual harassment at the workplace, which showed a woman fighting her case over several years. The women immediately picked up on the extended temporality of the case, remarking on how three judges had heard the case and the protagonist's child had grown to adulthood by the time the final judgment was passed.

When I asked the women for suggestions on films to watch together, some women asked for the 1993 Hindi film, *Damini*, about a woman fighting for justice on behalf of a raped domestic worker. The film, with its long, impassioned courtroom scenes depicting a layperson's disillusionment with the law, was part of our collective memory and cinematically mediated understanding of the law. Having grown up in India in the 1990s, I, too, had strong recollections of the film shattering my naivete about the criminal justice system, although unlike the detained women, I was fortunate to have not experienced the law and its delays first-hand. While discussing *Damini*, many women cited a monologue from the film when the protagonist's lawyer (played by popular Bollywood actor Sunny Deol) lambasts the Indian legal system for its inordinate delays in the form of "date after date" *("tareeq pe tareeq")* to the detriment of justice *(insaaf)*.[41] More than once, after watching a film about gender justice, the detained women compared the scene from *Damini* with their life at the shelter, asking, "Who will tell *our* story? The way we are given *tareeq pe tareeq*?"

There was no legal assistance at the shelter to help the women navigate these delays of law-as-bureaucracy. The Maharashtra State Rules implementing the ITPA prescribe the appointment of a "Duty Counsel" (along the lines of legal aid for prison inmates) to regularly visit the shelter, explain and track the status of the detained women's cases, and provide legal representation for them in court to appeal against their detention. Such legal aid is intended to provide institutionalized women access to the legal system (Muralidhar 1999). While monitoring the shelter after the escapes, the Bombay High Court too emphasized legal aid as a requirement the shelter was obligated to fulfill. However, this was only partly and symbolically implemented over the eight months I visited the shelter. Its provision rested upon yet another agency, the District Legal Services Authority (DLSA). The shelter did organize two legal aid "workshops," duly reported to the Bombay High Court. The DLSA sent judges and lawyers for an hour-long session where they gave the women a general overview about what most of them already knew – that release entailed a long and complicated verification process involving several agencies. While the women were able to ask questions, these workshops did not assist with specific cases.

Once, I accompanied Sarita, a government-appointed counselor and social worker well-liked by the women at the shelter, to a court in Thane (around 20 miles from Mumbai) one day. She was on a mission to explain the plight of a group of women from the shelter to a magistrate there whose vaguely worded order had led to this group languishing at the shelter for over five months. Preeti, the engineering student, was one of them. The detention order did not clarify whether all thirteen women were to be detained for one year or only the four among them who did not have guardians to claim their custody. In the absence of a legal aid advocate performing this task, Sarita made the hour-long train journey to try and speak with the judge.

The group of women in question had been forcibly "rescued" from a bar, where they said they worked as servers. While the police claimed they were being forced into prostitution there, they denied that they were doing anything except waiting tables, and were livid that they were being made to suffer while the bar owner was out on bail and had apparently already found replacements for them. Most of their "guardians" had appealed to the appellate sessions court, per procedure, to seek their custody – a long-drawn-out process – but four of the women had no guardians. Those four women wanted to ask the judge to set them at liberty to take

[41] Here is a longer translated excerpt from the monologue: "This is how it has always been, My Lord (addressing the judge). Date after date (phrase repeated four times with mounting frustration and anguish) is given [by the courts], but we have not got justice, all we have gotten is this 'date.'"

care of their children, who were being looked after by neighbors or relatives while they were at the shelter. On the appointed date of the court hearing in Thane, the case had been adjourned. The women had to return to the Mumbai shelter without being able to meet the judge. When Sarita made the second trip on her own to speak to the magistrate, he told her to go to the sessions court as he could not change his own order.

The delays of protective custody in India closely resemble lived experiences of immigrant detention. Undocumented detainees in the US endure both spatial exclusion from families and employment, and "dead" time that one is "not guilty of," but spends "just locked up" in administrative custody (Coutin 2010: 204). This systemic uncertainty and arbitrariness of waiting is also central to the lived experience of immigrant detention in the UK (Bosworth 2014; Turnbull 2016). Political anthropologists have also described how migrants and refugees experience "waiting zones" (Fassin 2005) and checkpoints (Poole 2004) along borders as sites governed by spatiotemporal uncertainties about their future, which hinges on decisions (or lack thereof) by laws and states (Ferme 2004).[42] As law and migration scholar Melanie Griffiths argues, "governance through uncertainty," even if not consciously designed, is normalized and critical to immigrant detention as it reiterates the state's power and indifference (2013: 280).

In Mumbai, while media reports highlighted *spectacular* violence and abuse at the shelter, my ethnographic research revealed how the arbitrariness and uncertainty of bureaucratic procedures enact *structural* violence (Gupta 2012). As anthropologist Akhil Gupta has shown, violence coexists with care in the routinized practices of state welfare (2012: 33). In shelter detention, the normalized bureaucratic practices causing inordinate delays subject those detained – ostensibly in the name of protection – to structural violence. Central to the enactment of disciplinary power is the "governance through uncertainty" that intensifies the impact of carceral institutions on those detained.

The role of NGOs is also worth noting here. The carceral protection, disciplinary power, and structural violence shelter detention enacts are shaped by what I described in Chapter 1 as an ever-expansive legal complex of both state *and* nonstate actors governing prostitution. NGOs, assisting with home verification and leading rehabilitation programs at the shelter, work within this regime of protection/detention and the structural violence of inordinate delays. Though the Mumbai shelter I researched was a state-run institution supported by NGOs doing home verification, rehabilitation, and so on, sometimes shelters are primarily run by NGOs. In the context of a shelter run by a US-funded anti-trafficking NGO in Hyderabad, Kimberly Walters finds that "bureaucratic indifference serves to deepen the harms of paternalism by disregarding and prolonging them in the name of procedural orderliness" (2020: 313).

[42] Though protective custody in India is not a site for border crossing, this sense of spatiotemporal powerlessness resonates with what I heard from the women detained there.

As Foucauldian sociolegal scholars remind us, along with the state, an entire legal complex of multiple regulatory authorities is enmeshed in the "bureaucratic workings of our over-governed existence" (Rose and Valverde 1998: 546).

Reform/Rehabilitation

Programming at the protective home implemented the ITPA's deeply connected projects of reform and rehabilitation through moralistic and gendered messages of self-improvement and NGO-assisted livelihood training. In this section, I will return to and expand upon the Foucauldian conceptual framework to show how these programs sought to create both the "docile bodies" of discipline and the "responsibilized" subjects of neoliberal governmentality who would earn a living outside of sex work after their release. At the Mumbai shelter, the state implemented reform and rehabilitation programs through its carceral and bureaucratic practices, while relying on NGOs – long involved in governing prostitution – to cultivate new subjectivities in the broader context of neoliberal empowerment (Roy 2022; Sharma 2008).

The shelter's main building had a large sign on it describing it as a *Swadhar Gruha* or "place of self-reliance," named after a federal government scheme for women's shelters. The Hindi word *Swadhar* closely resembles *sudhar*, which translates as reform or improvement. The term *Swadhar* in the shelter's description was frequently mistaken as *sudhar* by the detained women and the general public. As one woman quipped to me sarcastically during my first visit,

> There's such a big sign on the building saying "House of Improvement." Look! We have improved! We have learned everything! We accept that we did "inappropriate work." Now we have been punished, too. Let us go![43]

Decorating the shelter's sparse central hall was a framed painting of Savitribai Jyotirao Phule, a late nineteenth-century social reformer who, along with her husband, advocated for women's education and against caste discrimination in Maharashtra state. This image is labeled "Painting" in Figure 6.1. On major occasions such as a Hindu festival or national holiday, the shelter staff would center Savitribai's image more prominently on the wall and decorate it with ribbons and garlands. The image, featuring Savitribai's head partly covered with one end of her *sari*, was on display as the absolute antithesis of a sex worker. It evoked the type of gendered respectability the shelter wanted the detained women to aspire to, and formed the backdrop to speeches given by the superintendent or visiting guests (judges, state officials, and NGO representatives) or dance or music performances by the women.

During one of my visits, lawyers from an anti-trafficking NGO addressed the women at an information session at the shelter. What was reported to the High

[43] In Hindi, "*Itna bada* sign *laga hai yahaan, 'sudhar ghar' ka. Dekho hum sudhar gaye! Sab seekh liya. Maante hain ki galat kaam kiya. Ab sazaa bhi ho gayee. Yahaan se jaane do!*"

Court as a legal aid workshop to help the women understand the ITPA's release procedures often sounded like a "counseling" session aimed at reforming them.[44] The NGO lawyers explained to the women that the purpose of detention was not to treat them as criminals, but to "show them the right path." One of them, who also assisted the Special Court magistrate in conducting inquiries, invoked a gendered responsibility to one's family as the impetus for reform. She narrated the story of a woman who had put her son through engineering school with money she earned from the sex trade. "But when he found out what his mother did to support him, he was so disappointed in her. Think about this!" she addressed the women. Similarly, social workers and NGO representatives at the shelter sought to "change the women's mindsets" by explaining to them that "easy money" was detrimental to their health, honor (*izzat*), and their children's future.

At the end of the session, the shelter superintendent asked the women to sing a well-known redemption-seeking prayer in Hindi (from the 1986 Hindi film, *Ankush*), which they had been made to practice beforehand. Such performances of a willingness to take the "right path" were common to the shelter staff's presentation of the women to outsiders. Pulling up their *dupattas* (scarves) to cover their heads, they stood and sang:

> Give us the strength, that our mental faith may never be weakened. We are on a righteous path, may we never commit a wrong even by mistake.[45]

Seekhna versus Kamaana

Explaining the purpose of the protective home to me, the superintendent echoed what legislators had emphasized while debating the ITPA in 1956: bringing detained women into "mainstream society" (*aam samaj*) via economic rehabilitation. Rehabilitation programs worked within the shelter's overall moralistic ethos of improvement, while expanding its scope. NGOs provided tailoring, nursing, and beautician training, and occasional workshops in paper bag-making, spice-making, and the decorative arts of henna and *rangoli*,[46] all "decent," gendered, and low-paying forms of work aimed at disciplining "immoral" subjects into docile figures of feminine respectability.

Addressing a group of women participating in a *rangoli*-making workshop, the shelter superintendent thanked them for being *seekhne waale* ("the kind of people who learn"). She expressed appreciation for their willingness to learn "decent" skills – the desired outcomes of reform and rehabilitation. However, the cultivation of *seekhne waale* selves did not align with the detained women's socioeconomic realities. Many told me that they could ill-afford to devote time to learning (*seekhna*); their priority

44 See my discussion of legal aid in the previous section.

45 In Hindi, "*Itni shakti hamein dena daata, mann ka vishwas kamzor ho na. Hum chalein nek raste pe, hamse bhool kar bhi koi bhool ho na.*"

46 Floor decorations with colored powder.

was earning (*kamaana*). They were not convinced that the rehabilitation options offered at the shelter would provide enough income to sustain themselves and their families. Some retorted that they did sex work to feed their families, and asked where this "help" was when they really needed it.

Sarita, the shelter's state-appointed counselor, reported that the women asked why they were being asked to sit through the training instead of being released. Kalpana, the shelter's probation officer, said she spent much of her time trying, unsuccessfully, to "convince" the women to participate in livelihood training sessions:

> We have to explain to them to go and sit in the training, by saying "sit there, do this, you have to do this, it's good for your future." But they are not willing. We have to keep making them get up and go sit there.[47]

Notably, Kalpana's emphasis was on "sitting" in on the training, not on whether they were actually learning anything there, or benefiting from it. The detained women also referred to participating in the training sessions in this passive way. Sometimes, women who had said in their court inquiries that they worked at bars, parlors, or salons and were not sex workers at all would ask me to tell the Special Court magistrate that I had seen them "sitting" in the rehabilitation programs at the shelter. They hoped that a report of good behavior, based on their mere presence at these sessions, would help them get released sooner. Indeed, in response to some women's refusals to participate in the sessions, Kalpana and other staff threatened to inform the Special Court that they were reluctant to "learn" and "improve." They implied that if the court was not convinced of the women's good behavior, it would not release them from the shelter. The shelter's rehabilitation programs were thus both discursively and procedurally tethered to its carceral practices, and to the court that sent the women there.

The detained women resisted these programs, both because they did not consider them useful and because they were concerned that participating in them might result in a potentially longer stay at the shelter. Earlier in the chapter, I described how they refused to participate in the regime of power/knowledge that expected them to answer incessant questions from a revolving door of authority figures visiting the shelter while the women were unable to leave. Here, they refused to participate in a carceral regime of care that offered limited, untenable, and unviable forms of assistance.

NGOs held training programs at the shelter geared toward displacing responsibility for the women's welfare from the state (the Women and Child Department that ran the shelter) to the women's own initiative and entrepreneurial capacities. They taught the women livelihood skills with the aim to build their employability in

47 In Hindi, "Training *mein baitho, yeh karo, aapko yeh karna hai, aapke* future *ke liye achcha hai…aise samjhaana padta hai. Lekin taiyar nahin hotin. Unko manaana padta hai. Utha utha ke laake udhar baithana padta hai.*"

"decent work" so they could fend for themselves outside of the sex trade without state assistance upon release. Though the ITPA prescribes rehabilitation at shelters, it does not indicate the state's responsibility to facilitate the actual employment of women after their release.[48] I heard of some instances where NGOs had placed women in the beauty or hospitality industries. These were past examples and did not involve any women staying at the shelter during my fieldwork. My sense from talking to shelter staff and NGOs was that these placements were few and far between. In candid moments, some NGO representatives admitted that the rehabilitation options being provided were not sustainable or attractive, and recognized that women were not given options to train in lucrative fields or to pursue their preferred interests.

On the one hand, rehabilitation at the Mumbai protective home resembles neoliberal governmentality in other contexts. In the context of the transition from welfare to neoliberalism in Western Europe, governmentality scholars use the term "responsibilization" to describe how target populations are increasingly expected to advance their own welfare.[49] In the UK, Scoular and O'Neill discuss neoliberal "responsibilization" strategies where the state seeks to facilitate women's exit from prostitution by providing welfare support on the condition that they gain "useful employment." However, it does not provide jobs or tackle the poverty leading many women to sex work in the first place (2007). Along similar lines, NGOs at the Mumbai shelter (and in the economic rehabilitation of sex workers more generally) provide training in low-wage jobs and craft skills, urging women to find alternative employment, but do not help them to do so.[50]

On the other hand, reform and rehabilitation programs in the context of shelter detention do not merely instantiate neoliberal governmentality. They have a much longer history in the colonial and postcolonial governance of prostitution in India, as discussed earlier in the chapter, and deep connections to the state – specifically, the carceral space and disciplinary practices of shelter detention. It is also significant to note that neoliberal governmentality plays out differently in India than in Western Europe. In contemporary India, as anthropologist Aradhana Sharma (2008) points out, there is a coexistence of, rather than transition between, developmentalist and neoliberal logics in state and NGO collaborations to help marginalized women.[51]

48 In its description of activities protective homes are expected to undertake, the ITPA mentions "prospects of rehabilitation" and "imparting of training," without explaining what exactly these entail, or specifying the extent of the state's responsibility to facilitate women's employment.

49 Ballesteros-Peña 2018; Cruikshank 1999; O'Malley 1996; Scoular and O'Neill 2007.

50 Though unlike the UK, here no welfare support is provided on the condition of finding employment.

51 In the context of gender-based development programs, Sharma examines how the protectionist postcolonial Indian state struggles to reconcile its assumptions of passive female subjects in need of a benevolent hand, with neoliberal solutions in partnership with NGOs aimed to create active, responsible citizens. Sharma explains how the implementation of empowerment programs with NGOs enables the state to retain a welfarist face while building the capacities of marginalized actors to care for themselves. With its developmental functions being an inseparable part of its postcolonial identity and legitimacy, the Indian state cannot completely privatize these functions (2008: 59).

Rather than a transition from state welfare interventions to neoliberal projects, both are propagated simultaneously, not by a shrunken state that has dismantled welfare, but by multiple governmental bodies including NGOs.

Often, the detained women asked for more lucrative, stable, or glamorous work opportunities than the shelter provided.[52] The shelter superintendent once asked me to speak with the group of forcibly rescued bar servers from Thane about what rehabilitation options they wanted to explore. This group included Preeti, the engineering student who helped me with the film screenings and wondered why the delays of postrescue procedures were not shown. It was to advocate for this group's release that Sarita, the popular and conscientious staff counselor, had gone to the Thane court.

During my conversation with this group, thirty-year-old Anjali, exuding both confidence and weariness, was often the informal spokesperson. She said she worked at the bar, which the police insisted was a front for prostitution, to provide for her children. She was livid that the bar owner, after being arrested for running a prostitution racket, was out on bail and had resumed his business with a new set of women, while the "rescued" set languished at the shelter. For Anjali, a government job provided the possibility of financial security.

> I want a job in the municipality. I'll do anything. Get me a sweeper's job there. I'll do it. Can you or your *sansthas* [NGOs] do that? I don't think so.

Anjali's desire for a government job signaled her preference to pursue possibilities of long-term, secure employment, rather than the short-term training options being offered. However, the existing rehabilitation programs at the shelter could not facilitate this request. Anjali was asked to participate in the options offered at the shelter instead. Awaiting her release, she enrolled in nursing training and paper-bead making, with no guarantee of job placement or assistance with setting up a business.

Hema, another bar server from the group, had similarly specific aspirations that remained unmet. She wanted a job at the airport, so she could meet her favorite Bollywood actors.

> Madam, I have always wanted to work at the airport, I have heard that lots of glamorous people come there ... like Shah Rukh Khan, Hrithik Roshan, Madhuri Dixit.[53] I will do anything, even clean the bathroom there.

Again, the existing rehabilitation programs at the shelter could not accommodate this. When Hema was released early, an NGO encouraged her to come to their office for "job counseling." She never went. Instead, another woman from the

[52] As Bangladeshi women detained at shelters in India and Bangladesh have told researchers, the training shelters offer is for low wage work at best. With post-release employment options being limited to working in risky labor conditions in garment factories, many choose to return to sex work (Bose 2018; Ganguly 2016).

[53] Popular actors in the Hindi film industry.

group reported that Hema had returned to work at the bar. These examples demonstrate how existing rehabilitation programs can neither help those who wish to leave the sex trade explore viable or preferred alternatives, nor support those who might return to the sex trade.[54]

Bangladeshi Women: "From Maika *to* Sasuraal"

Two of the detained women whose roles are central to this chapter were from Bangladesh – Ruby and the woman who escaped and spoke to the media. Their accounts indicated very different migration trajectories and work experiences. Both willingly crossed the border to work in India, but Ruby was trafficked, while the woman behind the exposé said she worked in a bar by choice. Yet both, as Bangladeshi women, had endured prolonged stays at the shelter because their paperwork had not been processed. As I explained earlier in the chapter, even the involvement of NGOs and high-ranked government officials did little to speed up the process. In Ruby's case, the Bombay High Court's intervention fast-tracked her group's release from the shelter. This new level of scrutiny amid a temporary upswell of interest and attention provided a much-needed reprieve for some detained women at the Mumbai shelter. However, it did not alter the bureaucratic delays of the law in the longer term, especially in the case of women who crossed national borders.

Paula Banerjee poignantly describes the "in-betweenness" of women crossing the border from Bangladesh to India, with neither state willing to accept them or take responsibility (2012). A more colloquial take on this mutual lack of concern came from a magistrate familiar with ITPA cases who had considerable experience planning protective custody and rehabilitation programs for Bangladeshi women. This was the same magistrate who had explained her dual concerns around cross-border trafficking and illegal immigration to me in Chapter 5. When I asked her about why releasing Bangladeshi women from the shelter took especially long, she placed the blame squarely on the Bangladeshi government evading responsibility and not being "proactive" about helping them. She drew a parallel between India being the unfamiliar migration destination and a woman being an outsider at her in-laws' house (*sasuraal*) in the traditional South Asian context:

> See hypothetically I am saying, for them (Bangladeshi government) it's like the girl is in her *sasuraal* [in-laws' house]. If a girl goes from her *maika* (mother's house) to her *sasuraal*, her parents think it is OK, at least she is being fed there.

With this analogy, the magistrate extended the familial ideology discussed in Chapter 5 to the roles and stakes of nation-states in women's welfare. The analogy

[54] By training them in low-wage work, anti-trafficking rehabilitation programs return sex workers to the poverty that many seek to overcome through sex work (Walters 2016: 59), keeping them "mired in manual and menial low-wage work" (Shih 2023: 24).

references the prevalent patriarchal norm that once women are married, they are no longer seen as the responsibility of their natal family, and also remain outsiders at their in-laws' house even though they are expected to live there and care for their husbands and in-laws. Similarly, according to the magistrate's analogy, once women migrate, they are no longer seen as the responsibility of the country they left in search of a better life, and also remain outsiders at their migration destination, even if they live and work there. They are, therefore, caught "in between" two states that do not prioritize them.

Regardless of whether or not they were trafficked, many women, like Ruby, did not want to return to Bangladesh. The judges, NGO workers, and shelter staff I spoke to knew that economic need was the primary reason for this. Once they made it to India, Bangladeshi women wanted to stay on to find work that would pay more than they would earn in Bangladesh. As evident from the accounts of the three trafficked Bangladeshi girls I spoke to during an inquiry in Chapter 5, the wages paid by garment factories are not enough to make ends meet. If sent back to Bangladesh under repatriation procedures, many women try to return to India, as their material circumstances and options remain unchanged.[55] Indeed, Ruby explicitly voiced her intention to return to India to the magistrate who ordered her repatriation to Bangladesh. Grace, an Indian woman from a Christian NGO who regularly visited the shelter, recalled how one Bangladeshi woman had pleaded with her, "I will come back with a passport. Please get me a job."

For Bangladeshi women, the prolonged and uncertain temporality of shelter detention was caused both by the inordinate delays of bureaucratic procedures and, in some cases, by their own strategic denials of being from Bangladesh. In the context of inquiries in Chapter 5, I discussed how Bengali speaking women sometimes denied that they were from Bangladesh and provided unverifiable addresses in Kolkata, or no addresses at all. There is much to be critiqued about the culture of suspicion, anti-immigrant currents, and accusatory tactics framing inquiries. It is also important to recall that some Bangladeshi women who had been trafficked did not deny their nationality. However, some of them did strategically deny being from Bangladesh, which led to delays in initiating the procedure for their release. Some women admitted to being from Bangladesh only when detained at the shelter after inquiries, having realized that they would not be released until their addresses and families across the border could be verified.

In Chapter 5, I discussed the specter of criminality joining the possibilities of victimhood in judicial perceptions of Bangladeshi women because of their undocumented border crossing. Protective custody, too, was shaped by this anti-immigrant climate. Bangladeshi women were viewed through a specter of criminality that

[55] Bose 2018; Ganguly 2016; Ghosh 2015.

Indian women were not, even if they were also seen as exploited victims. My conversations with staff at the shelter about rehabilitation brought forth perceptions of Bangladeshi women as illegal immigrants less worthy of receiving support and assistance. Some among those implementing protective custody also expressed the view that Bangladeshi women were "not interested in learning anything." The magistrate who made the "*sasuraal*" analogy and expressed dual concerns around Bangladeshi women in Chapter 5 made the following comment.

> They are just spending their days there. Sometimes for two years, nothing is happening. They are not interested, not learning anything and they are also not allowing the rehabilitation to happen for the real victim girls.

In acknowledging that "nothing was happening" for two years, this magistrate evinced her awareness that Bangladeshi women's "lack of interest" in rehabilitation was due to procedural delays in their release. Yet she was one among many state actors who expressed concern that Bangladeshi women impeded the possibilities of rehabilitation at the protective home for those (Indian women) considered more deserving. Bangladeshi women were blamed both for not cultivating themselves into "learning" subjects (the *seekhne wale* selves the superintendent had lauded at the *rangoli* workshop) and for preventing the "real victim girls" from making the most of rehabilitation at the shelter. There was thus a not-so-implicit hierarchization of detained women – between those deemed deserving of support and those deemed undeserving as "illegal immigrants." Though on paper the Special Court magistrates prescribed rehabilitation for all detained women, Bangladeshi women's nationality thus factored into the kinds of targets of rehabilitation they were perceived to be.

As I have discussed in previous chapters, those implementing the ITPA viewed sex workers through the frameworks of criminality, immorality, and victimhood all together. This ambivalence was especially potent and discordant in the case of Bangladeshi women in protective custody. They were seen to embody extreme victimhood owing to their economic situation, and extreme criminality owing to their undocumented border crossing to leach away India's jobs and resources. Ironically, while magistrates and the shelter staff saw many Bangladeshi women as undeserving, unruly, and uninterested, they also spoke of some Bangladeshi women as more well-behaved and open to rehabilitation than Indian women. Ruby, as I have mentioned, was presented as the face of the shelter to visitors during her initial months there. Another Bangladeshi woman, Sultana, welcomed me to the shelter over nearly the entire eight months of my research, before she was sent back to Bangladesh. Considered more "well behaved" than the other detained women, Sultana participated in all the home's activities, served tea to visitors, and sewed beautiful clothes during the training programs and on her own time.

When I asked Kalpana, the probation officer, about whether any of the detained women were interested in rehabilitation, she categorized their likelihood to participate in the programs based on where they were from. In her view, women from Mumbai were usually released within three weeks or so, and therefore rehabilitation had "no meaning" for them. She contrasted them with Bangladeshi women, who had earned meager incomes from garment industry jobs back home. Unlike the magistrate's comments about Bangladeshi women being uninterested in rehabilitation and actively thwarting it, Kalpana felt that Bangladeshi women were docile subjects open to rehabilitation owing to their poverty.

> I shouldn't be saying this, but I am saying it anyway because you are asking me. That training for paper bag-making has started. I told all the girls to go and learn. The NGO people are saying they can earn Rs. 100 ($1.2) a day in that work. But the girls from Mumbai, they say, "We earn so much *outside* [i.e. from prostitution]. Rs. 3000 ($36) in a month is nothing for us." But Bangladeshi girls don't say this. Two of them are interested. They were trafficked. Now they want to do "good work." They go to the training sessions.

Kalpana's comments and my own observations indicated that some Bangladeshi women did participate in these sessions, in the hope that the skills being taught might help them earn higher incomes than they did in Bangladesh. But like the group of Indian women from the bar (Anjali and Hema), they had aspirations that the rehabilitation programs could not support and did not consider appropriate. Three Bangladeshi women I met at the shelter were talented dancers and wanted to learn modern dancing styles professionally to enter auditions in Mumbai's booming entertainment industry. They were denied this opportunity, both because dancing to earn a living was not considered a "decent" or sustainable rehabilitation option for women regardless of nationality,[56] and because of their Bangladeshi identities rendering their rehabilitation a low priority. The NGOs and shelter staff I asked about this replied that Bangladeshi women would eventually leave the shelter and cross the border into oblivion, with no way to follow them up, unlike Indian women whose rehabilitation could be continued and tracked by NGOs. This resonated closely with the extended familial ideology of the *sasuraal* comment. Thus, the reformist ethos of the shelter and of the broader Indian sociolegal context intersected with the anti-immigrant bias and *sasuraal* ideology around Bangladeshi women to narrow the already limited possibilities of rehabilitation and to whom they were made available.

AN ESCAPE, AN EXPOSÉ, AND JUDICIAL INTERVENTION

The media scrutiny and judicial intervention following the escapes in October 2012 deepened and expanded the multiple, intersecting forms of governance at the Mumbai protective home. The *Mumbai Mirror*, a city tabloid, foregrounded the allegations

[56] See my discussion of dance movement therapy in Chapter 4 and of concerns around dancing in Chapter 5.

of abuse and sexual violence that the Bangladeshi woman who had escaped made in her interview. It reported her account that the staff allowed armed men to come at night and rape women and tortured those who refused to have sex with these men, and that one woman became pregnant during her time at the shelter. In further reportage, the *Mirror* reports described the shelter's unhygienic living conditions and featured photographs of its filthy toilets, using terms such as "hell-hole" and "house of horrors." They highlighted the "insensitivity, corruption and callousness of the staff," who treated Bangladeshis as "scum," served irregular and inedible meals, beat the women, and took bribes from their families to release them (Sadhwani 2012).

Significantly, the *Mirror*'s exposé was part of a series of reports it carried about rape and abuse at other state-run residential institutions: an orphanage and a home for children with mental illness. Notably, those exposés were also done by the same reporter, Yogesh Sadhwani, and also prompted High Court scrutiny. This demonstrates how, while shelter detention is unique in its history and contemporary practices, it is also part of a broader set of state institutions meant to provide care but causing harm to marginalized groups. Further, the *Mirror's* role in these exposés reprises the role of the tabloid in framing and staging crime in the city, and participating in the ensuing legal theater (Prakash 2010: 2695, 3295).

In the context of prison escapes, Mahuya Bandyopadhyay observes that media reports temporarily disrupt the carceral institution's insulation from public view (2018: 45–49). She argues, further, that despite this disruption, escapes lead to the eventual reconstitution of prisons through increased surveillance and other punitive mechanisms (2018: 37, 41). At the Mumbai shelter, I observed how the escapes, followed by media coverage and judicial monitoring, similarly resulted in a reconstitution of shelter detention.

Concerned at the *Mirror*'s reports of abuse at the shelter, a local human rights activist emailed the reports to the Bombay High Court, which took it on as a public interest litigation (PIL).[57] PILs were introduced in India in the late 1970s by progressive lawyers, judges, and legal academics, relaxing the rule that only those whose rights have been violated may approach courts. The higher judiciary in India either acts on its own initiative or is approached by those acting out of concern for marginalized groups (though the scope of PIL has since expanded).[58] PILs have typically targeted both state repression (the violation of rights through the exercise of state power) and "governmental lawlessness" (the state's dereliction of legal duties) (Baxi 1985). Reflecting these features of PILs, the Bombay High Court's orders in the protective home case indicate that its intervention focused on two perceived problems.

[57] *Ms. Purnima Upadhyay vs State of Maharashtra* (2012).

[58] For an ethnographically informed exploration of expanding PIL jurisprudence in India, see Bhuwania (2017).

The first centered on the allegations of abuse and assault; that the shelter had failed to protect women. The second centered on the poor, inefficient, and "insensitive" management of the institution.

In PILs, courts typically appoint expert commissions of inquiry to ascertain the facts of the case, based on which they order state agencies to act. In this case, the Bombay High Court ordered the police and two committees to investigate and monitor the shelter. The police could not determine the veracity of the allegations of sexual assault in the *Mirror* interview, as the women who made the allegations could not be traced after their escape, and those who remained at the shelter could not corroborate them. The two committees focused on examining the shelter's space, staff, administration, and conditions, and their impact on those detained. The first committee, led by a psychiatrist and police officer, highlighted the staff's ill-treatment of the women, their "scare and subjugate" approach, lack of sensitivity and compassion, corruption, overcrowding, delays in repatriation, and unhygienic living conditions. The second committee, led by a judicial magistrate, provided a detailed action plan to improve the space, prevent overcrowding (by avoiding mass raids and speeding up release and repatriation with NGOs' assistance), and provide more and better rehabilitation options (again via NGOs).

Based on the two committees' reports, the Bombay High Court noted that the problem of overcrowding, attributed to mass raids filling it past capacity, had been addressed through the release of 200 women while the shelter was being monitored. The Justices also expressed appreciation for the proposed rehabilitation plan. The case was summed up as a matter where rights violations and a failure to protect had been caused by administrative incompetence and insensitivity, and a lack of coordination between agencies, which could be improved by better governance. At the final hearing of the case I observed in March 2013, the Chief Justice of the Bombay High Court told the shelter superintendent, "A little sensitivity is all we expect. That can make a difference to the entire system."

The High Court focused on improving the governance of the shelter and reducing abuse, not on questioning shelter detention itself. Usha Ramanathan describes the Indian judiciary's approach in PILs involving state institutions as "management jurisprudence," amounting to little more than a "bureaucratic exercise" (1996: 206). In this case, too, the judicial intervention resulted in efforts to ensure that the shelter was *managed* better. It extended the governance of sex workers to the governance of the shelter, reconstituting shelter detention as a site and practice that needs improving. The PIL did result in speedier release and repatriation during the monitoring period, thus addressing some of the problems with the ITPA's implementation. However, it subjected detained women to incessant questioning about the escapes, while their own questions about release remained unanswered. It also led to increased and intensified rehabilitation programs at the shelter, without questioning their moralistic premises or economic usefulness.

CONCLUSION

This chapter has situated "protective custody" within the Indian sociolegal context and at an intersection of multiple modalities of power governing prostitution. It has shown how state and nonstate actors enact the entwined projects of protection, detention, reform, and rehabilitation shaping shelter detention. It has also shown how shelter detention restricts the mobilities, relationships, and livelihoods of women removed from the sex trade, both through the law prescribing it and the uncertainties and delays marking its implementation. And it has demonstrated how the framing of Bangladeshi women as illegal immigrants impacts their treatment in protective custody, and their experiences of detention and rehabilitation.

Shelter detention combines disciplinary tactics of moral reform and governmental strategies of rehabilitation. In doing so, it reflects the ITPA's ambivalent treatment of sex workers as immoral subjects needing reform and victims needing assistance. In contrast, women such as Ruby, Anjali, and Hema sought their living in entirely different ways than the law's prescriptions of repatriation and rehabilitation. The refusals, escapes, and other strategies through which detained women resisted the Mumbai shelter go beyond condemning the reported abuse to foreground the structural violence of shelter detention permitted and, indeed, facilitated by law.

Beyond the analysis of shelter detention itself, the chapter has explored the incident of women escaping from the shelter, and its aftermath. It has argued that, in responding to shelters "gone wrong," media reports and judicial intervention ultimately reconstituted the carceral governance of women removed from the sex trade. Responding primarily to scandals, "insensitive" governance, inefficient administration, and callous staff, these interventions render shelter detention a target of improvement rather than repeal.

Conclusion

The ITPA and Beyond

Perhaps the biggest challenge of writing a book on a sociolegal issue of such complexity is keeping up with the ongoing plethora of legal developments around it. All the more so when both prostitution and trafficking continue to attract much political attention – both within India and globally – owing to the gendered moral panics around them. In this concluding chapter, I will reflect on some significant legal and policy developments – the newly expanded scope of anti-trafficking, the rehabilitation of sex workers, and the escalated targeting of Bangladeshi migrants – that have emerged since I did my ethnographic research. Through these updates, I will revisit some of the key themes I outlined in the Introduction and have tracked through the book: the excess of legality around the governance of prostitution and trafficking in India, the central role played by NGOs in this governance, and the impact of this governance on the women they target.

In the book, I have explored these themes using the intersections between anti-prostitution and anti-trafficking interventions as points of departure. The new developments I examine here shed further light on these themes, while also demonstrating the shifting intersections at which they emerge. The proposed legislations I am about to discuss are concerned with human trafficking more broadly. They intentionally and explicitly expand their mandate beyond the ITPA's focus on prostitution. There is, both in India and globally, a move to broaden the sexual humanitarianism through which trafficking was initially framed, to concerns around trafficking in labor sectors beyond the sex trade. At the same time, it is abundantly clear that the ITPA's long-standing framework governing prostitution continues to shape the broadened scope of anti-trafficking interventions in India. The proposed legislations signify both changes and connections between the governance of prostitution and anti-trafficking interventions in India over the past decade. While the legal framework of anti-trafficking now exceeds that of anti-prostitution, they continue to remain deeply connected, through the work of anti-trafficking NGOs and through existing models of intervention established under the ITPA.

EXPANDED SCOPE, OLD FRAMEWORK

As I was concluding my fieldwork in 2013, India adopted the United Nations (UN) Protocol's definition of human trafficking for the first time in its criminal law.[1] While the ITPA had only dealt with prostitution, Section 370 of the Indian Penal Code now criminalizes the trafficking of a person for the purpose of exploitation.[2] Two significant developments led to this amendment. For one, in 2011, before I began my fieldwork, India had ratified the UN Convention against Transnational Organized Crime and its supplementary Protocol to Prevent, Suppress and Punish Trafficking in Persons. India's adoption of the definition of trafficking in its criminal law reflected, in part, its effort to demonstrate its commitment to the UN Protocol.[3] Another major reason why India's criminal law was amended in 2013 was the unprecedented public furor over the widely reported and condemned New Delhi gang-rape incident of 2012.[4]

The criminal law amendment was followed by India's Ministry of Women and Child Development developing and circulating three draft anti-trafficking legislations in 2016, 2018, and 2021 with this broader definition of human trafficking. The draft legislations seek to place sex trafficking within an expanded framework of human trafficking (including issues such as child labor, bonded labor, forced marriage, and forced surrogacy). The draft 2016 Bill was revised into the 2018 Bill, which lapsed, and the 2021 Bill is yet to be introduced in Parliament at the time of writing (January 2024).[5] At the time I conclude this book, the ITPA and preexisting labor laws are still in force, and a new comprehensive anti-trafficking legislation has yet to be finalized.

Anti-trafficking NGOs supporting these new draft legislations have pointed out that they are required due to the limitations of the ITPA, which does not address trafficking beyond prostitution. Though these NGOs have long worked within the framework of the ITPA, along with other existing Indian laws, some have also expressed concerns about the hypocritical morality embedded in the ITPA's title. Nobel Laureate Kailash Satyarthi, whose child rights NGO receives US funding and uses an anti-trafficking framework, is reported to have questioned the moralizing approach framing the ITPA:

> Unfortunately, we have no proper law in India to combat trafficking. Even the nomenclature (of the ITPA) is ridiculous. As if some trafficking are (*sic*) moral, while others are not. (Banerjee 2022)

1 See Introduction, footnote 9.

2 See Kotiswaran 2013(a) for a comprehensive critique of this amendment.

3 As mentioned in Chapter 1, this ratification led to India being moved up in the US *Trafficking in Persons Report's* rankings.

4 See Chapter 1, footnote 29.

5 For a detailed discussion of these developments, especially the 2021 Bill, see Kotiswaran and Rajam (2023).

The ITPA's use of the term "immoral traffic," as opposed to "trafficking," brings anti-trafficking NGOs and pro-sex worker rights activists into rare agreement. Sex worker rights groups have also long pointed out that "the ITPA, with 'immoral' and 'traffic' in its very title, suggests that trafficking is an issue of morality rather than a criminal offense" (Pai et al 2018). However, this shared critique of the ITPA does not mean that anti-trafficking NGOs and pro-sex worker rights groups agree about the new proposed anti-trafficking Bills. Like the ITPA, these Bills have primarily been driven by anti-trafficking NGOs, and have excluded sex worker rights organizations. Unlike the ITPA's ambivalence around prostitution, the proposed Bills treat the "exploitation of prostitution" as an "aggravated form of trafficking in persons." Several pro-sex worker rights activists and scholars in solidarity with them have found that the proposed Bills conflate human trafficking with consensual sex work, and criminalize the facilitation of voluntary migration.[6]

The proposed anti-trafficking legislations also signify the *excess* of legality-and its attendant bureaucracy and paternalism – around prostitution and trafficking in India that I have explored through this book. This excess becomes especially clear when considering the relationship between the proposed Bills and other existing laws. Scholars and activists have questioned the need for new legislation, given the 2013 amendment to India's criminal law that already recognizes human trafficking (in all forms) as a crime. The proposed Bills' relationship to the ITPA and to multiple labor laws in India (e.g. on bonded labor or migrant workers) also remains unclear (Kotiswaran 2016 and 2018b). The 2021 Bill states that its provisions will override any existing laws if any inconsistencies arise (Agarwal 2021). However, several commentators have expressed concern that this multiplicity will lead, instead, to unnecessary overlap, confusion, and lack of coordination in the implementation of these laws.[7] Prasad (2018) points out that this will provide more scope for agencies to evade responsibility and not function effectively. When structures and entities have already been set up, via the ITPA, criminal law, and labor laws to address issues related to human trafficking, why multiply them? The new Bills will serve to further entrench the bureaucracy of law and governance I have described in this book. As a result, both voluntary sex workers and trafficked women will continue to face, even more intensely than before, the inordinate delays, uncertainties, and futilities of postrescue procedures.

It is also clear that anti-trafficking NGOs continue to be substantially involved in law reform as part of this expansion of focus from prostitution to trafficking. I have argued in the book that NGOs are central to a "governmentalized legal complex"

6 See, for example, Dasgupta (2018); Ghosh (2018); Kotiswaran (2013a, 2016, 2018a, 2018c, 2019); Lawyers Collective (2018); Pai and Sullivan (2018); Pattanaik and Sullivan (2018); Saikia (2018); Tandon (2018).

7 See, for example, Agarwal (2021); Kotiswaran (2018b); Prasad (2018).

that shapes, and is shaped by, the anti-prostitution ITPA. The draft anti-trafficking Bills have also been shaped by prominent US-funded anti-trafficking NGOs from across the country, through petitions they have brought to the higher judiciary and through the government's consultations with them.[8]

It is significant that anti-trafficking NGOs continue to shape law and policy and maintain strong working relationships with state agencies and policymakers, even in the current context in which the Hindu right-wing-led government of India, reflecting global trends of authoritarian regimes, has started to crack down on civil society organizations through increased regulation of foreign-funded NGOs. In this charged political context, several NGOs exposing the government for misconduct and abuse have, in the name of suspicions around "anti-national" or "anti-development" activities, lost their licenses and funding.[9] However, this targeting of NGOs in India does not seem to have impacted anti-trafficking NGOs, despite their foreign funding rendering them possible targets of state suspicion and regulation. Keeping in mind the central role nonstate actors have played in the history and contemporary implementation of the ITPA, this exception does not come as a surprise. In the context of prostitution, as I have illustrated in this book, Indian law *depends* upon a certain type of NGO intervention, which now extends, quite seamlessly, to trafficking.

To return to the proposed Bills and their expanded scope, I will briefly touch upon some broader points of critique, before turning to some specific provisions in light of this book's insights. This book has tracked how intersecting anti-trafficking and anti-prostitution interventions, implementing the ITPA, impact the women they target. Elsewhere, Kimberly Walters and I have argued that the regulation of prostitution continues to provide the framework for the proposed anti-trafficking legislation (2018). We have critiqued how the proposed legislation replicates the flaws of the existing ITPA framework by extending the harms of the raid–rescue–rehabilitation–repatriation model beyond sex work to other labor sectors.[10] Instead of acknowledging the harms of forced rescues, for instance, the Bill creates even greater scope for them to occur (Agarwal 2021). Police officers can, on mere suspicion that someone is being trafficked, conduct raid and rescue operations (Kotiswaran 2018b). Bringing my ethnographic insights from the book into this conversation, I want to take up three specific aspects of the proposed anti-trafficking Bills: the emphasis on a "victim-centered" approach, the reliance on

8 See Madhukalya (2016); Najar (2022); Pandit (2018).

9 Bornstein and Sharma (2016); Bornstein (2019); Ismail and Kamat (2018). As Bornstein and Sharma explain, "Nonstate actors in India have always had a dynamic and contested relationship with the postcolonial state. They have been courted and contracted by state institutions as partners in national development, albeit on statist terms. They have also opposed state agencies, forced policy reform, and been deemed anti-national forces" (2016: 86).

10 Prabha Kotiswaran also observes that several provisions of the 2018 Bill are formed "in the carceral mold of the ITPA" and applied to trafficking in other labor sectors (2018b).

"counseling," and continued institutionalization via protection homes and rehabilitation homes.

A "*Victim-Centered*" *Approach*

Those supporting the proposed anti-trafficking Bills describe them as "victim-centered." In an op-ed explaining her support for the 2018 Bill, the then Minister for Women and Child Development, Maneka Gandhi, emphasized that it centers the protection of vulnerable persons, especially women and children (2018). The Bills have an entire section on the care, protection, and rehabilitation of victims. They also stipulate that for recording the evidence of trafficked persons, designated courts should adopt "victim friendly court procedures" such as in-camera trials and video conferencing. The 2021 Bill states, under Section 48 (1) on Protection of Victims:

> The designated court … may, if satisfied that the life or safety of such a victim or any of his dependents or family members, or a witness, complainant or an informer is in danger, for reasons to be recorded in writing, take measures to protect such a victim or any of his dependents or family members, or a witness, complainant or an informer.

In light of my ethnographic observations, does this highly conditional scenario actually constitute a departure from the status quo of witness protection in the Indian criminal justice system? Why is the possibility of protection reserved only for those cases where the court is sufficiently "satisfied" that the victim or other witnesses are in danger? In Chapter 3, I discussed in detail why even survivors of trafficking (not just voluntary sex workers) refuse to testify, cannot be "traced," turn "hostile," or "compromise" owing to a lack of witness protection. Indeed, Sunaina Das and her family testified *despite* the constant threats they faced from the accused. Merely calling for protection to be provided to those who can "satisfy" the court of their need for it disregards the challenges that "victim-witnesses" endure just to come to court. The Bill's requirement that a written application be made to explain this perceived danger will, far from facilitating protection, place a greater burden on impoverished women and their families, and serve to exacerbate the labyrinthine bureaucracy of law that they already navigate.

Laws such as the ITPA and the proposed anti-trafficking Bills do not exist in a vacuum. They are (or will be) implemented within the criminal justice system. The 2021 Bill goes on to state, under Protection of Victims, that "witnesses, including victim-witnesses, shall have access to any existing witness protection measures or programmes" (Section 48 (4)). But such measures or programs are yet to be established. The conditional and limited witness protection the 2021 Bill envisages will remain, at best, in the realm of possibility, unless the Indian criminal justice system offers witness protection across the board. In 2018, the Indian government set up a witness protection scheme approved by the Supreme Court, pending the enactment of legislation on the matter, but the scheme has been critiqued for its short time frame of protection, screening of witnesses for threat perception, and other shortcomings (Gera and Makkar 2022).

The Bills also require the provision of legal aid among other forms of assistance. The need for legal aid, both for sex workers and survivors of trafficking, is especially evident from my discussion in Chapters 5 and 6 of how women navigate inquiries and shelter detention without legal assistance, sometimes relying on lawyers provided by the accused, which sends them further into debt. However, the Bills do not specify the mechanisms of when, how often, and by whom it will be provided, nor for what purposes, which Kimberly Walters and I have described as a missed opportunity (2018).

In a marked departure from the ITPA, the 2018 and 2021 Bills include, for the first time, provisions to compensate victims of trafficking from the property of the offenders, as well as "interim monetary relief." However, it remains unclear how this compensation will be administered (Dube et al. 2021: 232; Ramachandran and Walters 2018). As I found in Sunaina Das' case in Chapter 3, even when anti-trafficking NGOs help women pursue compensation ordered by courts, its disbursement is delayed, with victims and their families stuck between the courts and the Legal Services Authority. The 2021 Bill leaves it to Anti-Human Trafficking Committees to facilitate the provision of compensation, instead of streamlining this process and identifying the agencies responsible for disbursement. With this lack of specificity, it is hard to believe that survivors of trafficking will be spared from running pillar to post to actually receive the compensation they are due.

"Counseling"

When introducing the 2018 anti-trafficking Bill in the Lok Sabha (the lower house of the Indian Parliament), Maneka Gandhi made the following statement:

> The victim, who is counseled and rehabilitated, will be in a better position to support the prosecution.

The minister highlighted the Bill's rehabilitation-related provisions to make the claim that effective counseling would benefit not only the victim, but also the entire justice delivery process. Responding to this claim, Supriya Sule (Member of Parliament from the Nationalist Congress Party, in the Opposition), remarked:

> I welcome [rehabilitation] if everywhere we are going to get good and qualified counselors. But is India ready for such a [*sic*] good counseling? Who are going to be the counselors? Who is going to choose them?

This exchange[11] reminded me of how centrally "counseling" had featured in my research. Primarily conducted by women NGO workers, but also, occasionally, by

[11] Lok Sabha Proceedings 2018 (381, 451–452).

women police officers and magistrates, "counseling" was considered to hold the key to effective anti-prostitution and anti-trafficking interventions. Police, NGOs, and prosecutors explained that rescued women never revealed "the truth" at first, but would "gradually open up only with counseling." I have discussed at length how often I myself was reluctantly co-opted into conducting "counseling" across multiple sites and processes. Supriya Sule's questions reminded me of how, early on in my fieldwork, I often found myself wondering what exactly this practice, that NGOs and Indian legal actors alike saw as so potent, involved. Was it psychosocial counseling? What kind of expertise or skills did it call for?

The ITPA, enacted in 1956, does not define or mention counseling, though the practice was frequently mentioned to me as essential to its implementation. In contrast, half a century later, the 2018 and 2021 anti-trafficking bills explicitly mention counseling, qualified by a specific kind of expertise. The 2021 Bill states that "psychosocial counselors" should assist magistrates during inquiries, and that "psychological" support and assistance be provided to victims. This explicit mention of counseling reflects the growth of NGOs from their long-standing "social welfare" role to a newer image providing professional expertise, both within and beyond the contexts of prostitution and trafficking.

On the one hand, "counseling's" mention in the Bills and in the debates around them gestures to a specific form of expertise. On the other hand, however, in the implementation of the ITPA, where it is *not* thus defined, I have shown how "counseling" operates as an act of persuasion at which "respectable" women in positions of authority are deemed adept, regardless of specific expertise. I, too, as a researcher/volunteer with the perceived appurtenances of a "respectable" woman, rather than any particular skills, was seen as capable of "counseling." In the implementation of the ITPA, the purpose of "counseling" seemed to be to get rescued women to admit assumed "truths" about being trafficked or about being involved in prostitution, when they denied either possibility. As I have shown across the chapters, "counseling" often involved *dismissing* rescued women's narratives as lies or denials, and judging their choices as wrong or immoral. From postrescue procedures to court testimony, inquiries, and shelter detention, "counseling" was framed by moralistic and gendered presumptions and prescriptions, aimed to initiate a change in narrative, life choices, or future plans.

I do not know what prompted Sule's questions about counseling and counselors, but they have lingered in my mind as I wonder whether "counseling" will actually work differently if the 2021 anti-trafficking Bill is passed. Will a sociolegal context and history of social work structured by social hierarchies, paternalist assumptions, and deeply entrenched notions of gendered "respectability" prevail? Or will "counselors" really be selected for their psychosocial expertise? I am less inclined to believe the latter possibility, given how closely the procedures in the new draft legislations are modeled after the ITPA, and given the long-standing practices and hierarchies shaping "counseling" in the implementation of the ITPA. Besides, even if there is a greater emphasis on psychological or trauma counseling as an essential element of rehabilitation, how will it resolve the socioeconomic situations at the root of trafficking? In the next section, I will examine the related question of how the new proposed legislations envisage relief and rehabilitation.

It is also worth examining here the connection the minister drew between counseling, rehabilitation, and prosecution. The 2021 Bill includes a provision stating that the care, protection, or rehabilitation of victims should not be contingent upon their willingness to participate in the investigation or prosecution of the accused (Section 18). However, the minister's comment that counseling and rehabilitation will help survivors of trafficking better support the prosecution demonstrates a continued reliance on a criminal justice approach to trafficking. In Chapter 3, Sunaina Das' exceptional case of "victim-witness" testimony illuminated criminal justice's many limitations in serving survivors of trafficking.

Also implicit in the connection Maneka Gandhi draws between counseling, rehabilitation, and prosecution is the central role NGOs are envisaged to play in implementing the proposed anti-trafficking legislation. It indicates that the significance of NGOs in the "governmentalized legal complex" around prostitution now extends to trafficking writ large. My point here is not to argue that anti-trafficking interventions should only be the domain of state agencies. Instead, what I find interesting is the way a catch-all term such as "counseling" facilitates NGOs' expanded interventions into the realms of investigation and prosecution prioritized by their US donors. A practice such as "counseling" can be labeled as a specific form of professional expertise, yet implemented through the persuasive skills and moral righteousness of "respectable" women. It gives NGOs the opportunity to bridge their long-term involvement in social welfare and moral reform to curb prostitution, with newer donor-driven goals of working with the police and prosecution to curb trafficking.

Protection and Rehabilitation

The proposed anti-trafficking legislations are also set to extend shelter detention to newer target populations, expanding its scope and harms to survivors of "human trafficking" more broadly defined. The new Bills prescribe placing victims of *any* form of human trafficking in a "protection or rehabilitation home" as a judicial officer "may consider proper and required" for "such reasonable period as he considers suitable." The new Bills leave decisions about protection and rehabilitation to even greater judicial discretion, as the duration of time, which was specified under the ITPA, is now open to what a magistrate considers suitable. With this provision, the new Bills ignore the harms caused by the inordinate delays in ITPA shelters. The 2021 Bill appears to pay lip service to the well-documented abuses and violations at shelters discussed in Chapter 6, by merely stipulating that protection and rehabilitation homes be regularly inspected (Section 15). Such measures, as I have argued in Chapter 6, merely expand and extend the governance of shelter detention, leading to greater surveillance of the detained women. Protective custody itself not only remains unquestioned, but is now being extended beyond the ITPA to a much broader anti-trafficking context.

The 2021 Bill imposes time limits for the "repatriation" of victims back to their homes either within India or to the country of origin in the case of cross-border trafficking (Section 21 (5)). However, it does not impose time limits for the duration of shelter detention. Indeed, it makes release from shelters even harder than the ITPA through a provision by which the court can decide whether someone is contesting their detention voluntarily or under pressure (Section 7 (ii)). The new Bills also repeat the ITPA's requirement for the suitability of guardians to be determined before release. Rather than doing away with the "guardian" requirement, the proposed Bills now seem to infantilize all adults deemed to be trafficked in the same vein as the ITPA infantilizes women removed from the sex trade.

Though all forms of forced labor, such as bonded labor, now fall within the purview of human trafficking in the proposed Bills, the Bills' basic approach is markedly different from existing Indian labor legislation such as the Bonded Labor System (Abolition) Act, 1976 (BLSA) (Kotiswaran 2018b; Ramachandran and Walters 2018). The BLSA prescribes that bonded labor be set free, rather than detained in "protective custody" as in the ITPA. Instead of following this approach, the anti-trafficking Bills follow a model of institutionalizing victims, rooted in moral anxieties around "fallen" women and the perceived need to detain and reform them. Now, all categories of trafficked persons, including those subjected to bonded labor, are to be provided protection according to the ITPA's carceral model. It remains to be seen whether, in practice, male bonded labor, for instance, will actually be expected to produce "guardians" and sent into shelter detention under the proposed legislation. As some commentators have pointed out, despite the New Bills' broader definition of trafficking, their primary concern still seems to be sex trafficking (Prasad 2018).

Along with the new Bills, there has been another significant legal development around the rehabilitation of sex workers – a public interest litigation (PIL) in the case of *Budhadev Karmaskar vs State of West Bengal*. Before I began my fieldwork, the Supreme Court of India converted a criminal case involving the murder of a sex worker in Kolkata into this PIL focused on the economic rehabilitation of sex workers. I mentioned a previous order in this PIL in Chapter 1, while describing the Indian judiciary's moral ambivalence toward prostitution.[12] The court noted with concern that "sex workers obviously cannot lead a life of dignity as long as they remain sex workers."[13] Indeed, the court's orders, coauthored by Justice Markandey Katju, known for his literary departures, contain passages from Urdu poetry about chicks being hunted before they can fly and daughters in need of help while the custodians of morality are missing.

[12] Order dated August 2, 2011.

[13] Order dated February 14, 2011.

In its 2011 orders in this PIL, the Supreme Court ordered state governments across the country to provide details of schemes for the economic rehabilitation of sex workers. Interestingly, the court asked for specifics about who would provide the training, and proof of "concrete results" of how the training had helped women earn an income and find employment. This level of specificity seems to reflect the court's awareness of the futility of existing rehabilitation programs, soundly critiqued by the detained women whose experiences I discussed in Chapter 6. The court's subsequent orders in this PIL indicate its dissatisfaction with the information sent in by the state governments, which it described as "vague and too general." It criticized the central and state governments on this matter, while praising the work of anti-trafficking NGOs.[14] Though the court's instructions and critiques here are noteworthy, they continue to reflect an unquestioned belief in rehabilitation as something that all sex workers need, and that is to be paternalistically decided by NGOs and government agencies, rather than in conversation with individual women.

In line with how PILs have typically come to function, the court set up a panel to make recommendations in the *Budhadev* case through consultations with NGOs and government agencies. In a landmark move, the senior lawyer appointed to chair this panel also invited a major sex worker rights group to the table. Sex worker rights groups have long protested their exclusion from major legislative and policy developments around prostitution, such as the proposed ITPA amendment in 2006 I discussed in the Preface, and the new draft Bills. For the first time, despite much opposition from anti-trafficking NGOs, the *Budhadev* panel brought a sex worker rights group on board to provide input on a significant judicial intervention taking account of rehabilitation programs. Their inclusion has shaped the direction of the PIL in at least two significant ways. First, the court, while continuing to ask for better rehabilitation prospects, has recognized that rehabilitation should not be coercively imposed on sex workers,[15] or made conditional upon detention in protective homes.[16] Second, the court has recognized the need to not only provide sex workers livelihood options outside the sex trade, but also to create conditions for those who wish to continue sex work to live with dignity.[17] The latter recognition has caused much concern among anti-trafficking NGOs (and the central government ministries they work with closely), who have argued that this endorsement of voluntary sex work is contrary to the provisions of the ITPA (*The Hindu* 2012).

Eleven years later, the Supreme Court continues to issue directives in this PIL, pending the enactment of the proposed anti-trafficking legislations – which, the Indian government has claimed, incorporate the panel's recommendations on

[14] Order dated August 2, 2011.
[15] Ibid.
[16] Order dated August 24, 2011
[17] Order dated July 19, 2011.

rehabilitation. As part of its order on May 19, 2022, the court directed state governments to conduct a survey of ITPA protective homes, so that cases of adult women detained against their will could be "reviewed and processed for release in a time-bound manner." This ruling raised hope among sex worker rights groups that forced rescues had been called into question (National Network of Sex Workers 2022).

On the one hand, the Supreme Court's recognition of sex workers' right to live with dignity, coupled with this ruling calling for timely release from shelters, are welcome moves that demonstrate the foothold sex worker rights groups have now acquired in the realm of law. On the other hand, placing the latest *Budhadev* ruling in the context of my insights in Chapter 6, the Indian judiciary appears to view shelter detention yet again as something that needs better governance through surveys – another exercise of power/knowledge by the state. It acknowledges that adult women are detained "against their will," but focuses on speeding up their release, not on questioning forced rescues or protective custody. Significantly, just weeks after this Supreme Court ruling, eighty sex workers rioted against their detention in an NGO-run ITPA shelter in Hyderabad, though their escape was ultimately thwarted (Walters and Raghavendra 2022).

BANGLADESHI MIGRANTS

Chapters 5 and 6 have shown how Bangladeshi women and Indian Bengali women suspected of being from Bangladesh face additional surveillance, suspicion, biases, and delays owing to the anti-immigrant climate in which anti-prostitution and anti-trafficking imperatives played out. The "demographic anxieties" (Moodie 2010) and concerns with "detectability" (Ghosh 2019) around Bangladeshis in India have a long history that began to be entrenched in judicial rulings in the mid-2000s.[18] These sentiments were palpably prevalent and shaped the treatment of rescued Bangladeshi women at the time of my research. They have been greatly magnified and exacerbated in the decade since. During this time, the Hindu right wing has come into electoral power and retained it at the center and across several states, relying on a brand of Hindu nationalism that fuels and conflates a long-standing anti-Muslim political agenda with rhetoric and policies against Bangladeshi migrants, a majority of whom are Muslim.

In 2005, a politically motivated petition (*Sarbananda Sonowal vs. Union of India & Anr.*) raised concern about the "continuing influx of Bangladeshi nationals into India." The petitioner called into question a law in Assam that, according to him, made it difficult to prove that someone is not an Indian national and can be deported. In response, the court agreed that Bangladeshi "infiltration" is an "external aggression" to India and acknowledged the need to detect and deport "illegal

[18] See Chapter 5, footnotes 36, 39, and 40.

migrants." It ruled that the burden of proof should be placed on the person in question to prove that they are an Indian national and should not be deported.[19]

Motivated by the Hindu right wing's political ideology and building upon previous gains such as the *Sonowal* judgment, the Indian government made two major moves in 2019 to cement this growing anti-Muslim and anti-immigrant agenda. It brought about an amendment to the 1955 Citizenship Act (the Citizenship Amendment Act or CAA of 2019), which makes it possible for Hindus and non-Muslim minorities from neighboring South Asian countries (including Bangladesh) to apply for Indian citizenship. The Indian government went ahead with the amendment despite nationwide protests opposing the exclusion of Muslims from this newly defined access to Indian citizenship by religion in a nation built upon a secular constitution. Alongside, the government updated a documentary regime through the National Register of Citizens (NRC) that identifies those who cannot prove Indian citizenship and facilitates their detention and deportation (Chatterjee and Raheja 2020; Najar 2022). As Syantani Chatterjee has argued, the CAA and NRC have together weaponized suspicion against Muslims and migrants as a tactic of governance, and heightened the fear of arrest and deportation among Bengali-speaking Muslim migrants to an unprecedented extent (2020). Gender also plays a substantial role in the NRC's documentary regime and its exclusions (Ghosh and Moral 2020; Pisharoty 2019). Owing to gender discrimination and inequality, women, in particular, often lack state-issued documents or even bank accounts. In the context of postrescue procedures under the ITPA or the proposed anti-trafficking legislations, then, Bengali-speaking Indian Muslim women and Bangladeshi women who have lived in India a long time, now shoulder an even higher burden of proof than they did during the regime of suspicion I observed during my research.

Indeed, India's increasingly conspicuous, pervasive, and extensive entrenchment of anti-immigrant politics is also reflected in the proposed anti-trafficking Bills, which criminalize the facilitation of "illegal migration" as an aggravated form of trafficking (Najar 2022: 668, 680; Pattanaik and Sullivan 2018). Pattanaik and Sullivan have pointed out that the Bills thus conflate migrant smuggling with human trafficking and disregard the "dramatic mismatch" between the socioeconomic factors driving people's need to migrate and legally available migration opportunities (2018). By bringing a border control agenda into legislation purportedly aimed at curbing trafficking and protecting victims, the anti-trafficking Bills echo the carceral approach of the US anti-trafficking regime discussed in Chapter 1. In India's newly expanded anti-trafficking framework, preventing "illegal immigration" is a greater priority than protecting migrants' rights under international law or setting up support mechanisms for migrants to reduce their risk of being exploited and trafficked.

[19] The case is succinctly summarized by Kapur (2005): 134.

CONCLUSION

The accounts, stories, and choices of the women I met during my research call these new legal developments and forms of governance into question, just as they did with the ITPA and its implementation. As I contemplate the impact of these new developments, I am reminded of the several ways in which the women they target showed me the limitations and harms of the forms of assistance made available to or imposed upon them under the ITPA. Bishakha and Sunaina sought and received help, but ultimately made choices beyond the possibilities laid down by the law or needed assistance beyond what the law or NGOs could provide. Several women resisted rescue to begin with, Beauty from GB Road and the women from Meerut and Thane being cases in point. They also resisted the "governmentalized legal complex" around prostitution and trafficking by refusing to answer questions (an example being Ruby), or answering them selectively (as Rehana did during inquiries) and strategically (many denied being involved in sex work or being from Bangladesh). With very few exceptions, they questioned criminal justice's effectiveness as an anti-trafficking solution and the expectation to perform victimhood by refusing to appear or testify as "victim-witnesses" or by turning hostile if they did testify. After rescues, across the sites and procedures I observed, women sought a range of outcomes – returning home, returning to the sex trade, returning to India, marrying a former client, and making a living for themselves and their families (whether within or outside the sex trade). Regardless of whether they were trafficked or voluntary sex workers or denied being sex workers at all, they found ways to resist "protective custody" – by refusing to answer questions or participate in rehabilitation programs, by escaping if they could, and by speaking to the media. If only those drafting the new legislations would pay heed to their wide-ranging choices and experiences, more forms of support could have been envisaged beyond "counseling," vague mentions of "rehabilitation," and carceral forms of care.

Bibliography

Agarwal, P. (2021). Does India Really Need the New Trafficking in Persons Bill? *Open Democracy*, August 5. Retrieved January 30, 2024, from www.opendemocracy.net/en/beyond-trafficking-and-slavery/does-india-really-need-new-trafficking-persons-bill/

Agnes, F. (1996). Rescuing Mumbai's Child Sex Workers. *Economic and Political Weekly* 31 (14), 873.

Agnes, F. (2005, October). *Hypocritical Morality*. Retrieved January 14, 2007, from www.indiatogether.org/manushi/issue149/bardance.htm

Agnes, F. (2006, July). *The Right to Dance*. Retrieved August 10, 2016, from https://indiatogether.org/dancebar-society

Agnes, F., A. D'Mello and P. Sidhva (2014). The Making of a High Profile Rape Trial. *Economic and Political Weekly* 49 (29), 37–41.

Agrawal, A. (2008). *Chaste Wives and Prostitute Sisters: Patriarchy and Prostitution among the Bedias of India*. New Delhi: Routledge.

Agustin, L. (2007). *Sex at the Margins: Migration, Labour Markets, and the Rescue Industry*. New York: Zed Books.

Ahmed, A. and M. Seshu (2012). We Have the Right Not to Be "Rescued:" When Anti-Trafficking Programmes Undermine the Health and Well-Being of Sex Workers. *Anti-Trafficking Review* 1, 149–165. https://doi.org/10.14197/atr.201219

Alvarez, S. (1999). Advocating Feminism: The Latin American Feminist NGO "Boom." *International Feminist Journal of Politics* 1 (2), 181–209.

Amar, P. (2013). *The Security Archipelago: Human-Security States, Sexuality Politics, and the End of Neoliberalism*. Durham: Duke University Press.

Amin, S. (1987). Approver's Testimony, Judicial Discourse: The Case of Chauri Chaura, in R. Guha (ed.). *Subaltern Studies V*. New Delhi: Oxford University Press, 166–202.

Andrijasevic, R. and N. Mai (2016). Editorial: Trafficking (in) Representations: Understanding the Recurring Appeal of Victimhood and Slavery in Neoliberal Times. *Anti-Trafficking Review* 7, 1–10.

Aradau, C. (2004). The Perverse Politics of Four-Letter Words: Risk and Pity in the Securitisation of Human Trafficking. *Millennium: Journal of International Studies* 33 (2), 251–277.

Arondekar, A. (2012). Subject to Sex: A Small History of the Gomantak Maratha Samaj, in A. Loomba and R. Lukose (eds.). *South Asian Feminisms*. Durham: Duke University Press, 244–264.

Baker, C. (2013). Moving Beyond Slaves, Sinners, and Saviors: An Intersectional Feminist Analysis of U.S. Sex-Trafficking Discourses, Law and Policy. *Journal of Feminist Scholarship* 4 (Spring), 1–23.

Bales, K. (2012). *Disposable People: New Slavery in the Global Economy* (3rd edition). Berkeley: University of California Press.

Ballesteros-Peña, A. (2018). Responsibilisation and Female Imprisonment in Contemporary Penal Policy: "Respect Modules" ("Módulos de Respeto") in Spain. *Punishment and Society* 20 (4), 458–476.

Bandyopadhyay, M. (2010). *Everyday Life in a Prison: Confinement, Surveillance, Resistance*. New Delhi: Orient Blackswan.

Bandyopadhyay, M. (2018). Prison Escapes, Everyday Life and the State: Narratives of Contiguity and Disruption, in T. Martin and G. Chantraine (eds.). *Prison Breaks: Toward a Sociology of Escapes*. Camden: Palgrave Macmillan, 33–60.

Bandyopadhyay, M. and R. Mehta (eds.). (2022). *Women, Incarcerated: Narratives from India*. New Delhi: Orient Blackswan.

Banerjee, A. (2022). Need to Reform Old Anti-Trafficking Laws: Nobel Laureate Kailash Satyarthi. *The Times of India* (Kolkata Edition), July 29. Retrieved December 17, 2023, from https://timesofindia.indiatimes.com/city/kolkata/satyarthi-need-to-reform-old-anti-trafficking-laws/articleshow/93197144.cms

Banerjee, P. (2012). Chronicles of Trafficking. *The Hindu*, February 24. Retrieved January 30, 2024, from www.thehindu.com/features/metroplus/society/chronicles-of-trafficking/article2928155.ece

Barry, K. (1979). *Female Sexual Slavery*. New York: New York University Press.

Barnett, M. (ed.). (2016). *Paternalism Beyond Borders*. Cambridge: Cambridge University Press.

Basu, S. (2011). Impossible Translation: Beyond the Legal Body in Two South Asian Family Courts. *Law, Culture and Humanities* 7 (3), 358–375.

Basu, S. (2012). Judges of Normality: Mediating Marriage in the Family Courts of Kolkata, India. *Signs* 37 (2), 469–492.

Basu, S. (2015). *The Trouble with Marriage: Feminists Confront Law and Violence in India*. Berkeley: University of California Press.

Baxi, P. (2014). *Public Secrets of Law: Rape Trials in India*. New Delhi: Oxford University Press.

Baxi, U. (1985). Taking Suffering Seriously: Social Action Litigation in the Supreme Court of India. *Third World Legal Studies* 4 Article 6, 107–132.

Baxi, U. (1988). Beyond Prostitutional Platitudes, in S. C. Bhatia (ed.). *Social Audit of Immoral Traffic Prevention Act*. New Delhi: University of Delhi, 61–66.

Berman, J. (2010). Biopolitical Management, Economic Calculation and "Trafficked" Women. *International Migration* 48 (4), 84–113.

Bernal, V. (2017). NGO Fever and Donor Regimes: Tanzanian Feminist Activism within Landscapes of Contradictions, in A. Lashaw, C. Vannier and S. Sampson (eds.). *Cultures of Doing Good: Anthropologists and NGOs*. Tuscaloosa: University of Alabama Press, 37–55.

Bernal, V. and I. Grewal (eds.). (2014). *Theorizing NGOs: States, Feminisms, and Neoliberalism*. Durham: Duke University Press.

Bernstein, E. (2010). Militarized Humanitarianism Meets Carceral Feminism: The Politics of Sex, Rights, and Freedom in Contemporary Anti-Trafficking Campaigns. *Signs* 36 (1), 45–71.

Bernstein, E. (2018). *Brokered Subjects: Sex, Trafficking, and the Politics of Freedom*. Chicago: University of Chicago Press.

Berti, D. (2011). Courts of Law, in I. Clark-Deces (ed.). *A Companion to the Anthropology of India*. Malden, MA: Blackwell Publishing, 355–370.

Bhuwania, A. (2017). *Courting the People: Public Interest Litigation in Post-Emergency India*. New Delhi: Cambridge University Press.

Blanchette, T. G. et al. (2013). The Myth of Maria and the Imagining of Sexual Trafficking in Brazil. *Dialectical Anthropology* 37 (2), 195–227.

Bornstein, E. (2019). The Report: A Strategy and Nonprofit Public Good. *Humanity: An International Journal of Human Rights, Humanitarianism, and Development* 10 (1), 109–131.

Bornstein, E. and A. Sharma (2016). The Righteous and the Rightful: The Technomoral Politics of NGOs, Social Movements, and the State in India. *American Ethnologist* 43 (1), 76–90.

Bose, D. (2018). "There Are No Victims Here:" Ethnography of a Reintegration Shelter for Survivors of Trafficking in Bangladesh. *Anti-Trafficking Review* (10), 139–154, www.antitraffickingreview.org

Bosworth, M. (2014). *Inside Immigration Detention*. Oxford: Oxford University Press.

Brennan, D. (2005). *What's Love Got To Do With It? Transnational Desires and Sex Tourism in the Dominican Republic*. Durham: Duke University Press.

Brennan, D. (2014). *Life Interrupted: Trafficking into Forced Labor in the United States*. Durham: Duke University Press.

Brown, M. (2014). *Penal Power and Colonial Rule*. London: Routledge.

Brunovskis, A. and R. Surtees (2008). Agency or Illness – The Conceptualization of Trafficking; Victims' Choices and Behaviors in the Assistance System. *Gender, Technology and Development* 12 (1), 53–76.

Brunovskis, A. and R. Surtees (2010). Untold Stories: Biases and Selection Effects in Research with Victims of Trafficking for Sexual Exploitation. *International Migration* 48 (4), 1–37.

Budhadev Karmaskar vs. State of West Bengal, Supreme Court of India. Criminal Appeal No. 132 of 2010. Orders of the Supreme Court of India dated August 2, 2011 and May 19, 2022.

Butalia, U. (1993). Community, State and Gender: On Women's Agency during Partition. *Economic and Political Weekly* 28 (17), WS12–WS24.

Butalia, U. (2000). *The Other Side of Silence: Voices from the Partition of India*. Durham: Duke University Press.

Chacon, J. (2006). Misery and Myopia: Understanding the Failures of U.S. Efforts to Stop Human Trafficking. *Fordham Law Review*, 74 (6), 2977–3040.

Chapkis, W. (2003). Trafficking, Migration, and the Law: Protecting Innocents, Punishing Immigrants. *Gender and Society*, 17 (6), 923–937.

Chapkis, W. (2005). Soft Glove, Punishing Fist: The Trafficking Victims Protection Act of 2000, in E. Bernstein and L. Schaffner (eds.). *Regulating Sex: The Politics of Intimacy and Identity*. New York: Routledge, 51–66.

Chatterjee, P. (2004). *The Politics of the Governed: Reflections on Popular Politics in Most of the World*. New York: Columbia University Press.

Chatterjee, P. (2018). Governmentality in the East, in S. Legg and D. Heath (eds.). *South Asian Governmentalities: Michel Foucault and the Question of Postcolonial Orderings*. Cambridge: Cambridge University Press, 37–57.

Chatterjee, S. (2020). The Usual Suspects. *Political and Legal Anthropology Review (POLAR) Online*. https://polarjournal.org/2020/09/07/the-usual-suspects/

Chatterjee, S. and N. Raheja (2020). India's Citizenship Amendment Act (CAA): Citizenship and Belonging in India. *Political and Legal Anthropology Review (POLAR) Online*. https://polarjournal.org/2020/09/07/indias-citizenship-amendment-act-caa-citizenship-and-belonging-in-india/

Cheng, S. (2010). *On the Move for Love: Migrant Entertainers and the U.S. Military in South Korea*. Philadelphia: University of Pennsylvania Press.

Chimni, B. S. (2006). Third World Approaches to International Law: A Manifesto. *International Community Law Review* 8, 3–27.

Chuang, J. (2005). The United States as Global Sheriff: Using Unilateral Sanctions to Combat Global Trafficking. *Michigan Journal of International Law* 27, 437–494.

Chuang, J. (2010). Rescuing Trafficking from Ideological Capture: Anti-Prostitution Reform and Anti-Trafficking Law and Policy. *University of Pennsylvania Law Review*, 158, 1655–1728.

Clarke, K. M. (2006). *Fictions of Justice: The International Criminal Court and the Challenge of Legal Pluralism in Sub-Saharan Africa*. Cambridge: Cambridge University Press.

Coomaraswamy, R. (Special Rapporteur on Violence against Women). (2000, February 29). *Report on Trafficking in Women, Women's Migration and Violence against Women*. UN Doc. E/CN.4/2000/68 (The Special Rapporteur's Report). Retrieved October 29, 2009, available at www.unhchr.ch.html/menu2/7/b/mwom.htm

Coutin, S. (2010). Confined within: National Territories as Zones of Confinement. *Political Geography* 29, 200–208.

Cruikshank, B. (1999). *The Will to Empower: Democratic Citizens and Other Subjects*. Ithaca: Cornell University Press.

Darian-Smith, E. (2013). *Laws and Societies in Global Contexts: Contemporary Approaches*. Cambridge: Cambridge University Press.

Darian-Smith, E. and P. McCarty (2017). *The Global Turn: Theories, Research Designs, and Methods for Global Studies*. Berkeley: University of California Press.

Das, B. (2016). Who Would Like to Live in This Cage? Voices from a Shelter Home in Assam. *Economic and Political Weekly* 51, 44–45, 77–84.

Das, V. (2004). The Signature of the State: The Paradox of Illegibility, in V. Das and D. Poole (eds.). *Anthropology in the Margins of the State*. Santa Fe: School of American Research Press, 225–252.

Das, V. (2007). *Life and Words: Violence and the Descent into the Ordinary*. Berkeley: University of California Press.

Dasgupta, S. (2014). Sovereign Silence: Immoral Traffic (Prevention) Act and Legalizing Sex Work in Sonagachi. *Political and Legal Anthropology Review* 37 (1), 109–125.

Dasgupta, S. (2018). Indian Bill to "Protect" Trafficking Victims Will Make Sex Workers Less Safe. *The Conversation*, December 17. Retrieved December 17, 2023, from https://theconversation.com/indian-bill-to-protect-trafficking-victims-will-make-sex-workers-less-safe-104535

Dasgupta, S. (2019). Of Raids and Returns: Sex Work Movement, Police Oppression, and the Politics of the Ordinary in Sonagachi, India. *Anti-Trafficking Review* 12, 127–139.

De, R. (2018). *A People's Constitution: The Everyday Life of Law in the Indian Republic*. Princeton: Princeton University Press.

Delacoste, F. and P. Alexander (eds.). (1998). *Sex Work: Writings by Women in the Sex Industry*. San Francisco: Cleis Press.

Dell, H. (1999). *Hierarchies of Femininity: Sex Workers, Feminists and the Nation*. Unpublished doctoral dissertation, Duke University, Durham NC.

Deshpande, S. (ed.). (2014). *The Problem of Caste*. New Delhi: Orient Blackswan.

Dewey, S. and P. Kelly (eds.). (2011). *Policing Pleasure: Sex Work, Policy, and the State in Global Perspective*. New York: New York University Press.

Doezema, J. (2001). Ouch! Western Feminists' Wounded Attachment to the "Third World Prostitute." *Feminist Review* 67, 16–38.

Doezema, J. (2005). Now You See Her, Now You Don't: Sex Workers at the UN Trafficking Protocol Negotiation. *Social-Legal Studies*, 14 (1), 61–89.

Dottridge, M. (2007). Introduction, in *Collateral Damage: The Impact of Anti-Trafficking Measures of Human Rights around the World*. Bangkok: GAATW, 1–27.

Dube, D., A. Chakraborty and J. Winterdyk (2021). The Anti-Trafficking Bill, 2018: Does It Fulfill India's Commitment to the International Community? *Journal of Human Trafficking* 7 (2), 224–237.

Edelman, M. and A. Haugerud (2004). Development, in D. Nugent and J. Vincent (eds.). *A Companion to the Anthropology of Politics*. Malden, MA: Blackwell Publishing, 86–106.

Faleiro, S. (2014). The Ugly Prurience of R.R. Patil. *Livemint.com*, June 28. Retrieved April 4, 2014, from www.livemint.com/Leisure/NzNzl2MbgbDPU7ADbcR91I/The-ugly-prurience-of-RR-Patil.html

Farrell, A. et al. (2016). The Prosecution of State-Level Human Trafficking Cases in the United States. *Anti-Trafficking Review* 6, 48–70.

Fassin, D. (2005). Compassion and Repression: The Moral Economy of Immigration Policies in France. *Cultural Anthropology* 20 (3), 362–387.

Ferguson, J. and A. Gupta (2002). Spatializing States: Towards an Ethnography of Neoliberal Governmentality. *American Ethnologist* 29 (4), 981–1002.

Ferme, M. (2004). Deterritorialized Citizenship and the Resonances of the Sierra Leonean State, in V. Das and D. Poole (eds.). *Anthropology in the Margins of the State*. Santa Fe: School of American Research Press, 81–115.

Fernandes, L. (2006). *India's New Middle Class: Democratic Politics in an Era of Economic Reform*. Minneapolis: University of Minnesota Press.

Fisher, W. F. (1997). Doing Good? The Politics and Antipolitics of NGO Practices. *Annual Review of Anthropology* 26, 439–464.

Foucault, M. (1975). *Discipline & Punish: The Birth of the Prison*. New York: Vintage.

Foucault, M. (1982). The Subject and Power. *Critical Inquiry* 8 (4) (Summer, 1982), 777–795.

Foucault, M. (1991). Governmentality, in G. Burchell, C. Gordon and P. Miller (eds.). *The Foucault Effect*. Chicago: University of Chicago Press, 87–104.

Fukushima, A. (2019). *Migrant Crossings: Witnessing Human Trafficking in the US*. Palo Alto: Stanford University Press.

Gallagher, A. and E. Pearson (2010). The High Cost of Freedom: A Legal and Policy Analysis of Shelter Detention for Victims of Trafficking. *Human Rights Quarterly* 32 (1), 73–114.

Galusca, R. (2012). Slave Hunters, Brothel Busters, and Feminist Interventions: Investigative Journalists as Anti-Sex Trafficking Humanitarians. *Feminist Formations* 24 (2), 1–24.

Gandhi, M. (2018). Why I Pushed for Passage of the Anti-Trafficking Bill. *The Times of India* (New Delhi), July 30. Retrieved December 19, 2023, from https://timesofindia.indiatimes.com/india/why-i-pushed-for-passage-of-the-anti-trafficking-bill/articleshow/65190751.cms?utm_source=twitter.com&utm_medium=social&utm_campaign=TOIDesktop

Ganguly, B. (2016). "Next Time I Will Go to Dubai:" How Rescue and Rehabilitation Fails Women. *Economic and Political Weekly* 51, 44–45, 85–91.

Ganti, T. (2012). *Producing Bollywood: Inside the Contemporary Hindi Film Industry*. Durham: Duke University Press.

Gaurav Jain vs. Union of India and Others. Criminal Writ Petition Nos. 745-54 of 1950. Judgment of the Supreme Court of India dated July 9, 1997.

Gera, B. and K. Makkar (2022). Due to Major Loopholes, the Witness Protection Scheme Does Not Instill Confidence. *The Telegraph*, February 2. Retrieved December 17, 2023, from www.telegraphindia.com/opinion/due-to-major-loopholes-the-witness-protection-scheme-does-not-instil-confidence/cid/1685139

Germain, T. S. and S. Dewey (2017). *Women of the Street: How the Criminal Justice-Social Services Alliance Fails Women in Prostitution*. New York: New York University Press.

Ghosh, S. (2008). *Decriminalizing Sex Work*. Seminar no. 583, March 2008. Retrieved September 2010, from www.india-seminar.com/2008/583/583_shohini_ghosh.htm

Ghosh, S. (2015). Anti-Trafficking and Its Discontents: Women's Migrations and Work in an Indian Borderland. *Gender, Place & Culture* 22 (9), 1220–1235.

Ghosh, S. (2018). Anti-Trafficking Bill Ignores Consenting Sex Workers. *The Quint*, July 25. Retrieved December 17, 2023, from www.thequint.com/hotwire-text/anti-trafficking-bill-ignores-consenting-sex-workers

Ghosh, S. (2019). "Everything Must Match": Detection, Deception, and Migrant Illegality in the India-Bangladesh Borderlands. *American Anthropologist* 121 (4), 870–883.

Ghosh, S. and R. Moral. (2020). *The Slipperiness of Documents: Notes from India's Eastern Borderlands*. Retrieved October 29, 2023, from www.law.ox.ac.uk/research-subject-groups/centre-criminology/centreborder-criminologies/blog/2020/02/slipperiness

Global Alliance against Trafficking in Women (2007). *Collateral Damage: The Impact of Anti-Trafficking Measures of Human Rights around the World*. Bangkok: GAATW.

Golder, B. and P. Fitzpatrick. (2009). *Foucault's Law*. New York: Routledge.

Goodale, M. (2009). *Surrendering to Utopia: An Anthropology of Human Rights*. Stanford: Stanford University Press.

Goodey, J. (2004). Sex Trafficking in Women from Central and East European Countries: Promoting a "Victim-centred" and "Woman-centred" Approach to Criminal Justice Intervention. *Feminist Review* 76, 26–45.

Gothoskar, S. (2013). Women's Work, Stigma, Shelter Homes and the State. *Economic and Political Weekly* 48 (4), 10–13.

Govindan, P. (2013). Rethinking Emancipation: The Rhetorics of Slavery and Politics of Freedom in Anti-Trafficking Work in India. *Interventions: International Journal of Postcolonial Studies* 15 (4), 511–529.

Griffiths, M. (2013). Living with Uncertainty: Indefinite Immigration Detention. *Journal of Legal Anthropology* 1 (3): 263–286.

Guha, M. (2019). "Safe Spaces" and "Bad" Girls: "Child Marriage Victims" Experiences from a Shelter in Eastern India. *Gender, Place and Culture* 26 (1), 128–144.

Gupta, A. (2012). *Red Tape: Bureaucracy, Structural Violence, and Poverty in India*. Durham: Duke University Press.

Gupta, A. and A. Sharma (2006). Globalization and Postcolonial States. *Current Anthropology* 47 (2), 277–307.

Halley, J. et al. (2006). From the International to the Local in Feminist Legal Responses to Rape, Prostitution/Sex Work and Sex Trafficking: Four Studies in Contemporary Governance Feminism. *Harvard Journal of Law and Gender* 29, 335–423.

Hansen, T. B. and F. Stepputat (eds.). (2001). *States of Imagination: Ethnographic Explorations of the Postcolonial State*. Durham: Duke University Press.

Haynes, D. F. (2004). Used, Abused, Arrested and Deported: Extending Immigration Benefits to Protect the Victims of Trafficking and to Secure the Prosecution of Traffickers. *Human Rights Quarterly* 26, 221–272.

Heath, D. and S. Legg (eds.). (2018). *South Asian Governmentalities: Michel Foucault and the Question of Postcolonial Orderings*. Cambridge: Cambridge University Press, 37–57.

Hinchy, J. (2019). *Governing Gender and Sexuality in Colonial India: The Hijra c. 1850–1900*. Cambridge: Cambridge University Press.

Hlavka, H. and S. Mulla (2021). *Bodies in Evidence: Race, Gender, and Science in Sexual Assault Adjudication*. New York: New York University Press.

Hoefinger, H. (2016). Neoliberal Sexual Humanitarianism and Story-Telling: The case of Somaly Mam. *Anti-Trafficking Review* 7, 56–78.

Hua, J. (2011). *Trafficking Women's Human Rights*. Minneapolis: University of Minnesota Press.

Huckerby, J. (2007). United States of America, in *Collateral Damage: The Impact of Anti-Trafficking Measures of Human Rights around the World*. Bangkok: GAATW, 230–253.

Hull, M. (2012). *Government of Paper: The Materiality of Bureaucracy in Urban Pakistan*. Berkeley: University of California Press. Kindle Edition.

Human Rights Watch (1995, June). *Rape for Profit: Trafficking of Nepali Girls and Women to India's Brothels*. Human Rights Watch.

Hussain, N. (2003). *The Jurisprudence of Emergency: Colonialism and the Rule of Law*. Ann Arbor: University of Michigan Press.

India Today (2012, June 20). Court Orders Release of Women Arrested during Mumbai Police's Social Service op. (Online edition).

Ismail, F. and S. Kamat (2018). NGOs, Social Movements, and the Neoliberal State: Incorporation, Reinvention, Critique. *Critical Sociology* 44 (4–5), 569–577.

James, E. C. (2010). *Democratic Insecurities: Violence, Trauma, and Intervention in Haiti*. Berkeley: University of California Press.

Jauregui, B. (2016). *Provisional Authority: Police, Order, and Security in India*. Chicago: University of Chicago Press. Kindle Edition.

Jeffreys, S. (1997). *The Idea of Prostitution*. Melbourne: Spinifex Press

Jodhka, S. S. (2017). *Caste in Contemporary India* (2nd edition). New Delhi: Routledge.

Johari, A. (2020). *Child Protection Officers Aided Abusers in Muzaffarpur Home – Who Will Monitor the Monitors?* Retrieved February 26, 2022, from https://scroll.in/article/951017/muzaffarpur-shelter-home-abusers-have-been-convicted-but-who-is-monitoring-other-childrens-homes

Joshi, S. (2001). "Cheli-Beti" Discourses of Trafficking and Constructions of Gender, Citizenship and Nation in Modern Nepal. *South Asia: Journal of South Asian Studies* 24 (1), 157–175.

Kamat, S. (2002). *Development Hegemony: NGOs and the State in India*. New Delhi: Oxford University Press.

Kamat, S. (2003). The NGO Phenomenon and Political Culture in the Third World. *Development* 46 (1), 88–93.

Kamat, S. (2004). The Privatization of Public Interest: Theorizing NGO Discourse in a Neoliberal Era. *Review of International Political Economy* 11 (1), 155–176.

Kannabiran, V. and K. Kannabiran (2003). *Muvalur Ramamirthammal's Web of Deceit: Devadasi Reform in Colonial India*. New Delhi: Kali for Women.

Kaplan, M. (1995). Panopticon in Poona: An Essay on Foucault and Colonialism. *Cultural Anthropology* 10 (1), 85–98.

Kapur, R. (2005). *Erotic Justice: Law and the New Politics of Postcolonialism*. New Delhi: Permanent Black.

Kapur, R. (2007). *India. In Global Alliance against Trafficking in Women, Collateral Damage: The Impact of Anti-Trafficking Measures of Human Rights around the World*. Bangkok: GAATW, 114–141.

Kapur, R. (2010). *Makeshift Migrants and Law: Gender, Belonging, and Postcolonial Anxieties*. New Delhi: Routledge.

Kapur, R. and B. Cossman (1996). *Subversive Sites: Feminist Engagements with the Law in India*. New Delhi: SAGE.

Kara, S. (2017). *Sex Trafficking: Inside the Business of Modern Slavery*. New York: Columbia University Press.

Karim, L. (2011). *Microfinance and its Discontents: Women in Debt in Bangladesh*. Minneapolis: University of Minnesota Press.

Kashyap, A. (2013). Ensuring Witness Safety Central to Rule of Law. *The Hindu*, July 23.

Kempadoo, K. (1998). The Migrant Tightrope: Experiences from the Caribbean, in K. A. Kempadoo (ed.). *Global Sex Workers: Rights, Resistance, and Redefinition*. New York: Routledge, 124–138.

Kempadoo, K. et al. (eds.). (2012). *Trafficking and Prostitution Reconsidered: New Perspectives on Migration, Sex Work, and Human Rights*. New York: Routledge.

Kolsky, E. (2005). Codification and the Rule of Colonial Difference: Criminal Procedure in British India. *Law and History Review* 23 (3), 631–683.

Koppikar, S. (2013). ACP Dhoble: Both Hero and Villain. *Hindustan Times*, January 16.

Kotiswaran, P. (2001). Preparing for Civil Disobedience: Indian Sex Workers and the Law. *Boston College Third World Law Journal* 21 (2), 161–141.

Kotiswaran, P. (2011a). *Dangerous Sex, Invisible Labor: Sex Work and the Law in India*. Princeton: Princeton University Press.

Kotiswaran, P. (2011b). *Reader on Sex Work*. New Delhi: Women Unlimited.

Kotiswaran, P. (2013a). A Battle Half-Won. *Economic and Political Weekly* 48 (17), 9.

Kotiswaran, P (2013b). Sword or Shield? The Role of the Law in the Indian Sex Workers' Movement. *Interventions: International Journal of Postcolonial Studies* 15 (4), 530–548.

Kotiswaran, P. (2014). Beyond the Allures of Criminalization: Rethinking the Regulation of Sex Work in India. *Criminology and Criminal Justice* 14 (5), 565–579.

Kotiswaran, P. (2016). Empty Gestures: A Critique of India's New Trafficking Bill. *Open Democracy*, June 22. Retrieved December 17, 2023, from www.opendemocracy.net/en/beyond-trafficking-and-slavery/empty-gestures-critique-of-india-s-new-trafficking-bill/

Kotiswaran, P. (2018a). How Did We Get Here? Or a Short History of the 2018 Trafficking Bill. *Economic and Political Weekly Engage* 53 (29), n.p. Retrieved December 17, 2023, from www.epw.in/engage/article/how-did-we-get-hereor-short-history

Kotiswaran, P. (2018b). The Criminal Law as Sledgehammer: The Paternalist Politics of India's 2018 Trafficking Bill. *Open Democracy*, July 9. Retrieved December 17, 2023, from www.opendemocracy.net/en/beyond-trafficking-and-slavery/criminal-law-as-sledgehammer-paternalist-politics-of-india-s-2018-tr/

Kotiswaran, P. (2018c). Neoabolitionism's Last Laugh: India Must Rethink Trafficking. *Open Democracy*, March 20. Retrieved December 17, 2023, from www.opendemocracy.net/en/beyond-trafficking-and-slavery/neoabolitionisms-last-laugh-india-must-rethink-trafficking/

Kotiswaran, P. (2019). Has the Dial Moved on the Indian Sex Work Debate? *Economic and Political Weekly* 54 (22), 10–12.

Kotiswaran, P. (2021). The Sexual Politics of Anti-Trafficking Discourse. *Feminist Legal Studies* 29, 43–65.

Kotiswaran, P. and S. Rajam (2023). When Hypercriminalization Falls Afoul of the Constitution: The Need to Rethink the Trafficking in Persons (Prevention, Care and Rehabilitation) Bill 2021. *Indian Law Review* 7 (3), 299–321.

Kowalski, J. (2023). *Counseling Women: Kinship against Violence in India*. Philadelphia: University of Pennsylvania Press.

Kristof, N. (2004a). Girls for Sale. *New York Times*, January 17.

Kristof, N. (2004b). Going Home, with Hope. *New York Times*, January 24.

Kristof, N. (2015). Meet a 21st Century Sex Slave. *New York Times*, October 24.

Kumar, R. (2022). Witnessing Violence, Witnessing as Violence: Police Torture and Power in Twentieth-Century India. *Law and Social Inquiry* 47 (3), 946–970.

Lakkimsetti, C. (2016). "From Dance Bars to the Streets" Moral Dispossession and Eviction in Mumbai. *Positions* 24 (1), 206–230.

Lakkimsetti, C. (2020). *Legalizing Sex: Sexual Minorities, AIDS, and Citizenship in India*. New York: New York University Press.

Lal, V. (1999). Everyday Crime, Native Mendacity, and the Cultural Psychology of Justice in Colonial India. *Studies in History* 15 (1), 145–166.

Lashaw, A. (2012). How Progressive Culture Resists Critique: The Impasse of NGO Studies. *Ethnography* 14 (4), 501–522.

Lashaw, A., C. Vannier and S. Sampson (eds.). (2017). *Cultures of Doing Good: Anthropologists and NGOs*. Tuscaloosa: University of Alabama Press.

Law Commission of India (1975). *Sixty-Fourth Report on the Suppression of Immoral Traffic in Women and Girls Act, 1956*. New Delhi: Law Commission of India.

Lawyers Collective (2018). *We Don't Need the "Trafficking of Persons (Prevention, Protection, and Rehabilitation) Bill, 2018."* Retrieved December 17, 2023, from https://lawyerscollective.org/we-dont-need-the-trafficking-of-personsprevention-protection-and-rehabilitation-bill-2018/

Lee, M. (2014). Gendered Discipline and Protective Custody of Trafficking Victims in Asia. *Punishment and Society* 16 (2), 206–222.

Legg, S. (2009). Governing Prostitution in Colonial Delhi: From Cantonment Regulations to International Hygiene (1864–1939). *Social History* 34 (4), 447–467.

Legg, S. (2014). *Prostitution and the Ends of Empire; Scale, Governmentalities, and Interwar India*. Durham: Duke University Press.

Legg, S. (2023). Carceral and Colonial Domesticities: Subaltern Case Geographies of a Delhi Rescue Home. *EPD: Society and Space*, Online First.

Lemons, K. (2017). The Ethics and Politics of NGO-Dependent Anthropology, in A. Lashaw, C. Vannier and S. Sampson (eds.). *Cultures of Doing Good: Anthropologists and NGOs*. Tuscaloosa: University of Alabama Press, 194–211.

Leve, L. and L. Karim (2001). Introduction. Privatizing the State: Ethnography of Development, Transnational Capital, and NGOs. *Political and Legal Anthropology Review* 24 (1), 53–58.

Levine, P. (1994). Venereal Disease, Prostitution, and the Politics of Empire: The Case of British India. *Journal of the History of Sexuality* 4 (4), 579–602.

Levine, P. (2003). *Prostitution, Race, and Politics: Policing Venereal Disease in the British Empire*. London: Routledge.

Li, T. M. (2005). Beyond "the State" and Failed Schemes. *American Anthropologist* 107 (3), 383–394.

Li, T. M. (2007). *The Will to Improve: Governmentality, Development, and the Practice of Politics*. Durham: Duke University Press.

Liechty, M. (2002). *Suitably Modern: Making Middle-Class Culture in a New Consumer Society*. Princeton: Princeton University Press.

Lindquist, J. (2010). Images and Evidence: Human Trafficking, Auditing, and the Production of Illicit Markets in Southeast Asia and Beyond. *Public Culture* 22 (2), 223–236.

Lindquist, J. (2013). Beyond Anti-Anti-Trafficking. *Dialectical Anthropology* 37 (2), 319–323.

Lok Sabha (Parliament of India) Secretariat (1956). Lok Sabha Proceedings. Vol. IX (November 29, 1956), 1449–1588.

Lok Sabha (Parliament of India) Secretariat (2018, July 26). *Lok Sabha Debates (Uncorrected). Part II: Proceedings Other than Questions and Answers*, 373–555.

Madhukalya, A. (2016). New Anti-Trafficking Bill to Protect Victims. *DNA India* (Mumbai), May 31. Retrieved December 27, 2023, from www.dnaindia.com/mumbai/report-new-anti-trafficking-bill-to-protect-victims-2218256

Magar, V. (2012). Rescue and Rehabilitation: A Critical Analysis of Sex Workers' Anti-Trafficking Response in India. *Signs* 37 (3), 619–644.

Mahdavi, P. (2011). *Gridlock: Labor, Migration, and Human Trafficking in Dubai*. Stanford: Stanford University Press.

Mai, N. (2016). Assembling Samira: Understanding Sexual Humanitarianism through Experimental Filmmaking. *antiAtlas Journal* 1 [Online], April 13. www.antiatlas-journal.net/01-assembling-samira-understanding-sexual-humanitarianism-through-experimental-filmmaking

Mani, L. (1998). *Contentious Traditions: The Debate on Sati in Colonial India*. Berkeley: University of California Press.

Marcus, A. and E. Snadjr (2013). Introduction: Anti-Anti-Trafficking? Toward Critical Ethnographies of Human Trafficking. *Dialectical Anthropology* 37 (2), 191–194.

Massoud, M. (2014). *Law's Fragile State: Colonial, Authoritarian, and Humanitarian Legacies in Sudan*. Cambridge: Cambridge University Press.

Massoud, M. (2015). Work Rules: How International NGOs Build Law in War-Torn Societies. *Law and Society Review* 49 (2), 333–364.

Mathur, N. (2012). *Paper Tiger: Law, Bureaucracy and the Developmental State in Himalayan India*. Cambridge: Cambridge University Press. (Cambridge Studies in Law and Society).

Mathur, N. (2017). Eating Money: Corruption and Its Categorical "Other" in the Leaky Indian State. *Modern Asian Studies* 51 (6), 1796–1817.

Mazzarella, W. (2003). *Shoveling Smoke: Advertising and Globalization in Contemporary India*. Durham: Duke University Press.

Mazzarella, W. (2005). Middle Class, in Rachel Dwyer (ed.). *South Asia Keywords*. Retrieved July 2017, available online at http://d3qioqp55mx5f5.cloudfront.net/anthrolpology/docs/mazz_middleclass.pdfonline

Mazzarella, W. (2015). A Different Kind of Flesh: Public Obscenity, Globalisation and the Mumbai Dance Bar Ban. *South Asia: Journal of South Asian Studies* 38 (3), 481–494.

Mehta, R. (2016). Borders: A View from "Nowhere." *Criminology and Criminal Justice* 16 (3), 286–300.

Menon, R. and K. Bhasin (1993). Recovery, Rupture, Resistance: Indian State and the Abduction of Women during Partition. *Economic and Political Weekly* 28 (17), WS2–WS11.

Merry, S. E. (1994). Courts as Performances: Domestic Violence Hearings in a Hawai'i Family Court, in E. Mertz and M. Lazarus-Black (eds.). *Contested States: Law, Hegemony and Resistance*. New York: Routledge, 35–59.

Merry, S. E. (2000). Crossing Boundaries: Ethnography in the 21st Century. *Political and Legal Anthropology Review* 23 (2), 127–133.

Merry, S. E. (2001). Spatial Governmentality and the New Urban Social Order: Controlling Gender Violence through Law. *American Anthropologist* 103 (1), 16–29.

Merry, S. E. (2006). *Human Rights and Gender Violence: Translating International Law into Local Justice*. Chicago: University of Chicago Press.

Merry, S. E. (2016). *The Seductions of Quantification: Measuring Human Rights, Gender Violence, and Sex Trafficking*. Chicago: University of Chicago Press.

Mertz, E. and A. Timmer (2010). Introduction. Getting It Done: Ethnographic Perspectives on NGOs. *Political and Legal Anthropology Review* 33 (2), 171–177.

Mertz, E. and M. Goodale (2014). Comparative Anthropology of Law, in S. D. Clark (ed.). *Comparative Law and Society*. Northampton, MA: Edward Elgar Publishing, 77–91.

Mid-Day (2012). Unsocial Service of ACP Dhoble. Online Edition, May 11.

Miller, A. (2004). Sexuality, Violence against Women, and Human Rights: Women Make Demands and Ladies Get Protection. *Health and Human Rights* 7 (2), 16–47.

Ministry of Home Affairs, Government of India (2009). Advisory on Preventing and Combating Human Trafficking in India (September 9, 2009).

Mitra, D. (2020). *Indian Sex Life: Sexuality and the Colonial Origins of Modern Social Thought*. Princeton: Princeton University Press.

Modi, Dr. J. P. (2013). Personal Identity, in J. K. Kannan and Dr. K. Mathiharan (eds.). *A Textbook of Medical Jurisprudence and Toxicology* (5th edition). Nagpur: Lexis Nexis Butterworths Wadhwa, 247–248.

Mohanty, C. T. (1984). Under Western Eyes: Feminist Scholarship and Colonial Discourse. *Boundary* 12 (3), 333–358.

Molland, S. (2013). Tandem Ethnography: On Researching "Trafficking" and "Anti-Trafficking." *Ethnography* 14 (3), 300–323.

Montgomery, H. (2013). Commentary for Special Issue. Anti-Anti-Trafficking? Toward Critical Ethnographies of Human Trafficking. *Dialectical Anthropology* 37 (2), 313–317.

Moodie, M. (2010). "Why Can't You Say You are from Bangladesh?" Demographic Anxiety and Hindu Nationalist Common Sense in the Aftermath of the 2008 Jaipur Bombings. *Identities* 17 (5), 531–559.

Ms. Khushi Harkishan Malhotra vs. State of Maharashtra. Criminal Writ Petition No. 2037 of 2004. Judgment of the Bombay High Court dated September 8, 2005.

Ms. Purnima Upadhyay vs. State of Maharashtra. *Suo motu* Writ Petition no. 113 of 2012. Judgment of the Bombay High Court dated December 13, 2012.

Mulla, S. (2011). Introduction to Forging Family: Legal Documents as New Kinship Technologies. *Law, Culture and the Humanities* 7 (3), 352–358.

Mulla, S. (2014). *The Violence of Care: Rape Victims, Forensic Nurses, and Sexual Assault Intervention*. New York: New York University Press.

Muralidhar, S. (1999). The Case of the Agra Protective Home, in A. Dhanda and A. Parashar (eds.). *Engendering Law: Essays in Honor of Lotika Sarkar*. Lucknow: Eastern Book Company, 295–320.

Muralidhar, S. (2004). *Law, Poverty, and Legal Aid: Access to Criminal Justice*. New Delhi: Lexis Nexis Butterworths.

Musto, J. (2016). *Control and Protect: Collaboration, Carceral Protection, and Domestic Sex Trafficking in the United States*. Berkeley: University of California Press.

Mustt Sarabari Begum @ Syera vs. State of Assam & Ors. Civil Writ Petition no. 1094 of 2008. Judgment of the Gauhati High Court dated July 25, 2008.

Nair, V. (2018). An Eye for an I: Recording Biometrics and Reconsidering Identity in Postcolonial India. *Contemporary South Asia*, 26 (2), 143–156.

Nair, V. (2021). Becoming Data: Biometric IDs and the Individual in "Digital India." *Journal of the Royal Anthropological Institute* 27, 26–42.

Najar, J. L. (2022). Brahmanical Patriarchy and the Politics of Anti-Trafficking and Prostitution Governance: From Colonial to Contemporary India. *Third World Quarterly* 44 (4), 667–685.

Narmada Govind Kamble vs. State of Maharashtra. Criminal Appeal No. 1055 of 2004. Judgment of the Bombay High Court dated December 3, 2009.

Nataraj, S. (2022). The Thirunangai Promise: Gender as a Contingent Outcome of Migration and Economic Exchange. *Anti-Trafficking Review* 2022 (19), 47–65.

National Network of Sex Workers (2022, May 25). *Sex Workers Not to be Abused by Police, Rescued without Their Consent, and Press Council to Regulate Imagery around Sex Work, Directs Honourable Supreme Court of India*. Retrieved June 6, 2022, from https://nationalnetworkofsexworkers.medium.com/sex-workers-not-to-be-abused-by-police-rescued-without-their-consent-and-press-council-to-e89c10e3bd97

Oldenburg, V. T. (1990, Summer). Lifestyle as Resistance: The Case of the Courtesans of Lucknow, India. *Feminist Studies* 16 (2), 259–287.

O'Malley, P. (1996). Risk and Responsibility, in A. Barry, T. Osbourne and N. Rose (eds.). *Foucault and the Political Reason: Liberalism, Neo-Liberalism and the Rationalities of Government*. London: University College London Press.

O'Malley, P. (2008). Experiments in Risk and Criminal Justice. *Theoretical Criminology* 12 (4), 451–469.

Pai, A., M. Seshu et al. (2013). *Violence against People in Sex Work in India: Submission to the Special Rapporteur on Violence Against Women (Ms. Rashida Manjoo). Country Visit 2013: India*. Retrieved July 17, 2019, from http://nnswindia.org/upload/News/Press-Release/Final-Submission-SR-VAW-India-SW-CBOs-networks-17April13.pdf

Pai, A. et al. (2018, July 14). In Its Haste to Rescue Sex Workers, "Anti-Trafficking" is Increasing their Vulnerability. *Economic and Political Weekly* Online, 53 (28).

Pande, A. (2014). *Wombs in Labor: Transnational Commercial Surrogacy in India*. New York: Columbia University Press.

Pandit, A. (2018). Anti-Trafficking Bill Receives Mixed Response from Voluntary Organisations, Civil Society & Activists. *The Times of India* (New Delhi), July 27. Retrieved January 30, 2024, from https://timesofindia.indiatimes.com/india/anti-trafficking-bill-receives-mixed-response-from-voluntary-organisations-civil-society-activists/articleshow/65158566.cms

Parmanand, S. (2021). Salvation as Violence: Anti-Trafficking and the Rehabilitation of Rescued Filipino Women into Moral Subjects. *Journal of International Women's Studies* 22 (2), 78–91.

Parreñas, R. (2011). *Illicit Flirtations: Labor, Migration, and Sex Trafficking in Tokyo*. Stanford: Stanford University Press.

Pattanaik, B. and L. Sullivan (2018, July 4). India's "Anti-Trafficking" Bill Ignores Socio-Economic Realities of Trafficked Persons. *Economic and Political Weekly* Online 53 (28).

Pearson, E. (2002). Half-hearted Protection: What Does Victim Protection Really Mean for Victims of Trafficking in Europe? *Gender and Development* 10 (1), 56–59.

Peters, A. (2015). *Responding to Human Trafficking: Sex, Gender, and Culture in the Law*. Philadelphia: University of Pennsylvania Press.

Phadke, S. (2007). Dangerous Liaisons: Women and Men: Risk and Reputation in Mumbai, *Economic and Political Weekly* 42 (17), 1510–1518.

Pheterson, G. (ed.). (1989). *A Vindication of the Rights of Whores*. Seattle: Seal Press.

Pisharoty, S. B. (2019). Women Without Parents: An NRC Ground Report. *The Wire*, September 13. Retrieved September 20, 2023, from https://thewire.in/rights/women-without-parents-an-nrc-ground-report

Plambech, S. (2016). The Art of the Possible: Making Films on Sex Work Migration and Human Trafficking. *Anti-Trafficking Review* (7), 182–199. www.antitraffickingreview.org/index.php/atrjournal/article/view/206

Poole, D. (2004). Between Threat and Guarantee; Justice and Community in the Margins of the Peruvian State, in V. Das and D. Poole (eds.). *Anthropology in the Margins of the State*. Santa Fe: School of American Research Press, 35–66.

Prakash, G. (2010). *Mumbai Fables: A History of an Enchanted City*. Princeton: Princeton University Press, Kindle Edition.

Prasad, K. K. (2018, July 4). Will Trafficking Bill 2018 Harm Bonded Labourers? *Economic and Political Weekly* Online 53 (28).

Prerana vs. State of Maharashtra, Criminal Writ Petition No. 1694 of 2003. Judgment of the Bombay High Court dated April 18, 2007.

Puri, J. (2016). *Sexual States: Governance and the Struggle over the Antisodomy Law in India*. Durham: Duke University Press.

Rajagopal, B. (2008). Invoking the Rule of Law: International Discourses, in A. Hurwitz, and R. Huang (eds.). *Civil War and the Rule of Law: Security, Development, Human Rights*. Boulder, CO: Lynne Rienner, 47–68.

Rakshase, B. et al. (2022). *Identifying Changing Trends in the Sex Work Dynamics among Female Sex Workers (FSWs) in India*. Retrieved January 30, 2024, from http://naco.gov.in/

sites/default/files/Technical%20Brief%20on%20Changing%20trends%20in%20sex%20work.pdf

Ramachandran, V. (2019). Saving the Slaving Child: Domestic work, Labor Trafficking, and the Politics of Rescue in India. *Humanity* 10 (3), 339–362.

Ramachandran, V. and K. Walters (2018). A Recipe for Injustice: India's New Trafficking Bill expands a troubled Rescue, Rehabilitation, and Repatriation Framework. *Open Democracy*, July 30. Retrieved February 21, 2022, from www.opendemocracy.net/en/beyond-trafficking-and-slavery/recipe-for-injustice-india-s-new-trafficking-bil/

Ramanathan, U. (1996). Women, Law, and Institutionalization: A Manifestation of State Power. *Indian Journal of Gender Studies* 3, 199–223.

Ramberg, L. (2014). *Given to the Goddess: South Indian Devadasis and the Sexuality of Religion*. Durham, NC: Duke University Press.

Randeria, S. (2003). Glocalization of Law: Environmental Justice, World Bank, NGOs and the Cunning State in India. *Current Sociology* 51, 305.

Rao, U. and V. Nair (2019). Aadhaar: Governing with Biometrics. *South Asia: Journal of South Asia Studies* 42 (3), 469–481. Routledge.

Rhodes, L. A. (2001). Toward an Anthropology of Prisons. *Annual Review of Anthropology* 30 (1), 65–83.

Rose, N. and M. Valverde (1998). Governed by Law? *Social and Legal Studies* 7 (4), 541–551.

Rose, N. and P. Miller (1992). Political Power beyond the State: Problematics of Government. *The British Journal of Sociology* 43 (2): 173–205.

Roy, S. (2013, May 23). When Witnesses Go Hostile: From Jessica Lal to the Present. *Firstpost*. Retrieved May 27, 2014, from www.firstpost.com/india/when-witnesses-go-hostile-from-jessica-lal-to-varun-gandhi-809851.html

Roy, S. (2015). The Indian Women's Movement: Within and beyond NGOization. *Journal of South Asian Development* 10 (1), 96–117.

Roy, S. (2017). Enacting/Disrupting the Will to Empower: Feminist Governance of "Child Marriage" in Eastern India. *Signs* 42 (4), 867–891.

Roy, S. (2022). *Changing the Subject: Feminist and Queer Politics in Neoliberal India*. Durham, NC: Duke University Press.

Roychowdhury, P. (2015). Victims to Saviors: Governmentality and the Regendering of Citizenship in India. *Gender & Society* 29 (6), 792–816.

Roychowdhury, P. (2019). Illicit Justice: Aspirational-Strategic Subjects and the Political Economy of Domestic Violence Law in India. *Law and Social Inquiry* 44 (2), 444–467.

Roychowdhury, P. (2021). *Capable Women, Incapable States: Negotiating Violence and Rights in India*. New York: Oxford University Press.

Ruskola, T. (2013). *Legal Orientalism: China, the United States, and Modern Law*. Cambridge, MA: Harvard University Press.

Sadhwani, Y. (2012). Starved, Herded and Assaulted at State-run "Shelter." *Mumbai Mirror*, October 29.

Sadruddin, H. et al. (2005). Human Trafficking in the United States: Expanding Victim Protection beyond Prosecution Witnesses. *Stanford Law & Policy Review* 16 (2), 379–416.

Sahni, R., V. Kalyan Shankar and H. Apte (eds.). (2008). *Prostitution and Beyond: An Analysis of Sex Work in India*. New Delhi: SAGE.

Saikia, P. (2018). Anti-Trafficking Bill 2018: Comprehensive or Flawed? *Tehelka*, August 2. Retrieved February 18, 2022, from http://tehelka.com/anti-trafficking-bill-2018-comprehensive-or-flawed/

Salomi, V. and S. Shukla (2018). In Depth: Unraveling the Shelter Home Horrors of Uttar Pradesh and Bihar that Shocked the Nation. Retrieved February 18, 2022, from www.dnaindia.com/india/report-three-tales-of-shelter-home-terrors-2648667

Samaddar, R. (2008). Crimes, Passion and Detachment: Colonial Foundations of Rule of Law, in K. Kannabiran and R. Singh (eds.). *Challenging the Rule(s) of Law: Colonialism, Criminology, and Human Rights in India*. New Delhi: SAGE, 355–381.

Sanger, V. (2006). The Bar Girl Story: Dance, Dishonour or Death. *The Times of India*, January 15 (online). Retrieved January 3, 2007, from http://timesofindia.indiatimes.com/articleshow/1490127.cms

Sangram (2018). *Executive Summary, in Raided: How Anti-Trafficking Strategies Increase Sex Workers' Vulnerability to Exploitative Practices*. Retrieved September 20, 2023, from www.sangram.org/news/raided-e-book-4

Sarathi, V. P. (2006). *Law of Evidence* (6th edition). Lucknow: Eastern Book Company.

Sarbananda Sonowal vs. Union of India & Anr. Civil Writ Petition No. 131 of 2000. Judgment of the Supreme Court of India dated July 12, 2005.

Sarode, A. (2008). Contesting Legal Positions on Prostitution from a Human Rights Perspective, in R. Sahni, V. Kalyan Shankar and H. Apte (eds.). *Prostitution and Beyond: An Analysis of Sex Work in India*. New Delhi: SAGE, 32–38.

Satish, M. (2003). The Problem of Hostile Witnesses. *The Hindu*, September 2.

Satyogi, P. (2019). Law, Police and "Domestic Cruelty:" Assembling Written Complaints from Oral Narratives. *Contributions to Indian Sociology* 53 (1), 46–71.

Save the Children India (2014). *Socio Legal Factors Impacting Prosecution of Trafficking Crimes in Maharashtra*. Mumbai: STCI.

Schuller, M. (2007). Seeing Like a "Failed" NGO: Globalization's Impacts on State and Civil Society in Haiti. *Political and Legal Anthropology Review* 30 (1), 67–89.

Schuller, M. (2009). Gluing Globalization: NGOs as Intermediaries in Haiti. *Political and Legal Anthropology Review* 32 (1), 84–104.

Schuller, M. and D. Lewis (2017). Engagements with a Productively Unstable Category: Anthropologists and Non-Governmental Organizations. *Current Anthropology* 56 (5), 634–644.

Scott, D. (1995). Colonial Governmentality. *Social Text* 43, 191–220.

Scott, J. (1998). *Seeing Like a State: How Certain Schemes to Improve the Human Condition Have Failed*. New Haven: Yale University Press.

Scoular, J. (2010). What's Law Got to Do with It? How and Why Law Matters in the Regulation of Sex Work. *Journal of Law and Society* 37 (1), 12–39.

Scoular, J. and M. O'Neill (2007). Regulating Prostitution: Social Inclusion, Responsibilization and the Politics of Prostitution Reform. *British Journal of Criminology* 2007 (47), 764–778.

Sen, S. and P. M. Nair (2004). *A Report on Trafficking in Women and Children in India 2001–2003: Volumes 1 and 2*. New Delhi: Institute of Social Sciences, National Human Rights Commission, & UNIFEM.

Sengupta, A. (2010). Concept, Category and Claim: Insights on Caste and Ethnicity from the Police in India. *Ethnic and Racial Studies* 33 (4), 717–736.

Sex Workers Project (2009). *Kicking Down the Door: The Use of Raids to Fight Trafficking in Persons*. New York: Urban Justice Center.

Shah, S. (2013). True Sex and the Law: Prostitution, Sodomy, and the Politics of Sexual Minoritization in India, in S. Srivastava (ed.). *Sexuality Studies*. New Delhi: Oxford University Press, 161–183.

Shah, S. (2014). *Street Corner Secrets: Sex, Work, and Migration in the City of Mumbai*. Durham: Duke University Press.

Sharma, A. (2008). *Logics of Empowerment: Development, Gender, and Governance in Neoliberal India*. Minneapolis: University of Minnesota Press.

Shetye, S. (2014). *Implementation and Enforcement of Sex Trafficking Laws in Mumbai*. MPhil Dissertation, School of Social Sciences, Tata Institute for Social Sciences, Mumbai.

Shih, E. (2017). Freedom Markets: Consumption and Commerce across Human Trafficking Rescue in Thailand. *Positions* 25 (4), 769–788.

Shih, E. (2018). Duplicitous Freedom: Moral and Material Care Work in Anti-Trafficking Rescue and Rehabilitation. *Critical Sociology*, 44 (7–8), 1077–1086.

Shih, E. (2023). *Manufacturing Freedom: Sex Work, Anti-Trafficking Rehab, and the Racial Wages of Rescue*. Berkeley: University of California Press.

Simpson, A. (2017). The Ruse of Consent and the Anatomy of "Refusal:" Cases from Indigenous North America and Australia. *Postcolonial Studies* 20 (1), 18–33.

Singha, R. (1993). "Providential" Circumstances: The Thuggee Campaign of the 1830s and Legal Innovation. *Modern Asian History* 27 (1), 83–146.

Sinha, M. (2006). *Specters of Mother India: The Global Restructuring of an Empire*. Durham: Duke University Press.

Sivaramakrishnan, K. and A. Gupta (eds.). (2010). *The State in India after Liberalization: Interdisciplinary Perspectives* (Routledge Contemporary South Asia Series). New York: Routledge.

Skeggs, B. (1997). *Formations of Class and Gender: Becoming Respectable*. London: SAGE.

Smart, C. (1989). *Feminism and the Power of Law*. New York: Routledge.

Soderlund, G. (2005). Running from the Rescuers: New US Crusades against Sex Trafficking and the Rhetoric of Abolition. *NSWA Journal* 17 (3), 64–87.

Solanki, G. and G. Gangoli (1996). The Official Discourse around PITA. *Economic and Political Weekly* 31 (51), 3298–3300.

Soneji, D. (2011). *Unfinished Gestures: Devadasis, Memory and Modernity in South India*. Chicago: University of Chicago Press.

Soofi, M. (2012). *Nobody Can Love You More: Life in Delhi's Red Light District*. New Delhi: Penguin Books Ltd. Kindle Edition.

Spivak, G. (1988). Can the Subaltern Speak? in C. N. Grossberg (ed.). *Marxism and the Interpretation of Culture*. London: Macmillan, 271–313.

Srikantiah, J. (2007). Perfect Victims and Real Survivors: The Iconic Victim in Domestic Human Trafficking Law. *Boston University Law Review* 87, 157–211.

Srinivasan, A. (1985). Reform and Revival: The Devadasi and Her Dance. *Economic and Political Weekly* 20 (44), 1869–1876.

Starr, J. and M. Goodale (eds.). (2002). *Practicing Ethnography in Law: New Dialogues, Enduring Methods*. New York: Palgrave Macmillan.

State of Maharashtra vs. Anjali Shahaji Sul and others. Case no. 123 of 2010. Judgment of the Adhoc Additional Sessions Judge-1, Osmanabad District dated October 8, 2012.

State vs. Padma. Case no. 16 of 2012. Judgment of the Additional Sessions Judge, Special FTC-2 (Central), Tis Hazari Courts, Delhi dated September 25, 2013.

Sunder Rajan, R. (2003). *The Scandal of the State: Women, Law and Citizenship in Postcolonial India*. Durham: Duke University Press.

Sur, M. (2021). *Jungle Passports: Fences, Mobility, and Citizenship at the Northeast India-Bangladesh Border*. Philadelphia: University of Pennsylvania Press.

Tadros, V. (1998). Between Governance and Discipline: The Law and Michel Foucault. *Oxford Journal of Legal Studies* 18, 75–103.

Tambe, A. (2009). *Codes of Misconduct: Regulating Prostitution in Late Colonial Bombay*. Minneapolis: University of Minnesota Press.

Tandon, T. (2018). India's Trafficking Bill 2018 Is Neither Clear nor Comprehensive. *Economic and Political Weekly Engage* 53 (28), n.p. www.epw.in/engage/article/trafficking-ofpersons-prevention-protection-and-rehabilitation-bill-2018-is-neither-clear-nor-comprehensive

Tara vs State of Delhi. Criminal writ petition no. 296 of 2012. Judgment of the Delhi High Court dated April 13, 2012.

Thangaraj, M. (2019). Commodification in Multiple Registers: Child Workers, Child Consumers, and Child Labor NGOs in India, in K. Cheney and A. Sinervo (eds.). *Disadvantaged Childhoods and Humanitarian Intervention: Processes of Affective Commodification and Objectification*. Cham: Palgrave Macmillan, 87–112.

The Hindu (2012). Sex Workers Must Not be Allowed to Operate, Centre Tells Supreme Court. (July 13, 2012).

The State (D.B. Marg Police Station, Mumbai) vs. Subhash Birju Yadav & Ors. Case no. 604/PW/2010, Judgment of the Metropolitan Magistrate, Special Court for ITPA, 54th Court, Mazgaon, Mumbai dated August 1, 2013.

The State (Nagpada Police Station, Mumbai) vs. Prabha Shiva Gauda and Jamuna Keshar Gop, Case no. 136/PW/2008. Judgment of the Metropolitan Magistrate, Special Court for ITPA, 54th Court, Mazgaon, Mumbai dated October 5, 2012.

The State (V.P. Road Police Station, Mumbai) vs. Laxmi Nivrutti Patole and Baby Vakil Ahmed Khan, Case no. 781/PW/2011. Judgment of the Metropolitan Magistrate, Special Court for ITPA, 54th Court, Mazgaon, Mumbai dated April 5, 2013.

Thorat, A. (2002). *Wrecktifying ITPA*. Retrieved January 2010, available online at www.lawyerscollective.org/hiv-aids/publications/articles-wrecktifying-itpa

Ticktin, M. (2011). *Casualties of Care: Immigration and the Politics of Humanitarianism in France*. Berkeley: University of California Press.

Tuck, E. and K. W. Yang (2014). R-Words – Refusing Research, in D. Paris and M. T. Winn (eds.). *Humanizing Research: Decolonizing Qualitative Inquiry with Youth and Communities*. New York: SAGE, 223–247.

Turnbull, S. (2016). "Stuck in the Middle": Waiting and Uncertainty in Immigration Detention. *Time and Society* 25 (1), 61–79.

United Nations (2000, November 15). *Protocol to Prevent, Suppress and Punish Trafficking in Persons, Especially Women and Children*. 2237 UNTS 319.

United Nations Office on Drugs and Crime (2017). *Evidential Issues in Trafficking in Persons Cases*.

United Nations Office on Drugs and Crime and Government of India (2007). *Standard Operating Procedures on Investigating Crimes of Trafficking for Commercial Sexual Exploitation*. Retrieved June 20, 2009, from www.unodc.org/documents/humantrafficking/India_Training_material/SOP_on_Investigation_of_Crimes_of_Trafficking_for_Commercial.pdf

United States Department of State (2000–2021). *Trafficking in Persons Reports*. Washington, DC: US Department of State. Available at www.state.gov/g/tip/rls/tiprpt/

Valverde, M. (2008). *The Age of Light, Soap, and Water. Moral Reform in English Canada, 1885–1925*. Toronto: University of Toronto Press.

Valverde, M. (2010). Specters of Foucault in Law and Society Scholarship. *Annual Review of Law and Social Science* 6, 45–59.

Vanderhurst, S. (2017). Governing with God: Religion, Resistance, and the State in Nigeria's Counter-Trafficking Programs. *Political and Legal Anthropology Review* 40 (2), 194–209.

Vanderhurst, S. (2022). *Unmaking Migrants: Nigeria's Campaign to End Human Trafficking*. Ithaca: Cornell University Press.

Vijayakumar, G. (2021). *At Risk: Indian Sexual Politics and the Global AIDS Crisis*. Stanford, CA: Stanford University Press.

Vijayakumar, G. (2022). Labors of Love: Sex, Work, and Good Mothering in the Globalizing City. *Signs* 47 (3), 665–688.

Walkowitz, J. (1980). The Politics of Prostitution. *Signs* 6 (1), Women: Sex and Sexuality, Part 2 (Autumn, 1980), 123–135.

Walters, K. (2016). Humanitarian Trafficking: Violence of Rescue and (Mis)calculation of Rehabilitation. *Economic and Political Weekly* 51, 44–45, 55–61.

Walters, K. (2018). Scandals in Sex Worker Rescue Shelters: Is "Awful" Distracting from "lawful?" *Open Democracy*, December 12. Retrieved February 19, 2022, from www.opendemocracy.net/en/beyond-trafficking-and-slavery/scandals-in-indias-raid-and-rescue-shelters-is-awful-distracting-from/

Walters, K. (2020). Moral Security: Anti-Trafficking and the Humanitarian State in South India. *Anthropological Quarterly* 93 (3), 289–320.

Walters, K. and M. Raghavendra (2022). India's Supreme Court Rules in Favour of Sex Workers, and Women Rise Up. *Open Democracy*, July 27. Retrieved September 14, 2022, from www.opendemocracy.net/en/beyond-trafficking-and-slavery/indias-supreme-court-rules-in-favour-of-sex-workers-sparking-riot/

Weitzer, R. (2007). The Social Construction of Sex Trafficking: Ideology and Institutionalization of a Moral Crusade. *Politics and Society* 35, 447–475.

Whitehead, J. (1995). Bodies Clean and Unclean: Prostitution, Sanitary Legislation, and Respectable Femininity in Colonial North India. *Gender & History* 7 (1), 41–63.

Wilson, R. A. (2001). *The Politics of Truth and Reconciliation in South Africa: Legitimizing the Post-Apartheid State*. Cambridge: Cambridge University Press.

Zheng, T. (2008). Anti-Trafficking Campaign and Karaoke Bar Hostesses in China. *Wagadu: A Journal of Transnational Women's and Gender Studies* 5, 3–92.

Index

CAMBRIDGE STUDIES IN LAW AND SOCIETY

Books in the Series

Diseases of the Will: Alcohol and the Dilemmas of Freedom
Mariana Valverde

The Politics of Truth and Reconciliation in South Africa: Legitimizing the Post-Apartheid State
Richard A. Wilson

Modernism and the Grounds of Law
Peter Fitzpatrick

Unemployment and Government: Genealogies of the Social
William Walters

Autonomy and Ethnicity: Negotiating Competing Claims in Multi-Ethnic States
Yash Ghai

Constituting Democracy: Law, Globalism and South Africa's Political Reconstruction
Heinz Klug

The Ritual of Rights in Japan: Law, Society, and Health Policy
Eric A. Feldman

Governing Morals: A Social History of Moral Regulation
Alan Hunt

The Colonies of Law: Colonialism, Zionism and Law in Early Mandate Palestine
Ronen Shamir

Law and Nature
David Delaney

Social Citizenship and Workfare in the United States and Western Europe: The Paradox of Inclusion
Joel F. Handler

Law, Anthropology, and the Constitution of the Social: Making Persons and Things
Edited by Alain Pottage and Martha Mundy

Judicial Review and Bureaucratic Impact: International and Interdisciplinary Perspectives
Edited by Marc Hertogh and Simon Halliday

Immigrants at the Margins: Law, Race, and Exclusion in Southern Europe
Kitty Calavita

Lawyers and Regulation: The Politics of the Administrative Process
Patrick Schmidt

Law and Globalization from Below: Towards a Cosmopolitan Legality
Edited by Boaventura de Sousa Santos and César
A. Rodríguez-Garavito

Public Accountability: Designs, Dilemmas and Experiences
Edited by Michael W. Dowdle

Law, Violence and Sovereignty among West Bank Palestinians
Tobias Kelly

Legal Reform and Administrative Detention Powers in China
Sarah Biddulph

The Practice of Human Rights: Tracking Law between the Global and the Local
Edited by Mark Goodale and Sally Engle Merry

Judges beyond Politics in Democracy and Dictatorship: Lessons from Chile
Lisa Hilbink

Paths to International Justice: Social and Legal Perspectives
Edited by Marie-Bénédicte Dembour and Tobias Kelly

Law and Society in Vietnam: The Transition from Socialism in Comparative Perspective
Mark Sidel

Constitutionalizing Economic Globalization: Investment Rules and Democracy's Promise
David Schneiderman

The New World Trade Organization Knowledge Agreements: Second Edition
Christopher Arup

Justice and Reconciliation in Post-Apartheid South Africa
Edited by François du Bois and Antje du Bois-Pedain

Militarization and Violence against Women in Conflict Zones in the Middle East: A Palestinian Case-Study
Nadera Shalhoub-Kevorkian

Child Pornography and Sexual Grooming: Legal and Societal Responses
Suzanne Ost

Darfur and the Crime of Genocide
John Hagan and Wenona Rymond-Richmond

Fictions of Justice: The International Criminal Court and the Challenge of Legal Pluralism in Sub-Saharan Africa
Kamari Maxine Clarke

Conducting Law and Society Research: Reflections on Methods and Practices
Simon Halliday and Patrick Schmidt

Planted Flags: Trees, Land, and Law in Israel/Palestine
Irus Braverman

Culture under Cross-Examination: International Justice and the Special Court for Sierra Leone
Tim Kelsall

Cultures of Legality: Judicialization and Political Activism in Latin America
Javier Couso, Alexandra Huneeus, and Rachel Sieder

Courting Democracy in Bosnia and Herzegovina: The Hague Tribunal's Impact in a Postwar State
Lara J. Nettelfield

The Gacaca Courts, Post-Genocide Justice and Reconciliation in Rwanda: Justice without Lawyers
Phil Clark

Law, Society, and History: Themes in the Legal Sociology and Legal History of Lawrence M. Friedman
Edited by Robert W. Gordon and Morton J. Horwitz

After Abu Ghraib: Exploring Human Rights in America and the Middle East
Shadi Mokhtari

Adjudication in Religious Family Laws: Cultural Accommodation, Legal Pluralism, and Gender Equality in India
Gopika Solanki

Water on Tap: Rights and Regulation in the Transnational Governance of Urban Water Services
Bronwen Morgan

Elements of Moral Cognition: Rawls' Linguistic Analogy and the Cognitive Science of Moral and Legal Judgment
John Mikhail

Mitigation and Aggravation at Sentencing
Edited by Julian V. Roberts

Institutional Inequality and the Mobilization of the Family and Medical Leave Act: Rights on Leave
Catherine R. Albiston

Authoritarian Rule of Law: Legislation, Discourse and Legitimacy in Singapore
Jothie Rajah

Law and Development and the Global Discourses of Legal Transfers
Edited by John Gillespie and Pip Nicholson

Law against the State: Ethnographic Forays into Law's Transformations
Edited by Julia Eckert, Brian Donahoe, Christian Strümpell and Zerrin Özlem Biner

Transnational Legal Ordering and State Change
Edited by Gregory C. Shaffer

Legal Mobilization under Authoritarianism: The Case of Post-Colonial Hong Kong
Waikeung Tam

Complementarity in the Line of Fire: The Catalysing Effect of the International Criminal Court in Uganda and Sudan
Sarah M. H. Nouwen

Political and Legal Transformations of an Indonesian Polity: The Nagari from Colonisation to Decentralisation
Franz von Benda-Beckmann and Keebet von Benda-Beckmann

Pakistan's Experience with Formal Law: An Alien Justice
Osama Siddique

Human Rights under State-Enforced Religious Family Laws in Israel, Egypt, and India
Yüksel Sezgin

Why Prison?
Edited by David Scott

Law's Fragile State: Colonial, Authoritarian, and Humanitarian Legacies in Sudan
Mark Fathi Massoud

Rights for Others: The Slow Home-Coming of Human Rights in the Netherlands
Barbara Oomen

European States and Their Muslim Citizens: The Impact of Institutions on Perceptions and Boundaries
Edited by John R. Bowen, Christophe Bertossi, Jan Willem Duyvendak, and Mona Lena Krook

Environmental Litigation in China: A Study in Political Ambivalence
Rachel E. Stern

Indigeneity and Legal Pluralism in India: Claims, Histories, Meanings
Pooja Parmar

Paper Tiger: Law, Bureaucracy and the Developmental State in Himalayan India
Nayanika Mathur

Religion, Law and Society
Russell Sandberg

The Experiences of Face Veil Wearers in Europe and the Law
Edited by Eva Brems

The Contentious History of the International Bill of Human Rights
Christopher N. J. Roberts

Transnational Legal Orders
Edited by Terence C. Halliday and Gregory Shaffer

Lost in China? Law, Culture and Society in Post-1997 Hong Kong
Carol A. G. Jones

Security Theology, Surveillance and the Politics of Fear
Nadera Shalhoub-Kevorkian

Opposing the Rule of Law: How Myanmar's Courts Make Law and Order
Nick Cheesman

Ironies of Colonial Governance: Law, Custom and Justice in Colonial India
James Jaffe

The Clinic and the Court: Law, Medicine and Anthropology
Edited by Ian Harper, Tobias Kelly, and Akshay Khanna

The World of Indicators: The Making of Government Knowledge through Quantification
Edited by Richard Rottenburg, Sally E. Merry, Sung-Joon Park, and Johanna Mugler

Contesting Immigration Policy in Court: Legal Activism and Its Radiating Effects in the United States and France
Leila Kawar

The Quiet Power of Indicators: Measuring Governance, Corruption, and Rule of Law
Edited by Sally Engle Merry, Kevin E. Davis, and Benedict Kingsbury

Investing in Authoritarian Rule: Punishment and Patronage in Rwanda's Gacaca Courts for Genocide Crimes
Anuradha Chakravarty

Contractual Knowledge: One Hundred Years of Legal Experimentation in Global Markets
Edited by Grégoire Mallard and Jérôme Sgard

Iraq and the Crimes of Aggressive War: The Legal Cynicism of Criminal Militarism
John Hagan, Joshua Kaiser, and Anna Hanson

Culture in the Domains of Law
Edited by René Provost

China and Islam: The Prophet, the Party, and Law
Matthew S. Erie

Diversity in Practice: Race, Gender, and Class in Legal and Professional Careers
Edited by Spencer Headworth, Robert L. Nelson, Ronit Dinovitzer, and David B. Wilkins

A Sociology of Constitutions: Constitutions and State Legitimacy in Historical-Sociological Perspective
Chris Thornhill

A Sociology of Transnational Constitutions: Social Foundations of the Post-National Legal Structure
Chris Thornhill

Genocide Never Sleeps: Living Law at the International Criminal Tribunal for Rwanda
Nigel Eltringham

Shifting Legal Visions: Judicial Change and Human Rights Trials in Latin America
Ezequiel A. González-Ocantos

The Demographic Transformations of Citizenship
Heli Askola

Criminal Defense in China: The Politics of Lawyers at Work
Sida Liu and Terence C. Halliday

Contesting Economic and Social Rights in Ireland: Constitution, State and Society, 1848–2016
Thomas Murray

Buried in the Heart: Women, Complex Victimhood and the War in Northern Uganda
Erin Baines

Palaces of Hope: The Anthropology of Global Organizations
Edited by Ronald Niezen and Maria Sapignoli

The Politics of Bureaucratic Corruption in Post-Transitional Eastern Europe
Marina Zaloznaya

Revisiting the Law and Governance of Trafficking, Forced Labor and Modern Slavery
Edited by Prabha Kotiswaran

Incitement on Trial: Prosecuting International Speech Crimes
Richard Ashby Wilson

Criminalizing Children: Welfare and the State in Australia
David McCallum

Global Lawmakers: International Organizations in the Crafting of World Markets
Susan Block-Lieb and Terence C. Halliday

Duties to Care: Dementia, Relationality and Law
Rosie Harding

Insiders, Outsiders, Injuries, and Law: Revisiting "The Oven Bird's Song"
Edited by Mary Nell Trautner

Hunting Justice: Displacement, Law, and Activism in the Kalahari
Maria Sapignoli

Injury and Injustice: The Cultural Politics of Harm and Redress
Edited by Anne Bloom, David M. Engel, and Michael McCann

Ruling Before the Law: The Politics of Legal Regimes in China and Indonesia
William Hurst

The Powers of Law: A Comparative Analysis of Sociopolitical Legal Studies
Mauricio García-Villegas

A Sociology of Justice in Russia
Edited by Marina Kurkchiyan and Agnieszka Kubal

Constituting Religion: Islam, Liberal Rights, and the Malaysian State
Tamir Moustafa

The Invention of the Passport: Surveillance, Citizenship and the State, Second Edition
John C. Torpey

Law's Trials: The Performance of Legal Institutions in the US "War on Terror"
Richard L. Abel

Law's Wars: The Fate of the Rule of Law in the US "War on Terror"
Richard L. Abel

Transforming Gender Citizenship: The Irresistible Rise of Gender Quotas in Europe
Edited by Eléonore Lépinard and Ruth Rubio-Marín

Muslim Women's Quest for Justice: Gender, Law and Activism in India
Mengia Hong Tschalaer

Children as 'Risk': Sexual Exploitation and Abuse by Children and Young People
Anne-Marie McAlinden

The Legal Process and the Promise of Justice: Studies Inspired by the Work of Malcolm Feeley
Jonathan Simon, Rosann Greenspan, Hadar Aviram

Gift Exchanges: The Transnational History of a Political Idea
Grégoire Mallard

Measuring Justice: Quantitative Accountability and the National Prosecuting Authority in South Africa
Johanna Mugler

Negotiating the Power of NGOs: Women's Legal Rights in South Africa
Reem Wael

Indigenous Water Rights in Law and Regulation: Lessons from Comparative Experience
Elizabeth Jane Macpherson

The Edge of Law: Legal Geographies of a War Crimes Court
Alex Jeffrey

Everyday Justice: Law, Ethnography, and Injustice
Sandra Brunnegger

The Uncounted: Politics of Data in Global Health
Sara L. M. Davis

Transnational Legal Ordering of Criminal Justice
Gregory Shaffer and Ely Aaronson

Five Republics and One Tradition
Pablo Ruiz-Tagle

The Law Multiple: Judgment and Knowledge in Practice
Irene van Oorschot

Health as a Human Right: The Politics and Judicialisation of Health in Brazil
Octávio Luiz Motta Ferraz

Shari'a, Inshallah: Finding God in Somali Legal Politics
Mark Fathi Massoud

Policing for Peace: Institutions, Expectations, and Security in Divided Societies
Matthew Nanes

Rule of Law Intermediaries: Brokering Influence in Myanmar
Kristina Simion

Lactation at Work: Expressed Milk, Expressing Beliefs, and the Expressive Value of Law
Elizabeth A. Hoffmann

The Archival Politics of International Courts
Henry Redwood

Global Pro Bono: Causes, Context, and Contestation
Edited by Scott L. Cummings, Fabio de Sa e Silva and Louise G. Trubek

The Practice and Problems of Transnational Counter-Terrorism
Fiona de Londras

Decoupling: Gender Injustice in China's Divorce Courts
Ethan Michelson

Anti-Constitutional Populism
Martin Krygier, Adam Czarnota and Wojciech Sadurski

Lawyers in Conflict and Transition
Kieran McEvoy, Louse Mallinder and Anna Bryson

The Ghostwriters: Lawyers and the Politics behind the Judicial Construction of Europe
Tommaso Pavone

The Sentimental Court: The Affective Life of International Criminal Justice
Jonas Bens

Practices of Reparations in International Criminal Justice
Christoph Sperfeldt

Seeking Supremacy: The Pursuit of Judicial Power in Pakistan
Yasser Kureshi

The Power of the Jury: Transforming Citizens into Jurors
Nancy S. Marder

Undue Process: Persecution and Punishment in Autocratic Courts
Fiona Feiang Shen-Bayh

Discounting Life: Necropolitical Law, Culture, and the Long War on Terror
Jothie Rajah

Clean Air at What Cost? The Rise of Blunt Force Regulation in China
Denise Sienli van der Kamp

Law and Precarity: Legal Consciousness and Daily Survival in Vietnam
Tu Phuong Nguyen

Prosecutors, Voters and The Criminalization of Corruption in Latin America: The Case of Lava Jato
Ezequiel A. Gonzalez-Ocantos and Paula Muñoz Chirinos

Entangled Domains: Empire, Law and Religion in Northern Nigeria
Rabiat Akande

The Social Constitution: Embedding Social Rights Through Legal Mobilization
Whitney K. Taylor

Out of Place: Fieldwork and Positionality in Law and Society
Edited by Lynette J. Chua and Mark Fathi Massoud

Negotiating Legality: Chinese Companies in the U.S. Legal System
Ji Li

For EU product safety concerns, contact us at Calle de José Abascal, 56–1°, 28003 Madrid, Spain or eugpsr@cambridge.org.

www.ingramcontent.com/pod-product-compliance
Lightning Source LLC
LaVergne TN
LVHW011810200926
848484LV00005B/1140

* 9 7 8 1 0 0 9 4 9 0 2 9 0 *